M000111249

# SCREENWRITING
# UNCHAINED

# SCREENWRITING UNCHAINED
Reclaim Your Creative Freedom and Master Story Structure
With the *Story-Type Method*®
By Emmanuel Oberg

ISBN: 978-0-9954981-0-5 (e-book),
978-0-9954981-1-2 (paperback), 978-0-9954981-2-9 (hardcover with colour interior)

**Already published in the Story-Type Method Series**
*The Screenwriter's Troubleshooter* by Emmanuel Oberg

**Coming Soon**
*Writing a Successful TV Series* by Emmanuel Oberg

*The Story-Type Method*® Series Editor: Naomi Telford
Author photograph by Barbara Leatham Photography
Cover and interior design by JD Smith Design

See **If You Want to Find Out More...** at the end of this book to get a free sampler of *The Screenwriter's Troubleshooter,* the second volume in the series

**Screenwriting Unchained** by Emmanuel Oberg – 1st ed.
Published in Great Britain in 2016 by

**SCREENPLAY**
*Unlimited*
PUBLISHING

10, Orange Street, Haymarket, London WC2H 7DQ United Kingdom

Read more at www.screenplayunlimited.com

Emmanuel Oberg

# SCREENWRITING
# UNCHAINED

## Reclaim Your Creative Freedom and Master Story Structure

With  The **STORY-TYPE METHOD**®

# Contents

# Acknowledgements

The list of people who inspired me to write this book is too long for me to name them all, but I'll try to mention the most significant ones.

Aristotle, of course, for starting the whole thing with his *Poetics*; Edward Mabley for the seminal *Dramatic Construction*; Frank Daniel, renowned screenwriting teacher at Columbia University and USC, who passed his knowledge to so many students including Yves Lavandier and who, along with Mabley, inspired him to write the excellent *Writing Drama*. These, added to my own experience as a screenwriter, were my main references for writing the *Developing a Plot-Led Story* section of this book and I highly recommend you read their work. These theoreticians brilliantly explain the way the dramatic three-act structure works for many plays and movies, including its fractal aspect and essential tools like dramatic irony or planting and pay-off.

The *Developing a Character-Led / Theme-Led Story*, *Developing Something Else* and *Bringing It All Together* sections of this book, the new idea of applying Abraham Maslow's Hierarchy of Needs to screenplay development, as well as the *Story-Type Method®* itself, represent a much more personal take on screenwriting and story structure. However, I was inspired a long time ago by Linda Seger's *Making a Good Script Great,* which triggered the association between character evolution and story structure, planting one of the early seeds for the *Developing a Character-Led Story* chapter of this book. And more recently by Paul Haggis and Bobby Moresco, who made me cry like a baby with *Crash*, forcing me to find a way to clarify how multi-stranded narratives work. This brought me to the notion of theme-led stories, just in time to make the most of *Game of Thrones*.

Christopher Vogler, for his take on applying Joseph Campbell's work to screenwriting in *The Writer's Journey* and for providing us with useful tools when developing a story with a mythical element.

David Howard, for adapting Mabley's work in *The Tools of Screenwriting* – an essential book which, unlike *Dramatic Construction*, is still in print – and of course for giving us the hilariously entertaining *Galaxy Quest*.

Colin Young, former chairman of the School of Theatre, Film and Television at UCLA, first director of the British National Film and Television School, founding director and senior script consultant of ACE, who patiently but relentlessly reformed my plot-led approach while I worked with him as a consultant and lecturer for ACE and who encouraged me to explore a more character-led vision of screenwriting.

All the friends who gave precious comments on the various incarnations of the *Story-Type Method* up to and including this book; especially Yves-Marie Le Bescond, Eileen Horne, Gregory Kourilsky, Mercy Sword, Hans Dobson, Lucy Telford and Lorna Hobbs, who provided not only the most constructive criticism but unabated enthusiasm and encouragement over the years.

The participants from all over the world at my *3-day Advanced Development Workshop*, who kept pushing me to clarify my thoughts – and are still doing so today. I might never have written this book had they not kept asking me to do it so persuasively.

Most importantly, I owe everything to all the filmmakers I love and admire. Enjoying watching their work, trying to understand how they do what they do, hoping to find a way to match a fraction of their talent and skill is what truly keeps me going.

Leading them, screenwriter William Goldman who wrote – besides some of the best screenplays ever written – two sentences that remain absolute truths in this business: *Structure is everything*, and *Nobody knows anything* (that would include me). It was after reading his *Adventures in the Screen Trade* that I stopped believing there was such a thing as objectivity when assessing a screenplay, which completely changed my approach to script development and greatly impacted on the *Bringing It All Together* chapter of *Screenwriting Unchained*.

Finally, I want to thank for their indefectible support: my multi-talented wife, editor and business partner, Naomi, my gorgeous daughters, Eloise and Juliette, my wonderful mother, Nicole, my many sisters and last but not least my agent extraordinaire, Rachel Holroyd, who graciously put up with me while I was writing this book.

*"I can't give you a sure-fire formula for success, but I can give you a formula for failure: try to please everybody, all the time."*

—Herbert Bayard Swope

# Introduction

When I considered writing about screenwriting and story structure, I knew the first question I would be asked is why.

It's not as if there weren't an abundance of books on the subject written by talented and insightful authors.

In fact, most of us would agree that we need another book on screenwriting like we need a hole in the head.

So why bring more noise to an already confusing arena?

As much as I'd like to offer a concise, witty answer, I'm afraid this one needs a bit of background.

Over the last two decades, as I was making my way through the film and TV industry, starting as a reader then progressing to script consultant, senior development executive, co-writer selling a first project to Warner Bros and getting hired by StudioCanal or Gold Circle, then getting solo writing gigs with Working Title / Universal or quirkier outfits like Film4, I had many opportunities to think about story structure and screenplay development from different perspectives.

I gradually realised that a significant shift had come about towards the end of the twentieth century: some story theoreticians had drifted away from the classical, *dramatic* three-act structure and taken a *logistical* approach to it. I'll try here to give a brief overview of what I mean by this, but we'll spend a lot more time on it later.

Let's first quickly define what I call the *dramatic* three-act structure. We have three *dramatic* acts in a story if we have a main dramatic action: someone is trying to do something about a problem, consciously or not. In that case, dramatic Act 1 is what happens before we understand this problem; Act 2 shows the attempts of a protagonist to solve the problem; Act 3 shows what happens once the problem is solved.

Before, during and after a main dramatic action; this is what defines three acts when a story uses the *dramatic* three-act structure. There are no rules to dictate the duration of these three acts in pages or minutes, and this makes it a flexible tool.

The dramatic three-act structure is in fact much more complex and powerful than this. We can use it to structure a main *evolution* as well as a main *action,* and we can use it to design not only the whole story but also its parts: dramatic acts, sequences, scenes and even strands in a multi-stranded narrative. Again, more on this later.

So what about the *logistical* three-act structure? Well, more and more theoreticians decided to impose an arbitrary, rigid *logistical* shape on every story, based on page numbers and not dramatic, structural elements. Not only was every screenplay supposed to have three acts, these acts were also expected to have a fixed length and include mandatory plot points or beats at pre-determined moments.

This *logistical* separation between acts, determined by an arbitrary number of minutes or pages – and supposedly the same for every story – didn't match the more flexible boundaries of the *dramatic* three-act structure still used as an underlying framework most of the time. Also, this *logistical* approach only applies to the story as a whole, not its parts. These theoreticians could state precisely *what* we had to do and *when,* but they had regrettably lost the connection with the *why* and *how.*

For a while, this *logistical* approach was enthusiastically embraced because it gave a simple, reassuring map to follow on what is always a perilous journey: the writing of a screenplay. Creating something out of nothing is incredibly difficult, so of course writers – particularly newcomers – will take any help they can get, especially if it makes their task seem easier.

Unfortunately, these artificial constraints, while not preventing talented writers from producing original screenplays, started to disconnect the way story structure was explained and discussed from the way it actually works, making it more difficult, not easier, for many to write original yet effective stories – which is in the end what everyone wants.

All this because the *logistical* three-act structure, as taught in many books, film schools and workshops around the world, had grown further and further away from the original, *dramatic* three-act structure.

Feeling this disconnection between practice and theory, many filmmakers turned their backs on this revisionist version of the three-act structure which they felt – and rightly so – was too limiting.

In response, theoreticians themselves started to move away from what had become "the" three-act structure, either rejecting it entirely or building on it, adding more artificial, dogmatic constraints with no structural justification. On top of three logistical acts of fixed lengths, all screenplays suddenly had to have eight sequences, fifteen beats or twenty-two steps according to the fad of the day. Three-act structure bashing was "in", yet many of these variations were still based on a flawed, logistical interpretation of the classical three-act structure, hence building on flaky foundations anyway.

So, beyond the personal enjoyment it brought me – I'm ridiculously passionate about storytelling – I wrote this book in reaction to this fairly recent evolution, as an attempt to knock down this wobbly tower of confusion and start again, going back to the roots of story structure in a resolutely modern way.

I'm not a big fan of theory for the sake of theory, so here is what I aim to achieve at a more practical level. First, offer an alternative approach to screenwriting that should be useful not only to writers but to everyone involved in the development process; second, initiate a move away from formulas telling filmmakers *what* is supposed to happen *when* in every screenplay to a method that concentrates on *why* some principles have stood the test of time, and *how* to use them flexibly yet powerfully today; third, introduce a versatile toolbox that brings freedom from all the artificial rules and dogmas accumulated over the last few decades yet grants more creative power to all involved through a deeper understanding of story structure. Hence the title, *Screenwriting Unchained*.

Such a paradigm shift should help filmmakers, and more generally, storytellers, to reconcile theory and practice, to reconnect the way story structure is discussed and taught with the way it actually works and to increase the potential to reach a wide audience, at home and abroad, while still telling original, meaningful, moving and entertaining stories.

Of course, the usual disclaimer applies. Reading a book – any book – won't make screenwriting easy. Developing a good screenplay requires, beyond talent, a great deal of hard work from all involved. It should, however, give you more clarity about story structure and an advanced understanding of the craft. This will, in turn, help you to develop the best possible version of each project you're attached to and hopefully, with the required amount of luck, get it made.

So here's the plan.

I'm first going to explain the limitations of the logistical approach to the three-act structure and, by extension, many of the more recent theories tacked onto it. I'll tackle these flaws, one by one, and I'll describe how the alternative, which I call the *Story-Type Method*®, can help overcome these limitations.

I'll then explain why we're usually dealing with one of three main types of story (story-types) when developing a screenplay – **plot-led, character-led, theme-led** – and how we can use just one set of tools to develop any story.

I'll introduce a brand new way to apply Abraham Maslow's Hierarchy of Needs to screenplay development and I'll detail how it relates to the target audience, genre and story-type of any project. I'll also explain, through a few examples, how what I call the M-Factor can increase the chances for a film to reach a wider audience at home and abroad.

I'll develop how we can use each story-type as a structural model. I won't list arbitrary page numbers, mandatory plot points or archetypical characters, which too often lead to predictable screenplays. I'll just provide flexible tools that can be used to shape a unique, original yet efficient story. For each story-type, I'll provide detailed case studies from various genres, time periods and countries. Movies such as *Gravity*, *Billy Elliot*, *Misery*, *Silver Linings Playbook*, *The Intouchables*, *Crash* and *Cloud Atlas*.

For good measure, I'll pick a few examples that show how some of the most successful movies – both artistically and commercially – can be hybrids or exceptions that don't clearly fit any of the main story-types we've just defined, and still work beautifully because they use the same set of tools, the same principles, just in a less classical way. Amongst these, films like *Edge of Tomorrow*, *The Lives of Others*, *Birdman*, *The Secret in Their Eyes* and *L.A. Confidential*.

Finally, in *Bringing It All Together*, I'll explain how we can apply the *Story-Type Method* during the development process, for all involved, ending with a tactical send-off, *The Rewrite Stuff: 12 Ways to a Stronger Screenplay*.

That's about it.

Irrespective of your level of experience, if you're looking for more clarity regarding story structure and practical yet flexible tools to apply to your craft, *Screenwriting Unchained* should transform the way you write, read, pitch, design and assess screenplays, both for film and TV.

Great screenplays all share one virtue: clarity. Some achieve this through simplicity; some, through complexity. But simplicity doesn't have to be simplistic, and confusion shouldn't be mistaken for complexity.

So let's look for clarity and tell some exciting stories...

# 1. The Story-Type Method®: A New Framework for Developing Screenplays

# 1.1 What's Wrong with the Three-Act Structure?

As discussed in the introduction, nothing and everything is wrong with the three-act structure. It depends which one we're talking about.

I started out looking at story structure the way it's explained in the books we've all read and learnt from. Gradually, I started to see a widening gap between these theories and my own evolving practice as a screenwriter, consultant and development executive. I felt an increasing need to come up with something more flexible, more versatile, less prescriptive to define story structure not as it was used centuries or even decades ago but as a wide variety of talented filmmakers practise it today.

I was thrilled by *The Bourne Trilogy*, *Gravity*, *Finding Nemo* just as much as I loved *Silver Linings Playbook*, *The Intouchables* or *Groundhog Day*, was moved by *Crash*, *Magnolia* or *Cloud Atlas* and was blown away by *Birdman*, *The Secret in Their Eyes* or *The Lives of Others*.

I wanted to define an inclusive theory that would offer a way of looking at these very different movies and explain how even the so-called exceptions use the same structural tools. Principles that work when developing the next mainstream blockbuster just as well as when designing the quirky sleeper that takes everyone by surprise.

I also wanted to go beyond the study of screenwriting tools and explore ways to improve the script development process itself.

This is why I came up with the *Story-Type Method*®, an innovative framework that never tells you what should happen when and to whom in a story, but reveals instead how tools used by talented filmmakers really work, and how to use them (or not, it's your choice). A method that takes into account the specificity of each project, instead of insisting on a one-size-fits-all model.

Looking at thousands of films or TV shows and as many screenplays, I identified three main story-types – **plot-led**, **character-led** and

**theme-led** – linked to the location of the main problem in the story. Here is how it works.

If the main problem lies outside the protagonist and comes from other characters or nature, what leads the narrative is the plot, the main dramatic *action*, and we're dealing with a **plot-led story**.

If the main problem lies within the protagonist, what drives the narrative is the protagonist's *evolution*, and we're dealing with a **character-led story**.

Finally, if the main problem lies in society or if the writer tries to make a moral, philosophical or spiritual point, what dominates the narrative is a theme or *vision*, and we're dealing with a **theme-led story**, usually multi-stranded.

I'll explain the way these three main story-types impact on the structure of any project – illustrating this with many examples and case studies – and how, using a single set of story tools, we can generate original, structurally sound screenplays.

One of these story tools is the *dramatic* three-act structure, which I started to define in the introduction. It is significantly different from the *logistical* 30–60–30 paradigm you might be familiar with (the one stating that a two-hour movie should be structured in three acts of roughly thirty, sixty and thirty minutes). In fact, the difference is quite fundamental, so I'll spend the first few sections trying to make it as clear as possible.

Of course I didn't invent the dramatic three-act structure. That part of the *Story-Type Method* approach to story structure goes all the way back to Aristotle's *Poetics*, relayed and built upon by theoreticians like Edward Mabley, Frank Daniel or Yves Lavandier and, more importantly, by all the playwrights and filmmakers who have used the dramatic three-act structure to shape their work: Sophocles, Moliere, Shakespeare, Ibsen, Chaplin, Capra, Lubitsch, Wilder, Hitchcock and, more recently, filmmakers as different as James Cameron and Jacques Audiard, Diablo Cody and Kathryn Bigelow, William Goldman and Paul Haggis, Nora Ephron and Jane Goldman or Alfonso Cuarón and David O. Russell.

However, the art of writing drama has evolved a lot since Aristotle, mainly because our understanding of the human psyche has changed. Aristotle hadn't met Freud, so he had no clue that we might not be in control of our subconscious mind. He hadn't met Copernicus or Galileo and wasn't aware that our Earth isn't the centre of the universe.

These crucial discoveries – along with many others – shifted the way human beings see themselves and relate to each other. Therefore, it also changed how characters are expected to behave in fiction to allow a story, play or screenplay to be moving, meaningful and entertaining.

Regarding screenwriting, while many principles remain the same, the practice of writing screenplays has changed drastically since the invention of cinema, especially over the last few decades.

If existing theories based around the usual paradigms have helped you, that's great.

If you have rejected them because you found them too limiting, more power to you!

Either way, you might want to take a look at a more flexible and less prescriptive way to approach screenwriting, which drastically changes the way we can handle the script development process.

What's so different in the *Story-Type Method* approach to story structure? Here are the five most important points:

## The Story-Type Method®

### Five Key Points About Story Structure

1. Story structure is **flexible**: act breaks have nothing to do with fixed page numbers.
2. The **fractal aspect** of story structure: the *dramatic* three-act structure can be used to design both the whole story and its parts.
3. Story structure is **versatile**: the *dramatic* three-act structure is used differently in a plot-led and a character-led story.
4. The *dramatic* three-act structure is **optional**: theme-led stories and other exceptions prove that it doesn't have to be used, at least not to structure the whole story.
5. The *dramatic* three-act structure is **only one side of structure**: writers use other tools to manage information, which can be part of structure.

Sounds good? Great, let's dive in!

# Key Point 1: Story Structure Is Flexible

*Drama* is the Greek word for action, and Aristotle defines the art of drama as being the imitation and representation of a human action.

Classically, this means a protagonist pursuing a unique goal over most of the story, meeting obstacles and experiencing conflict. In other words, we only have a dramatic action if someone is trying to do something about a problem, consciously or not (please see *Managing Conflict* in *Behind the Scenes* if you're not already familiar with this notion).

This dramatic action provides the backbone of a classically structured screenplay *if* the writer chooses to use the protagonist–goal–obstacle device to focus the attention of the audience, create a strong identification link and manage most of the conflict in the story.

In that case, you have three *dramatic* acts because you have what happens **before** we – the audience – understand what the main dramatic action is going to be (Act 1), what happens **during** the main dramatic action (Act 2) and what happens **after** the main dramatic action is resolved (Act 3). This is the foundation of the *dramatic* three-act structure.

Having a clear main dramatic action has many advantages. It helps to clarify what's at stake in the movie and to sustain the attention of the audience over a long period of time, to generate conflict and emotions not only for your protagonist but also for the audience through the identification link; it can even help you to convey more clearly the meaning of your story. Although it's not something you have to do – as we'll see in *Key Point 3* and *Key Point 4* – when writers focus on one main dramatic action, they use the *dramatic* three-act structure to shape their story.

Of course, most writers know intuitively that you'd better start the main action way earlier than around minute thirty in a two-hour feature film. Some movies define the main action as soon as minute one. Imagine a classic western starting with a cowboy coming back home to find his ranch burnt, his wife dead and his daughter gone. The main action starts as soon as we understand that the goal of the protagonist is to find and rescue his daughter. This means that in this example our first act lasts only a couple of minutes.

The primary reason for clarifying the main action early is to generate conflict and focus the interest of the audience as soon as possible, i.e. before they leave, fall asleep, switch channels or move on to the next script. But if you find other ways to generate conflict and interest early on, you can get away with a longer first act. In other words, if you know what you're doing, the three-act structure is much more flexible than the 30–60–30 logistical paradigm.

Similarly, many writers know instinctively that the main hook keeping the audience interested in a classically structured movie is the dramatic question: Will the protagonist reach the goal or not? Once you answer that question, the show is over and everyone wants to go home. There are some exceptions, but this means that, usually, dramatic Act 3 is very short. Dramatic Act 3 of Spielberg's *Duel*, for example, is only one circular long shot, showing the elated protagonist relieved to have escaped death by truck. Dramatic Act 3 of Hitchcock's *North by Northwest* (everything that happens once Cary Grant rescues Eva Marie-Saint on the top of Mount Rushmore) lasts forty-six seconds. Dramatic Act 3 of *Mission Impossible: Rogue Nation* is also just a couple of minutes long.

Although we are then often left with a second act which takes up most of the movie, this way of explaining the three-act structure can at least be justified dramatically: before the action, during the action, after the action.

**Once you understand the *dramatic* three-act structure, everything falls into place.**

The **inciting incident** is the dramatic event, usually located in Act 1, that triggers the protagonist's goal and raises the dramatic question: Will the protagonist reach the goal? I say usually, because it can take place before the beginning of the movie and only be revealed towards the end, as in *Once Upon a Time in the West*. We can also have an inciting action rather than an isolated incident, as in *Misery* or *Alien*. More on this in *Inciting Incident vs Inciting Action* in *Craft the Draft*.

The **climax** is the dramatic event at the end of the movie which answers the dramatic question: *Yes*, the protagonist succeeds, or *no*, the protagonist fails to reach the goal. The climax is usually close to the very end of the film, at the end of the last dramatic sequence of Act 2. In fact, *logistical* Act III for many theoreticians (the last thirty minutes of the film) is often made of the last sequence of dramatic Act 2, the climax and dramatic Act 3 (which shows the consequences of the action of the protagonist). Sometimes, the climax takes place earlier, when there is a modified structure (I call it an *Encore Twist*), which gives two successive answers to the same dramatic question (for example in *Gravity*, *Alien or Misery*), but we'll discuss this later in *Craft the Draft*.

**So what do many theoreticians do?** They confuse dramatic acts and logistical acts. They help us cut a long, scary thing (a screenplay) into more manageable chunks (logistical acts). This is helpful from a superficial point of view, but it's unhelpful dramatically because it creates confusion over the true structure of a story.

Some of them, frustrated with the fact that their second act is twice as long as the others, go further and state that there should be a significant "midpoint" in every movie, leading to four parts with an equal length of thirty minutes (logistical Act I, first half of Act II, second half of Act II, Act III). Saying that there is a midpoint in every movie because in every good script something significant happens around page sixty is misleading. In a good screenplay, something significant happens every few pages. However, we can use a mid-act climax, which helps to shape a story when it's difficult to use the same dramatic goal for the protagonist over the whole story. We'll discuss this crucial difference in *Midpoint vs Mid-Act Climax* in *Craft the Draft*.

The truth is, most movies don't have a mid-act climax or significant midpoint. What happens around page sixty is often the climax of the last dramatic sequence, or the inciting event of the next one (more on this in *Key Point 2*).

If your approach is logistical, having four parts with an equal length of thirty minutes can be satisfying. But if your approach is dramatic, this is just another unnecessary constraint which takes the writer away from the structural reality of the story.

This crucial difference between the two approaches could be illustrated like this:

## *Dramatic* Acts vs *Logistical* Acts

### The *Dramatic* 3-Act Structure

**Act 1**
(before the action)
No fixed length
Usually 5–15 min

**Act 2**
(main dramatic action)
No fixed length
Most of the movie

**Act 3**
(after the action)
No fixed length
Usually very short

Inciting incident
(anywhere in Act 1)

Optional
mid-act climax

Climax
(end of Act 2)

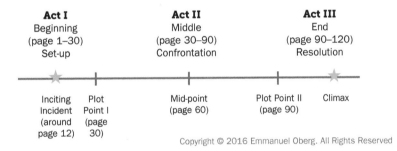

### The *Logistical* 3-Act Structure

**Act I**
Beginning
(page 1–30)
Set-up

**Act II**
Middle
(page 30–90)
Confrontation

**Act III**
End
(page 90–120)
Resolution

Inciting
Incident
(around
page 12)

Plot
Point I
(page
30)

Mid-point
(page 60)

Plot Point II
(page 90)

Climax

Many theoreticians define their three-act structure with a logistical approach, which is why some say – incorrectly in my opinion – that if the movie is significantly longer than two hours, more acts are required, and if it's notably shorter, it should be just one or two acts long.

This same misconception leads to the belief that TV movies in the U.S. are structured in seven acts. They are not structured in seven dramatic acts, but seven logistical acts, because they have six commercial breaks. It's the job of the writer(s) to add enough cliffhangers (unresolved conflict) and other dramatic hooks at the end of each act to make sure that the audience comes back to the same show after each commercial break. Yes, these TV movies are structured in seven *logistical* acts, but they are dramatically structured in three if they use – and most of them do – a *dramatic* three-act structure. It's the same with a one-hour TV drama: three commercial breaks, hence four *logistical* acts, but three *dramatic* acts.

Another example can be found in the past. When Moliere or Shakespeare wrote a play in five acts, it doesn't mean that they were designing it with five *dramatic* acts. All their plays are structured in three dramatic acts. The stage at the time was lit with candles, and these candles had to be as long as possible so they wouldn't have to be replaced too often, but not too long or they would burn the actors' clothes. Hence five *logistical* acts – those which show as act breaks when you read the play – because the candles had to be changed four times, but three *dramatic* acts – those used by the writer to design the main dramatic action. Logistical act breaks could also be needed simply to change the set, which takes time in the theatre and can't be done easily or elegantly in front of an audience.

*Hamlet*, for example, is a play in five *logistical* acts which is structured in three *dramatic* acts. Before Hamlet learns that his father was killed by his uncle (Act 1, which is pretty short, in fact shorter than logistical Act I); while Hamlet procrastinates over avenging the death of his father (Act 2, the main dramatic action/evolution which takes most of the play until the very end); and once Hamlet has finally managed to overcome his internal flaw and kill Claudius (Act 3, a few minutes before the end of logistical act V, in fact just the time needed to close all the subplots still left open at that point).

On the one hand, the 30–60–30 paradigm makes it easier for the writer because it cuts a long script into more manageable logistical units; on the other hand, it makes it more difficult because it disconnects the script from its true dramatic structure. This logistical approach also offers no explanation as to why we should have three acts in every screenplay.

Now here is a valid question. Why would the dramatic three-act structure be useful if it leaves us with a gigantic second act taking up most of the movie? You could argue that it might be useful theoretically, but practically, how does it help us write a screenplay? Isn't it more helpful to have four manageable units of thirty pages?

This is when the second point comes in handy, and it's one of the building blocks of the *Story-Type Method*: Story structure has a *fractal* aspect, which means that you can use the dramatic three-act structure to design not only the whole story but also its parts.

So let's discuss this next.

# Key Point 2: The Fractal Aspect of Story Structure

A *fractal* is "a natural phenomenon or a mathematical set that exhibits a repeating pattern that displays at every scale". To read more about fractals, which are related to things as diverse as a snowflake, a Russian doll or a Romanesco broccoli, please look it up in Wikipedia. It's a fascinating subject, but we don't have the space here to discuss it in detail. Instead we'll concentrate on how fractals apply to story structure.

What's really liberating about the three-act structure when it's used as it should be – which is dramatically rather than logistically – is that we can use it to structure not only the whole story but also each part. We don't *have* to (we'll discuss this in *Key Point 4*), but we *can*. This is the fractal aspect of story structure and one of the building blocks of the *Story-Type Method*. It uses a repeating pattern – the dramatic three-act structure – at every level: whole story, dramatic acts, dramatic sequences, dramatic scenes as well as subplots and strands.

For example, we can structure a fifteen-minute sequence in the middle of Act 2 in three dramatic acts, in exactly the same way we can structure the whole screenplay. In order to do so, we simply have to clarify what the main dramatic action is during this sequence: Who is the protagonist of the sequence and what is the dramatic goal? Often this action will represent a subgoal, which is a way for the protagonist to reach the main goal.

This is how we'll be able to cut the second act of a classically-structured story into more manageable units. Once we have identified the main goal of the protagonist, we explore different ways the protagonist can try to reach the goal (usually failing until the very end). Each of these subgoals defines a dramatic sequence, which can be structured in three dramatic acts.

If we go back to our illustration of the dramatic three-act structure, it would look like this:

# The *Fractal* Aspect of Structure

## The *Dramatic* 3-Act Structure

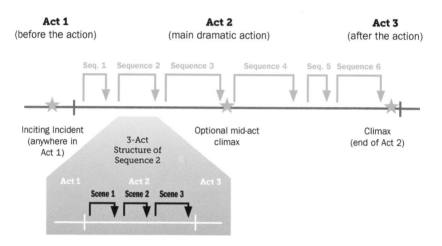

**Act 1**
(before the action)

**Act 2**
(main dramatic action)

**Act 3**
(after the action)

Seq. 1    Sequence 2    Sequence 3         Sequence 4       Seq. 5  Sequence 6

Inciting Incident
(anywhere in
Act 1)

3-Act
Structure of
Sequence 2

Optional mid-act
climax

Climax
(end of Act 2)

Act 1        Act 2        Act 3

Scene 1   Scene 2   Scene 3

This is a crucial aspect of the dramatic three-act structure compared to the logistical 30–60–30 paradigm.

Just as we can cut the whole screenplay into dramatic acts instead of logistical acts, we can also cut our second act into dramatic sequences (any number, usually between four and six) instead of logistical blocks (two half acts). That way, instead of having a vague idea of what a section of our screenplay is about, we know exactly which subgoal our protagonist is trying to reach during each dramatic sequence, usually as a way of reaching the main goal.

**A dramatic sequence is a group of scenes connected dramatically because they show the attempts of a protagonist (of the sequence) to reach a subgoal.** This protagonist of the sequence is usually the protagonist of the whole film, but not always. In *Misery*, for example, one of the last sequences of the movie is structured around Buster, the cop, who tries to investigate Annie once she has raised his suspicion.

Logistical Act I usually includes dramatic Act 1 and the first dramatic sequence of Act 2. Logistical Act II includes two to four dramatic sequences (subgoals) in dramatic Act 2. Logistical Act III usually includes the last dramatic sequence of dramatic Act 2, the climax and dramatic Act 3.

There can also be a dramatic sequence in Act 1, before the main dramatic action starts. In most action/adventure movies, we start with a sequence which is often only indirectly related to the main action. For example, *Raiders of the Lost Ark* starts with the great temple action sequence, which introduces two main characters in the movie (protagonist Indy and rival archaeologist Belloq). But we're still in Act 1 as the main problem of the story (getting the Ark of the Covenant before the Nazis) hasn't been introduced yet. Most *Bond* or *Mission Impossible* instalments are designed this way.

**Similarly, we can structure each scene (or rather, as many scenes as possible) in our screenplay using the *dramatic* three-act structure,** which has nothing to do with pages and everything to do with a main dramatic action.

In *Misery*, one of the first dramatic sequences in dramatic Act 2 is the "hairpin sequence", when Paul Sheldon tries to use a hairpin to escape. This sixteen-minute sequence is designed in three dramatic acts: the first act is everything that happens in the sequence until Paul Sheldon sees the hairpin on the floor; this inciting incident triggers his subgoal over most of the sequence, which is "trying to escape using the hairpin". The second act shows him attempting to use this hairpin to escape, then dealing with the consequences of this attempt (there is a mid-act climax in the sequence). The third act shows the consequences of this dramatic action, mainly that he's failed to escape but managed to grab some pills which he's going to use later.

Let's go down one more level. Sheldon's first sub-subgoal in this sequence, which structures the first dramatic scene of the hairpin sequence, is to get Annie out of the house. This comes before he even tries to pick up the hairpin which lies on the floor (that's the next dramatic scene). This sub-subgoal, "getting Annie out of the house", defines the first dramatic scene of the first dramatic sequence of the second dramatic act of *Misery* (phew!).

**So the dramatic three-act structure is used in *Misery*:**

1.  To structure the whole film, with a main dramatic action showing a main protagonist (Paul Sheldon) trying to survive and escape from the antagonist (Annie Wilkes);

2.  To design the five dramatic sequences which form the second act of *Misery*, including the one we've just discussed;

3.  To shape many dramatic scenes in the movie, if not most, defining a clear local protagonist and goal for each scene, therefore a clear dramatic action and a local three-act structure (before, during and after the local action).

If we go back to our illustration of the dramatic three-act structure, it would now look like this:

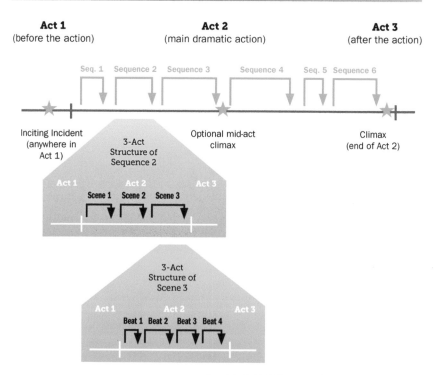

We can also use the dramatic three-act structure this way to design a short film, a thirty-minute TV episode or a one-hour TV drama.

So yes, if we think about the three-act structure in a logistical way, as many theoreticians do, we can't have three acts if our script is longer or shorter than two hours, because we're thinking in pages or minutes, not in dramatic units. Shorter and it becomes two logistical acts (or less). Longer and it becomes four logistical acts (or more).

However, if we forget about the logistical approach, we can use the dramatic three-act structure to design a three-minute scene in a feature film, a ten-minute short film, a fifteen-minute sequence in a feature film, a thirty-minute sitcom episode, a one-hour drama, a ninety-minute TV movie, a two-hour feature film, a three-hour movie like *Gandhi* or *JFK* or a five-hour play like *Hamlet*, irrespective of how many logistical acts you want them to have.

## 2. The *Fractal Aspect* of Structure

### We Can Use the Same Tools to Structure a:

- 3 min scene
- 10 min short film
- 15 min sequence in a feature film
- 30 min sitcom episode
- 60 min drama
- 90 min TV movie
- 120 min feature film

The *dramatic* three-act structure doesn't tell us on which page number we have to put our act breaks, which makes it more flexible. It also allows us to design parts within the whole, making it more powerful.

Fully understanding the fractal aspect of story structure allows us to design our story and its parts dramatically rather than logistically. Dividing a main dramatic goal into subgoals and a main dramatic action into dramatic sequences and scenes also helps us to identify what's not working much more precisely. For this reason, it's one of the core aspects of the *Story-Type Method.*

If we know what a character wants specifically in a scene or sequence, it's much easier for the writer to create obstacles and generate the relevant conflict for this character, and for the audience to be involved emotionally, wondering: "Will the character be able to...".

It's also incredibly useful for actors (and directors), who need to know what's at stake in each scene to be able to stage/act it. If you read Stanislavski's method of acting, you'll see that actors are expected to decode what the dramatist/writer has encoded. They are asked to find out what the main dramatic goal of their character is over the whole play/film, but also in each scene. It's much easier to do so if it has been encoded by the writer in the first place. Otherwise actors – or directors – have to invent it, when possible.

Finally, it's a fantastic way to keep the audience involved. Sure, we need to know what the protagonist wants (or needs) over the whole film, but we also need to know how the protagonist can do something about the main problem, practically, as the story unfolds. This is when sequences become really handy. Terry Rossio (co-writer of *Shrek* and *Pirates of the Caribbean*) has written a great article on Wordplayer.com about this very concept. What I call dramatic sequences, he calls tasks, but we're talking about the same concept (ways to cut Act 2 into dramatic units). See http://tinyurl.com/rossiotask and *Sequence the Action* for more details.

Using dramatic sequences is also the best way to avoid the dreaded sagging middle syndrome, when the story loses steam in the middle of the screenplay. If we cut our dramatic Act 2 into four to six dramatic sequences, which we can then handle as mini-movies, we have more manageable units to work with – dramatic rather than logistical ones – and we're less likely to get lost in the middle of the story, because we have a map to get us out of the woods.

Don't panic if this feels like a lot to take in. I'm trying to cover a lot of ground quickly in these five key points, but we'll look at many examples and case studies in the next chapters.

Now, all of this is very useful when a character (or a group of characters) consciously wants something in the story, and if that defines a clear, main dramatic action. But what if my protagonist doesn't want anything, at least consciously? What if what my protagonist *wants* is far less important than what my protagonist *needs*? If that unconscious need defines what's at stake in the story or my protagonist is passive or reactive? Does that mean I have a bad story? Or that I have to force my story into what we've just described?

Fortunately, no, because **the dramatic three-act structure is a versatile tool. It isn't used the same way in plot-led stories and in character-led stories.** So let's see how we can handle them differently, which is when the *Story-Type Method* really starts to come into its own.

## Key Point 3: The Difference between a Plot-Led and a Character-Led Story

Although I'm convinced that the dramatic three-act structure is an essential tool, the way we have discussed it until now – before, during, after a main dramatic action – is very much plot-led (or plot-driven).

A character having a unique goal over most of the film, meeting obstacles and experiencing conflict on the way is a useful device when structuring a plot-led movie like the vast majority of action or disaster movies (say *The Bourne Identity*, *Gravity* or most action-hero movies), but also for more intimate movies in which the main goal is plot-led like *Goodbye Lenin* or *Billy Elliot*.

However, this leaves out a large number of movies in which we can identify a main character but not necessarily a clear, unique, conscious goal for that character over the whole film. Movies like *As Good As It Gets*, *The Beat That My Heart Skipped*, *Groundhog Day*, *Something's Gotta Give* and many others.

This is because the classical protagonist–goal–obstacles device is mostly applicable to plot-led movies.

It's based on the notion that main characters know what they want. But what if they don't? Or, more precisely, what if their unconscious *need* is far more important than their conscious *want*?

This is why filmmakers developing character-led movies find most story theories frustrating. Even the approach developed by theoreticians who better understand the dramatic three-act structure – like Edward Mabley or Frank Daniel – leaves them wanting. These theoreticians are more helpful because they get the difference between dramatic acts and logistical acts, and they are aware of the fractal aspect of story structure. But still, their approach is more plot-led than character-led. If your protagonist doesn't have a clear, conscious goal, you're more or less on your own.

So how do we overcome this with the *Story-Type Method*? The first thing we have to do is identify the type of story we're dealing with, and this comes down to a simple question: What is a good story?

The most inclusive answer I can offer is that **a good story is a meta-phor for a problem-solving process**. If we don't have, somewhere in our story, a problem to be solved, and someone – a character or a group of characters – doing something about it or struggling with it, consciously or not, we might not have a movie. Whether it is to escape and survive, like Paul Sheldon in *Misery*, to become a better person, like Phil Connors in *Groundhog Day* or to deal with racial tension in Los Angeles, like all the main characters in *Crash*, if you can't isolate a main problem, you might be in trouble.

The next step is to locate the main problem.

**If the main problem in our story lies outside our protagonist and comes from other characters or nature, we're dealing with a plot-led movie**. Our character – or group of characters if we have co-protagonists sharing the same goal – consciously wants to solve the problem and doesn't need to change, because the main problem isn't within the character, but outside. That's Paul Sheldon (James Caan) in *Misery*, or Ryan Stone (Sandra Bullock) in *Gravity*. The character might need to grow – like Stone in *Gravity* who needs to move on from her daughter's death – but what holds the story together and defines its direction is one main dramatic *action*, making it plot-led.

**If the main problem lies inside our protagonist, we're dealing with a character-led movie**. Our character needs to change in order to solve the problem, and often wants this unconsciously, but is usually unaware of the problem, or denies its existence, and therefore can't have the conscious goal of solving it. That's Phil Connors (Bill Murray) in *Groundhog Day* or Melvin Udall (Jack Nicholson) in *As Good As It Gets*, Pat (Bradley Cooper) in *Silver Linings Playbook* or P.L. Travers (Emma Thomson) in *Saving Mr Banks*. What holds the story together and defines its direction is the main character's *evolution*, making it character-led.

**Finally, if the main problem lies in society, or if the movie tries to make a moral, philosophical or spiritual point, we're probably dealing with a theme-led story, usually a multi-stranded narrative**, in which we show different individuals confronted with the same problem (or variations of the same problem). We need more than one main character to make it clear that the problem is not unique to one specific character. What holds the story together is the exploration of a unique *vision* or *theme*, making it theme-led. We'll discuss theme-led stories next in Key Point 4, as they tend to be an exception rather than the rule in movies, but it doesn't mean they should be neglected, especially in TV writing where they are very common.

# 3. *Plot-Led* vs *Character-Led* Story

- In a **plot-led** movie, what ties the story together is the **dramatic action** of the protagonist, defined by a clear conscious *want*. The main problem lies **outside** of the protagonist (other characters, nature).

- In a **character-led** movie, what ties the story together is the **evolution** of the protagonist, defined by an **unconscious** *need*. The main problem lies **within** the protagonist.

Establishing this difference between a conscious *want* and an unconscious *need* is crucial for most movies, because although both types can use the dramatic three-act structure, I don't believe we can design a plot-led movie and a character-led movie in the same way. This is what makes the *Story-Type Method* so powerful and flexible.

**To structure a plot-led movie,** we decide *who wants what and why.* This defines the main dramatic action of the protagonist, so we have a three-act structure showing the conscious attempts of our protagonist (whether it's one character or a group of characters sharing the same objective) to reach a goal. The protagonist reaches the goal (or fails) and the story is over. Of course the protagonist may have some internal obstacles, which make it more difficult to reach the goal. For example, Jason Bourne doesn't remember who he is, making it more challenging for him – and more interesting for us – to defeat his former employer and survive. Overall what needs to be solved lies outside, not within the protagonist. The plot rules; the character follows. The protagonist can *grow* – and often does – but there is no need to *change* because there is nothing wrong with the protagonist.

**To structure a character-led movie**, we decide *who needs what and why*. This defines the main evolution of the protagonist, and we have to make this evolution believable, (especially if the protagonist manages to change and solve the internal problem) satisfying and meaningful (particularly if the protagonist fails). Because human beings resist change and evolve most when experiencing conflict, we design the plot so that while trying to reach one or more conscious goals, the protagonist experiences external conflict which forces an internal change. What's primarily at stake is not whether the protagonist will reach the conscious goal(s), but whether the protagonist will change.

**When we structure the second act of a plot-led movie**, we try to define four to six dramatic sequences showing the protagonist's attempts to reach a conscious goal. We generate conflict to increase the difficulty for the protagonist, making the action more interesting for the audience and helping to create a strong identification. The protagonist's goal is the same over most of the movie, although it's usually broken down into subgoals, each of which defines a dramatic sequence. We use a *dramatic* three-act structure: before, during and after the *action* of the protagonist.

**When we structure the second act of a character-led movie**, we try to define four to six main emotional or psychological steps mapping the evolution of the protagonist, and we design dramatic sequences to generate the conflict that will force the protagonist to change. The evolution of the protagonist is focused on the same character flaw over most of the movie, although it's usually broken down into steps which define dramatic sequences. If there is one clear evolution, it will feel like one story. In a character-led movie, we don't need one main action if we have one main evolution. This is because what's mainly at stake is not the conscious *want* but the unconscious *need* of the protagonist. Again, we have a *dramatic* three-act structure: before, during and after the *evolution* of the protagonist.

In a well-structured plot-led movie, we enter Act 2 when we – the audience – understand who **wants** what and why, i.e. what the conscious goal of the protagonist is. This will define the main *action*.

In a well-structured character-led movie, we enter Act 2 when we – the audience – understand who **needs** what and why, i.e. what the unconscious need of the protagonist is. This will define the main *evolution*.

In other words, **plot-led movies are *action*-driven** (as in dramatic action, not car chases or fighting scenes), **while character-led movies are *evolution*-driven.**

**This is why well-structured character-led movies can be quite episodic.** In *Groundhog Day*, we don't have one main conscious goal which determines the direction of the movie. We have one main evolution which defines what's at stake in the whole film: Will Phil Connors (Bill Murray) manage to change, to become a better person?

**This is also why good character-led movies are often road movies.** A change of scene can create new situations which can force an evolution, and the lack of a conscious dramatic drive is supplemented by a clear geographical destination. That's what we have in *Sideways* for example.

Now all of this is great, and hopefully it starts to define a clearer picture, but what if we don't want to use the dramatic three-act structure at all to shape the whole film? What if we're writing a multi-stranded narrative, like *Crash* (Haggis), *Cloud Atlas* or *Magnolia*? Or a TV series like *ER*, *Friends*, *Deadwood*, or *Game of Thrones*? Most theoreticians would probably find a way to fit these into their paradigm. However, we know that we can't use the dramatic three-act structure because there isn't just one main dramatic action or one main evolution for one main protagonist, but many equally important characters defining as many story lines. Then what?

Understanding how the dramatic three-act structure works is essential if we choose to use it to design the whole story, but it's just as important to master it if we choose not to, for example because we can't reduce our story to one main dramatic action or evolution without losing something in the process.

This is when the *Story-Type Method* fully kicks into gear, because if you're writing *Cloud Atlas* or *Magnolia*, most of the usual story theories have left you by the side of the road as they primarily deal with a main protagonist and a main dramatic action.

So let's discuss how the *Story-Type Method* allows us to **use the dramatic three-act structure... even if we'd rather *not* use it to shape the whole story.**

## Key Point 4: Theme-Led Stories, or Why the Three-Act Structure Is Optional

Let's say you're writing a multi-stranded narrative with five main characters. No one character is more important than the others, so you don't have a main character. No single character experiences more conflict than the others, so you don't have a clear protagonist. And they don't share the same goal (in which case they could be co-protagonists in a plot-led movie with a classical three-act structure, as in *Alien*, *The Full Monty* and *Seven Samurai* or its remakes *The Magnificent Seven* and Disney's *Bugs*).

No, you're Paul Haggis writing *Crash* with Bobby Moresco; Paul Thomas Anderson writing *Magnolia*; Richard Curtis writing *Love Actually*; Robert Altman writing *Short Cuts* with Frank Barhydt; Guillermo Arriaga writing *Babel*; Lowell Ganz, Babaloo Mandel and Ron Howard writing *Parenthood*; or the Wachowskis adapting *Cloud Atlas* with Tom Tykwer from David Mitchell's novel (which is not only multi-stranded but also non-linear). What interests you is primarily thematic, and you feel that a multi-stranded narrative is better suited to telling your story.

In this case, there is no reason to use a dramatic three-act structure to design your story because you can't isolate one main dramatic action or evolution.

What holds these stories together is the theme they explore. The problems they illustrate tend to lie in society rather than within the protagonist or coming from another character or groups of characters who would act in an antagonistic way. The many characters in this type of movie are used to illustrate different facets of the same problem, a problem which usually goes beyond any individual and cannot be solved by the end of the story.

Therefore, there is no dramatic three-act structure shaping the whole story, simply because there is no before, during and after a main dramatic action or evolution.

There is no main protagonist either, because the story is multi-stranded.

And you know what? That's fine! None of the movies listed above fit a conventional paradigm or use the dramatic three-act structure to shape the whole movie.

**A good screenplay doesn't have to be structured in three acts. The three-act structure is optional, at least as far as structuring the whole story is concerned**.

However, thanks to the fractal aspect of story structure, nothing prevents us from using the dramatic three-act structure to shape parts of an unclassically structured story, or using other structural tools like dramatic irony (more on this in *Key Point 5*).

For example, we can give each strand a protagonist, with a clear want/need. This means we can use the dramatic three-act structure to design some (or all) strands and dramatic sequences in our multi-stranded narrative.

# 4. The Three-Act Structure Is *Optional*

- In a **theme-led** movie, what ties the story together is a unique *theme* exploring a problem that lies in society, usually a moral, spiritual or philosophical issue.
- There is **no three-act structure** over the whole story, because there is no main dramatic **action** or **evolution**.
- There is **no main protagonist** either, because the story is multi-stranded.
- However **each strand** can be structured as **plot-led** or **character-led** using the *dramatic* three-act structure and its **fractal** aspect.

This is often how we approach a long-running TV series, for example in *Game of Thrones*. Each episode might not be structured in three dramatic acts because we are interweaving different plots which might have started a few episodes back or might end in episodes to come. However, we can still use the dramatic three-act structure to shape each plot with a main dramatic action as it unfolds over many episodes.

In a close-ended TV series (say most episodes of *CSI*) we have a more classical three-act structure for each episode, with a main plot in three acts and one or more subplot(s) often in three acts as well. Occasionally the problem will be strong enough to justify developing it over a few episodes.

**Once we master the *dramatic* three-act structure, we can use it to design classically structured stories, and even unclassically structured ones.**

This is why the *dramatic* three-act structure is so much more powerful than its *logistical* sibling: 1) You don't have to use it to shape the whole story; 2) If you do, you can design the whole story and its parts with it; 3) If you decide not to use it for the whole story, you can still use it to structure its parts (acts, sequences, scenes, subplots and/or strands).

In many theme-led stories, each strand is designed around one main character, and can be plot-led or character-led. In a well-structured multi-stranded narrative, each strand is connected to the same theme or vision to give it some coherence. This is what makes the story theme-led. The evolution (or the action) of each character moves the story (the theme) forward.

While most movies tend to be either character-led or plot-led, theme-led movies are an exception we need to be able to properly identify and handle. Many theoreticians don't pick up on the difference between the three main story-types and try to force all screenplays into a one-size-fits-all theory, which ends up causing a lot of frustration during the development process.

Let's try a car analogy. Imagine that the story is a car we're driving to a distant but exciting destination (production!). How likely are we to arrive if we don't first check the type of fuel our engine needs? Petrol, diesel and electricity are the equivalent of story-types. You can have pure types or hybrids, but you need to identify what the car runs on if you want to get to the finish line. Fill it up with the wrong type of fuel and you can cause serious damage...

This is what makes the *Story-Type Method* so efficient: identifying the story-type of each project early on helps us to avoid many structural issues during the development process. Get the story-type right and you'll have your story engine firing on all cylinders. Get it wrong and all sorts of problems will ensue.

In *If We Know the Problem, We Know the Story-Type*, we'll explore in more detail how to identify the story-type of a project as it's such a core aspect of the method, but for now let's tackle Key Point 5 and explain why **even the *dramatic* three-act structure is only one aspect of story structure**.

# Key Point 5: The Three-Act Structure Is Only One Side of Structure

Managing conflict is a crucial part of story structure. Using the dramatic three-act structure to define a main dramatic action/evolution and generate a strong identification link is the most efficient way to manage conflict in a dramatic story, which is why it's still so prevalent.

However, managing conflict is only one aspect of structure. Managing information is at least as important because it can have a significant impact on the structure of the story (and sometimes generate even more conflict).

To manage information in a story – which can also be seen as defining the audience's point of view – we use three main tools: dramatic irony (often used to generate suspense), mystery and surprise.

Later on, we'll take a closer look at how each of these tools work, but here is the gist:

**Dramatic irony** is when we give a piece of information to the audience which at least one character on screen isn't aware of. This character is known as the victim of the dramatic irony, and while the victims may not experience conflict directly, we feel conflict for them because of what we know and they don't. Dramatic irony can be used to create comedy or drama, to generate laughter or thrills. It's one of the most powerful tools at the writer's disposal. As such, it needs to be fully understood because it can be used in a structural way, to supplement and sometimes even replace the dramatic three-act structure.

**Mystery** is when we provide enough information for the audience to understand there is something that they don't know but not enough for them to know exactly what it is. It's a great hook, especially at the beginning of a story, and while it can be overused or overrated, it's a popular tool. On its own, it tends to work better in literature than on screen, so it's usually a good idea to avoid relying on mystery alone (and a final surprise). Instead, try to combine it with other tools.

**Surprise** is when we suddenly reveal an unexpected piece of information to the audience. Most good stories have at least a couple of strong surprises, because while we enjoy knowing where the story is heading, we enjoy even more being surprised by the way we get there. Whether a surprise happens during the movie or at the end, it casts a new light on the story. When we look back over the narrative with this new information, it still has to make sense.

# 5. The Three-Act Structure Is *Only One Side of Structure*

- Story structure uses other tools, such as **dramatic irony,** which are part of structure.

- Movies like *Infernal Affairs* and its remake *The Departed, Tootsie, Victor Victoria, Titanic, Back to the Future, The Apartment, Goodbye Lenin, Avatar, The Court Jester, La Cage Aux Folles, Amadeus* or *The Lives of Others* use dramatic irony in a structural way.

Let's take two examples that deal with information differently, but in which managing information is as important as managing conflict, precisely because most of the conflict is generated through the way information is handled.

In *Sleuth* (Mankiewicz), although there is a succession of three-act structures, as we understand the evolving motivations and goals of the two main characters, it's the different mysteries and main surprises that generate most of the conflict. They shape the film. We want to know what's going to happen next, not because someone wants or needs something, but because of what we've just learnt, what we feel we're about to learn or what we know and at least one character on screen isn't aware of.

We don't identify with the same character over the whole story. Depending on who is perceived to be experiencing the most conflict, we empathise with one character or the other. Our allegiance changes a few times during the film. Overall, Milo Tindle (Michael Caine) is probably the protagonist more than Andrew Wyke (Laurence Olivier), as he experiences more conflict.

So, most of the interest and conflict is generated through a combination of mystery and surprise. It's very similar to *Psycho* in this respect, although *Psycho* uses dramatic irony more. We know there's a killer in the motel, but most characters don't, except Norman Bates (Anthony Perkins).

At the other end of the spectrum, movies like *The Departed*, *It's Complicated*, *The Court Jester* or *Tootsie*, almost entirely based on dramatic irony, only use the dramatic three-act structure and the dramatic question – will the protagonist reach the goal or not? – as a starting point. The ironic question – how and when will the victim(s) of the dramatic ironies find out? – is much more important in shaping the story and building the audience's desire to find out what's going to happen next.

For example, in *Tootsie*, actor Michael Dorsey's (Dustin Hoffman) main problem at the beginning of the film is that he's out of work. No one wants to hire him. So he's trying to raise $6,000 to finance a friend's play that he will star in. As soon as he's hired as Dorothy Michaels, that financial problem is solved. For a while, his problem becomes "keeping the job", followed by "finding a way to leave it". So what is shaping the movie? From a plot-led point of view, he tries to face the dilemma created by his lie (Will he keep the job or tell the truth?). This is dramatised by the fact that he falls in love with Julie (Jessica Lange) and tries to seduce her, which is more difficult because of who he pretends to be. In reality, *Tootsie* is a character-led movie. Michael's main problem is to become a better man especially regarding his relationships with women. He will achieve this by exploring how different he would feel if he had been born a woman.

But if we leave the story-type aside for a while, there is a strong ironic question in *Tootsie*: How will Julie react when she finds out – along with the other characters – that he's a man and not a woman? This is almost more important than the dramatic question. A lot of the conflict in the story is generated by this dramatic irony and its consequences. Indeed, the climax of the movie takes place when Julie – with the others – finds out and rejects him, feeling betrayed (even though she changes her mind at the very end and forgives him).

Managing information also offers more subtlety when it comes to generating conflict.

While a plot-led attitude to generating conflict (a character – the protagonist – wants something but faces obstacles, therefore experiences conflict) is definitely useful, limiting conflict to this leads some screenwriting gurus to say that you have to: "Put your character in a tree and throw rocks at him". This also leads many writers to have people fighting or arguing for no real reason, because they believe this is the only way to stir up conflict in a story. How many times have you seen people shouting at each other in a movie and found the situation artificial, or wondered in which way the argument moved the plot (or the characters) forward?

This is where dramatic irony becomes so useful. **When we use dramatic irony, we can generate a lot of conflict without any of it being apparent, which often makes the situation more interesting.**

For example, if we tell the audience that a female character is about to leave her partner, but he doesn't know this yet, we generate a lot of conflict both for the characters and the audience. We can feel the impending conflict for the male character – who might be discussing their wedding plans with enthusiasm – and the conflict for the female character who is internally struggling to find the best way to tell him their relationship is over.

Take Hitchcock's famous example of the bomb under the table. Two characters are discussing the weather but we – the audience – see that there is a bomb under the table. Suddenly, although there is no apparent conflict between the two characters, we feel a lot of conflict for them, because we know something that they don't: the presence of a life-threatening danger.

This works at scene level, but it also works at story level. For example, *Infernal Affairs* and its remake *The Departed*, *Back to the Future*, *Cyrano de Bergerac*, *Tootsie*, *The Lives of Others*, *Goodbye Lenin*, *Avatar* and *Psycho* are all heavily based on dramatic irony. Even super-hero movies use dramatic irony a lot. The real identity of the protagonist (Batman, Superman, Spider-Man, Iron Man, Wonder Woman, etc) is usually a secret for most, except the audience and maybe a confidant or love interest.

So, while managing conflict using the dramatic three-act structure allows us to answer the question: "Who *wants* what and why?" or "Who *needs* what and why?", managing information deals with this other essential aspect of storytelling, which is: "Who *knows* what and when?". Managing information is therefore part of structure, and I don't believe it's possible to analyse the structure of the movies we've just mentioned without taking it into account.

Some theoreticians do discuss dramatic irony in more or less vague terms, but few of them - one exception being Yves Lavandier – realise how structural dramatic irony can be, and how an ironic question can be as important as the dramatic question in shaping the story and generating most of the conflict. This is a key aspect of the *Story-Type Method*.

# 1.2 So What Do We Need to Get It Right?

## A New Approach to Story Structure

I see structure as a combination of **character, theme** and **plot**, as well as managing **conflict** and **information**.

When we work on a story – which is, as stated earlier, a metaphor for a problem-solving process – we first need to identify what the main problem is.

We only have drama – *action* in Greek – if someone is trying to do something about a problem, consciously or not. The location of this main problem will lead us to the story-type: plot-led, character-led or theme-led.

**This is the backbone of the *Story-Type Method*:** leaving behind the one-size-fits-all story theories and adapting the development process to the story-type of each individual project.

So let's summarise what we've established so far:

**If the main problem lies outside the protagonist, we're dealing with a plot-led story:**

- The protagonist has a strong, conscious want: the goal to resolve or overcome the main problem in the story.

- The protagonist can be a character or a group of characters sharing the same conscious goal.

- The whole story is shaped in three acts because we have *before, during* and *after* a main dramatic *action*.

- There is no need for the protagonist to change, because the main problem doesn't lie within the protagonist.

- The character's need, when present, only adds substance or subtlety. It's not the meat of the story; it's the gravy.

- The character might need to grow – a change in attitude rather than a radical evolution – in order to reach the goal, or might change as a consequence of having experienced the story, but the character doesn't need to change fundamentally.

- However, we're trying to make the journey as entertaining, funny or challenging as possible. We'll design the character to serve the plot, for example by defining the protagonist so that some character traits make it more difficult to achieve the goal.

- The dramatic three-act structure is prominent here, because the story is plot-led.

- What's at stake is primarily what the protagonist *wants*, not what the protagonist *needs*.

- What interests the audience most is: "Will the protagonist reach the goal?".

- Most of the conflict comes from external characters, so we usually need an antagonist (a character or group of characters whose goal is in direct opposition to the protagonist's goal) or antagonistic forces such as nature in disaster movies – storms, twisters, volcanos, earthquakes, mountains, outer space, seas and oceans – or monsters/killers in monster/horror/slasher movies.

- Examples of plot-led stories are all the *Indiana Jones* and *James Bond* movies (except maybe *Skyfall*), most action films (like the *Bourne* trilogy), most thrillers, horror and disaster movies (think *Gravity*, *Taken*, *Misery*, *Alien*, *Jaws*, *The Day after Tomorrow*) but also some independent movies like *The Full Monty*, *Billy Elliot* or *Goodbye Lenin*.

**If the main problem lies within the protagonist, we're dealing with a character-led story:**

- The protagonist has a strong, unconscious *need* to resolve a main psychological problem or flaw.

- If we can see a glimmer of hope for the protagonist, we want the character to change, so we'll give the character the unconscious goal of changing in order to overcome the internal problem.

- Often, the character has this goal, unconsciously, but is resisting this change for most of the movie.

- The whole story is shaped in three dramatic acts because we have *before*, *during* and *after* the main *evolution* of the character.

- The protagonist doesn't have to pursue a unique goal because what holds the story together isn't a conscious goal defining a main dramatic action (who *wants* what and why), but an unconscious need defining a main *evolution* (who *needs* what and why).

- We are trying to map this *evolution* of our character and find the most relevant conflicts to make that change happen (or not).

- In this case, the priority is our character *evolution*, and the plot – the main dramatic action – becomes a tool to shape it. We use the character's conscious goal, which determines the plot, to organise the conflicts which are going to force the character to change.

- What interests the audience most is: "Will the character find a way to change?". This is the main dramatic question.

- What's at stake primarily is related to what the protagonist *needs* rather than what the protagonist *wants*.

- Most of the conflict comes from within the character, so the protagonist *is* the antagonist in character-led movies. Other characters tend to be catalysts, characters who force the protagonist to change, rather than antagonists.

- Examples of character-led stories are *As Good As It Gets, Silver Linings Playbook, Groundhog Day, The Intouchables, The Beat That My Heart Skipped, The Apartment, Little Miss Sunshine, Saving Mr Banks*.

Many original movies are carefully balanced between two story-types (hybrid cars in our analogy). For example, *Se7en* is a fascinating thriller because although it's plot-led like most thrillers – will Sommerset (Morgan Freeman) and Mills (Brad Pitt), the two co-protagonist cops, catch serial killer John Doe (Kevin Spacey)? – it develops a strong character-led subplot: Will Mills manage to control his anger? This brings most of the substance of the story and makes it compelling to watch. Although the co-protagonists reach their primary goal (to catch the killer) and therefore solve the main problem in the story, they fail on three counts: 1) Mills fails to control his emotions and kills Doe out of revenge; 2) Sommerset fails to stop him; 3) This allows Doe to win as he completes his series with the last murder he had planned: his own. This is what gives *Se7en* a powerful ending and makes it such an original thriller.

Another fascinating example is *The Bourne Identity*, an action thriller with Bourne (Matt Damon) as the protagonist trying to survive, escape and understand who wants to kill him. Bourne's got a fantastic internal problem: he doesn't remember who he is. Although each movie in the trilogy introduces a new set of villains (and each external problem is solved by the end of each instalment), it's the internal problem that shapes the trilogy. It's only when most of the mystery related to Bourne's past is solved that the story truly ends.

**Finally, if the main problem lies in society – or if the movie makes a moral, philosophical or spiritual point – we're dealing with a theme-led story, usually a multi-stranded narrative:**

- We don't have a clear protagonist or a main character, as no character (or group of characters) experiences more conflict or is more important than the others. There is no main plot, only subplots (strands).

- Each strand of the story follows a character or group of characters confronted with the same problem, in a different way.

- Each strand, which can be plot-led or character-led, illustrates one aspect of this problem.

- Each character is facing the same problem, but they are not consciously trying to resolve it together (otherwise they would be co-protagonists sharing the same conscious goal and we would have a plot-led story).

- We don't have *before*, *during* and *after* a main dramatic *action* or *evolution*. We therefore don't have a dramatic three-act structure shaping the whole story and that's fine because the three-act structure is optional.

- Thanks to the fractal aspect of story structure, nothing stops us from using the dramatic three-act structure to design each strand as a plot-led or character-led story.

- For a multi-stranded narrative to work, all the strands need to be connected thematically. What holds the story together is a main *theme* or *vision*, rather than a main dramatic *action* or *evolution*.

- We end up with a kind of *thematic* three-act structure, because there is a) before we understand the main theme; b) while the main theme is explored; c) what we can learn or take away from the journey.

- However, while a main dramatic action (or evolution) is a dynamic element able to drive a story, a theme merely states a *vision*, a point of view on society. As a result, theme-led stories tend to be more difficult to handle and require a specific talent to get right. Designing and weaving many strands together while still telling one effective story isn't easy.

- In a theme-led story, the problem is rarely resolved in the end as it wouldn't be believable. In the least depressing ones, at least one of the strands shows how you can find a way to deal with it at a personal level, even if the problem itself still exists in society (or in the world of the story). For example, in *Crash* (Haggis), racial tension still exists in L.A. at the end of the film, but some of the strands have found a positive resolution.

- What interests the audience most is: "How are these apparently disconnected stories going to be meaningfully connected, and what can I learn from them?". This defines the *thematic* question.

- *Crash* (Haggis), *Magnolia, Traffic, Babel, Parenthood, Cloud Atlas* or the TV series *Friends, Deadwood* and *Game of Thrones* are great examples of theme-led stories.

Let's not forget that the dramatic three-act structure is only one way to manage conflict. Managing information (using tools like dramatic irony, mystery, suspense or surprise) generates a lot of conflict too, and often makes for a large part of the structure of a good screenplay.

**If you asked me to show visually how I see structure, I would come up with something like this:**

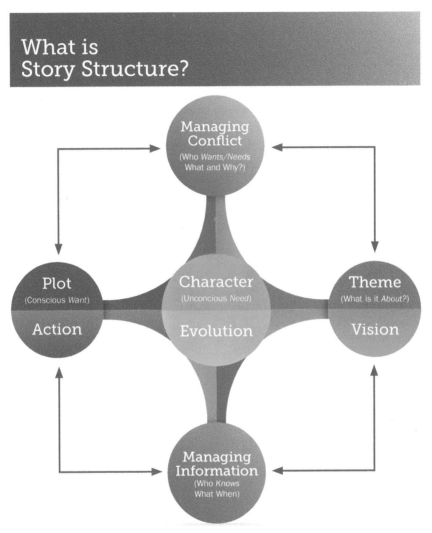

Most great movies flex all of their dramatic muscles and work as much on character as plot or theme, as well as managing conflict and managing information. <u>All of this</u> is structure.

I try to suggest this in the illustration above, which also shows that each story structure element is connected with the others (please don't take the arrows too literally, they're only meant to suggest this intercon-nection). Depending on the primary focus of the story design (a main dramatic *action*; a main dramatic *evolution*; the filmmaker's *vision*), the story will be either plot-led, character-led or theme-led. If there is no clear focus, it might be a hybrid or an exception or it might be a story that needs work. Managing conflict (who *wants/needs* what and why) and managing information (who *knows* what when) apply to all stories, including hybrids and exceptions, though in slightly different ways.

The key here is to know what's primarily at stake and design the story accordingly. If you obsess about the plot, or the plot-led aspect of structure, you might miss the most fundamental part of your design in a character-led or theme-led story. If you're trying to force a protagonist to change because supposedly "The protagonist is the character who changes most", you might be doing a disservice to your plot-led story. If the main problem lies outside the protagonist, there is no reason for the protagonist to change.

Similarly, if you try to analyse movies like *Infernal Affairs* or its remake *The Departed, Tootsie, Back to the Future, Cyrano de Bergerac, Psycho, The Court Jester, Sleuth, Amadeus, The Lives of Others, Goodbye Lenin or Avatar* purely from a managing conflict point of view, you miss a large part of the structure of these movies because they are built primarily on the way they manage information.

Take *Titanic* for example. So many critics missed the point. They said: "But we already know the ending!". That's because they don't un-derstand dramatic irony. Yes, we know that the boat is going to sink, and that's precisely what makes the story compelling. When Jack Dawson (Leonardo DiCaprio) wins his ticket at the beginning and is so happy to board the ship, we feel for him because we know he's just won a ticket to a guaranteed disaster!

In *Titanic*, a lot of the conflict is generated through management of information, thanks to the strong dramatic irony: absolutely everyone in the audience knows that the ship is going to sink. However, we don't know who is going to survive – we know she does, but will he? – and that's what keeps our interest alive. If, for example, we knew for a fact that there were no survivors of the Titanic disaster, it would be much more difficult to engage with the two main characters; it's our hope that both of them will survive that keeps us involved emotionally and it's only at the very end of the movie that we get the answer to that question.

**I hope this introduction starts to clarify the theory behind the *Story-Type Method***

- How **flexible and powerful the dramatic three-act structure** can be when we use it to design not only the whole movie in a plot-led or character-led story but also its parts, including its acts (especially dramatic Act 2), sequences and scenes, or its strands in a theme-led story (ensemble films and many TV series). This makes it much more flexible and powerful than the logistical 30–60–30 paradigm. I also explained how it was used differently in plot-led and in character-led stories.

- How **the fractal aspect of story structure** makes it possible to design not only the whole story but also its parts (acts, sequences, scenes, subplots). The *dramatic* three-act structure can therefore be used to shape the strands in theme-led stories, even when it's not used to design the whole story.

- How **story structure goes well beyond the three-act structure, even the dramatic one**, and involves working both on managing conflict (*who wants/needs what and why*) and managing information (*who knows what when*); knowing what the protagonist *needs* (which drives the *evolution* of the character) as well as what the protagonist *wants* (which drives the plot and defines the *main dramatic action*); and being able to handle an unclassical overall structure, especially when the story is theme-led and driven by a strong *vision*.

- Finally, **how using the *Story-Type Method* as early as possible in the script development process** will allow you to identify the *story-type* of your project and adjust the development process accordingly, making it easier, faster and hopefully leading to stronger screenplays.

# The Story-Type Method Overview

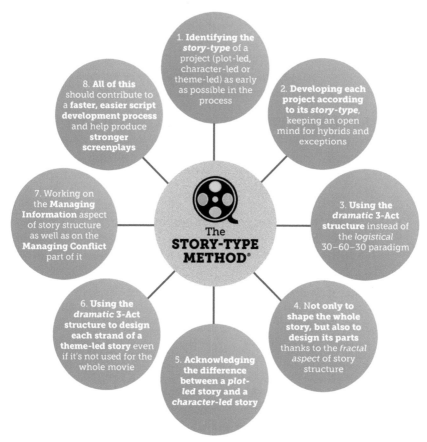

1. **Identifying the story-type** of a project (plot-led, character-led or theme-led) as early as possible in the process

2. **Developing each project according to its story-type**, keeping an open mind for hybrids and exceptions

3. **Using the dramatic 3-Act structure** instead of the logistical 30–60–30 paradigm

4. **Not only to shape the whole story, but also to design its parts** thanks to the fractal aspect of story structure

5. **Acknowledging the difference between a plot-led story and a character-led story**

6. **Using the dramatic 3-Act structure to design each strand of a theme-led story** even if it's not used for the whole movie

7. Working on the **Managing Information** aspect of story structure as well as on the **Managing Conflict** part of it

8. **All of this** should contribute to a **faster, easier script development process** and help produce **stronger screenplays**

The **STORY-TYPE METHOD®**

Mastering these concepts should help you develop original and powerful stories, which won't feel like they've been forced into a predictable, artificial formula yet will be based on solid dramatic foundations. While there is no formula that guarantees a creative or commercial success, the *Story-Type Method* tries to strike the right balance between efficiency and originality.

**This is what the *Story-Type Method* is about. Helping you break free of artificial constraints and instead offering you flexible yet powerful**

tools to develop original, structurally sound screenplays, in a faster, easier way, for a global audience.

So let's discuss how we can do just that!

# If We Know the Problem, We Know the Story-Type

Because it's such a crucial aspect of the *Story-Type Method*, I'd like to both recap and expand on the first step in the process.

So, how do we identify the story-type of our project?

As explained in *Key Point 3*, if we agree that a good story is a metaphor for a problem-solving process, we first need to define the main problem in the story. Once we've identified the main problem and can see where it lies, we know which story-type we're dealing with.

**If the main problem lies outside the protagonist**, in other characters or nature, we're developing a *plot-led story*, which focuses on a main dramatic *action*.

**If the main problem lies within the protagonist**, we're developing a *character-led story*, which focuses on the *evolution* of a main character.

**If the main problem lies in society**, explores a political or philosophical problem, we're developing a *theme-led* story – usually a multi-stranded narrative – which focuses on a main theme or *vision*.

**If the main problem is unclear**, we might have to define it more precisely, or we might be developing *something else*, a hybrid or an exception.

Here's a way to visualise this decision process and its impact on story structure:

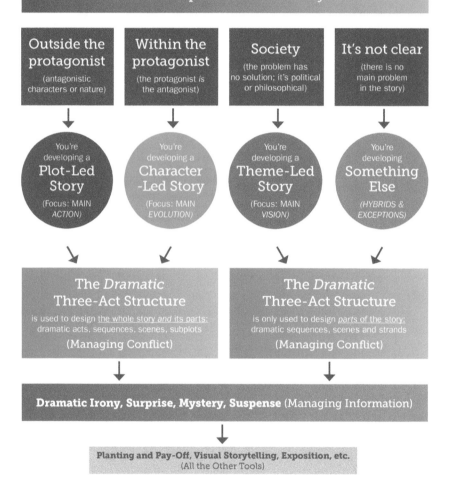

The Story-Type Method®

A good story is a metaphor for a problem-solving process.
Where does the main problem in the story come from?

| Outside the protagonist | Within the protagonist | Society | It's not clear |
|---|---|---|---|
| (antagonistic characters or nature) | (the protagonist *is* the antagonist) | (the problem has no solution; it's political or philosophical) | (there is no main problem in the story) |

You're developing a
**Plot-Led Story**
*(Focus: MAIN ACTION)*

You're developing a
**Character -Led Story**
*(Focus: MAIN EVOLUTION)*

You're developing a
**Theme-Led Story**
*(Focus: MAIN VISION)*

You're developing
**Something Else**
*(HYBRIDS & EXCEPTIONS)*

The *Dramatic* Three-Act Structure
is used to design the whole story *and* its parts: dramatic acts, sequences, scenes, subplots
(Managing Conflict)

The *Dramatic* Three-Act Structure
is only used to design *parts of the story:* dramatic sequences, scenes and strands
(Managing Conflict)

**Dramatic Irony, Surprise, Mystery, Suspense** (Managing Information)

**Planting and Pay-Off, Visual Storytelling, Exposition, etc.**
(All the Other Tools)

If you have a specific story in mind and its main problem is already well-defined, you should be able to tell which story-type your project belongs to. Looking at the examples for each story-type provided earlier in *Key Point 3* might help you with this.

In that case you're good to go and might be tempted to skip to the chapter that directly concerns your story-type.

I suggest instead that you read the next three chapters in full and in sequence. Developing a character-led story relies on many of the same tools and concepts detailed in *Developing a Plot-led Story*, and developing a theme-led story requires a clear understanding of both plot-led and character-led story-types. That's why I have chosen to approach them in this order.

If you're unclear about your story-type, I've designed a free interactive video guide called *The Structurator®*, which is available at www.thestructurator.com, to help you identify the type of the story you're working on. You could give it a try.

If you're still struggling to identify your story-type, it could mean one of a few things.

First, I could be wrong. The theory itself could be flawed, or the way I have put it into words could be flawed. Either way, it doesn't mean that there is necessarily something wrong with your story. Trust your instinct and press on.

Second, your story could be a plot-led story with a strong character-led element, like *The Bourne Identity, Midnight Run, Billy Elliot* or *Se7en*; or a character-led story disguised as plot-led, like *Silver Linings Playbook, Two Days, One Night, Little Miss Sunshine* or *Ridicule*.

Third, your story could be a hybrid or an exception which, while not clearly fitting any of the story-types briefly defined above and discussed at length in the next three chapters, still works. It could be a movie like *Citizen Kane, Psycho, The Lives of Others, The Shining, L.A. Confidential, Memento, The Usual Suspects, Birdman, Gone Girl, The Secret in Their Eyes, Edge of Tomorrow* and many, many others. If that's the case, congratulations! These working exceptions can be the most exciting, interesting, challenging and successful movies, and I'm looking forward to watching yours. I briefly analyse a few of them in *Developing Something Else*, because understanding how they work – using the tools and templates we're about to describe, just in a less classical way – might help you create your own.

Finally, there could be something amiss in the way you've designed your story, and hopefully the *Story-Type Method* will help you fix this. If you don't know what the main problem in your story is, whether it lies inside your protagonist, outside your protagonist or in society, if you can't identify what's primarily at stake in your story, you might be in trouble. If you're not sure how you manage conflict or information in your story, you might have a problem, but reading the rest of the book should help you solve it.

This is why I suggest you simply go on reading, whether you've been able to identify the story-type of the project you're working on or not. As we look at each story-type in more depth and explain how a few essential tools work along the way, you should be able to identify your story-type, clarify the structure of your screenplay and solve many of its problems. It might even lead you to realise that your story-type isn't what you initially thought it was, or that your story might be a hybrid or a working exception...

But before we explore how to develop each project according to its story-type, I'd like to introduce a brand new concept that applies to all stories, inspired by the work of psychologist Abraham Maslow.

# 1.3 Is Maslow Running the Show?

The Hierarchy of Needs is a psychological theory proposed by Abraham Maslow in his 1943 paper, *A Theory of Human Motivation*. Maslow suggests a pattern describing the way human motivations generally evolve, defining the following levels of needs: Physiological, Safety, Belongingness and Love, Esteem and Self-Actualisation.

I've always been interested in Maslow's theory and realised gradually that it can be very useful as the foundation for a framework to help us think about key elements of story design, in a very practical way.

When I share this concept of applying Maslow's Hierarchy of Needs to screenwriting with other filmmakers, for example when I run my three-day Advanced Development Workshop, it seems to resonate with everyone involved in the creative process, not just screenwriters. Producers and development executives, especially, tell me they find it to be a very powerful tool when they apply it to their projects. I hope you'll find it useful too.

Let's start with the original Hierarchy of Needs, then we'll see how we can use Maslow's theory to improve key story elements before defining what I call the M-Factor and illustrating all this with a few examples.

## Maslow's Hierarchy of Needs

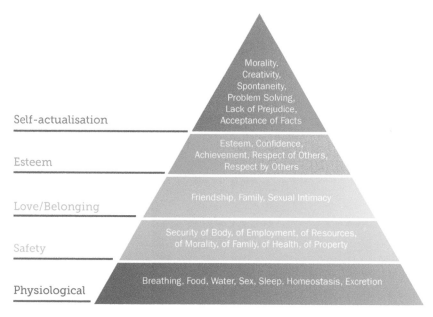

The general principle of Maslow's theory, as illustrated above, is fairly simple. Lower needs have to be satisfied before we can move up the pyramid. The four lower needs – physiological, safety, love/belonging, esteem – have to be satisfied before we can reach the highest one, self-actualisation.

Note that professional artists, specifically writers, often break this rule, but for most people it's kind of true. We're only able to consider a creative hobby seriously when our more basic needs are satisfied. Do you really feel like learning how to sculpt when the bank is about to repossess your house? Unless said hobby is just an excuse to get a lower need satisfied, for example taking an acting or a painting class just to get laid. But who does that?

What's all this got to do with storytelling, and more specifically with the *Story-Type Method*? Well, if we agree that a good story is a metaphor for a problem-solving process, let's see where the main problem – what's at stake in the story – lies in Maslow's pyramid, and how this relates to audience, genre, story-type and identification.

## Audience

What's really interesting here from a story point of view is that if the main problem in the story hangs at the top of the pyramid, the story is likely to provide primarily intellectual gratification. As you go down, the gratification becomes more and more emotional, until it reaches a basic, primitive stage.

This is not a formula, but roughly speaking, the higher the main problem sits in the pyramid, the more limited the potential audience, the lower the largest. It doesn't mean that making a movie about people eating, farting and having sex means a guaranteed commercial success or that anything philosophical can only be appreciated by a handful of people. It just means that *if* the nature of your project – according to where the main problem lies in Maslow's pyramid – limits its potential audience, then the design and development of the story should ideally take this into account, so that in some ways the story reaches down to lower levels in the pyramid.

Similarly, if your story is anchored at the bottom, you might want to find ways to explore higher needs so that a more sophisticated part of the audience can relate to it more easily. This is what Pixar does brilliantly with most of its animation movies. A base layer in the story – the main problem / what's at stake – is accessible to anyone, including its core audience of young people. Some jokes, themes and references are present in higher layers designed to hook an older, more sophisticated audience – in this case their parents.

In relation to this, and a key point to remember if you're interested in crossing borders: the lower in the pyramid, the more universal the story is. Every human being, irrespective of age, gender, social origin, nationality or spoken language can understand and relate to the lowest level (physiology). Most can relate to the level just above (safety). This is why a film like *Apocalypto* can reach audiences all over the world, despite being shot in a language that almost no one understands. Rooting the story at the lowest levels of Maslow's Hierarchy of Needs and using all the dramatic tools we've discussed is what gives it universality, allowing it to reach such a wide audience. As you go up the pyramid, the influence of education, social origin, culture and language become more prominent and can make it more difficult for the story to cross borders. It doesn't mean that films addressing such issues shouldn't be made. It just helps if we're aware of this and design the story so that it also explores lower levels in the pyramid. *Crash* is a great example of that, as we'll see.

Finally, it's very interesting to investigate how our needs change with age.

A 1981 study looked at how Maslow's hierarchy might vary across age groups. A survey asked participants of varying ages to rate a set number of statements from most important to least important. The researchers found that children had higher physical need scores than the other groups: the love need emerged from childhood to young adulthood; the esteem need was highest among the adolescent group; young adults had the highest self-actualisation level; and while old age had the highest level of security, it was needed across all levels comparably. The authors argue that this suggests Maslow's hierarchy may be limited as a theory for developmental sequence since the sequence of the love need and the self-esteem need should be reversed according to age.

Regardless of this possible flaw in Maslow's theory, if you're writing for children, it might be a good idea to check that what's at stake in the story is anchored in the lowest two levels. If you're writing for teenagers, checking that the main problem is directly or indirectly related to esteem can help. Finally, if you're aiming at young adults, self-actualisation might be a good theme to be aiming for.

Again, I'm not trying to reduce storytelling to an equation or a formula. The point I'm trying to make is that working on the dramatic structure, on the design of a story, can help us reach a wider audience without losing our intellectual or cultural integrity. Filmmakers with important things to say, who are eager to communicate them, can increase their chances of meeting a large audience at home and abroad if they use story structure to their advantage.

To illustrate this further, let's see how we can use Maslow's theory in relation to genre and story-type.

## Genre

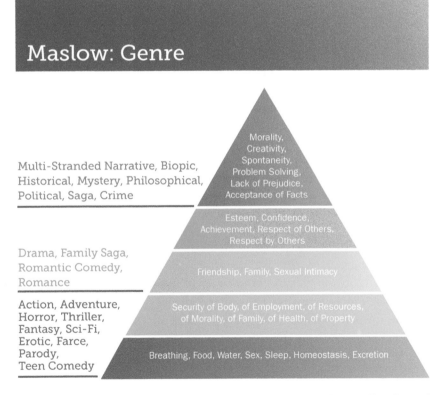

Maslow: Genre

Multi-Stranded Narrative, Biopic, Historical, Mystery, Philosophical, Political, Saga, Crime

Morality, Creativity, Spontaneity, Problem Solving, Lack of Prejudice, Acceptance of Facts

Esteem, Confidence, Achievement, Respect of Others, Respect by Others

Drama, Family Saga, Romantic Comedy, Romance

Friendship, Family, Sexual Intimacy

Action, Adventure, Horror, Thriller, Fantasy, Sci-Fi, Erotic, Farce, Parody, Teen Comedy

Security of Body, of Employment, of Resources, of Morality, of Family, of Health, of Property

Breathing, Food, Water, Sex, Sleep, Homeostasis, Excretion

Again, this is an artificial classification and there will always be hybrids and exceptions, but let's see if Maslow can help us with genre when we look at where the main problem lies in the pyramid.

At the top of the pyramid, we find the most intellectual genres, like multi-stranded narratives, historical, political or philosophical subjects, biopics, crime (whodunits based on mystery), etc. These are often designed to provide primarily an intellectual gratification.

In the middle, we have drama, family sagas and romantic comedies, which tend to be more emotional, even if they usually also deliver some kind of intellectual gratification.

At the bottom, we find more "commercial" genres: action, adventure, horror, thriller, fantasy, sci-fi. These can reach a wider audience simply because the problems they deal with are relevant to more people. Even those having reached higher needs can relate to problems associated with lower needs, while the opposite is less likely. An intellectual gratification isn't impossible – it's often expected with genres like science-fiction for example, as demonstrated by *Blade Runner*, *Interstellar*, *The Matrix* or *Inception* – but it's not required.

At the very bottom, we have mostly low-brow genres: erotic, farce, parody, as well as most teen comedies. These are based on the most fundamental needs in the audience. Not only is intellectual gratification not expected in these, it's often counter-productive to include any. Of course some thrillers or horror movies reach down to this visceral level, especially when breathing, food, water or homeostasis are involved (space thrillers like *Gravity*, horror / thrillers like *Misery*, survival stories like *127 Hours* etc).

So look at your project and try to see where the main problem sits in Maslow's pyramid, due to the nature of the theme it explores and the way the story is told. Does this help you identify its genre? Does this genre match your intention for the project? Does it tally in terms of audience and budget?

Then, especially if it sits too high in the pyramid, is there something you can do with its dramatic structure – i.e. in the design of the main characters, of the plot or in the way you manage conflict and information – to make it more accessible to a wider audience?

This is where understanding story-types becomes crucial, so let's move to the next point.

## Story-Type

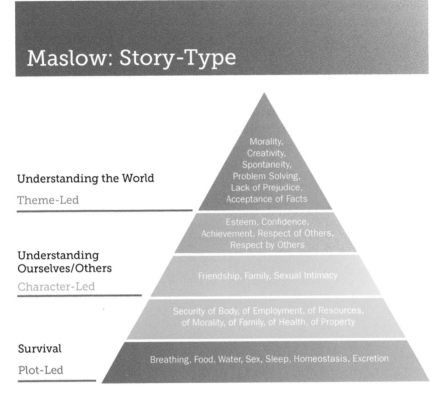

Provided you're not dealing with a hybrid or an exception, looking where each story-type tends to lie in Maslow's pyramid can be extremely useful, if only to make sure that you have chosen the right story-type for your project according to its genre, intended audience and budget.

At the bottom of the pyramid, we find **plot-led movies**. The main problem in the story lies outside of the protagonist, usually in a character, a group of characters or nature. These can reach the widest possible audience because they are about **survival**, one way or the other; they are the most universal stories because almost everyone, irrespective of the spoken language or the culture portrayed, can relate to them.

In the middle we find **character-led movies**, which can still reach a wide audience because they tend to focus on a problem located within the main character, in connection with the universal notions of esteem, love and belonging. The more universal the problem, the wider the potential audience. These stories are about **understanding ourselves and others**, which is why they are often the fictional equivalent of self-help books, and why they can be so popular.

At the top of the pyramid we find **theme-led movies**. In these, the main problem tends to be located in society. These stories help us **understand the world, society** (like most multi-stranded narratives) or **one person's life** (biopics). While these are more difficult to handle because they tend to be more limited to the subject, the culture, the society they explore, developed properly they can still reach a wide audience. They just require a very specific writing talent (and preferably a well-known director and stellar cast) to improve their chances of crossing over.

If the writer doesn't find ways to make the story relevant to a wider potential audience through its design, the movie may struggle for commercial success. This is why producers and executives know intuitively they have to beef up other elements to make up for the perceived weakness of the story-type.

This leads us to the next section, which deals with *identification* and what we might have to do to get a film made...

# Identification and Talent:
# The Key to Getting It Made

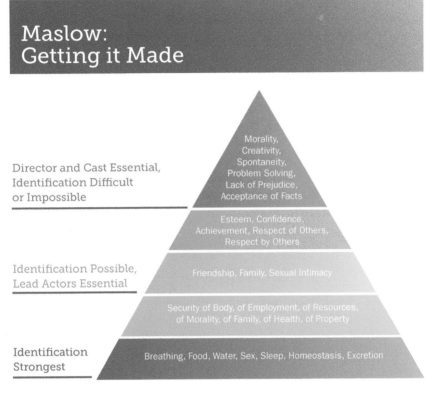

Maslow:
Getting it Made

Director and Cast Essential,
Identification Difficult
or Impossible

Morality,
Creativity,
Spontaneity,
Problem Solving,
Lack of Prejudice,
Acceptance of Facts

Esteem, Confidence,
Achievement, Respect of Others,
Respect by Others

Identification Possible,
Lead Actors Essential

Friendship, Family, Sexual Intimacy

Security of Body, of Employment, of Resources,
of Morality, of Family, of Health, of Property

Identification
Strongest

Breathing, Food, Water, Sex, Sleep, Homeostasis, Excretion

When dealing with a **plot-led story,** we can have an unknown director and cast if the script is good because what's at stake is relevant to everyone and a strong emotional identification with the characters is possible. This is why so many new actors and directors get their break in horror movies and thrillers. You can sell the story with the pitch so you don't need big names to get the movie financed – and seen. The fact that these genres can also be very economical in locations, scale and special effects also helps to keep the budget low and increase the chances for newcomers to get the film made.

When we deal with a **character-led story,** the casting of the main parts becomes crucial, especially because the lead is often *not* sympathetic. Think of *Groundhog Day* without Bill Murray and Andy McDowell, or

*As Good As It Gets* without Jack Nicholson and Helen Hunt or *Silver Linings Playbook* without Bradley Cooper and Jennifer Lawrence. We need a charismatic lead to make up for the lack of immediate sympathy we often have for the character. We'll soon have empathy as we start to understand the problem, but we need the actor to make us want the character to get better. In romantic comedies, the chemistry between the two main actors is one of the keys to the movie's success, as the whole story is based on the audience wanting them to end up together, even if they initially hate each other. No chemistry between the two means no movie. Because character-led movies are usually about family, love, friendship and relationships or self-esteem, achievement and respect (of others, by others), a strong identification is possible. We don't need names as much as for theme-led stories, but they definitely help (as always).

At the top of the pyramid, we're usually dealing with **theme-led stories**. We need a director able to assemble a stellar cast for these multi-stranded narratives. We need a director stars will fight to work with, preferably for a lower than usual salary because there will be so many of them. We need Robert Altman, Steven Soderbergh, Paul Thomas Anderson, The Wachowskis, Paul Haggis, Oliver Stone... Because the problem is in society, we need the director and the stars to get the audience to come watch the film, at least to start with, because the pitch itself rarely sells. Often, there isn't even a pitch. What's at stake isn't clear, or is too intellectual/theoretical/philosophical/sociological.

Of course we shouldn't take any of this literally. Again there is no formula for commercial or artistic success, but if you understand the story-type of your project (or in which way it's a hybrid or an exception that works), and where its main problem sits on Maslow's Hierarchy of Needs, it might become easier to develop and sell because you'll be able to handle it for what it is.

Now, enough theory. It's time to get more practical and look at some examples to illustrate these concepts.

## M-Factor and a Few Examples

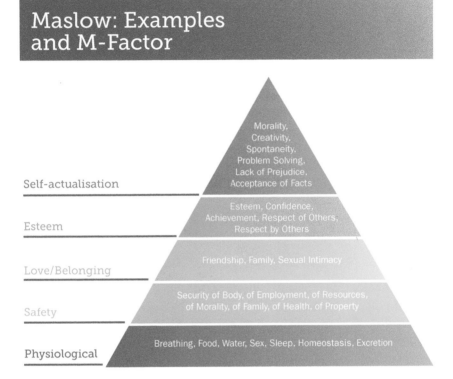

Maslow: Examples and M-Factor

Self-actualisation — Morality, Creativity, Spontaneity, Problem Solving, Lack of Prejudice, Acceptance of Facts

Esteem — Esteem, Confidence, Achievement, Respect of Others, Respect by Others

Love/Belonging — Friendship, Family, Sexual Intimacy

Safety — Security of Body, of Employment, of Resources, of Morality, of Family, of Health, of Property

Physiological — Breathing, Food, Water, Sex, Sleep, Homeostasis, Excretion

Just as hanging at the top of the pyramid doesn't guarantee an intellectually satisfying movie or artistic success, being stuck at the bottom doesn't necessarily secure a commercial hit. This is the way arthouse and commercial cinema are traditionally separated and opposed, but great movies often transcend this artificial line.

The best way to use Maslow's Hierarchy of Needs in screenplay development is not to focus solely on where the main problem lies in the pyramid. If the main problem is stuck at the top in abstract or intellectual layers, check if some aspects of the story explore problems that a wide audience can relate to on a more emotional level. If the main problem is anchored at the bottom, check if the story explores elements that give it more depth, that increase its heart and substance. This will allow a more thorough evaluation.

I call this the **M-Factor** (short for Maslow Factor). It's not a mathe-matical formula, just the way a story scores regarding Maslow's Hierarchy of Needs in relation to the main problem and other story elements, like each strand in a theme-led movie or subplots in a plot-led or character-led movie. I suggest using five "grades" for the M-Factor: low, low-medium, medium, medium-high and high. If your project scores medium to high, you're probably doing okay. If it scores low to medium, you might want to take another look at its design.

Remember: *"Nobody knows anything"* as far as commercial success is concerned. A bad screenplay is a bad screenplay and a high M-Factor won't change that. But if a screenplay is good (as in well-written, well-de-signed), looking at the M-Factor can be a way to check if its *potential* audience lines up with its budget level and genre, and also possibly find ways to widen it without losing any intellectual, artistic or cultural integ-rity in the process.

For example, *Crash* (Paul Haggis) is a theme-led movie. Its main problem lies in society (racial tension in Los Angeles). This places it at the top of Maslow's pyramid: morality, lack of prejudice and respect of others, respect from others. It has no identifiable genre, except maybe drama or ensemble film, and neither of these qualifies as a genre. All this helps it to do well with critics and festivals. However, every single strand in the movie, while exploring the same theme, is plot-led or character-led. What's at stake in each subplot lies much lower in the pyramid. Most problems are about relationships and safety: security of body, family, employment, resources, morality, property. In other words, while the main thematic problem – what the story is about – lies high up in the pyramid, the dramatic problems – what the characters struggle against in each strand – anchor the story in a much more concrete reality, which greatly increases its chances of reaching a wider audience. Overall, I would give *Crash* a medium-high M-Factor.

Let's take a completely different example: *Gravity*. Like all disaster movies, it's plot-led as the main problem in the story is external to the co-protagonists. Nature, in this case outer space, is the antagonist. What's at stake in the movie is the survival of astronauts Stone and Kowalski. Breathing, one of the most basic physiological human needs, is constantly under threat. The only thing keeping them from instant death for most of the story is their fragile space suit or some damaged structure – a space station on fire, a pod about to disintegrate, etc. So the main problem is firmly anchored at the very base of the pyramid: it's all about survival. As such, it's positioned as a mainstream thriller / disaster movie. However,

Stone also has an internal problem related to the death of her daughter, which gives her more depth as a character as well as internal conflict when it weakens her and tempts her to give up. This character-led subplot contributes to making the story less basic and helps us to care more about her and her survival. She needs to move on, and what she experiences during her survival ordeal will allow her to do just that. In fact, this is what the movie is about, thematically: rebirth and transformation. So from a Maslow point of view, it's almost the opposite of *Crash*: A main problem lying at the bottom of the pyramid to give it tension and suspense, a subplot that flirts with the middle to give it heart and a theme that explores the top to give it substance. The end result is the same: a great combination of meaning, entertainment and emotion. I'd give *Gravity* a high M-Factor as the main problem is so universal and visceral.

Another example: **Billy Elliot**. The main problem in the story is Billy's father's opposition to his son's aspiration to become a ballet dancer. The main problem sits at the top of the pyramid: It's about self-actualisation (creativity and art) and self-esteem (respect from others). However, to compensate for this, the film is set in a working class background, during the miners' strike of the 1980s. This allows the story to explore problems sitting much lower in the pyramid, in relation to safety (security of employment, resources, morality, family, health). There would be much less drama (and conflict) if Billy's family was well-off and from a more privileged background. In fact, there probably would be no story at all, or a very different one. A large part of the story is also about Billy's relationship with his father, and how they manage to move on. This important character-led aspect explores the middle of the pyramid (love/belonging/family). Overall, while *Billy Elliot*'s main problem and theme sit at the top of the pyramid, the story explores problems and issues anchored lower in the pyramid, allowing a much wider audience to relate to the characters and their struggles. Another effective cocktail of meaning, entertainment and emotion. I'd give it a medium-high M-Factor.

It's all about what's at stake, not necessarily about the problem itself or the protagonist's goal. For example, **Bicycle Thieves** portrays a very poor family trying to make ends meet in ruined Italy, post-World War II. The protagonist's goal over most of the film is to get his bicycle back after it's stolen. This sounds fairly unimportant and banal, but the story makes it very clear that without a bicycle, he loses his job. In fact, the overall goal of the protagonist is to protect his family. For the father, getting the bicycle back is literally a matter of life and death and defines the main dramatic action in the film. It's a survival story. When you look at it this way, the story is anchored right at the bottom of Maslow's pyramid, as it's all about safety (security of employment, of resources, of morality, of the family, of health), despite the apparent banality of the goal. This doesn't prevent it from exploring interesting themes and delivering a poignant testimonial about a very specific time and place. Overall I would give *Bicycle Thieves* a high M-Factor.

Again, if you happen to develop a story with a main problem hanging at the top of the pyramid, and you're interested in widening your potential audience, try to develop elements which explore problems in a lower layer (as for each strand in *Crash*) or boost the background of the story (like the subplots in *Billy Elliot*). Or add a romantic comedy element to make the story about love and relationships, as in *Silver Linings Playbook*, instead of keeping it in the serious drama sphere.

Similarly, if you're developing a thriller or an action movie with a main problem firmly anchored at the bottom of the pyramid, as it should be, you might want to try to add more depth and substance through a character-led subplot as in *Gravity* or an original theme as in *The Matrix*.

The following elements all contribute to the M-Factor: how far the stakes stretch through the pyramid; whether the main problem lies in the appropriate part of the pyramid; whether this defines a potential audience on a par with the budget level and genre of the film. Low stakes and/or mismatch, and you get a low M-Factor. High stakes, wide span through the pyramid and potential audience matching budget level and genre, and you get a high M-Factor.

We'll discuss some of the above examples and a few others in more depth in the next three chapters, but this should already show how Maslow's Hierarchy of Needs can help identify the core story elements that might require further development or clarification to increase our chances of reaching a wider audience. This is the main takeaway of this section: profitability has little to do with budget level. A more expensive movie isn't necessarily more profitable. A low budget movie with a high M-Factor like *Crash*, *Billy Elliot* or *The Intouchables* might stand a better chance of commercial success than a high budget movie with a low M-Factor.

Before we start looking more closely at the way to develop each story according to its story-type, let's see if a bit of practice can help solidify this theory.

# 1.4 Hands-On: What's Your Type?

You'll find below a list of ten well-known movies or TV shows.

For each one, describe who the protagonist is (if applicable), identify the main problem and where it lies (within the protagonist, outside the protagonist in other characters / nature or in society) and write down the story-type: PL for Plot-Led, CL for Character-Led, TL for Theme-Led.

Then, let's try to define where the main problem lies in Maslow's Hierarchy of Needs and check if there are other elements in the story (for example, strands in a theme-led movie, or subplots in a character-led or plot-led movie) which allow the story to reach lower or higher layers in the pyramid, and if all this tallies with the genre, budget and intended audience for the movie. This will give you its M-Factor.

For example, Hitchcock's *North by Northwest* is a classic thriller, in which protagonist Roger Thornhill (Cary Grant) first tries to understand who wants to kill him, and once he's identified that it's a group of foreign spies led by Philip Vandamm (James Mason), goes head-on after them to rescue Eve Kendall (Eva Marie-Saint), the secret agent he's got into trouble. The main problem and main source of conflict is the antagonist, Vandamm and his men, who directly threaten the life of the protagonist, making the film a plot-led story (as for almost all thrillers). The main problem lies right at the bottom of Maslow's pyramid (it's about survival, both for Roger and Eve, the woman he loves) although the love story also explores a higher level (love/belonging). Like most good thrillers, it has a high M-Factor. *North by Northwest* has become the archetype of the plot-led movie as championed by Hitchcock and his writers, with its inventive, entertaining, but fairly old-school storytelling. It's classical three-act structure at its best. Story-type, genre, intended audience and budget all tally.

Another example, the Dardenne Brothers' *Two Days, One Night* is a drama about Sandra's (Marion Cotillard) self-worth, her ability to be happy again, to get out of depression. It's disguised as a plot-led story (around the conscious goal of getting her job back), but the main problem lies within her (her depression, her inability to believe in herself, to see her worth, to be happy). She needs to change, so it's a character-led story. While the real problem hangs at the top of Maslow's pyramid (esteem and self-actualisation), the apparent main problem is anchored all the way down to survival: keeping a job, keeping a house. Love and belonging is also explored through her relationship with her husband and her colleagues. This contributes to widening its potential audience, without preventing the movie from exploring the social issues at its core or leading it to lose its intellectual, cultural and even political integrity. It's a drama, not a genre movie, yet the main problem in the pitch: "She has only one week-end to convince her colleagues to give up their bonuses so she can keep her job (and her home)" is universal. As a result, *Two Days, One Night* has a medium-high M-Factor, which helped it to reach a significant crossover audience, both at home and abroad, while still pleasing festivals crowds and critics. Without the external job-seeking dramatic action featuring such a strong time-lock, it would probably have ended with a low to medium M-Factor, a far less exciting pitch and likely a much smaller, strictly arthouse and less international audience.

Now, let's identify the story-type and M-Factor of the following movies or TV shows:
*Jaws*
*Silver Linings Playbook*
*Parenthood*
*Game of Thrones*
*Billy Elliot*
*Saving Mr Banks*
*Traffic*
*Interstellar*
*Little Miss Sunshine*
*Finding Nemo*

You'll find my take at the end of the book, in the *Hands-On Solutions* section.

Hands-on

Now, you might want to have a look at your own project. Try to identify its story-type, protagonist – if applicable – and where the main story problem lies in Maslow's Hierarchy of Needs.

Once you've clarified this, can you make any adjustments to try to reach a high or at least medium-high M-Factor? For example, if the main problem in the story hangs at the top of Maslow's hierarchy, can you check that some parts of the story deal with problems lying lower in the pyramid, so that a potentially wider audience can relate to the story?

Similarly, if you're designing a children's story with a main problem anchored at the bottom of the pyramid so that it explores issues a young person can relate to, can you add some layers to the story so an older audience can appreciate more sophisticated elements, without taking away the clarity of the main plot and losing your core audience (or your U rating)?

Finally, do the story-type, genre, intended audience, budget and M-Factor of your project seem to match? A low-budget drama with a medium M-Factor isn't necessarily an issue, but a high-budget genre movie targeted at a mainstream audience with a low M-Factor probably is.

# 2. Developing a Plot-Led Story

## First Up

**We're going to use *Misery, Billy Elliott and Gravity* as examples during this chapter, so it's highly recommended you watch these films before reading on.**

While no screenplay is easy to write, a plot-led story – in which the main problem lies outside the protagonist – is probably the most common and simplest story-type. It's by far the most classical, the one most story theoreticians since Aristotle have focused on.

This is why many screenwriting gurus even today confuse structure and plot and put so much emphasis on having a unique protagonist, with a unique goal, meeting many obstacles. They fail to notice that more and more stories (especially movies since the second half of the twentieth century) are character-led or theme-led. More and more filmmakers are becoming frustrated with this plot-led approach.

This being said, simple doesn't mean simplistic. When developed properly, a plot-led story can be original, moving and entertaining. It can even be meaningful. Think about movies like *The Pursuit of Happyness, Goodbye Lenin, The Bourne Identity, Billy Elliot, Alien, Misery, There's Something about Mary, Gravity, Jaws, Life Is Beautiful, Back to the Future*: all plot-led stories, in many different genres. All great movies.

Fairy tales and myths are usually plot-led, which is why some plot-led stories – the most famous example being *Star Wars* – can benefit from mythical storytelling theories inspired by the work of Joseph Campbell (and his student Christopher Vogler). But not all plot-led stories have a mythical journey or characters who conform to mythical archetypes. Let's see how plot-led stories are built and which story tools are applicable to all of them, not just those with a mythical aspect.

In fact, most of these tools - for example, all those explored in

*Behind the Scenes* and *Craft the Draft* - can also be used in character-led and theme-led stories, as well as hybrids and exceptions. Therefore, as explained earlier, this chapter should be read as a first layer, not as an independent block. Each chapter builds on the one before. We have to start somewhere, and because they are structurally simpler, it makes sense to start with plot-led stories.

We'll also take a closer look at the fractal aspect of the *dramatic* three-act structure and discuss the most important structural tools at scene level, before seeing how we can apply them at sequence level, and finally how we can use them to structure a whole script. This doesn't mean that this is the order in which every writer should develop a screenplay, and we'll discuss this in the next section, but it should make it easier to understand and master these concepts.

One limitation in most screenwriting books is that they ask the reader to analyse and apply concepts at script level right away, which is incredibly difficult initially, especially for writers (as understanding a concept is far easier than applying it). Explaining the concepts at scene level, and then expanding their use gradually at higher levels, makes it much easier to understand how they work and master them progressively.

In *Behind the Scenes*, we're going to look at the concepts behind the main structural tools, then we'll write scenes to put them into practice. We'll focus on the design, not on the writing style or dialogue, which means that not only writers, but everyone involved in the development process is invited to give it a go. Even if only to realise that understanding a concept intellectually is one thing; putting it into practice in a skilful, creative and original way is another. We'll also look at many examples, taken from very different movies (not only plot-led ones as the tools can be used for any story-type).

In *Sequence the Action*, we'll see how we can break down our second act into dramatic sequences using subgoals and we'll discuss subplots (yes, they are two different things!).

Finally, in *Craft the Draft* we'll weave it all together and discuss a few global concepts like genre, story world, theme and characterisation.

Before we dive into scene writing though, I'd like to clarify a few things regarding the kind of writer you are, or might be working with...

## Are You (or Are You Working with) an Ascending or a Descending Writer?

Writers come in all shapes and forms, but the way I see it, as a screen-writer myself and having worked with dozens of other writers as a script consultant/development exec or co-writer, we tend to be one of two main types: *ascending* writers and *descending* writers.

Nothing to do with the writer's career, and everything to do with a less painful development process.

**Ascending writers** start with an idea, then they structure their story, using many short documents like step outlines, index cards, beat sheets, scene breakdowns, character breakdowns, evolution maps, relationship maps. They design a story like a house, starting with plans, then with the foundations, the walls, roof and last, decoration. Once they've designed the story, they write a first draft. Like all first drafts, it's flawed in many ways, but if the writer is experienced and talented, it's usually a draft to build on for the rest of the development process. If an ascending writer is given three months to write a first draft, he or she will spend eight to ten weeks designing it using shorter documents, a couple of weeks writing the actual draft and one or two weeks to self-revise it before delivery. The development process, especially in TV, is designed for them and around them. They can be themselves and thrive.

**Descending writers** are different animals. They start with a theme, a character, a situation, and before they can start designing, they have to get all their ideas down in a first intuitive draft, which we'll call a draft zero. It doesn't take very long to write. Usually a couple of weeks, a month maybe. That's what helps them to find out about their characters, the theme, the story. Nothing can be built on this draft zero, because it has little design. Instead, we have a lot of dialogue, too much exposition and backstory. Once they have this big mess of a script, if they are talented and experienced, they can do the design – it usually takes about the same amount of time as when doing the design first – and get to a sound first draft. They often start the story much later and cut the first two thirds of the script. They are usually reluctant to use technical documents like step outlines and scene breakdowns which are sometimes forced upon them by well-meaning producers, story editors and development execs. They tend to have to work on the script, and on some apparently random, messy notes jotted by hand on a napkin. But their first draft will be just as good as that of an ascending writer. These writers would never deliver a draft zero as a first draft. They know the draft zero is just for them.

Robert M. Pirsig, in *Zen and the Art of Motorcycle Maintenance*, writes an insightful description of the difference between what he calls a classical mode and a romantic mode. Motorcycle maintenance being classical; motorcycle riding being romantic. If we translate this to screenwriting, I would say that ascending writers tend to favour the classical mode: good at logic, causality, problem-solving and story design, sometimes struggling with characters and dialogue. Descending writers tend to be drawn to the romantic mode: intuitive, with a solid handle on characters and dialogue, full of ideas, occasionally struggling to organise them. The challenge, for many writers, is to identify their dominant mode and develop the other one (or seek a co-writer with a complementary talent). The most accomplished writers are those who command both aspects of creativity, who switch seamlessly between classical and romantic modes during each phase of the creative process and deliver a well-designed screenplay, full of original ideas.

The development process isn't built for descending writers, especially in the TV industry. They often try to become more of an ascending writer to fit better with step deals, just as left-handed people in the past were forced to become right-handed.

**If you're a writer**, it's crucial that you identify which type you belong to.

There are no hard rules, but ascending writers tend to write plot-led stories; descending writers tend to be drawn to character-led or theme-led stories.

If you're an ascending writer, it doesn't mean you write better scripts, but you're quite lucky because the way you work naturally is more or less the way the industry expects writers to work.

If you're a descending writer, you might need to work around your methodology. Ascending writers may get there faster, but they are not better writers. What you need to understand and accept is that when a producer commissions a first draft, he or she means a first draft, which can be built upon. Not a draft zero. You have to write that draft zero for yourself, do the design and deliver the real first draft. If someone insists you write a step outline or a scene breakdown before you "go to draft", cheat. Write your intuitive draft zero in a couple of weeks, then write and deliver the requested step outline or scene breakdown. It's best not to just break down your draft zero as it's most likely flawed from a story structure point of view, but work on the design as you break it down.

There may be some writers who, like Mozart (allegedly), do all the design in their head so that writing the draft is simply a matter of putting to paper a perfectly formed story, but I haven't met one yet. Although the closest to this might be Sylvester Stallone. In a 1979 NY Times interview, Stallone explains that it took him three and a half days to write the script of *Rocky*, but he then adds that once he first got the idea – after watching the 1975 fight between Chuck Wepner and Muhammad Ali – he took a month to think about it and ten months to incubate it. What sticks in people's minds are the three and a half days to write the screenplay, forgetting about the eleven months of design preceding this productivity feast.

**If you're a creative producer, a story editor or a development exec**, try to identify the kind of writer you're working with. If they are ascending writers who revel in step outlines, beat sheets and scene breakdowns, work with them on these documents if they need/want you to. But if you're working with a descending writer, let them write this intuitive draft zero first, very quickly, instead of insisting they go through a methodology that doesn't suit them. You can't teach a dolphin to fly, but it swims much better than an eagle. What's important isn't how we get there, it's the result.

Another thing you really have to be able to identify is whether this draft you have in front of you is a first, second or third draft or simply a first, second or third version of a draft zero. Different but not better. You can't build on this because there are no foundations. It's as if you were building on sand. As soon as you try to add another floor, the house collapses. For the project to improve significantly, it has to have a strong structure. That means a *real* first draft.

As long as descending writers are not expecting to be paid for a first draft on delivery of a draft zero and accept that the design has to be done at some point, and if producers, development execs and story editors don't force an ascending methodology on descending writers, quite a few development problems can be avoided. We'll talk more about methodology later, but it might be useful to flag this right away, both for writers and non-writers.

This is also important for the structure of this book, especially the next three sections (*Behind the Scenes, Sequence the Action* and *Craft the Draft*). Depending on the kind of writer you are, you would either start writing random scenes, and then organise them into sequences as you work on the overall story structure, or you would do exactly the opposite, start with the overall structure, design dramatic sequences and only then write scenes. I'm starting with scene writing because it allows us to start playing with the tools at scene level, then go up to sequence level and finally work on the overall structure. While it makes sense from a teaching point of view, it's certainly not the only/best way to approach methodology. Remember, the best methodology is the one that works for you / your writer, although it doesn't hurt to experiment.

For now, though, first things first. In the beginning was the scene...

# 2.1 Behind the Scenes

Writing great scenes is the best way to write great scripts.

This is especially true for comedy where the three-act structure can be looser if the gags are good and the scenes are well-written.

Of course, some comedies have a very strong structure. *Tootsie* for example combines wonderful characters, a powerful dramatic irony, a tight plot and a rich theme making it at the same time entertaining, moving and meaningful. But comedies like *The Court Jester*, *Bean*, *Airplane* or *Parenthood* – which are hilarious if you enjoy the kind of humour they carry – mainly work because of the quantity and quality of the gags and the way other tools (usually dramatic irony) are used. The overall three-act structure is a kind of excuse to shape the story, but certainly not what we care about most as we watch the movie.

Improving the writing at scene level can make a huge difference to the overall quality of the scripts you develop, irrespective of their story-type, and is based on exactly the same concepts used at sequence or script level. Get your scene writing right and you're halfway to a great script!

## Managing Conflict

### Protagonist–Goal–Obstacle–Conflict–Emotion

The first concept we can use at scene level is the most important, as it's the most efficient way to generate and manage conflict. It's the idea that we can define a main dramatic action in a scene by defining (and being aware of) who wants what and why in the scene, what he/she/they try to do about it and what stands in his/her/their way.

This is the basic Aristotelian notion of protagonist–goal–obstacle that you are probably already familiar with:

## Structure (Plot-Led Story)

**Protagonist – Goal – Obstacles – Conflict – Emotion**

The basic form of drama:

- A character, the **protagonist,**
- tries to reach a **goal** (conscious *want*);
- meets **obstacles** and
- experiences **conflict** and **emotion,**
- which often leads the character to *grow.*

While I'm not convinced that the protagonist–goal–obstacle device should always be used at script level unless you're developing a purely plot-led story, nothing prevents you from structuring most scenes with a clear dramatic action, irrespective of the overall story-type of the movie itself. There are a few reasons for this.

1. It defines something clearly at stake in the scene; therefore, it makes it more interesting to watch for the audience. We want to know whether the protagonist of the scene will reach the local goal. When you raise a dramatic question over the whole film in a plot-led movie by defining who is trying to do something about the main problem, you lead the audience to wonder whether the protagonist will reach the goal. Similarly, you can raise a dramatic question over most scenes by defining who is trying to do something about a smaller problem (often related to the bigger one, as we'll see in *Sequencing the Action*), or who is trying to achieve something that gets them closer to the main goal (resolving the main problem). The protagonist of a scene doesn't even have to be the protagonist of the movie. It can be any character, including the antagonist if there is one. If we define a main dramatic action, we have a three-act structure in the scene, for the same reasons we can have one over the whole movie:

# Structure (Plot-Led Story)

## Why Three Acts?

1. The first act lasts until **the audience understands the goal of the protagonist** (conscious *want*).

2. The second act shows **the attempts made by the protagonist to reach this goal** (the dramatic action).

3. The third act shows **the consequences of the action.**

2. It generates conflict for the protagonist of the scene, which means that we start to care for the character. This is a crucial notion to understand. In a plot-led (or a character-led) movie, we don't necessarily identify (empathise) with the nicest character. We empathise with the character who experiences the most conflict. If you have a protagonist in your film, the way to get the audience to care is not to make them nice, it's to make sure that the protagonist experiences more conflict than the other characters. It's true at script level for the protagonist of the entire movie, and it's true at scene level for the protagonist of the scene. Therefore, if you have a protagonist in the movie, you're going to try to make that character the protagonist of most scenes, so they become the character who experiences most conflict overall. In a plot-led movie, this will be the character – or group of characters – trying to consciously solve an external problem. In a character-led movie, it will be the character trying to unconsciously solve an internal problem.

3. The conflict generates emotion, both for the protagonist and, through the identification link, the audience. There is a great scene in *Birdman* which illustrates this perfectly. Riggan Thomson (Michael Keaton), the protagonist, has hired his daughter, Sam,

as his assistant because she's just out of rehab and he's trying to keep her from bad influences. She's more resentful than grateful for this, so when Riggan tells her off for smoking cannabis (his goal in the scene is to protect her from herself), she tells him a few hard-to-hear truths, mainly that he doesn't matter and that what he's doing doesn't matter. It's all vanity. We feel his pain, but it's also a strong conflict and emotion for Sam, when she realises how far she's gone and starts to regret it. The scene is loaded with conflict, but it's the emotion that matters.

4.   It makes the scene much easier for the actors involved. As mentioned earlier, Stanislavski and his student Michael Chekhov (nephew of Anton), who have taught and inspired countless actors and are behind the Actor's Studio and its Method, suggest that actors try to understand what their goal and motivation is over the whole play or film, but also in each scene. It's much easier to do that if the writer has done the work and it's already there, encoded in the scenes and screenplay. Aimless scenes are difficult for actors to handle because they don't know why they are on stage or on the set and what they are trying to achieve. So defining clearly what's at stake in each scene, who is trying to do something about what, and who or what is standing in their way makes it easier for both the audience and actors. And as actors often get movies financed, this is a pretty important thing to do.

# Structure (Plot-Led Story)

## The Right Goal

In order to be efficient, the protagonist's goal in a plot-led-story should be:

- known and understood by the audience
- unique
- motivated
- hard to reach
- an absolute necessity for the protagonist

In a plot-led story, the protagonist's conscious goal should be **known and understood by the audience**, because this is what's going to help us understand the main direction of the story: **Who wants what**.

Usually **the goal is unique** so we get a clear sense of what's at stake in the story and we can root for the protagonist. A unique goal – dealing with the external problem – is what defines the main dramatic action. One protagonist, one goal is the essence of a plot-led story, because it's what gives it its backbone. This rule is broken all the time in character-led stories (in which a unique unconscious need linked to a unique evolution is what defines the main dramatic action), and even more in theme-led stories in which we have no main action, no unique protagonist and many strands. But in plot-led stories, this is how it tends to work. Of course it can be broken in a few working exceptions like *Psycho*, but usually when you break this rule in a plot-led story, it becomes more difficult to handle. Sometimes, as in *Alien*, the goal evolves as the antagonist evolves, and it's not an issue as long as the main problem in the story remains the same. We'll see how this works in more detail in *Sequence the Action*.

We should also **understand the motivations to reach the goal**. Sometimes they are obvious, sometimes not. If we don't understand why it's crucial for this character (or group of characters) to achieve a certain goal, then there is nothing at stake and we don't really care if the protagonist fails or succeeds. But if we do understand the character's motivation, **now we know who wants what and why.**

**The goal should be hard to reach** because if it's easy, there is no conflict for the protagonist and when there is no conflict, there is little interest and no emotional identification. This is closely linked to the strength of the obstacles we're going to put in the way of the protagonist. Now we **know who wants what and why, as well as what stands in the way.**

Finally, **the protagonist should be determined to reach the goal.** It's fine if they aren't fully committed to start with, or even if they first refuse the call-to-action as Christopher Vogler suggests in *The Writer's Journey*. After all, trying to avoid a problem can be a way of not having to solve it. This often happens in character-led stories, but in a plot-led story, at some point, the protagonist usually commits to solving the problem or there is no dramatic action. **A good protagonist in a plot-led story is one who doesn't give up despite all the obstacles thrown in his or her way.** They can have a wobble; they can have doubts or feel despair in the darkest moments of the story (as Ryan Stone does in *Gravity*), but a good protagonist doesn't give up until they have conclusively tried everything and failed, or succeeded.

We're going to use all these tools and principles that work at script level and apply them at scene level.

One last thing to discuss, though, before we give it a try: obstacles.

## Structure (Plot-Led Story)

### Obstacles

There are three main sources of obstacles:

- External Obstacles (from other characters, nature, society)

- Internal Obstacles (from within the protagonist)

- External Obstacles with an Internal Origin (when the protagonist is responsible for an external obstacle)

You're probably already familiar with the first two common sources.

**External obstacles** come from other characters, nature or society and stand in the way of a protagonist trying to reach a goal, making it more difficult and sometimes impossible for this character to succeed. This is Billy's father in *Billy Elliot*, space in *Gravity*, and parents, clans, gangs or tribes in *Romeo and Juliet* or *West Side Story*, *Mad Max*, etc.

With obstacles, it's quality rather than quantity that matters. Better a few well-chosen and well-exploited obstacles than a multitude of random ones. Also, delaying a protagonist is not the same as exploiting an obstacle. An external obstacle, ideally, makes it difficult for the protagonist to reach the goal, because that's how we'll generate the conflict that is going to make the story, the situation, the scene more interesting and will help the audience empathise with the character. It doesn't simply make it longer, which wouldn't help generate interest or identification.

**Internal obstacles** are a flaw or weakness in a protagonist, making it more difficult for a character to reach a goal. This is Ryan Stone's lack of experience as an astronaut in *Gravity*; Billy's own prejudice at the beginning of *Billy Elliot*; Chief Brody's fear of the sea in *Jaws*.

We're usually talking psychological rather than physical when defining the source of an obstacle, so the fact that Paul Sheldon is disabled due to his injuries and stuck in a wheelchair is an external obstacle in *Misery*, even if it's his own body. However, in *Cyrano de Bergerac*, Cyrano's lack of confidence in love because of his physical appearance is an internal obstacle. What stands in the way of Cyrano's goal of seducing Roxane is psychological – his lack of confidence – rather than physical. John Merrick's appearance in *The Elephant Man*, on the other hand, is an external obstacle which feeds the way society rejects him. While his deformed body prevents him from being part of society initially, the way he deals with his deformity allows him to become part of society in the end. The true obstacle is society, not his body.

Fear is an internal obstacle for gunman Lee (Robert Vaughn), one of the *Magnificent Seven*. He manages to overcome his fear in the end (paying with his life), but his goal is initially the same as his co-protagonists: to help the villagers stand up against antagonist Calvera (Eli Wallach). His fear is only revealed later in the story. Or Captain John H. Miller (Tom Hanks) whose reasonable fear only makes him more human and his actions more heroic in *Saving Private Ryan*.

Of course an internal source of conflict in a plot-led movie doesn't have to be fear. Jason Bourne tries to find out in *Bourne Identity* who is trying to kill him and why. The protagonist's amnesia is an internal obstacle but the main source of conflict in the story comes from Treadstone and its operatives. Just like David Mills (Brad Pitt) who struggles against his anger as he's trying to stop serial killer John Doe in *Se7en*. All these are plot-led movies (what's at stake primarily lies in a problem external to the protagonist, who consciously wants to do something about it). The internal source of conflict only makes reaching the conscious goal more difficult; it doesn't define what's primarily at stake in the movie.

Finally, let's take a bit more time to discuss the last source:

**External obstacles with an internal origin**. With these, the protagonist is the source of an external obstacle, which usually makes the story or the situation more interesting, gripping or funny. For example, when writer Paul Sheldon has to deal with Annie Wilkes in *Misery*, he's clearly facing an external obstacle – a deranged nurse – but this obstacle has two internal origins. First, she's a fan of his books. Had he not written them, he probably wouldn't have to deal with such a dangerously infatuated fan. He's not responsible for the fact that she's a homicidal maniac, but he's indirectly responsible for creating her as an obsessive fan. Second, if he had not made the decision to kill Misery, the heroine of his series of popular novels, to make room for writing something more personal, he wouldn't have made Annie so angry towards him and might have literally walked away. So while Annie is an external antagonist, Paul has to deal with something he's partially responsible for, both regarding the character and the situation he's facing, which makes the story more interesting and is connected to its theme (extreme fanboyism and creativity). If Annie were simply a random killer, even if she were still a nurse, the story wouldn't be as rich, complex, ironic and entertaining.

This external obstacle with an internal origin isn't necessarily a different character. For example, Dorothy Michaels gradually becomes one for Michael Dorsey (Dustin Hoffman) in the second half of *Tootsie*, just like *The Hulk* becomes one for Bruce Banner, or Mr Hyde for Dr Jekyll.

There isn't much more to it, really, so let's put all this into practice.

*Hands-on*

First, I'd like you to design a scene which will be three to seven minutes long (that's three to seven pages including dialogue if you follow the formatting industry standard), involving three characters, at most, in a single location. There should be a clear protagonist (one character or a group of characters sharing the same goal) trying consciously to do something about a problem which is either introduced at the beginning of the scene, or which we understand at the beginning of the scene even if the protagonist is already aware of it as the scene starts.

It can be a brand new, self-standing scene, like a mini-movie, or it can be a scene from a story you're developing right now.

During the scene, we'll be aware of a dramatic question: Will the protagonist reach the goal (solve the problem)? By the end of the scene, a climax will have brought an answer to this question: *Yes*, the protagonist reached the goal; *no*, the protagonist didn't. This will define a *dramatic* three-act structure in the scene: before, during and after the protagonist's action.

**Note:** The protagonist can have internal obstacles (some internal flaw or weakness that leads the character to experience more conflict on the road to the goal), but the main problem in the scene should be external to the protagonist (other characters or nature).

We have an antagonist if most of the conflict and obstacles for the protagonist come from one character (or group of characters sharing the same goal) in direct opposition to the protagonist. This is not always necessary. Obstacles and conflict can stem from various sources, in which case there is no antagonist (in the story or in the scene).

As you can see, over a short scene, we are dealing with all the structural elements we'll have to use at sequence and script level. Except that because it involves only a few characters and a simple dramatic action, it will be much easier to identify whether it works or not.

You can write the dialogue if you want to, but it's not essential. In fact, it could be a purely visual scene, without any dialogue. What's important here is the structural design of the scene.

To give you an idea of what we're after, have a look at the example from *Misery* in the next subsection and come back.

Ready? It shouldn't take you more than thirty minutes, and when you're done, we'll see if we can improve the result. Don't cheat. You have to try to design this scene, whether you are a writer or not. I promise you'll thank me later.

* * *

Okay, so now you have your scene, let's check a few things:

1.   **Did you make sure the audience was aware of the pro-tagonist's conscious goal early in the scene?** Remember, we only enter dramatic Act 2 when we – the audience – understand what the problem is, what's at stake, and who is trying to do something about it. So in a five-minute scene, you have less than a minute to introduce the characters and set up the main dramatic situation. In a screenplay, the dramatic situation is often set up in a previous scene, so you have a very short or nonexistent first act and you can start the scene in Act 2, but in this exercise we'll include a first act. This can either be what happens before the protagonist becomes aware of a problem and tries to do something about it, or it can last until we understand what an already active protagonist is trying to do. But that first act should be fairly short in relation to the whole scene.

2.   **If the above isn't obvious in the scene, can you try to show an inciting incident, a moment which triggers the protag-onist's goal, at the beginning of the scene?** Does that help?

3.   **Is the protagonist actively trying to solve the problem / reach the goal?** A passive or reactive protagonist can be tricky to handle in plot-led movies, so let's make sure we start with an active one.

4.   **Did you check that it was difficult for the protagonist to reach the goal, i.e. that the problem wasn't solved too**

quickly or easily? Did you make sure that the protagonist of the scene is the character who experiences the most conflict? Otherwise, you might have chosen the wrong protagonist and might have to rethink the structure of the scene.

5. **Did you make sure that it was getting harder for the protagonist to reach the goal as the scene progressed?** This is called a *crescendo*. The protagonist has to overcome increasingly challenging obstacles to maintain the audience's interest in the dramatic question.

6. **Did you check that you were using obstacles and sources of conflict related to the protagonist and the goal itself, and not obstacles which would be a problem for anyone or come out of nowhere?** For example, if a random tree falls on the protagonist or they get a flat tire, that's not as good as an obstacle related to the action and situation. Delaying the protagonist isn't enough.

7. **Did you try to make the protagonist at least partially responsible for the problem,** or did you try to find something in the protagonist, a character trait, that would make it more difficult for this protagonist to achieve this specific goal?

8. **Do you have a clear climax in the scene, i.e. a clear moment when the protagonist is facing the biggest obstacle and either succeeds or fails to reach the goal?** In other words, do you provide a clear answer to the dramatic question: *Yes*, the protagonist reaches the goal; *no*, the protagonist doesn't reach the goal.

9. **Did you show in a brief Act 3 (after the dramatic action) one or more consequences of the protagonist's action?** Usually, when someone tries hard to achieve something and either succeeds or fails, it has some consequences.

10. **Did you try to convey as much as possible in the scene through visual storytelling rather than dialogue?** Did you try to show rather than tell? For example, showing an important character trait visually, or using a picture to convey backstory?

As you can see, all these questions would be relevant at script level if we were developing a plot-led story, but we can check these very same things at scene level to improve the clarity and efficiency of each scene, irrespective of the project's story-type.

That's the beauty of the fractal aspect of story structure. If we get better at scene level, we get better at sequence and screenplay level as well. This is why improving your scene writing is one of the best ways to enhance your writing (or development) skills. The other benefit is that we'll need this skill for any screenplay, not only in plot-led stories.

If you think that any of the above could be improved in the scene, please go back and rewrite it to make it better.

\* \* \*

Is your scene better? I know it's just an exercise, but I hope it's been fun and it's becoming clearer how the *dramatic* three-act structure can be used in most scenes – and sequences – even if you're not interested in using it for the overall structure of the story.

Now let's take a look at *Misery* for an example of a well-structured scene, then we'll go through a few essential questions about managing conflict.

## Paul Tries to Save His Manuscript in *Misery* (Local Three-Act Structure)

Let's look at the scene in *Misery* when nurse Annie Wilkes (Kathy Bates), the antagonist of the movie, asks writer Paul Sheldon (James Caan), the protagonist, to burn the manuscript of a new book he's just written, about thirty-three minutes into the movie.

In this scene, Paul does everything he can to avoid this (we know it's the only copy), until he realises that Annie is going to kill him if he doesn't comply, so he's left with no choice.

It's a great scene, fantastically written, with a clear protagonist (Paul). His goal in the scene is to save his manuscript. It is triggered when he understands that Annie wants him to destroy it. That's the end of the first act of the scene, and the beginning of Paul's dramatic action.

The second dramatic act of the scene shows Paul's attempts to save his work: He first tries to lie, pretending he doesn't care, that it's not the only copy (subgoal 1). He fails; Annie knows it's the only copy (obstacle, therefore conflict for Paul). He then tries to bribe her, promising half the proceeds when it's auctioned (subgoal 2). But he fails; Annie isn't interested in money, only about decency, purity and God's will (obstacle/conflict). He then tries to convince Annie that he won't publish it, that he'll keep it to himself (subgoal 3). He fails; Annie believes he won't be free until he destroys it (obstacle/conflict). The climax of the scene (when Paul faces the biggest obstacle and we get an answer to the dramatic question: "Will Paul manage to save his manuscript?") is when Annie starts pouring petrol on his bed, clearly threatening his life if he persists in refusing. Paul, dejected, has to destroy his manuscript to save his life. He fails to reach his goal in the scene in order to survive, which is his goal in the film. The third act is very short, simply showing the burnt bits of charred paper threatening to set fire to the rest of the room (conflict for Annie), until they are drowned in water, making them look even more pathetic (conflict for Paul).

There is an antagonist in the scene (a unique source for the obstacles and conflict that the protagonist experiences in the scene) and that's of course Annie, who happens to be the antagonist of the movie as well.

Annie also has a goal: to convince Paul to destroy his manuscript. While she experiences conflict as well – Paul doesn't agree right away and tries to resist – the reason Paul is the protagonist of the scene is simply because the conflict he experiences (being forced by a deranged nurse to burn his beloved manuscript) is stronger than the conflict she experiences (a writer she admires refuses to burn a book he's written in a way she doesn't approve of).

Like him, Annie has motivations and a fitting backstory. She isn't a cardboard villain. That's what makes *Misery* such a great psychological thriller.

Change a few details in the situation – for example make Paul a serial killer who has written a book about his exploits and have Annie force him to burn his manuscript before he pays with his life for having killed her only daughter – and obviously we will not identify with the same character in the scene.

Finally, while the scene isn't directly connected to the "escaping" part of Paul's overall goal, it is related to the "survival" part. He's forced to burn the sole copy of his manuscript to survive a physical threat.

## Five Essential Questions Regarding Managing Conflict

If you agree with the idea that a good story is a metaphor for a problem-solving process, it has many practical consequences.

The first is that it allows you to think about five essential questions related to story structure and especially to the managing conflict side of it. As soon as we've identified the main problem in the story, we can address these crucial questions:

1. **Who is struggling with the problem / trying to do something about it (consciously or not)?** This gives us our story *protagonist* (a single character, or a group of characters sharing the same goal).

2. **Where is the problem located?** This gives us our *story-type* (*plot-led* if the problem is external to the protagonist and lies in other characters or nature; *character-led* if the problem lies within the protagonist; *theme-led* if the problem lies in society).

3. **What can be done about it?** This defines the main dramatic *action* or *evolution*, (or the various strands united by the filmmaker's *vision* in a theme-led story).

4. **How can it be done?** This gives us *dramatic sequences*, defined by *subgoals* (conscious tasks in a plot-led story), *psychological/ emotional steps* in a character-led story or *strands* exploring various aspects of the same problem in a theme-led story.

5. **What happens if the problem isn't solved?** This is possibly the most important question, because it defines *what's at stake*. To be emotionally involved in a story, we have to feel that it would be a catastrophe if the protagonist fails (to reach a conscious goal or to change). If we're not able to identify what's at stake, we're unlikely to care about the outcome. In *plot-led stories*, what's at stake is related to the main dramatic *action*. In *character-led* stories, it's about the main character's *evolution*. In *theme-led* stories, because the problem explored in various strands is usually not solvable in a believable way, you have to make sure that there is something at stake in each strand to make up for that, therefore making as many strands as possible plot-led or character-led.

These are the most important questions you can ask yourself about your story from a managing conflict point of view.

## Managing Conflict

### Five Essential Questions Regarding Managing Conflict

1. Who is struggling/trying to do something about a problem (consciously or not)? *Protagonist*
2. Where is the problem? *Story-Type*
3. What can be done about it? *Action/Evolution*
4. How can that be done? *Sequences/Subgoals*
5. What happens if the problem isn't solved? *What's at stake*

Now that we've had fun with this essential part of story structure, we're going to look at the tools we can use to handle another essential aspect, which is *managing information.*

# Managing Information

### Dramatic Irony

To manage information in a story – or in a scene – we use primarily three tools:

## Managing Information

**Each piece of information to be shared with the audience can be revealed or exploited as:**

• Dramatic irony

• Surprise

• Mystery

Managing information is also crucial to generate **suspense**.

We'll discuss all the other tools in the next section, but I'd like to spend some time on dramatic irony first, as it's both one of the most powerful and most overlooked tools, especially in relation to story structure.

If we think about a man walking towards a cliff, it's not dramatic. But as soon as we realise that the man is blind, it becomes more interesting, and our natural reaction is to want to shout a warning. This is because we know something that the blind man – the victim of the dramatic irony – doesn't know.

This is called dramatic irony, and it can be used to generate comedy, suspense, drama, tears, laughter, thrills... It's present in almost every great screenplay. Think about *Back to the Future* (we know that Marty comes from the future; most of the other characters in the past, including his own mother and father, don't), *Amadeus* (we know that Salieri wants to destroy Mozart, but his wife Constanza thinks he's a friend), *Tootsie* (we know that Michael Dorsey is a man pretending to be a woman; most of the other characters don't know that), *Psycho* (after Marion Crane's murder, we know that there is a killer in the motel; most of the characters – except Norman Bates – don't), *The Dark Knight* (we know that Bruce Wayne is the Batman; most of the other characters don't), *The Lives of Others* (we know that Georg Dreyer and Christa-Maria Sieland, the theatre couple, are under surveillance, but they don't. Later we know that Gerd Wiesler, the Stasi agent, is trying to help them; they don't), *Cyrano de Bergerac* (we know that Cyrano loves Roxane; she and Christian don't. We know that Cyrano writes Christian's letters; Roxane doesn't), *Infernal Affairs* and its remake *The Departed* (we know that Sullivan, the cop – Damon – is an infiltrated gang member and that Costigan, the gang member – Di Caprio – is an undercover cop). We could find countless examples in contemporary cinema, classic movies and stage plays. Dramatic irony is almost everywhere.

It works so well because the audience enjoys being in the know. In life, we usually find out about crucial things when it's too late. With dramatic irony, we can have a god-like experience and know about significant events before they happen, or as they happen. That's extremely gratifying for the audience.

How does it work? Well, it usually works in three steps.

**First step**: We set up the dramatic irony, i.e. we give the audience information that at least one character on screen will not be aware of. This is when we show that the man walking towards the cliff is blind, or reveal the presence of the bomb under the table without letting the characters see it. The character who doesn't know is the victim of the dramatic irony. It can be one character, or more. Sometimes, as in some of the movies listed earlier, most of the characters in the movie are victims of one or more dramatic ironies over most of the story.

**Second step**: We exploit this dramatic irony, which means that we're making the most of the conflict we can see coming for the victim. For example, show that the characters about to walk away from the bomb are delayed, or come back having forgotten something. A single dramatic irony can be exploited over the whole story, a sequence, a scene, down to just a single shot.

**Third and last step**: We resolve the dramatic irony: the victim(s) discovers the piece of information that we've known about since the set-up.

Sometimes the resolution is called a must-do scene (or obligatory scene) because the audience would be disappointed if we forgot to resolve the dramatic irony. We usually want to see how the victims react when they find out. In *Tootsie*, all the characters – especially Julia (Jessica Lange) or her father (Matt Donahue) – have to find out that Dorothy Michaels is a man, and we want to see their reactions. In *City Lights*, the flower girl has to find out that her benefactor isn't a millionaire but a tramp. In *The Lives of Others*, the director has to realise what the Stasi cop has done for them, and how he became a "good man". Roxane has to find out that Cyrano wrote Christian's love letters. But in other instances, dramatic ironies are not resolved, and it's not a problem. For example, Mozart dies thinking Salieri is still helping him, and Marty comes back from the past without any character – except Doc – having realised that he was from the future.

## Managing Information

### Dramatic Irony

A tool that works in three steps:

1. Set-Up

2. Exploitation

3. Resolution

While dramatic irony is often used to make us feel pity and fear for the victim, it can also generate humour. For example, in the famous balcony scene in *Cyrano de Bergerac*, which we'll analyse fully later, we laugh when Roxane doesn't realise that Christian is repeating Cyrano's words without even understanding them, but we feel Cyrano's pain when he helps to send his rival into the arms of the woman he loves.

Dramatic irony is also used to generate suspense, especially when the victim of the dramatic irony is the antagonist. In this case, we fear the consequences of the victim finding out. For example, in *Misery*, when Paul sends Annie away to get him some paper while he tries to escape,

Annie isn't aware of his escape attempt. We fear what's going to happen if she finds out – and rightly so as when she finds out, she hobbles him!

We could spend a whole chapter discussing dramatic irony – and this is exactly what Yves Lavandier does brilliantly in his excellent *Writing Drama* – but the best way to understand how it works is to use it.

**Hands-on**

I'd like you to design a scene during which you set up, exploit and resolve a local dramatic irony.

Same constraints as before: one location, three to seven minutes, three characters maximum.

If you need some inspiration, or want to find out more about the set-up, exploitation and resolution stages, you'll find some examples from a few different movies over the next few pages.

*   *   *

Now that you have your scene based on dramatic irony, let's check a few things to see if we can improve it:

1.  **Have you given the information to the audience clearly during the set-up?** Dramatic irony is all about sharing as much information as possible with the audience. So don't be shy. Give the information as clearly as you can, if possible visually. Then exploit it to create tension, humour or conflict.

2.  **What emotions does your dramatic irony generate?** Is it humour? Drama? Suspense? Try to milk it as much as possible. As soon as we set up a dramatic irony, the audience is anticipating trouble for the victim. You're opening a door leading to a lot of juicy conflict: Don't disappoint. The worst thing you can do is not to exploit a dramatic irony you've set up, or resolve it too early.

3. **Are you aware of the three-act structure in the scene, if there is any?** Does the dramatic irony work with it, or against it? For example, if the protagonist of your scene is character A, but character B is the victim of a strong dramatic irony, do we identify more with the victim of the dramatic irony than with the protagonist? Or, if the victim of the dramatic irony is the protagonist, can we still identify with the protagonist despite the fact that we have more information? Usually this isn't an issue at scene level, but it can become one at script level, when a dramatic irony is exploited over a long period of time. Finally, if the victim of the dramatic irony is an antagonistic character, do we fear the consequences of the resolution? In this case, suspense comes from the expected conflict for the protagonist when/if the antagonist finds out.

4. **When we design a clear protagonist-goal-obstacle structure in a scene** (or in a script), we raise a dramatic question: Will the protagonist reach the goal? When we set up a dramatic irony, we raise an ironic question: How and when will the victim of the dramatic irony find out? Make sure these two questions work hand in hand and do not cause issues in your scene.

5. **During the resolution, do you show the victim's reaction?** This is a gratifying moment, a moment we've been waiting for, so make the most of it. Think about the flower girl's face at the end of *City Lights*, or Roxane when she finds out it was Cyrano who wrote Christian's love letters, or the reaction of all the characters in *Tootsie* when they realise that Dorothy Michaels is a man. It's not by chance that all the victims are watching that specific episode in the film. If you decide not to show the resolution, make sure you know why it's better than showing it; otherwise, the audience might be disappointed. For example, the victims of the dramatic irony in *Back to the Future* (especially Marty's parents) don't find out that Marty comes from the future, but there is still a huge pay-off in dramatic Act 3, once Marty is back and sees his world changed thanks to his actions in the past. This makes up for the non-resolution of the main dramatic irony for its victims.

Check if there is anything you can improve in your scene in the areas discussed above, and come back when you're done.

* * *

Dramatic irony is one of the most important tools, so mastering it is crucial, in any genre. You can use it to shape the whole story, as in the movies mentioned earlier, but you can also use it locally, in a scene or sequence, to spice up a section of your script, or even give a dramatic backbone to an otherwise spineless sequence.

Sometimes, we can't avoid a few episodic moments in a screenplay – moments that might not fit under one main dramatic action for whatever reason. One way to strengthen such a section might be to set up, exploit and resolve a dramatic irony as you deal with the disconnected plot points. There may be no unifying dramatic action over the sequence, but an ironic question might be all we need for the audience to overlook this structural weakness. So dramatic irony is a tool you might benefit from even if the general structure of your screenplay isn't classical.

## Local Set-Up, Exploitation and Resolution: *Heat*

In *Heat* (1995), towards the end of the movie at 02:15, Chris (Val Kilmer) – a member of the gang led by Neil (Robert De Niro) – drives back to his wife Charlene (Ashley Judd) after a bank heist that went horribly wrong, as he doesn't want to leave town without her.

There is very little apparent conflict in the scene. But thanks to dramatic irony, we feel a lot of conflict for the two main characters, because of how skilfully information is managed.

In an earlier scene, at 02:03, the police have forced Charlene to set a trap for Chris, using her son to convince her that if she goes to jail, Dominick ends up in foster care and his life goes downhill from there. If she helps them to arrest Chris, she doesn't go to jail and keeps her son. So she agrees to makes the call and tell Chris where to meet them. This initial scene is the set-up. Chris doesn't have this information, which makes him the victim of a dramatic irony.

So when Chris stops his car under Charlene's window, there is tension because we know where the danger is: the police in the apartment and in the street, waiting to hear from Charlene if it's Chris or not so they can arrest him. We're not sure what Charlene will do as it's such a dilemma for her. They have a rocky relationship. She was about to leave Chris for another man, so we don't know if she's going to betray Chris or if she'll try to save him, putting her and her son at risk. We know she loves her son and doesn't want to lose him, but does she still love Chris?

Chris doesn't know about the danger, but we do. It's a classic "bomb under the table" example where dramatic irony is used to generate tension. We feel a lot of conflict for Chris, but also for Charlene who is struggling with her dilemma.

There is another dramatic irony at play here. The antagonists – the police – are also victims of a dramatic irony. We know it's Chris; they don't. Therefore, we fear the resolution because we fear the consequences of the antagonists finding out. In this case, Chris could be arrested or killed by the police, and Charlene could go to jail and lose her son if she lies to them. This is also used to generate suspense and tension in the scene.

When Charlene finally signals Chris not to come up and tells the police that it's not him, we have the resolution of the main dramatic irony. Chris is now aware of the presence of the police. We feel relieved for Chris – he can drive out of danger – and moved for both of them. It's also a great proof of love from her. It's done without a word, using visual storytelling, which makes the moment cinematic and powerful.

As often, the resolution of this dramatic irony (Chris finding out that the police are there) sets up another one. We know that he's now aware of the police presence, but the police don't know he's found out. This dramatic irony, along with the fact that the police, misled by Charlene, believe it's not Chris – even after they check his ID, which is fake – and let him go, is never resolved (and it's not an issue here).

Dramatic irony is used in the scene primarily to create suspense/ tension, and also to generate intense emotions. The scene is short, with little to no dialogue, but it's one of the strongest scenes in the movie from an emotional point of view, all thanks to dramatic irony (and visual storytelling). There is no apparent conflict – no one is fighting, arguing or yelling at each other – but because of the way information is managed, we feel a lot of conflict for the two main characters in the scene. This is the power of dramatic irony: using the management of information to create subtler forms of conflict and yet very strong emotions.

## Set-Up Scene: *Bolt*

After a brilliant opening action sequence showing Bolt (John Travolta) fiercely protecting his young owner Penny (Miley Cyrus) with his impressive super powers (which he believes are real), the truth is revealed to the audience: This is a TV show, Penny is an actress, everything is fake and Bolt is just a normal dog. This nice surprise immediately sets up a dramatic irony: Bolt doesn't know that he has no super-powers. This strong dramatic irony is going to be exploited over a large part of the movie, generating both humour and tension.

This is a technique often used when managing information: reveal something as a surprise to the audience, but keep it from at least one character (in this case, Bolt, the protagonist of the movie), then exploit it as a dramatic irony. This is not specific to genre movies or animation. The device is used the same way in a movie like *The Apartment*, in which we know that Fran Kubelik (Shirley McLane) is Sheldrake's (Fred McMurray) mistress, when C.C. Baxter (Jack Lemon) doesn't.

So the short scene eleven minutes into the movie between the director of the show and "Mindy from the network" is essential. It sets up this important dramatic irony and justifies the concept. It also explains why the premise is possible and helps us to suspend our disbelief. If we didn't know why it's so essential that the dog doesn't know, we would question the TV production going to such lengths to make sure that everything looks real to the dog, thus making the dramatic irony possible.

This dramatic irony not only generates a lot of humour, it also increases our identification with Bolt. We feel for him because he isn't aware of something so important about himself and we fear the moment he'll find out (we know it has to happen at some point, as we expect the resolution). It also puts him in danger because he overestimates his abilities, so we feel a lot of conflict for him, even if he doesn't experience as much himself.

Finally, it gives a strong character-led aspect to the story, which adds depth. While Bolt's conscious goal is to find his owner, Penny, after he's shipped away in a crate by mistake, he also needs to find out the truth about himself. As such, dramatic irony is part of the structure of the movie. In *Bolt* as in many other movies like *Tootsie*, *The Lives of Others* or *Avatar*, managing information is as important as managing conflict. Its structure can't be analysed without a clear understanding of how dramatic irony helps to shape it.

So getting the set-up right is essential in *Bolt*, and that's what this short scene achieves brilliantly.

## Exploitation Scene: *Cyrano de Bergerac*

Note: I'm using for reference Jean-Paul Rappeneau's version (with Gerard Depardieu as Cyrano) because it's one of the most recent but almost any version faithful to the original play is designed the same way, as is the play itself.

The so-called "balcony scene" in *Cyrano de Bergerac* is one of the most famous scenes in the whole repertoire. Of course, the dialogue is funny and poetic, but what really powers the scene is the way it's structured.

The scene starts at 01:08. It has a strong three-act structure and also exploits two dramatic ironies which have been set up earlier in the story. This is the complex dramatic engine of the scene.

Let's look at the three-act structure aspect first.

Before the balcony scene, Christian tells Cyrano that he doesn't need him anymore, that Roxane loves him and he's fine on his own now. But when he next sees Roxane and is talking to her without Cyrano's help, she finds him dull and doesn't want to see him anymore. Indeed, he tells her he loves her, and when asked for more, he says he loves her... a lot. Not enough for Roxane. So Christian goes back to Cyrano and begs him to help him win Roxane back.

As the balcony scene starts, we already have clear co-protagonists, Christian and Cyrano, and their goal is to win Roxane back for Christian.

However, we know that Cyrano loves Roxane, and would like her for himself. In fact, Cyrano is the protagonist of the story, and his goal is to seduce Roxane for himself. He's only using Christian to talk to her, because he's as insecure in love – he finds himself ugly – as he's brave in combat.

There is a clear conflict between Cyrano's overall goal of trying to win Roxane for himself and Cyrano as a co-protagonist of the scene, trying to win her back for Christian. As for the rest of the story, Cyrano is using the fact that he can hide behind Christian to tell Roxane how he feels about her. Problem is, it works too well and she ends up in the arms of his rival.

There is no first act in the scene, because we already know from the previous scene who the co-protagonists are (Christian and Cyrano) and what their goal is (to win Roxane back for Christian).

That's how the three-act structure works in the scene, which also exploits two main dramatic ironies. Both have been set up earlier in the story and will be resolved later. First, we know that Christian is using Cyrano's words to seduce Roxane, and she doesn't know that. Second, we know that Cyrano loves Roxane, and both Christian and Roxane are unaware of this.

It's interesting to look at the different emotions generated by these two dramatic ironies, and how they alternate as Cyrano moves back and forth between his local goal in the scene and his overall goal in the story.

We start the scene with Christian talking to Roxane in the shadows under her balcony. When we see Cyrano feeding him lines, the first dramatic irony is exploited: Roxane has no idea that Christian's words come from Cyrano. This dramatic irony mainly generates humour. We also feel they are making progress on the road to their local goal (winning Roxane back for Christian).

When Roxane becomes suspicious and Cyrano takes the opportunity to speak to her directly, concealing his identity in the darkness, we start exploiting the second dramatic irony. We know he's in love with her while neither Christian nor Roxane are aware of that. This is when Cyrano is making progress on the road to his own goal, which is to seduce Roxane for himself. It's the first time he speaks to her directly, even if she doesn't know it's him, and it's a great success for Cyrano: "I never hoped for that much. I can die now". This dramatic irony is more poignant. We're not laughing anymore. We feel sorry for Cyrano and his inability to speak as himself to the woman he loves.

When Christian feels that they are going off track and forces Cyrano to re-focus on their local goal, asking for a kiss, we go back briefly to the first dramatic irony, the funny one, until Cyrano reluctantly manages to get Christian up the balcony and into Roxane's arms for the night. This is the climax of the scene (the answer to the local dramatic question is *yes*, they do win Roxane back for Christian) and while it's a success for the co-protagonists of the scene, it's mainly a success for Christian. For Cyrano, it's a huge blow. To experience his biggest success to date (the opportunity to tell Roxane how he feels about her), he's thrown his rival into the arms of the woman he loves.

In the last moments of the scene, we switch back to the second dramatic irony, and again we feel a lot for Cyrano when he looks at them kissing each other and disappearing into her room. The third act of the scene is just this moment showing Cyrano looking at the consequences of their dramatic action.

In the balcony scene, beyond the surface which is full of witty, poetic dialogue, we have a very strong structure which uses both the dramatic three-act structure and dramatic irony to create a complex but powerful combination. The scene is both funny and moving, and it allows us to feel very close to the protagonist, Cyrano, and share his emotions.

## Classical Misunderstanding: *There's Something about Mary*

*There's Something about Mary* uses dramatic irony a lot, both locally in scenes or sequences, and over most of the movie for the most important ones. For example, we know that a few stalkers are spying on Mary (Cameron Diaz), but she doesn't; we know that Healy (Matt Dillon) is lying to our protagonist Ted (Ben Stiller), but he doesn't. We also know that Ted is sincere and never intends to take advantage of her, but Mary doesn't.

The Farrelly brothers are masters of using dramatic irony to generate humour just as Hitchcock was a master of using dramatic irony to generate suspense. They use the tool brilliantly, in the pure tradition of Vaudeville – as Labiche did in the theatre, going all the way back to Moliere – but with their own modern style, of course.

There is one sequence about sixty-six minutes into the movie, when they create a situation in which a double dramatic irony leads to a classical misunderstanding. It's the police interrogation scene, when Ted is questioned about "the hitchhiker".

"The hitchhiker" means two different things for Ted and for the police.

For Ted, it simply means a hitchhiker he picked up before stopping at a rest area. When Ted was arrested in the police raid, the hitchhiker escaped, leaving his bag behind.

For the police, who have found a hacked-up body in the bag left in Ted's car, "the hitchhiker" means the victim of a murder.

Because of what happened before the interrogation scene – we saw Ted with the hitchhiker a few scenes ago, and we heard the police officers briefly discussing the case just before the interrogation – both parties in the scene are victims of a dramatic irony.

1.  Ted doesn't know that the police officers are talking about committing a murder – not hitchhiking;

2.  the police officers don't know that Ted is talking about hitchhiking – not about committing a murder.

The audience is the only party to know exactly what the misunderstanding is, which generates hilarity in the scene.

The situation is resolved a few scenes later, when the police, having arrested the real killer, apologise to Ted as they release him from jail.

## Resolution Scene: *City Lights*

In *City Lights*, the Tramp (Charlie Chaplin) has fallen in love with a blind flower girl (Virginia Cherrill) who, due to a misunderstanding, believes he's a very rich man. It's a plot-led movie and the Tramp spends the whole film trying to help her by finding money for an eye operation which could restore her sight, and paying for her rent before her landlord kicks her out. At the end of the movie, he gets the money, gives it to the girl but is sent to jail because he's wrongly accused of theft.

We're in dramatic Act 3 as he's achieved his goal, but we know the story isn't over because there are two strong dramatic ironies that still need resolving. First, the Tramp doesn't know that the eye operation has been successful and that the flower girl has got her sight back. Second, she doesn't know that the benefactor who helped her was a penniless tramp and not a millionaire.

The first dramatic irony is resolved when the Tramp, who's just been released from jail, meets the girl working in her new flower shop and realises she can see. The second is resolved when she ironically wants to give him some money, and as she holds his hand realises who he really is.

This pure moment of cinema is wonderfully moving because it uses a combination of three writing tools. It's the resolution of a dramatic irony (the flower girl realises how selfless the Tramp has been and how hard it must have been for him to raise the money for her operation); it's a pay-off for everything that happened in the movie before; lastly it's done visually as it's when she touches his hand that she understands (he could have told her, even in a silent movie, but that would have been out of character and weaker).

There is great talent behind such a moving ending. Technically, it's made possible because Chaplin mastered the craft and knew how to use the tools. Using dramatic irony and planting/pay-off allows him to generate emotion. Using visual storytelling instead of dialogue enables him to bypass our intellect and speak directly to our emotional brain, amplifying the effect. We'll discuss planting/pay-off and visual storytelling later as they are both essential tools.

Dramatic irony is an integral part of the structure of *City Lights*, and the ending wouldn't be so moving if it weren't for the resolution of the main dramatic irony.

## Surprise, Mystery and Suspense

While **dramatic irony** means sharing as much information as possible with the audience to bring them closer to the filmmaker, there are other ways to manage information in a story.

With **surprise** – which is simply an unexpected plot point, also called a twist – we hold information back until we reveal it to the audience. This can create very strong moments in a story, as long as the surprise is believable, which means that it's been discreetly planted in the story before the reveal. It's easy to surprise the audience with something that comes out of the blue at the end of the movie. For example, the two lovers in a romantic comedy are about to kiss when suddenly... a UFO lands and aliens abduct them. It's surprising, but it's not really satisfying if it's not been planted before.

The first thing we do when we're surprised in a movie is go back to see if it makes sense. If it does, most will enjoy the surprise. If it doesn't, some might reject it as a cheap trick. For example, at the end of *The Sixth Sense*, we discover – with the protagonist Dr Malcolm Crowe (Bruce Willis) – that he was dead all along. It's a shock to him – and to most of us – and it works because, as he does, we go back through the movie and suddenly we see scenes in a different light, which make the surprise not only believable but moving. We feel what the protagonist feels.

At the end of *The Usual Suspects*, we realise that Verbal Kint (Kevin Spacey) has lied to us and cop Dave Kujan (Chazz Palmintieri) during the whole movie and that he *is* Keyser Soze. While it's a surprise that many enjoyed – we realise that we've been tricked and we find it satisfying – some feel it's an easy trick not only because some of the lies have been filmed (for example the scene in which Verbal Kint, hiding behind ropes on a boat, sees Keyser Soze), but also because the character we have empathised with all along is the one who lied to us. That's a huge betrayal! It doesn't make the rest of the movie less enjoyable – at least not to me – and overall *The Usual Suspects* remains a very entertaining movie, but it illustrates that we have to be careful not to lie to the audience or pull a surprise out of a hat.

Most movies have at least one or two surprises or twists that suddenly change the way we understand the story, or the direction in which the story is heading. For example, in *Chinatown*, when we realise that Evelyn's sister is also her daughter. Or in *Psycho*, when the first protagonist, Marion Crane, is killed half an hour into the movie. Or in *The Silence of the Lambs*, when we realise that Hannibal Lecter has taken the place of one of the guards he's killed to escape.

A final twist, as in *The Sixth Sense, The Usual Suspects, Don't Look Now* or *The Sting*, when the action seems over but a surprise sheds new light on it, is also a classic. If well-planted, it can be very effective.

Many movies also have a fake ending, with a first climax when everything seems over, until – surprise! – the antagonist isn't dead yet and the same dramatic action resumes for a last *encore*, as in *Gravity, Misery* or *Alien*. This twist towards the end of dramatic Act 2 can be a bit predictable, so if you use it, make sure it's a real surprise – even if only in the way it happens – and not an expected twist which might feel a bit contrived. We'll discuss the *Encore Twist* in more detail a bit later in this chapter as it can be a fun tool to use.

With **mystery**, we reveal just enough to make it clear that the audience doesn't know something important. It's a tease. Like all teases, it works for a while, but if we overuse it, it can get boring.

So mystery can be a great hook, especially at the beginning of a movie, because it pulls us into the story, forcing us to wonder what's going on. Nothing stops us from having a mystery over a whole movie only to resolve it at the end, but in that case it's usually beneficial to use other tools to manage information as well, for example dramatic irony and surprise, so that we don't feel like we're being kept in the dark over the whole movie just for the benefit of a huge final surprise. This is what a movie like *Psycho* achieves brilliantly. There is a significant amount of mystery in the movie: Who is the killer? Who is the mysterious mother in the house? Why don't we ever see her? But there is also a lot of dramatic irony. After Marion Crane's murder, we know there is a killer in the motel, but the other characters don't (Arbogast, the detective, and Marion's sister and boyfriend). There are also a couple of huge surprises: the murder of Marion Crane, our first protagonist, so early in the story (talk about breaking the rules!). The final surprise in the cellar, of course, is another big one.

Usually mystery on its own, over the whole story, works better in literature than in drama, because it's an intellectual rather than emotional gratification. For this reason, "whodunits" or murder mysteries work fine in novels or on TV (see *True Detective*) but tend to fall a bit flat on the big screen if they are not pumped up with other tools. For example, Agatha Christie novels are entertaining to read, but their big screen adaptations are not that great. One of the reasons why the recent reboot of *Sherlock Holmes* was so successful is that Guy Ritchie and his writers went beyond the murder mystery and completely reshaped the characters and plot to deliver a very entertaining action movie, which wasn't about "who [has] done it" but about survival and crushing evil.

A good way to look at managing information is to think about every piece of information in the story and ask yourself: What is the best way to dramatise this? Is it simply to tell it flat to the audience? Make a mystery of it? Reveal it suddenly as a surprise? Exploit it as a dramatic irony? Combine all of this and make a mystery out of it for a short while, then reveal it in a surprising way to the audience but not some of the characters, and then possibly exploit it as a dramatic irony? The possibilities are endless, and great writers are often those who become masters at managing information to generate humour, drama or thrills.

To visualise these options, think about a shop in the street. The curtain is closed. What's behind the curtain is the information (and we suppose that it's not what it should be, for example it's an alien or a dead body, not a cake in a bakery). The passers-by in the street are the audience. With *surprise*, we keep the curtain closed until we decide to suddenly lift it. The passers-by are shocked by the unexpected discovery: there is an alien eating the croissants! With *mystery*, we lift the curtain just enough for the audience to see something weird or unexpected (a puddle of green, slimy stuff or drips of blood-red liquid) but not enough for the audience in the street to understand what it is. With *dramatic irony*, we invite the audience into the shop, while keeping the curtain closed, so people in the shop can see what lies behind the curtain, but those still in the street can't.

One last element is **suspense**. Dramatic irony is often used to create suspense, and Hitchcock's "bomb under the table" is the most famous example. We only have suspense if we are aware of a danger (physical or psychological), so if we tell the audience about the danger without telling some of the characters, we can use dramatic irony to generate suspense. But we don't need dramatic irony to have suspense. The characters and the audience can be aware of the danger, so you can also have suspense without dramatic irony. A classic example of this can be found at the end of *Olympus Has Fallen*. As soon as the protagonist (Gerard Butler) finds out about the last threat, everyone knows the nuclear missiles are about to go off, so we have suspense without dramatic irony. However, suspense *is* related to managing information, and the important thing to bear in mind is that we can't have suspense if we hold back too much information. New writers are frequently scared of losing control of the story, so they try to keep hold of as much information as possible, often overusing mystery instead of combining it with surprise and dramatic irony. This leads to development teams thinking they are developing a thriller, when they are in fact developing a murder mystery. We need to know enough about the danger threatening the characters to be afraid.

To create suspense, the audience has to know where the danger is coming from. No clear understanding of where the danger is coming from, no suspense and no thriller.

**Hands-on**

Enough theory. Time for a little practice. I'd like you to design a scene which starts with a mystery, and then introduces a surprise which solves the mystery for the audience but not for at least one of the characters in the scene. This will create a dramatic irony you're going to exploit and then resolve. 1) Mystery; 2) Surprise that solves the mystery and sets up a dramatic irony; 3) Exploitation; 4) Resolution. It can be a funny, a dramatic or scary/tense scene. Still one location, three to seven minutes and three characters max. You can have a protagonist in the scene, as well as a dramatic three-act structure, but it's optional, not mandatory.

\* \* \*

Okay, now you've done that, let's have a look at a few key things we might want to improve in the scene:

1.  **Did you try to set up the mystery visually?** You don't have to, but it's a good habit to develop. You can describe something we see in such a way that it sets up a mystery. For example, the subjective steady-cam shots of the attacker in *Wolfen*.

2.  **Did you try to resolve the mystery visually?** Showing something in a close-up can create mystery, and simply widening the shot can reveal what it was to the audience. Or vice-versa, something might look banal until the camera closes in on a detail, for example, the shot of the sleigh with the Rosebud inscription at the end of *Citizen Kane* or the face of Jack Torrance in the old picture in the last shot of *The Shining*. Or when Verbal Kint stops limping at the end of *The Usual Suspects*.

3. **Did you try to exploit the dramatic irony – milk the situation – as much as possible?** Once you've solved the mystery for the audience and are starting to exploit it as a dramatic irony, do you generate as many gags/thrills/drama from the situation as you can?

4. **Did you try to resolve the dramatic irony visually?** Using an action, or an object to convey a specific meaning? We'll discuss this in the next section about planting, pay-off and visual storytelling. It's a very powerful way to resolve dramatic irony. Not easy to pull off in just one scene, but who said this was easy?

5. **Who is the victim of the dramatic irony?** If it's a "positive" character like the protagonist, we'll want the resolution because we want to see the victim's reaction. If it's a "negative" character, like the antagonist in a thriller or horror movie, we'll fear the resolution because we'll fear the consequences of the antagonist finding out. Are you making the most of this in your scene?

If any of this could improve the scene, then try a little rewrite and come back when you're done.

* * *

I hope you're starting to enjoy playing with managing information as much as with managing conflict. Can you see how much conflict you can generate with the way you manage information? How it can allow you to create hilarious, dramatic situations that are subtler than scenes in which characters yell at each other or physically fight, and yet are still full of tension or emotion?

We want to know what the story is about, what's at stake, where the story is heading because that's how we get emotionally involved in the process, but we also want to be surprised and entertained along the way. Managing conflict (who *wants/needs* what and why) defines a story in two dimensions. Managing information (who *knows* what when) gives it a third one. This is why managing information is so important.

Sometimes, a strong dramatic irony can shape a whole story,

much more than the classical protagonist–goal–obstacles device. So look at the way information is managed in your story, make sure you have at least a couple of big surprises, that they are believable and have been seeded – but not telegraphed – throughout the story. Check that you don't rely exclusively on mystery but also use suspense and surprise. Finally, if you're thinking of developing a comedy or a thriller, you have no choice but to become a master of dramatic irony.

## The Opening of *Scream*

The opening of *Scream* illustrates the way mystery, surprise and suspense can be combined to generate a lot of tension, fear and excitement. There is little dramatic irony in the scene, which shows that although it's often used to create suspense, it's not needed as long as we know where the danger is coming from. The main use of dramatic irony in this opening sequence is to generate humour using references to various horror films and serial killers.

The film starts with a mystery: Who is this mysterious caller, and what does he want from the babysitter (Drew Barrymore)? Those who have seen other slasher/horror movies – especially *When a Stranger Calls* – know that he should be taken seriously as a threat, so there is a small dramatic irony at the beginning of the scene, as we're more aware of the probable threat than the protagonist who seems to take it quite lightly.

Then, as the danger becomes clearer (this isn't a joke) and as the babysitter starts to panic, we have suspense (we know where the danger is coming from), but we still have some mystery (we don't know who the killer is or what his motivations are, beyond playing cat and mouse with the babysitter).

Then we have a couple of surprises. First, the boyfriend, tied up and gagged in front of the house. It's a shock (both for us and for the protagonist of the sequence), but it also makes it clear that the danger is real, that it's not just a prank call. This helps raise the tension.

Then there are a few more surprises, for example the gruesome way the boyfriend is killed, or how various things are done to terrify the girl (classics like a smashed window or the sudden appearance of the killer on the other side of the window).

The killer is only gradually revealed. We first see a distant silhouette, and only later do we get a closer look. Even when the killer is close, because of the mask and costume we still don't know who he is, which is both important now (it makes the killer scarier) and for the rest of the story (there is a strong whodunit – who is the killer, who's done it? – element in *Scream*).

Because there is a clear protagonist in the sequence – the babysitter – and because what's at stake is life or death – the sequence is rooted at the bottom of Maslow. It's about survival and integrity of the body – there is an immediate, strong identification with her. In fact, the identification is so strong that when she does get killed, it's a gratifying shock.

The opening sequence of *Scream* feels like a condensed version of the beginning of *Psycho*, when the star (Janet Leigh in *Psycho*; Drew Barrymore here) gets killed right away. Shock, horror! We thought she'd be the protagonist of the film.

Note that while there is strong suspense – will she manage to save her life? – because we know where the danger comes from, there is little dramatic irony in the sequence. She knows as much as we do. This is what allows us to identify closely with her. If we knew more than she did, we wouldn't be able to experience the terror through her eyes.

This is something crucial in thrillers/horror. You can make the antagonist the victim of a dramatic irony (for example, we know that the protagonist is trying to escape, but the antagonist doesn't, as in *Misery*) because we can keep the emotional point of view of the protagonist and fear the consequences of the resolution (when the antagonist finds out).

But making the protagonist victim of a dramatic irony over a long period of time changes the nature of the identification link. We know more, so we can't be the protagonist anymore. It works fine in drama or comedy (*The Apartment*; *There's Something about Mary*) because that distance can help with identification – we feel sorry for the protagonist. It's more difficult to make it work in thrillers and horror, in which you want the audience to *be* the protagonist in order to experience terror and fear from their point of view. Of course it works locally, for example if we see the protagonist walking towards a house in which we know the antagonist is waiting with an axe. However, stretching over a long period of time a dramatic irony whose victim is the protagonist can be tricky to pull off. As always, there are no hard rules; it's just something worth keeping in mind.

So when you're looking for a visceral rather than intellectual involvement from the audience, be careful how you use dramatic irony in relation to the protagonist. The opening sequence of *Scream* illustrates perfectly how you can use a mix of mystery, surprise and suspense to get the audience on the edge of their seats, without using dramatic irony.

While we could come up with a version of the sequence with dramatic irony (for example, we could see before her that the caller is outside the house, that the danger is real, while she could still think it's a joke), the sequence wouldn't be as emotionally intense if only mystery was used.

This is another crucial thing to take into account with thrillers and horror movies. If you want to create fear or terror, mystery isn't enough. With mystery, you can create an intellectual involvement. You get a whodunit. At best, a chiller. To get fear, we need to know where the danger is coming from and that it's real. That doesn't stop you from keeping some mystery. For example, in *Scream*, we only find out who the killer is towards the end of the story. But we have a lot of surprises, suspense and even dramatic irony during the film.

## Five Essential Questions Regarding Managing Information

*Managing information* is part of story structure, especially when using tools like dramatic irony over most of the movie (i.e. not just locally, in a scene).

Here are the five most important questions you can ask yourself regarding managing information in a story:

1. **Is the story predictable?**

   Understanding who wants or needs what and why, what stands in the way and what's at stake in a story is important for the audience, yet it tends to define a straight line between the starting point and the goal. We need this to be able to follow the story and be involved emotionally, but we also want to be surprised along the way.

   So, do you have at least one or two big surprises in your story, events or news that throw the story into a completely different direction, without necessarily changing the goal? For example, making it look much more difficult to reach or forcing the protagonist to explore a different way of reaching it?

2. **Are we missing an opportunity for dramatic irony?**

   Many writers, especially beginners, tend to favour mystery over dramatic irony. They try to keep it all to themselves for as long as possible, thinking it makes the story more interesting. Most of the time, it doesn't. Mystery is a great tool, but it often works best in combination with dramatic irony and surprise.

For example, instead of having mystery, mystery, mystery and a big surprise at the end, we can have mystery, a surprise that sets up one or more dramatic ironies, another surprise in the middle which might reverse a dramatic irony and a final surprise at the very end. More variety in the way information is managed usually wins.

3. **Are we revealing too much?**

   Just like keeping too much information to yourself can be off-putting for the audience, revealing too much can also make a story flat. Try to think about a few key pieces of information that you could use as a mystery or save as a surprise.

4. **Are we guilty of over-exposition?**

   Often we start a story with everything we think we have to tell the audience. This involves a lot of backstory about the characters, explanations about situations, etc. The advice here is to cut and dramatise. The audience probably needs less than you think in order to get the story, and a lot of the fun comes from putting the pieces of the puzzle together.

   Just as it's usually a good idea to enter a scene late and leave early, try to make the difference between what the writer needs to know to be able to write the story (a lot) and what the audience needs to know to be able to enjoy the story (very little). Cut what's not needed, and try to place what's actually needed later in the story, possibly to reveal it as a surprise or a twist. That way you won't end up with a boring first act. Start right in the action or just before the action, and give us just enough information to understand what's happening. This is why the pilot in a TV series is often thrown away. If it only serves to introduce the main characters, it's pretty boring. Great TV series like *Breaking Bad* start right in the action, even if they jump back afterwards to introduce the characters. Some movies go further than that and give a form of amnesia to the protagonist so we start out knowing nothing and feel even closer to the character. We'll see a few examples of this in the *Cold Start* section of *Craft the Draft*.

Finding the right balance between what we need to know to get involved emotionally (and intellectually) in the story and what's not needed is a key aspect of writing.

5. **Is the way we handle information causing structural issues?**

As soon as you set up a dramatic irony in which the victim is the protagonist, it's not possible anymore to see the story through their eyes. In *Bolt*, which we discussed earlier, it's not a problem, but this kind of dramatic irony could be a problem in a thriller, when we want the audience to be as close to the protagonist as possible, so that they can experience the same emotions. You have to handle this really well, as in *The Hand That Rocks the Cradle*, to produce an involving emotional journey.

Another possible way to cause a structural issue is to set up a strong dramatic irony in which the victim is not the protagonist, before the main problem / main goal has been defined. Because we give the victim the goal of finding out, it can lead us to start identifying with the wrong character.
So, to sum it up:

## Managing Information

### Five Essential Questions Regarding Managing Information

1. Is the story **predictable**?
2. Are we missing an opportunity for **dramatic irony**?
3. Are we **revealing too much, too early**?
4. Are we guilty of **over-exposition**?
5. Is the way we manage information **causing structural issues**?

As always, no hard rules here, just things to be aware of. *Managing information* is part of structure because the identification process is strongly connected to the way information is managed, just as much as it is connected to the way conflict is managed.

## Visual Storytelling

Visual storytelling is the art of showing rather than telling. It's been part of the essence of cinema since the silent era when we had little choice but to find visual ways to move the story forward.

Vince Gilligan, original writer and show runner of *Breaking Bad*, who used to write for film before he joined the *X-Files* writing team and branched out to TV, nails it in a recent WGAW interview:

> *"Film – or television – is a visual medium. The idea of getting across a story through images rather than dialogue... Dialogue is great, it's important, it's crucial, but the more you can put across through images, the more film becomes universal, the more people around the world can enjoy it, the fewer subtitles you have to read".*

So how do we tell a story through images?

Often, as we'll see with *The Apartment*, planting can be used to assign a specific meaning to an object or action, so that we can achieve visual storytelling during the pay-off. We'll discuss this in detail in the next section.

Sometimes, we don't even need planting to achieve a great effect, for example at the end of the original *Planet of the Apes*. When the arm of the Statue of Liberty is revealed on the beach, we understand that this is not another distant planet, but Earth, and that mankind did this to itself. Beyond the perfect symbol, it's a very powerful way to create a strong final surprise both for protagonist Taylor (Charlton Heston) and the audience, using visual storytelling. In this case just about everyone knows what the Statue of Liberty looks like and where it's located, so it doesn't need to be planted during the movie.

## Visual Storytelling

### To Show Rather Than Tell

- **Use planting and pay-off** to assign a specific meaning to an element so that seeing that element means something.

- **Dialogue is the last resource to use.** Structure and causality are more meaningful.

- **Cut dialogue** as much as possible and trust actors and actions to convey meaning and emotion.

Hands-on

Let's put this into practice in the usual three-to-seven-minute scene exercise, with three characters max and one location. What you have to do now is use visual storytelling to convey exposition, show a character trait or reveal an unexpected piece of information. You can use planting and pay-off if needed (see the next section), and of course nothing stops you from using a local three-act structure, dramatic irony, surprise, mystery and so on. If you want to score bonus points for extra difficulty, you can try to write a scene without any dialogue, using only visual storytelling. Your scene still has to tell a dramatic story with at least one strong moment of visual storytelling. Something that could have been told using dialogue but which is instead shown visually. For example, showing a character running in the street isn't visual storytelling; it's just physical action. However, if a character sees a police car and starts to run, it usually means that he or she has done something wrong.

If you need some inspiration, you can take a look at the few examples in the next section. I've chosen the opening three minutes of three very different movies (*Rio Bravo*, *The Breakfast Club* and *As Good As It Gets*) to illustrate how much we can show about characters with little to no dialogue.

* * *

Done? Great. Let's take a look at what you have and how we can improve it.

1. **Look at every single line of dialogue in your scene**. Can you think of a way to convey some or all the information using visual storytelling? For example, if a character says that another character is jealous, can you think of a way to show it instead? Try to use conflict to show character traits. We're all the same when everything goes well. It's when conflict strikes that we reveal our true nature. Conflict here can be as small as a friend asking your honest opinion on their appalling haircut, or as big as experiencing a terrorist attack. Just try to find the situation, the moment that will reveal a character trait.

2. **Does your scene still have a lot of dialogue?** Try to identify how much of the dialogue is needed because of the design of the situation. For example, starting late in a story or in a scene is great as long as it doesn't mean too much exposition (telling us about what happened in the past). Can you redesign the scene so that you need less exposition and can therefore cut down the amount of dialogue? For example, would starting a bit earlier allow you to show more and tell less?

3. **Does your protagonist have something to do in the scene?** A clear dramatic action is the best way to allow visual storytelling, because we can show what the character does. Can you clarify or beef up the dramatic action in the scene, so that the protagonist – and any other character – has practical things to do in order to reach a goal / solve a problem? Actors and directors will love you for it!

4. **If you use planting to assign a specific meaning to an object**, a character, a song or a line of dialogue, have you disguised the planting using conflict to take our attention away from the planting itself?

5. **If you are not using planting in such a situation**, are you sure that the moment will be meaningful for everyone, and not just for those in the audience who share your cultural references? If not, consider planting as a way to make sure everyone reaches the same understanding during the visual pay-off, or find something more universal.

Now it's time to rewrite!

\* \* \*

Did this improve your visual storytelling? If you try to use every tool you can before relying on dialogue, your writing will shine and even your dialogue will improve.

This is true at scene level, but all the above applies to the screenplay as a whole. If you take your screenplay and do a pass focusing on these tips to improve your visual storytelling, your script won't only become more visual, which might help it to cross borders, you'll improve its structure with more causality through planting and pay-off.

## The First Three Minutes of...

I've chosen the opening three minutes of three very different movies to illustrate visual storytelling:

- *Rio Bravo* (H. Hawks)

- *The Breakfast Club* (J. Hughes)

- *As Good As It Gets* (J. L. Brooks)

These three movies do a great job of introducing the main character(s) using visual storytelling, the first one using no dialogue at all. They also introduce the theme of the movie right away, which is always useful.

I chose these because they are not action movies. Most action/adventure movies – from *James Bond* to *Indiana Jones* to *The Expendables* to *Mission Impossible – Rogue Nation* start with an action sequence also featuring little to no dialogue, but we don't learn that much about characters or story in these entertaining opening sequences. They are designed to start the movie right in the action and give the impression that their protagonists are always in the middle of an adventure.

So watch the following three movies to see how visual storytelling can be used to say a lot more than dialogue. Hopefully the first three minutes will make you want to watch the whole film.

In ***Rio Bravo* (1957),** the three main characters are introduced without a single line of dialogue. Sheriff John T. Chance (John Wayne), bad guy Joe Burdette (Claude Akins) and the drunk Dude (Dean Martin). A succession of visual storytelling moments sketch a stereotypical but very clear picture of who these characters are. For example, when Burdette sees how desperate the Dude is for a glass of alcohol, he throws a coin in a spittoon. This shows how cruel he can be. But then when the Dude is readying himself to recover the coin, it shows how desperate he is and how little self-respect he has. When Chance kicks the spittoon out of his reach, it shows that he cares for his friend and won't let him fall that low. But when the Dude knocks him out, it shows he doesn't see it that way (the frustration of the addict clearly overcoming the gratitude of the friend). When Burdette shoots a man who is trying to stop him from beating up the Dude, it shows that the bad guy in the movie has no respect for human life.

These moments are so strong that they are almost clichés, which is fine in *Rio Bravo* because it's kind of a spoof of a western (it was made by Hawks in reaction to *High Noon*). But being stereotypical doesn't stop these moments from being very efficient at conveying the essence of these three characters. They'll be revealed as having more depth – well, at least the Dude and Chance – than this purely visual introduction allows, but as a quick start it's very efficient.

In ***The Breakfast Club* (1985)** the main characters are also introduced mostly visually. For example, the way John Bender (Judd Nelson), the "criminal", crosses the street in front of a car without even looking, forcing it to stop, shows how much of a careless rebel he is. The way Allison Reynolds (Ally Sheedy), the "basket-case", tries to talk to her parents as they drive away, shows how deep the lack of communication is between them, and that she's not the only guilty party. The other characters are introduced with a bit more dialogue, but the brief conversation with their parents is also used to show who they are, or at least who they appear to be: a spoilt princess, a geek under pressure, an athlete with a bully of a father.

In *As Good As It Gets* (1997) protagonist Melvin Udall (Jack Nicholson) is introduced as he gets rid of his gay neighbour's dog. He then has a short altercation with his neighbour and his African-American agent, which efficiently conveys the fact that Melvin not only suffers from severe OCD but also that he's homophobic and racist. While there is some dialogue in the second half of the sequence, the first half shows the extent of Melvin's anti-social problem through visual storytelling.

This scene also illustrates the anti "save the cat" approach to storytelling. If you have a character who isn't nice, like Melvin Udall, and when it's the essence of your story, as it is in *As Good As It Gets*, don't try to make him more sympathetic conceptually by having him do something nice. Embrace the badness – the problem – and explore how it's solved through the story. Use conflict to force the audience to identify – empathise – with the character, even if we don't approve of his or her actions, or don't like who he or she is at the beginning of the film. Use conflict to force the character to change. Saving a cat won't redeem Melvin Udall or Salieri. Instead, get them to get rid of a dog, or claim they have killed Mozart. That will raise our interest, as long as the writer knows how to use conflict to deal with unsympathetic protagonists.

I'm not choosing these moments to suggest that visual storytelling is only or should only be used at the beginning of movies, but to illustrate how much a well-chosen piece of visual storytelling can convey about a character when we don't know anything about them. Yes, it's a first impression and as such it's only part of the truth, but it's nevertheless some of the truth.

We'll see a few other examples in the next section about planting and pay-off, showing that visual storytelling can be used during a movie (*The Apartment*) or towards the end (*Crash*) with great effect.

Cinema is a visual medium. Visual storytelling is its essence. Use it all the time, as often as possible.

# Planting and Pay-Off

Planting and pay-off is another essential story design tool. It usually works in two steps:

## Planting and Pay-Off

### A Tool That Works in Two Steps

1. First an element (character trait, object), is **planted**, using conflict to disguise it so that the audience won't guess it's going to pay off later.

2. Then the element **pays off**, just once or many times (for example as a running gag).

It's used to achieve a few different things in a screenplay and some of these are quite structural, so let's have a quick look at them.

The first, most obvious way we can use planting is **to avoid a *deus ex machina***. A *deus ex machina* is any kind of help (ability, object, weapon, character) which hasn't been planted before, and comes out of the blue when you need it to get the protagonist out of trouble. It's usually not something we want to have in a movie, especially not at the end, unless of course you make fun of it as in *Adaptation*.

One way to avoid a *deus ex machina* is to plant the help earlier in the story, making sure we're not telegraphing it. This is usually achieved using conflict to distract the audience while the future help is planted.

For example, at the end of *Finding Nemo*, Nemo instructs all the fish to swim down so that he can free Dory and himself from the fishermen's net. If the ability of the fish to swim together in a specific direction had not been foreshadowed before, this would have felt like a *deus ex machina*. This ability was planted when Marlin and Dory encounter the fish earlier in the story, and is disguised using conflict (the fish making fun of Marlin), so we don't think "Okay, this is going to be used later". The real reason for this situation is to show Marlin's evolution, as he lets Nemo swim into the net to help Dory (allowing his son to take a risk, which is a big step for an overprotective father), but the planting is still valid, even if the pay-off serves multiple purposes.

Another example, at the end of *Aliens*, Ripley steps into an exoskeleton and uses it both for protection and as a weapon as she fights the mother alien during the climax of the film. If not only the presence of the exoskeleton in the space ship but also Ripley's ability to drive that loader had not been planted earlier in the movie, it would have been rejected by the audience as a *deus ex machina*. James Cameron uses conflict to distract us when the help is planted (we're more interested in the G.I.'s macho attitude than in the fact that she can drive a loader at this stage), and he also makes sure that it's difficult for Ripley to use the loader during the climax. The planting only makes it possible for the protagonist to reach the goal; it doesn't make it easy.

To use planting to avoid a *deus ex machina*, we need to 1) Plant the ability, object, character that is going to help the protagonist later; 2) Plant it earlier in the story, well before we need to use it; 3) Disguise the plant using conflict to distract the audience and avoid telegraphing; 4) Make sure the protagonist is active in using the help; 5) Make sure it's still going to be difficult for the protagonist to overcome the obstacle, especially if this is the climax of the movie.

Also make sure you don't get into the habit of planting things unnecessarily. Some writers plant everything, which wastes a lot of screen time. You only need to plant something if the audience is likely to reject it as "Too easy!" or "Where did that come from?". So if Ben Stiller is supposed to be able to defeat a six-foot-tall Kung Fu master, or if The Rock is supposed to be able to gracefully dance a ballet number, better plant it; otherwise, if it goes with the character or the situation, just save time or make fun of it. Over-planting can be boring, so always ask yourself: Do I really need to plant this?

Planting is also used along with **visual storytelling** to assign a very specific meaning to an object or action to make the pay-off both moving and visual. More often than not, this is also linked to the resolution of a dramatic irony. We've already discussed this with the ending of *City Lights*, but one of the best known examples of this happens in *The Apartment* (1960), in the broken mirror sequence. We're going to look at this sequence in detail because it's a wonderful demonstration of the use of all the tools we've discussed.

Finally, planting is used **to make the pay-off moving**. For example, at the end of *The Wrestler*, when Randy "The Ram" Robinson (Mickey Rourke) leaps to certain death because he'd rather die doing what he loves than live a meaningless life, we're moved because the meaning of this action has been planted by what happened before in the movie. This is mainly because we know Randy has a heart condition that makes it impossible for him to fight professionally, and that he can't adjust to "normal" life. Planting, in this case, helps to generate an emotion during the pay-off. In fact, almost every moving moment in a film is a pay-off for something that has been planted before. One of the best examples of this is the ending of *City Lights* that we used to illustrate the resolution of a dramatic irony. It's a pay-off for the whole movie, and it's hugely moving.

## Planting and Pay-Off

### The Three Main Types of Planting

- To make the audience accept an element that would be rejected otherwise (weapon, ability, helping character, coincidence);

- To assign a specific meaning to an object, gesture or dialogue, for visual storytelling,

- To increase the emotional involvement of the audience.

All right, enough theory. Let's practice.

Hands-on

You know the drill: one location, three-to-seven-minute scene, three characters max. I'd like you to design a scene in which you use visual storytelling to plant a negative character trait in the protagonist of the scene (jealous, gluttonous, uncaring, overprotective, etc). Make it so that it causes a problem that has to be solved and then use an object introduced while you planted the negative character trait to resolve the situation.

* * *

Okay, so you've got your scene. Now let's have a look at it.

1. **As you've introduced a negative character trait in your protagonist, does this have an effect on our ability to empathise with the character?** Remember, we identify with the character who experiences the most conflict, not the nicest character. So did you make sure that your negative protagonist was the character in the scene who experienced most conflict?

2. **When planting the negative character trait along with the object that will be used to resolve the problem, did you make sure you added conflict to take our attention away from the planting?** Remember that a gag is also a conflict (as it usually shows a character confronted with a human limitation), so you can use humour to disguise a plant. What's important is that we focus on something other than the object/weapon/ability you are planting, so you don't telegraph the pay-off.

3. **Did you check that while the plant makes it possible to solve the situation, it doesn't make it easy?** Also make sure that the protagonist is active in using the help you've planted, and that it's still difficult to overcome the obstacles and resolve the problem.

4. **Can you look at the way you manage information in the scene** and see if you can use dramatic irony, surprise and mystery, even if very briefly, to make the scene more exciting?

5. **Do you have a point of view about the negative character trait at the core of the scene?** Is this point of view expressed clearly through the outcome of the scene? If the protagonist succeeds at the end of the scene, does it contradict your point of view? How could you re-think the scene so that it conveys your point of view?

If any of the above could help improve the scene, then take the time to do so and come back.

\* \* \*

Any better? I know it's hard to think about all of this in one single scene, but again, who said screenwriting was easy? While it's difficult to keep all this in mind, it's still much easier to do this at scene level with one location and a few characters than at sequence or script level.

Feel free to design a couple more scenes, or variations of the ones we've already designed, just for a bit more practice.

For example, you could try the following exercises before we move to *Sequencing the Action*.

1. **Design a scene with no dialogue** which still shows a clear dramatic action (a protagonist, with a clear goal, overcoming one or more obstacles, and either succeeding or failing to reach the goal).

2. **Design a "super-scene" featuring all the tools we've discussed**: a protagonist-goal-obstacle defining a *dramatic* three-act structure in the scene, a dramatic irony set-up, exploited and resolved, some mystery, at least one surprise, one element of visual storytelling and one planting/pay-off. That one can be up to ten minutes long, so almost a sequence. A couple of great examples of such a super scene can be found in *Crash*: the climax of the Daniel and Farhad strand and the sequence in which Ryan rescues Christine after her car crash are both

discussed in the detailed analysis of *Crash* at the end of the *Developing a Theme-Led Story* chapter. We'll also a look at the climax of the Daniel and Farhad strand to illustrate planting and pay-off in this section.

3.   **Design a scene without any of the tools discussed**, and see if still works. If it does, can you say why?

For more inspiration, here are a few examples that illustrate the main ways to use planting and pay-off. The first comes from a plot-led movie, *Gravity*; the second, from *The Apartment*, a character-led movie; the third, from a theme-led movie, *Crash*, to illustrate that planting and pay-off can serve different purposes and be used in very different movies.

## Avoiding a Deus Ex Machina: *Gravity*

Towards the end of *Gravity*, protagonist Ryan Stone realises that she won't be able to reach the Chinese station from the trajectory of her Soyuz pod. So she grabs a fire extinguisher and uses it as a jetpack to steer her to the station. Had this fire extinguisher not been planted earlier, this would probably have been rejected by the audience as a *deus ex machina*: an external, unplanted help coming out of the blue to solve the problem of the protagonist. So let's see how this is avoided in *Gravity*.

At 00:44, once she's reached the Soyuz, Stone has to overcome the fire planted at 00:40, which itself helps to plant the fire extinguisher she's going to need later.

It's not only the object itself which is planted, but also its possible use in a gravity-free environment. It works like a jetpack, pushing Stone backwards and almost knocking her out when she tries to use it to put the fire out. It makes sense to try to use a fire extinguisher to stop a fire and take it with you if it blocks the airlock. The future help is planted, but conflict is used – the fire, the knocking out, the blocking of the airlock – to disguise the plant and distract the audience so that the help isn't telegraphed.

Planting it skilfully before it's needed, using conflict to disguise it, makes it possible for the audience to accept the help when it's needed, during the pay-off. The writers also make sure that Stone is active using the help, and that it only makes a resolution possible. It doesn't make it easy.

## Visual Storytelling and Moving Pay-Off: *The Apartment*

**Massive spoilers to follow, so if you've never watched *The Apartment*, please do so before reading on.**

As planting is usually done a while before the pay-off is needed, it's difficult to find both in the same scene, except for some very local gags or surprises. So we're going to analyse the broken-compact-mirror sequence from *The Apartment* (1960), a screenplay by Billy Wilder and I.A.L. Diamond, directed by Wilder.

This fifteen-page sequence features one of the most classical and powerful examples of planting using visual storytelling to generate an emotion during the pay-off. It also perfectly illustrates how dramatic irony works. All this brilliance includes top-notch dialogue, so it's an ideal sequence to wrap our *Behind the Scenes* section. The quality of the screenwriting craft and talent on display in this film is simply out of this world.

The analysis is based on the shooting script as published by Irvington in *Classic Screenplays – Film Scripts Three*. There are a few minor differences between the script and the movie as shot and edited, but overall the screenplay is very close to the finished film. Page numbers refer to the printed screenplay in the book, scene numbers to the scenes as numbered in the screenplay and minutes to the running time in the Blu-ray. For simplicity, we'll say "Wilder" when referring to the writers, while we should of course mention both writers.

Here is a brief summary of the beginning of the story:

C.C. "Bud" Baxter (Jack Lemmon) is a small cog in a large insurance company. Hoping to get a faster promotion, he lends his apartment to his office superiors, giving them a place to entertain their mistresses and have fun.

Bud is attracted to Fran Kubelik (Shirley MacLaine), an elevator girl in the same company. He fears that she may not be available or possibly that he's not worthy of her, and is not able to approach her.

One day, Bud's boss, Jeff D. Sheldrake (Fred MacMurray), calls him to his office. Bud is initially confident he's going to be promoted, but Sheldrake tells him he has discovered the little game going on with his apartment. Bud expects to be fired but finally understands that his boss would like to benefit from the apartment as well. Sheldrake also has a mistress that he'd like to take there tonight.

Bud, relieved, is happy to oblige. In exchange for the key to his apartment, Sheldrake gives him two tickets for *The Music Man* that same evening.

His confidence boosted, Bud finds the courage to invite Fran to the show. She already has an early evening date, but she promises to join Bud later at the show.

When Fran meets her date at a Chinese restaurant, we discover that she's Sheldrake's mistress. She wants to break up with him, convinced that their affair was only a summer fling for him. Sheldrake tells her he loves her, and promises to divorce soon.

Fran, who is clearly in love with Sheldrake, agrees to spend the night with him in Bud's apartment.

Bud waits in vain for Fran at the theatre entrance, and finally leaves after having thrown both tickets away.

* * *

The sequence we're about to analyse starts about forty-two minutes into the film (which is one hundred and twenty-five minutes long). The entire sequence lasts about ten minutes.

**Sc. 80** is a pay-off for the whole beginning of the movie. From the start, Bud's conscious goal is to get a promotion. As a direct consequence of his action, he is promoted. This could be the end of the story, but that's not what's at stake in the film. We know that getting Fran is more important for him, even if he doesn't know that yet himself. Getting Fran may not be what he *wants* (his conscious goal), but we know it's related to what he *needs* (his unconscious goal). *The Apartment* is the story of a man who needs to become a "mensch", which is his neighbour's expression to say "a real man". It's a character-led movie. Therefore, we want to know whether he'll learn to become a "mensch". Will he choose the girl or the job? So the main dramatic question has not been answered yet and won't be until the end of the movie.

**Sc. 81** briefly exploits a minor dramatic irony. We know that Bud got the promotion because he's now lending his apartment to Sheldrake. His old friends don't know that.

We also find a plant for a background gag in scene 84: The Volkswagen is mentioned to make us laugh when we hear the other side of the story, from Sylvia, Kirkeby's girlfriend, a bit later.

Then the scene shifts to a different tone when Bud and Sheldrake are left alone.

We have an important line in the middle of page 101, when Bud says about Miss Olson, Sheldrake's secretary: "Is she... the lucky one". This is a different kind of planting, to establish that Bud still doesn't know who Sheldrake's mistress is (he could have found out in the meantime). We know it's Fran, but he doesn't. The dramatic irony is simply reinforced.

Then comes the most important plant of the sequence: the broken mirror. Wilder has taken an incredible amount of care in this process.

First, he needs to assign a specific meaning to a common object, because he wants the protagonist to learn a devastating piece of information through visual storytelling, not through dialogue: his boss's mistress, the one Sheldrake takes to his own apartment, is the girl he's in love with. This moment gives us a specific piece of information: for Bud, that mirror belongs to Sheldrake's mistress.

We've already seen Fran use the mirror at the Rickshaw. But Wilder re-establishes it now, in relation to Bud.

Then, because Wilder wants us (and Bud) to be able to recognise the mirror without any possible doubt, he gives it a special pattern (the film is in black and white and Wilder knows he cannot write "a red mirror"). And it's broken too, to make sure that people who don't see the pattern are not lost or in doubt, which would prevent full emotional involvement.

Furthermore, Wilder knows that if planting isn't handled properly, the audience will guess that the mirror is going to pay off later.

So, he does two things. First, our attention is immediately distracted by something else, using a strong conflict for Fran and a dramatic irony. We know Sheldrake is just playing with her, but she doesn't. Then, to make sure our attention won't be drawn towards the sudden appearance of a specific object, Wilder plants the planting! Earlier in the story, he establishes (he shows us) that Bud frequently finds objects in his apartment (combs, and things like that). So, to us, the mirror isn't *the* one. It's only one object amongst others. Everything has been carefully designed so the audience is emotionally manipulated and prepared but has no way of knowing it.

Then we have a few straightforward scenes to establish time passing (**sc. 82**) and the present time and mood (it's Christmas Eve).

In **sc. 84**, we have the pay-off for the plant in **sc. 81**, with the Silvia/car gag. If you look at it closely, it's not simply a gag. It also serves the purpose of convincing the audience that the world of the film is coherent from every POV. We have strong causality, even within the smaller details. Somebody says something in a scene, and we later incidentally hear a different version. This kind of detail contributes to making the whole film ring true.

Then, we have a logical consequence from the scene when Fran stood Bud up (right before the beginning of the sequence). These two have some explaining to do.

Later on we have an important plot point. Fran discovers what we've known for a long time: Sheldrake is playing with her. It's the resolution of a dramatic irony whose victim (Fran) is not the protagonist. And that's why Wilder, amongst the different tools that he masters, chooses to resolve it through dialogue. The moment is strong, but Fran isn't our protagonist, so he wants us to react on a slightly more intellectual than emotional level. The moment is much stronger emotionally for Fran than it is for us.

The resolution of this dramatic irony instantly sets up a new one. We know that a devastated Fran has discovered the truth about Sheldrake, but Bud doesn't. This dramatic irony will be exploited until the end of the sequence. We feel even more conflict for Bud, who is the victim of this new dramatic irony through these scenes.

The end of **scene 84** and beginning of **scene 85** include some very subtle planting. We don't want Fran simply to take her broken mirror out of her purse – to redo her make-up, for example – in order for Bud to understand that she's Sheldrake's mistress. That would be clumsy. Fran is not in any state to think about her make-up. We need coherence. Everything must be logical, from each character's POV. This is why Wilder gives her a good reason, from the beginning of the scene, to get it out. She has to give it to Bud so he can see his new hat. This is the main purpose of the hat in the scene. But it's linked to character, to the situation.

The scene then further exploits two dramatic ironies:

1.  We know that Fran is Sheldrake's mistress, but Bud doesn't.

2.  We know that Fran is devastated by the news, but Bud doesn't.

Finally, we have the *"point d'orgue"* of the scene, the climax:
Bud discovers that Fran is Sheldrake's mistress.
This single sentence is all you'd need to describe the scene in a step outline or beat sheet.

Yet with craft and talent, Wilder has found the best way to tell it visually.

In this moment, he uses a combination of three powerful tools (just as in *City Lights*):

It's the resolution of a dramatic irony. For a long time, we've wanted to know when and how Bud would discover this crucial fact. When is now, and how is great, because:

It's through visual storytelling, not dialogue.

It's a pay-off. The broken mirror has a very specific meaning, set up earlier using planting, which means the information can be given to Bud visually.

This moment is technically the same as a few scenes earlier, when Fran discovers the truth about Sheldrake's feelings. It's the resolution of a dramatic irony. However, this time the victim isn't one of the main characters – Fran – but our protagonist, the character we identify with. Wilder uses visual storytelling through careful planting to allow us to be as emotionally close to Bud as possible. At this point in the film, we are Bud. We feel what he feels, without the need for any dialogue. Because he was the victim of a strong dramatic irony, we were a little above him on the information ladder. At this moment, he catches up with us and we are back at the same informational – and emotional – level.

This resolution establishes another dramatic irony. We know that Bud knows about Sheldrake and Fran, but Fran doesn't (and Sheldrake doesn't either). The game goes on...

The scene finally ends with another pay-off and a wonderful line of dialogue. When Bud remarks that the mirror is broken, Fran replies: "I like it that way – makes me look the way I feel". This is the intellectual climax of the scene, which allows us to recover emotionally from what's just happened and plants Fran's suicide attempt later.

* * *

While these few pages show how much work was involved in the design of the sequence, most of it wasn't conscious. Great writers like Diamond and Wilder "just do it". Their understanding of the craft is intuitive, based on hands-on experience, trial and error, not theoretical study. Of course, it's much better to have Wilder and Diamond's talent and an unconscious understanding of the craft than an extensive conscious understanding of the craft and little talent. To illustrate this and as a conclusion, here is what Wilder himself had to say about the broken mirror moment (from the excellent *Conversations with Wilder* by Cameron Crowe):

*CC: You've often used mirrors as a clever way of revealing a story point, but the most powerful instance has to be the broken-compact-mirror shot in* The Apartment.

*BW: Yes. When Baxter sees himself in the mirror, he adds up two and two. He gave it to the president of the insurance company [MacMurray], the big shot at the office, now he knows what we know. And we see it in his face in the broken mirror. That was a very elegant way of pointing it out. Better than a third person telling him about the affair – that we did not want to do. This was better. This gave us everything in one shot. Some ideas came easy, like that one. It was good; it came easy. That's why it was good.*

## Increasing the Emotional Involvement of the Audience: *Crash*

**Massive spoilers to follow, so if you've never watched *Crash*, please do so before reading on.**

In *Crash*, written by Paul Haggis and Bobby Moresco, directed by Haggis, there is a beautiful use of planting to increase the emotional involvement of the audience in the "impenetrable cloak" scene. Quite early in the story, locksmith Daniel Ruiz (Michael Peña), protagonist of one of the eight strands in the film, comes home and finds his young daughter, Lara, hiding under her bed.

We understand that they have recently moved from a bad neighbourhood to a safer one – nice piece of exposition, by the way – but Lara is still frightened that she could get hit by a stray bullet (one came through her window in her old home). Daniel invents a sweet story about a fairy who gave him an invisible, impenetrable cloak when he was five. He was supposed to give it to his daughter when she turned five, but he forgot. He gives it to Lara, after reassuring her that he doesn't need it anymore, and she feels safer.

This scene is great in itself, showing what a good father Daniel is and completely turning around our perception of him – like Jean Cabot, the D.A.'s wife, some of us might have thought that because of his tattoos, he's a gang member. However, when they came up with the scene during the writing of the screenplay, writers Paul Haggis and Bobby Moresco knew that the impenetrable cloak story had to pay off later.

So towards the end of the movie, when Daniel's strand reaches its conclusion after it collides with Persian shopkeeper Farhad's strand, the writers found a very effective way to make it pay off, using planting to enhance the emotional involvement of the audience. When Farhad points a gun at Daniel, asking for money because he holds Daniel responsible for the damage in his shop, we feel danger for Daniel. When Lara sees her father in danger, she realises he doesn't have the impenetrable cloak, as she's wearing it. So she runs towards her dad, trying to protect him, and just as Farhad shoots, she throws herself between them and takes the bullet.

This is a hugely emotional moment in the film – one of many – because we know what she is doing and why. The fact that Daniel might have involuntarily caused her death makes the situation even more poignant. At that point, we are him completely. We feel what he feels: shock, pain, injustice, anger. And when we realise, with him, that she's still alive, we also feel what he feels: surprise, relief, incredulity, gratitude. All these emotions are not only made possible but amplified by the planting. The pay-off is moving because thanks to the planting, we know what the characters do, why they do it and we can fully share their emotions. The planting of the impenetrable cloak also sets up a strong dramatic irony, which enhances even further the emotional impact of the scene. We know that Lara believes the cloak is impenetrable, while we – and Daniel – know it doesn't exist.

There are many other examples of emotional moments in *Crash* which are pay-offs of a previous scene, for example when LAPD officer John Ryan (Matt Dillon) rushes to a burning car to rescue Christine Thayer (Thandy Newton), the woman he sexually abused a few scenes earlier. *Crash* doesn't use a classical dramatic three-act structure over the whole movie – it's a theme-led, multi-stranded narrative – but it uses many other tools like dramatic irony and planting/pay-off to deliver strong, well-crafted strands, sequences and scenes. This contributes to making *Crash* a moving, entertaining and meaningful movie. See *Developing a Theme-Led Story* for a detailed analysis of *Crash*.

# 2.2 Sequence the Action

The next step in improving a plot-led story is to design clear dramatic sequences, especially in dramatic Act 2. A dramatic sequence can be defined as a group of scenes exploring the same subgoal, a way for the protagonist to reach the overall goal.

This provides more manageable units while we write or rewrite the screenplay, as well as a way to clarify what's at stake at all times. In other words, what the protagonist can do about the story problem.

This is what I call *sequencing the action* in a plot-led movie. An essential step which few screenwriting books mention, as many of them focus on *logistical* ways to cut down the screenplay (in chunks of pages / minutes) rather than on *dramatic* ways to divide the main action into more manageable units.

## Structure (Plot-Led Story)

### Sequence The Action

- Clarify the main action / overall three-act structure.

- Break down the main action into subgoals or tasks to define dramatic sequences.

- Structure and develop each sequence.

- Don't forget the subplots.

Understanding how you can cut dramatic Act 2 into sequences is the best way to avoid the "sag in the middle" syndrome, a problem in many screenplays. When the action runs out of steam in the middle of Act 2, it's usually because the protagonist's main goal hasn't been cut down into dramatic sequences, i.e. practical things that the protagonist has to do in order to achieve the goal and solve the external problem.

As mentioned earlier, screenwriter Terry Rossio (*Aladdin*, *The Mask of Zorro*, *Shrek*, *Pirates of the Caribbean* with co-writer Ted Elliott) came up with a great way of looking at these dramatic sequences in his excellent website – sadly inactive as of now – Wordplayer.com. He calls them *tasks*, and they are exactly the same thing as what we're going to call *subgoals*. His article, *The Task*, can be found at: http://tinyurl.com/rossiotask.

Before we can split our acts into sequences – especially dramatic Act 2, but often in Act 1 and occasionally Act 3 when we use an *Encore Twist* (more on that in *Craft the Draft*) – we first need to clarify the main action, the overall structure of our plot-led story.

This means finding the best protagonist, the best goal and the best obstacles for our story.

Then we'll try to clarify what's at stake and, if necessary, raise the stakes in the movie.

Only then will we be able to break down the main goal into dramatic subgoals – and as many dramatic sequences – in order to develop each sequence almost as a mini-movie in itself, with its own dramatic three-act structure.

Finally, we'll talk about subplots, which are not mandatory in a plot-led story, but which can be very useful, especially to convey thematic elements. This is why theme-led movies have only subplots and no main-plot: it's the theme (usually an issue in society) that defines what's at stake, not a main dramatic action or evolution.

## Clarify the Main Action
## (Overall Three-Act Structure)

Unless you're dealing with a short film (thirty minutes at most) or a TV series episode which could have just one main dramatic sequence, you're going to have to design the overall structure before you can break the story into subgoals / dramatic sequences. Otherwise you'll end up with an episodic story with little causality, in which any sequence could be swapped with another, which is rarely satisfying.

We'll discuss how to design this overall structure with character-led and theme-led stories in the next chapters, so for now let's concentrate on the main dramatic action in a plot-led movie.

There are three main elements to figure out when structuring a plot-led movie: finding the best protagonist, finding the best goal and finding the best obstacles, as these are the main structural components of our story from a managing conflict point of view. Let's look at each of these and then we'll see how we can clarify and raise the stakes in the story as well.

## Structure (Plot-Led Story)

### Clarify the Main Action / Overall Three-Act Structure

• Choosing the **best protagonist**

• Deciding on the **best goal**

• Designing the **best obstacles**

• Clarifying and **raising the stakes**

Of course, this only deals with the managing conflict side of a plot-led story. We will have to work on characters and theme, as well as on the managing information side of structure, but we'll discuss this later.

## Choosing the Best Protagonist

Who is the best protagonist in a story?

This is a key question which isn't that easy to answer if we go beyond the simplistic notions of hero or main character.

A hero is a positive central character on a plot-led quest. That's a fairly limiting definition. It works fine for fairy tales, animations (say *Finding Nemo*) and some plot-led stories, especially those involving super-heroes, but it doesn't help you to qualify a character like Salieri in *Amadeus* or a group of characters like the crew of the Nostromo in *Alien*.

The main character is the one that generates the most interest. It's often the character whose story we're telling, but it's not necessarily the protagonist. Sometimes it is, but not always.

We need to go back to the definition of a protagonist (from the Greek word *protagonistes*, the one who fights in the first row) to stand a chance of identifying or creating the best one for our story.

So here is our definition: **The protagonist is the character** – or group of characters sharing the same dramatic goal – **who experiences the most conflict in our story**.

This is because in life, we often see ourselves as the person who experiences the most conflict, therefore in fiction we tend to identify with the character who is most like us, hence the character who experiences the most conflict. Also, conflict generates interest, so the character experiencing more conflict becomes more interesting than the others.

It's essential to define a protagonist like this because it allows us to use conflict to force the audience to identify – empathise – with a character, even with a conceptually negative character, such as Salieri in *Amadeus*. Yes, even a villain can be the protagonist, as shown by Maleficent (Angelina Jolie) in... *Maleficent*. We can identify emotionally – as in feeling some empathy – with a character without approving of his or her actions.

In fact, we will be more likely to identify emotionally with a negative character who experiences a lot of conflict than with a positive character who doesn't experience enough conflict, especially if other characters in the story experience more.

When you look at your story, first try to put aside the notion of hero and main character. Is there a character who experiences significantly more conflict than the others? Conflict that we can understand and relate to? If so, that's your protagonist.

Otherwise, you either need to create a character – or a group of characters sharing the same dramatic goal – who will experience more conflict than the others, or you need to balance the conflict so that the character you want to be the protagonist – the character with whom you want the audience to empathise – experiences more conflict than the others.

Most importantly, your protagonist doesn't have to be conceptually nice. We don't need to feel sympathy for the protagonist. We can disapprove of what the protagonist does or tries to achieve, but we can feel empathy if we understand the conflicts the character experiences and his or her motivations. Again, *Maleficent* is a perfect example of that.

Very often, when we don't care about the protagonist in a story, some will suggest making the character nicer conceptually. That's the very flawed "save the cat" principle. While increasing sympathy can help initially, it's rarely enough to make us care about the character. In fact, identification has little to do with how nice the character is. It's how much conflict the character experiences, either trying to reach the goal (in a plot-led story) or resisting change (in a character-led story) that leads us to feel empathy. A great example of this is *Heat* (1995). It's almost impossible to decide which of the two main characters is the protagonist and which, the antagonist. They represent two different points of view; they have opposite moral standpoints, but they are very similar and we can root for both because they experience the same amount of conflict.

What makes us root for a character, what makes us care about a character, isn't that they look like us, are the same age or have the same skin colour. It's because the character suffers like us, because they experience conflict we can understand and relate to.

Otherwise, we wouldn't be able to identify with Wall-E, John Merrick in *The Elephant Man*, E.T. or Jaguar Paw, the hunter-turned-warrior in *Apocalypto*.

Another important point is that the protagonist should be able to do something, consciously or not, about the main problem in the story.

If our protagonist is simply suffering and there is nothing that can be done about it (defining a dramatic action or an evolution), this is likely to be alienating for the audience. Drama is action; we want to see someone doing something about a problem, or someone struggling to change. Otherwise, there simply is no drama.

So if our main character isn't very active, or is active in a way we can't condone, for example self-destruction (which is often the case in a character-led movie), it might be a good idea to try to find a better emotional point of view for the audience. For example, this is why Sera (Elisabeth Shue) is such an important character in *Leaving Las Vegas*. It would be unbearable to watch Ben Sanderson (Nicolas Cage) drinking himself to death if we didn't have the point of view of another character trying to rescue him – despite their initial agreement. Sera is a kind of substitute protagonist, providing a less alienating point of view into the story for the audience, because there is nothing that can be done about Ben's death wish, other than watch him spiral down.

So again, in a plot-led movie the best protagonist is the character – or group of characters sharing the same dramatic goal – who experiences the most conflict on a journey towards a conscious goal.

When we have co-protagonists – two characters or more sharing the same dramatic goal – some of the conflict comes from within the protagonists, because they might disagree on the way to reach the goal or have very different personalities. This is how some buddy movies (*Planes, Trains and Automobiles*) or some romantic comedies (*The African Queen*) work.

So take a look at your story, and check that your protagonist is the character who experiences the most conflict, and not simply the hero (positive, heroic character) or the main character (most interesting character in the story; character whose life you're telling; character who has the most screen time). If that's not the case, you might have to restructure to either make sure that your protagonist does experience most of the conflict (so we can identify with that character emotionally) or create a new character in order to tell the life of your main character from a different emotional point of view (as with Salieri to tell Mozart's life story in *Amadeus*).

## Choosing the Best Goal

Let's start with the right goal as discussed earlier in the *Behind the Scenes* section:

# Structure (Plot-Led Story)

## The Right Goal

In order to be efficient, the protagonist's goal in a plot-led-story should be:

- known and understood by the audience
- unique
- motivated
- hard to reach
- an absolute necessity for the protagonist

Building from there, we can add a few things to help design the best possible goal in a plot-led story.

First, it really helps to make a distinction between the main goal in the story and the ambition of the character (what they'd like to achieve in life). Also, a protagonist sometimes starts the story with a goal which isn't the goal of the story, just a first goal which is quickly reached or abandoned. What we're looking for is the goal triggered by the main problem in the story.

It also helps if the goal defines a dramatic action. It's not by chance that "rescuing the princess" or "surviving" are two of the most common goals in plot-led movies. If the protagonist's goal defines an idea, a thought or a principle rather than a dramatic action, it's more likely to lead to a pamphlet than to a dramatic, exciting story.

Of course, looking at where the goal sits in Maslow's pyramid will be useful too, especially if we take the genre into account.

For example, a thriller, horror or slasher will almost always involve a survival element, which anchors the goal at the bottom of the pyramid. This is common in movies such as *Gravity*, *Apocalypto*, *Misery* or the *Bourne Trilogy*.

In many action movies, the main goal might not be to survive. Still, trying to reach the goal will lead to physical danger (whether it's saving the world as in super-hero movies or protecting/rescuing a son or daughter as in *Run All Night* or *Taken*). Sometimes, the audience might be more concerned about the protagonists' survival than the protagonists themselves, for example when the goal is linked to revenge as in *John Wick* or rescue/protection as in *Jaws* and many disaster movies. In these, the heroic protagonists are ready to sacrifice their lives for the greater good.

In stories that are not about physical survival, the goal might be connected to the survival of another character, as in *Goodbye Lenin*, or economic survival, as in *Pursuit of Happyness* or *Two Days, One Night*.

What matters most is whether the goal is clear, and whether it defines the stakes. Do we care if the protagonist reaches the goal or not? This is where story structure is connected to characterisation. If we don't care about the characters, we won't care about the story.

One way to force us to care about the characters is to get them to experience conflict. And the best way to generate conflict is to put obstacles in their way as they try to reach their goal, which explains why the protagonist–goal–obstacle principle works so well. We will usually do this for the protagonist's main goal, once the main problem has been defined. But if we have a longer than usual first dramatic act, we need to generate conflict earlier, to start creating an identification *before* the main action starts.

We'll see in the next section how it's done in *Alien*, in which the protagonists have a first goal in Act 1 (to investigate the possibility of non-human life on LV426), before the main problem is introduced as a consequence of this action: they *do* find an alien and spend the rest of the story trying to deal with the consequences of this discovery.

## Choosing the Best Obstacles

With obstacles, quality is usually more important than quantity. A few well-chosen and well-exploited obstacles tend to be more satisfying than a random selection of weak ones.

There are a few ways to discuss obstacles, but the least effective obstacles are those that simply delay the protagonist rather than creating true conflict, and those that seem to come out of the blue, just because we've been told to put obstacles in the way.

The most interesting obstacles are usually those which come from the protagonist (internal obstacles) or are indirectly generated by the protagonist or the protagonist's action/decisions (external obstacles with an internal origin). We've already discussed this in more detail in the *Behind the Scenes* section, so feel free to go back for a refresher.

## Structure (Plot-Led Story)

### Obstacles

There are three main sources of obstacles:

• **External Obstacles** (from other characters, nature, society)

• **Internal Obstacles** (from within the protagonist)

• **External Obstacles with an Internal Origin** (when the protagonist is responsible for an external obstacle)

From there, the most important thing to keep in mind is that obstacles have to be strong enough to generate conflict for the protagonist, but not too strong (if we think there is no chance the protagonist can reach the goal, we lose interest in the story) or too weak (if we think the protagonist is bound to succeed, we also lose interest).

There is a great example of this need to balance the strength of the obstacles versus the strength of the protagonist in Patrice Leconte's *Ridicule*.

The story starts like a plot-led story: Baron Pontceludon de Malavoy (Charles Berling) needs help from the King to save his peasants from dying of disease. He's a positive protagonist, with a positive goal. As soon as he starts his journey, he experiences conflict (his horse and money are swiftly stolen from him) which helps us to identify with him.

Then our protagonist starts meeting ministers to put his case forward and finds a closed door every time: they won't help him. These are strong obstacles, but soon we start to feel that Pontceludon stands little chance of resolving his problem. He doesn't seem to have what it takes to overcome the obstacles he's facing.

Then we discover that he has a weapon – his wit – that can be of great use in court. We realise he's stronger than we thought and we believe, again, that he might succeed. The dramatic question (Will Pontceludon manage to save his peasants?) remains open, but a character question is opened (How much will Pontceludon have to change to reach his goal?) which feeds the theme (Does the end justify the means?). All this renews our interest in the story, which starts to become more character-led than plot-led.

One of the most important tasks for the writer is not only to find the best obstacles for the protagonist in each story, but also to make sure that the strength of the protagonist and the strength of the obstacles are well-balanced over the whole movie. It should be hard for the protagonist to reach the goal, but not impossible. We need to fear failure, but we also need to hope for success. If the story shifts too much one way or the other, we tend to lose interest because we're able to answer the dramatic question before the end of the movie. In other words, Pontceludon needs wit like Superman needs Kryptonite.

## Clarifying and Raising the Stakes

Now this is something that many writers forget to do.

They think they have a strong structure because they believe they have covered the basics:

Clear protagonist? Check.

Clear goal? Check.

Clear motivations? Check.

Strong obstacles? Check.

We know who wants what and why and it's hard to get, so it generates conflict. That means the structure is good, right?

Wrong. If we don't care about the outcome, you can have all the above and still end up with a boring story.

The best way to define what's at stake in a plot-led story is to answer the question: What happens if the protagonist fails?

This should define something that is so negative, so unbearable, so dreadful, so scary for the protagonist that we don't want it to happen. This means that there is something at stake.

Often, it's death. Literally or otherwise.

It might be a loss (of a loved one, job, house, anything that matters for the character, preferably lying as low as possible in Maslow's pyramid).

In a plot-led movie, it has to be a problem that the protagonist can do something about or it's likely to be alienating.

Overall, if we don't care about the outcome of the movie (what's at stake in the story), we won't be emotionally involved.

Of course this is truer of some movies than others. In a parody, we don't care too much about what's going to happen, as long as the gags are funny and make us laugh. But in most stories, we should care about the outcome.

As the story unfolds, it's often useful to raise the stakes. We start with a significant problem and as the protagonist tries to solve it, we realise that the problem is much worse, wider and more difficult to solve, with even more negative consequences.

As long as the protagonist has grown during the story and we feel there is still a chance of success, even if the odds are low, raising the stakes usually renews our interest. It also gives the story a bit of a boost and forces our protagonist to act in a more extreme way out of desperation, which is always good for drama.

For example, in *Jaws*, Chief Brody (Roy Scheider) has to overcome his fear of the sea and get on a boat. His goal (shared with his co-protagonists) is to hunt and capture the great white shark that has claimed the life of a few victims already. What's at stake is the life of Amity Island's citizens and the future of its tourism industry. But when the shark damages the boat and claims the life of hunter Quint (Robert Shaw) after having apparently gobbled oceanographer Hooper (Richard Dreyfus), the stakes are raised. Chief Brody has to get *into* the sea and face the shark one on one to survive.

Raising the stakes goes along with the idea that we should have stronger and stronger obstacles until the climax, which should be the most conflictual sequence of the story.

*Back to the Future* provides another very good example of raising and clarifying the stakes. Marty McFly (Michael J. Fox) first simply wants to go back to the future because that's where his life – mostly his girlfriend – is, but when he realises that he has prevented his parents from falling in love, it's his own survival that's at stake. If he doesn't find a way to make sure they meet, he won't be born and neither will his siblings. So staying in the past isn't even an option. This is shown visually towards the end of the movie, as he fades away from a photograph. It makes the film more interesting thematically – his own mother is falling in love with him, which could lead to his death! – and it adds a lot of tension and suspense, especially in the last third of the movie.

Hands-on

Take a look at your story, and check that we always know what's at stake, not only over the whole film but also most sequences and scenes. Every time the protagonist wants to achieve something, are you making it clear what will happen if the protagonist fails?

Also, if you can, try to raise the stakes at least once or twice in the story to give it a boost. It will not only make it more efficient dramatically and emotionally, it might also make it more interesting thematically.

## Break Down the Main Goal into Subgoals

Once we've identified the main problem in the story, we need to decide what the protagonist can do, practically, to resolve it. Each of these subgoals defines a dramatic sequence. This will allow us to develop a strong dramatic action in Act 2, which usually contains four to six sequences.

In a plot led-story, the goal can also evolve or change slightly. As long as the problem remains the same and each goal or subgoal explores a way to deal with it, there is no structural issue.

A key thing to keep in mind is to try to raise the stakes as we move from one subgoal to the next. Things should get more difficult, not easier for the protagonist.

We'll see in detail how this is done in plot-led movies (where the main problem in the story is external to the protagonist) with our detailed analyses of *Gravity*, *Billy Elliot* and *Misery*, but just to illustrate this crucial point let's take a quick look at how it's done in *Alien*.

## Subgoals in *Alien*

**Massive spoilers to follow, so if you've never watched *Alien*, please do so before reading on.**

Written by Dan O'Bannon and Ronald Shusett, directed by Ridley Scott, *Alien* perfectly illustrates how acts can be cut into dramatic sequences using subgoals. As in most horror movies, the main problem is external to the protagonist: it's the monster, the alien, like the shark in *Jaws* or nurse Annie in *Misery*. So it's a plot-led story.

Because the alien – the antagonist, main source of conflict in the story – evolves over the course of the movie, the goal of the protagonist (the crew of the Nostromo) changes too. And because the alien kills them one by one, the protagonist evolves too – it shrinks in numbers, as happens in most horror/slasher movies – until Ripley (Sigourney Weaver) is left as the sole survivor – with Jones the cat.

The story starts when Mother, the ship computer, wakes up the crew early – they are halfway to Earth – because it has detected an unknown radio transmission, as we understand around 00:11. This isn't *the* inciting event of the movie because it doesn't start the main dramatic action. There is no clear problem yet, just an intriguing situation, with some mystery and anticipation of conflict. We've seen the poster and read its promising tagline: "In space, no one can hear you scream". We know that it's not going to be a spacewalk in the park.

This first inciting event does trigger a first goal though, as their contract forces them to investigate any possibility of non-human life. This is what they agree to do – reluctantly for some, especially Parker (Yaphet Kotto) and Brett (Harry Dean Stanton), from 00:14. **This action defines the**

**first and only dramatic sequence in Act 1**. We're still in Act 1 because there is nothing really at stake, except their bonuses. The main problem in the story – the alien – hasn't been introduced yet. Their motivation is to be done with the exploration of LV-426 so they can resume their journey home. This is why in *Alien*, as in many stories including *Misery*, we have an *inciting action* over most of Act 1 rather than an isolated *inciting event*. This first dramatic action is resolved when they find the lost vessel with its giant mutilated bodies. The answer to the dramatic question is *yes*, they have found evidence of non-human life on LV-426.

Dramatic Act 2 starts at 00:35 when they discover the alien eggs and a *facehugger* attacks Kane (John Hurt). This is the inciting event which triggers their main goal in the movie. From that moment on, they – the whole crew of the Nostromo, protagonist of the film – are trying to deal with an evolving, shape-shifting antagonist: the alien, main source of external conflict and main problem in the story. What's at stake at first is Kane's life, but it quickly becomes the survival of the entire crew.

They are going to argue, quite often, about the best way to deal with the problem (internal conflict for the protagonist). For example, Ripley refuses to let them in when they bring an infected Kane back to the ship, while the rest of the crew insists she does so, to save his life. Or some think they should freeze Kane with the *facehugger* still on, though others want to try to take it off Kane first. When they attempt to do this, it reveals a strong defence mechanism: it has acid for blood, which is going to restrict what they can do to deal with it.

**The first dramatic sequence of Act 2, triggered by the attack on Kane, is about dealing with the *facehugger***. Should they let it in or not? Should they freeze it with Kane or not? Should they attempt to take it off Kane or not? Dealing with the *facehugger* is their first subgoal.

After failing to remove it from Kane's face, they find that the *facehugger* isn't attached to Kane anymore. They look for it in the medical room until they find it dead (climax of the first sequence of Act 2 at 00:49). It looks like the problem has resolved itself: Kane seems to have recovered and there is no threat anymore. It's as if we had started dramatic Act 3 and were back to normal. The crew are having a last meal before resuming their journey back to Earth. Only dramatic irony keeps the story going at this stage. We know this can't be the end of the film; it's way too early.

When the *chestburster*, implanted by the *facehugger*, leaps out of Kane's ribcage – killing him – and escapes at 00:57, this is a huge surprise which forces them to resume the same goal: finding a way to deal with the alien. Structurally, this is more like an early *Encore Twist* than a mid-act climax, because the goal is the same. Logistically, this might be the midpoint (more on all these elements in the *Craft the Draft* section).

The alien has changed shape for the first time in the story, and as it's still relatively small, they declare a new subgoal: **They are going to try to find the alien, catch it and get rid of it.** They can't kill it with conventional weapons as its acid-blood could damage the ship. This new subgoal, triggered by a shocking inciting incident, defines the **second sequence of Act 2: catching the** *chestburster*. But the alien has changed shape for the second time; it's fully grown now – a surprise then exploited as a dramatic irony – and when the creature takes Brett, it's the climax of sequence two. They have failed to find the alien, catch it and get rid of it.

Brett's death at 00:68 is not only the climax of the second sequence of Act 2, it's also the inciting incident of the next sequence which starts at 00:69. Using nets and electric cattle prods won't do against a fully grown alien; they have to try something else. So here comes the **third sequence of Act 2, defined by their next subgoal: trying to flush the alien outside using flamethrowers.** But at 01:14 they fail again and the alien takes Dallas (Tom Skerritt), which is the climax of the sequence.

Desperately looking for a solution, **Ripley tries to find out more about their situation (fourth subgoal, defining the fourth sequence of Act 2).** She discovers from Mother that Ash (Ian Holm) was ordered to bring the organisms back to Earth for study, and that the company considers the crew expendable. She confronts Ash who tries to kill her (climax of the sequence, 01:20-01:22). She's rescued by Parker and Lambert (Veronica Cartwright) and it's revealed that Ash is an android. They interrogate him before incinerating him, at 01:25. This is their first success. They have rid the team of its most important internal obstacle. Ash was a constant threat as his goal was the protection of the alien, not the survival of the crew. This is why he let Kane get into the ship with the *facehugger* in the first place, or stopped Parker from killing the *chestburster* during the gory breakfast scene.

They immediately decide to **escape from the Nostromo before blowing it up (fifth subgoal defining the fifth and last sequence of Act 2).** Lambert and Parker are killed at 01:31, but Ripley manages to escape in the shuttle with Jones the cat just before the Nostromo explodes (climax of the sequence and first climax of the film at 01:43).

We are now in dramatic Act 3: Ripley has reached her goal. She has apparently defeated the alien and saved her life, although all her co-protagonists are now dead. Structurally, this moment is similar to what we experienced earlier in the film, when the *facehugger* died and the problem seemed to be solved, except that now we could believe that the film is over. Just as we start to relax, we have an *Encore Twist*: a surprise – the alien has managed to sneak into the shuttle – which re-launches the same dramatic action at 01:46. **Ripley has to face the alien one last time** until she blows it out of the airlock and fries it with the shuttle engine at 01:51. We'll discuss the *Encore Twist* in more detail in *Craft the Draft* as it's a commonly used structural device, especially in genre movies. Briefly, it's a surprise at the beginning of Act 3 that works as an inciting event when we thought the action was over, leading the same protagonist to resume the same goal. This defines a mini three-act structure in dramatic Act 3 and a last dramatic sequence or scene.

So in *Alien*, the main goal which defines the overall three-act structure of the movie (dealing with the alien) can be split into five subgoals, five tasks: dealing with the *facehugger* (apparently self-resolves), trying to capture the *chestburster* (they fail), trying to flush the fully-grown alien out (they fail), getting more information from Mother and Ash (they succeed), blowing up the ship and escaping with the shuttle (Ripley succeeds). These five subgoals define as many dramatic sequences in Act 2. We can see how each evolution of the antagonist raises the stakes for the protagonist, leading to a change of subgoal.

Overall, *Alien* has seven main dramatic sequences: one in dramatic Act 1; five in dramatic Act 2 until the first climax; one in dramatic Act 3, which features an *Encore Twist* and a second climax providing a second answer to the same dramatic question.

Here is an illustration to help visualise this dramatic structure:

# The *Fractal* Aspect of Structure

## *Dramatic* 3-Act Structure of ***Alien***

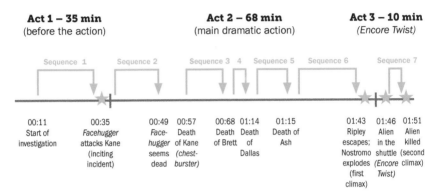

**Act 1 – 35 min**
(before the action)

**Act 2 – 68 min**
(main dramatic action)

**Act 3 – 10 min**
*(Encore Twist)*

Sequence 1    Sequence 2    Sequence 3  4    Sequence 5    Sequence 6    Sequence 7

| 00:11 | 00:35 | 00:49 | 00:57 | 00:68 | 01:14 | 01:15 | 01:43 | 01:46 | 01:51 |
|---|---|---|---|---|---|---|---|---|---|
| Start of investigation | *Facehugger* attacks Kane *(inciting incident)* | *Face-hugger* seems dead | Death of Kane *(chest-burster)* | Death of Brett | Death of Dallas | Death of Ash | Ripley escapes; Nostromo explodes *(first climax)* | Alien in the shuttle *(Encore Twist)* | Alien killed *(second climax)* |

Sequence 1 (24 min): Investigating the possibility of non-human life
Sequence 2 (14 min): Dealing with the *facehugger*
Sequence 3 (10 min): Capturing the *chestburster*
Sequence 4 (5 min): Flushing out the alien using flame-throwers
Sequence 5 (10 min): Finding out more about the situation
Sequence 6 (18 min): Escaping with the shuttle and blowing up the ship
Sequence 7 (5 min): Facing the alien in the shuttle one last time

Funnily enough, *Alien*'s logistical three-act structure (30 min, 60 min, 30 min) is not too far from its dramatic structure because it has an extended dramatic sequence in Act 1, thanks to a first goal which makes the first act unusually long. It also has an *Encore Twist* in Act 3 which makes the last dramatic act longer than usual. This is more an exception than the rule though. Usually, dramatic Act 2 is much longer, often lasting most of the film.

Hopefully, looking at *Alien* makes it clear how dramatic acts are cut into more manageable units (dramatic sequences) using subgoals. This allows the writer to handle them as mini-movies, complete with their own dramatic three acts, thanks to the fractal aspect of story structure.

Getting rid of the *logistical* three-act structure and embracing the *dramatic* three-act structure, in order to cut down your second act into dramatic units instead of logistical units, is what's going to help clarify what's at stake at all times and avoid the dreaded yet so common soft belly in the middle of Act 2.

*Alien* also shows very clearly how the threat grows in intensity. We first have to deal with a *facehugger*, then a *chestburster*, then a fully grown alien. We can't swap these around without making the story less interesting and involving. Thinking about subgoals (dramatic tasks) and making sure that the obstacles faced by the protagonist in each dramatic sequence get stronger and stronger – thus raising the stakes – can also help to improve a screenplay.

In *Alien*, the antagonist evolves over the course of the story as it changes shape, keeping some mystery – what's coming next? – while increasing the suspense – the danger gets stronger and stronger. In *Jaws*, *Terminator* or *Misery*, the antagonist doesn't change or evolve that much, it's our perception and understanding of the antagonist that changes, increasing the threat as the story unfolds.

The protagonist also evolves. It goes from the full crew to the last survivors, Ripley and her cat, as all the crew members are killed by the antagonist (a common structure in horror/slasher movies). While the decrease in number weakens the protagonist, the increase in strength – Ripley becomes stronger as the story moves forward – partially makes up for it. The strength of the obstacles and the strength of the protagonist are perfectly balanced. We get more and more conflict as the situation gets worse and worse, yet we still *just* believe in the protagonist's chances to succeed.

We'll take a look at a few more case studies at the end of this chapter to illustrate again how we can break a main goal into subgoals, as it's a key point to master when developing plot-led stories. It's just as important for character-led and theme-led stories, but it's used in a slightly different way as we'll see in the chapters dedicated to these story-types.

Now that we've seen how we can break down a dramatic act – especially Act 2 – into sequences using the fractal aspect of story structure, let's go one step further and break down sequences into mini-movies also using the fractal aspect of story structure to design them in three dramatic acts, just as we did for the whole movie.

# Structure and Develop Each Sequence

As we've seen in the former section, once the main conscious goal – related to the main external problem – is defined, we can break it down into subgoals, also called tasks, i.e. practical things to do to achieve the goal and attempt to solve the main problem.

Once we have our subgoals, each one often defines a dramatic sequence, like a mini-story within the story. Thanks to the fractal aspect of the dramatic three-act structure, we can then design each sequence in three dramatic acts, and develop it accordingly.

Usually in a plot-led or character-led movie, the protagonist of most sequences will be the protagonist of the whole film, but in theme-led movies – multi-stranded narratives – each strand will probably have a different protagonist: the character or group of characters experiencing the most conflict in the strand.

Sometimes, the protagonist of some of the sequences isn't the protagonist of the movie, especially when the protagonist is unable to be active for some reason. For example, in *Misery*, Buster the sheriff is the protagonist of a sequence towards the end of the film as we'll see in *Don't Forget the Subplots*.

So what we're going to do for each sequence is the same as we've done for the whole movie: identify the best protagonist, the best goal, the best sources of obstacles and develop each sequence as a series of scenes, connected by the same subgoal, the same dramatic action.

Then we can structure each of these scenes in three dramatic acts, as we did in *Behind the Scenes*. Not every scene has to be structured this way, but defining a clear dramatic action with a clear protagonist, goal and obstacles usually helps to make a scene more exciting and effective.

We should also look at the way we manage information in each sequence. We might be exploiting an overall dramatic irony which was set up earlier and will be resolved later, but we could also use dramatic irony to shape a sequence, especially if it's difficult to have an active protagonist over the whole sequence. We could structure it with a dramatic irony, and instead of a dramatic question (Will the protagonist of the sequence reach the goal?), have an ironic question (How and when will the victim of the dramatic irony find out?). For example, at the beginning of *Misery* we know more than Paul Sheldon early on in the movie, which shapes an "ironic" sequence in Act 1, before Paul Sheldon becomes aware of the extent of the problem and tries to resolve it more actively.

We can also combine both. In the "Using the hairpin to escape" sequence, we have both a clear protagonist (Paul, the protagonist in the movie) and a victim of a strong dramatic irony (Annie, who doesn't know he's trying to escape). This often happens in thrillers. The victim of the dramatic irony is the antagonist, which generates a strong suspense as we fear the consequences of the antagonist finding out. Let's take a closer look at how this dramatic sequence is built.

## The Hairpin Sequence in *Misery*

When Paul realises that he's in more trouble than he thought after Annie's second outburst of violence and first clear threat (If I die, you die), he tries to escape from his room briefly and fails when he finds that the door is locked. This is a fairly short scene.

The first proper sequence in dramatic Act 2 in *Misery* starts around 00:40, just after the scene in which Annie forces Paul to burn his manuscript.

This sixteen-minute sequence has a short first act, then a second act divided in two parts with a mid-act climax (more on this in the *Craft the Draft* section) and many scenes using sub-subgoals, and finally a short third act. The subgoal defining the sequence and leading to these three dramatic acts is "using the hairpin to escape".

To help visualise this analysis, here is what the three-act structure of the sequence looks like (for the three-act structure of the whole film, see the detailed analysis of *Misery* in *Case Studies* at the end of the chapter):

# The *Fractal* Aspect of Structure

## The Hairpin Sequence in *Misery*

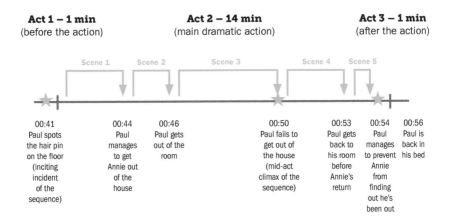

| Act 1 – 1 min | Act 2 – 14 min | Act 3 – 1 min |
|:---:|:---:|:---:|
| (before the action) | (main dramatic action) | (after the action) |

Scene 1 (3 min): Trying to get Annie out of the house
Scene 2 (2 min): Trying to get out of the room
Scene 3 (5 min): Trying to get out of the house
Scene 4 (3 min): Trying to get back to his room before Annie's return
Scene 5 (1 min): Trying to prevent Annie from finding out he's been out

Let's see how it's designed in more detail:

00:40, Annie gives Paul a table, a chair and a typewriter, as well as a wheelchair. She expects him to write a new book for the series, in order to bring Misery back to life: *Misery's Return.* This is the first act of the sequence, before the dramatic action.

00:41, Paul spots a hairpin on the floor and this inciting event for the sequence triggers a new subgoal which shapes the dramatic action for the next fifteen minutes: **using the hairpin to escape**. We enter the second act of the sequence. Annie becomes the victim of a dramatic irony because unlike the audience she doesn't know that Paul has potentially found a way to escape.

00:42, the *first sub-subgoal* from here is *to get Annie out of the house.* Paul uses the paper excuse and manages to convince Annie, but he pays a price (more pain!). First success for Paul.

00:45, Paul now has *to get out of the room (second sub-subgoal)*. He first needs to get the pin, then to open the door.

00:46, new success: Paul's out of the room. He can now *try to find a way out of the house (third sub-subgoal)*. But the front door is closed. The phone is a fake.

00:47, Annie is on her way back. Because she's a victim of a dramatic irony (she doesn't know that Paul is trying to escape) and she's the antagonist, we fear the resolution of that dramatic irony (How is she going to react when she finds out?). Paul is also victim of a dramatic irony: we know Annie is on her way back, but Paul doesn't. These two elements generate a lot of suspense and tension in the sequence.

00:48, Paul manages to catch the falling penguin, but he puts it back facing the wrong direction. This foreshadows the way Annie will find out about his escape attempts (and sets up a minor dramatic irony).

00:49, Paul visits the "pharmacy" and gets more pills.

In the kitchen, Paul has to give up the wheelchair (more pain), but the back door is locked too. It feels like the end of his sub-subgoal. He's giving up on finding a way out. This is in fact the mid-act climax of the sequence. The answer to the local dramatic question is **no**, the hairpin won't allow him to escape. Just as he spots a knife, which would trigger a new sub-subgoal (*to get a weapon*), he hears that Annie is back on the farm. We enter the second half of the second act of the sequence: Paul has to deal with the consequences of his action in the first half of the sequence. We'll talk more about the mid-act climax in *Craft the Draft* as it can also be used to structure the whole story.

00:51, Annie's return triggers his *fourth sub-subgoal in the sequence: getting back to his room before Annie finds out*. There is a strong time-lock (more on this in *Craft the Draft*), which adds to the tension of the end of the sequence. He has to get back in the wheelchair, make his way back, close all the doors and lock his bedroom door, in just a few minutes. Success on this sub-subgoal, but...

Small local dramatic irony: we see that the pills are visible, but he doesn't. Just as Annie comes into the room, Paul realises that the pills are poking out, which triggers his last sub-subgoal: *preventing Annie from finding out he's tried to escape*. He manages to cover the pills with his hands and send her away before she puts him back to bed, which allows him to hide the pills better. Success on this sub-subgoal. We enter the third act of the sequence.

00:54: Annie apologises about her bad temper; Paul jokes about it. This is linked to the drama of pretending all is fine in order to keep as good a relationship as possible with Annie and prevent one of her bad-tempered outbursts.

00:56: Paul is back in his bed. **This is the end of the "hairpin" sequence.** He's failed on the subgoal "using the pin to find a way to escape", but his exploration of the house has allowed him to get more pills, and he's managed not to get caught.

As we can see, in *Misery* the fractal aspect of the three-act structure is used to structure the whole film, each dramatic sequence and many scenes, meaning we always know what's at stake not only in the whole film, but also at every moment. This really helps to increase our emotional involvement and identification with the protagonist, an essential element in a thriller.

## Don't Forget the Subplots

A subplot is a dramatic action that's less important than the main dramatic action but connected to it in some way (dramatically or thematically, ideally both).

Depending on the story-type, we can have anything ranging from no subplot at all in very pure, action-filled plot-led stories (*High Noon*, *Duel*) to a single, minor subplot (*Gravity*) to just subplots with no main plot in theme-led stories / multi-stranded narratives (*Crash*, *Parenthood*, *Game of Thrones*).

Thanks to the fractal aspect of story structure, subplots can also be structured in three dramatic acts around a dramatic *action* (the subplot is plot-led) or an *evolution* (the subplot is character-led). Of course using the dramatic three-act structure to design a subplot is optional, just as it is for the story as a whole.

The protagonist of a subplot doesn't have to be the protagonist of the whole story. In fact, it's often another character. Subplots are frequently used in plot-led stories to show a parallel action (like the sheriff, Buster, investigating Paul Sheldon's disappearance in *Misery* as we'll see in a moment) or to explore/convey a theme (say everything related to the rise of fascism in the first half of Roberto Benigni's *Life Is Beautiful*, which is an interesting example as in this movie the subplot in the first half becomes the main plot in the second half).

Often, a character-led subplot will add some depth to a plot-led story, and will carry most of the theme and meaning, like the subplot in *Midnight Run* about Jack Walsh's (De Niro) backstory. The Duke (Grodin) tries to find out what happened to Walsh, what made him the grumpy, jaded man he is today. Although the Duke is the apparent protagonist of this subplot, the one who consciously wants to find out, the actual protagonist is Walsh because he's the one experiencing the most conflict and resisting change, the one who needs to realise that what he's doing is wrong. He's the protagonist of the character-led subplot just as he's the protagonist of the plot-led main plot.

This subplot allows us to find out essential things about our protagonist, and leads to the solution for his moral dilemma (Should Walsh deliver the Duke and take the bounty, or do the right thing and let him go?). It's only in the climax that we find out, through Walsh's final decision, who he really is, which also concludes the character-led subplot. In *Midnight Run* as in many good plot-led stories, the character-led subplot is really what the movie is about. Without it, we'd have only fist fights and car chases, which could still be entertaining but would be far less interesting.

Generally, **in a plot-led story**, each subplot is connected to the main plot (dramatic action of the protagonist). For example, in *Gravity*, the dead daughter subplot leads to the protagonist being tempted to give up. **In a character-led story**, subplots tend to be connected to the evolution of the main character, as with Pat's father's subplot in *Silver Linings Playbook*. **In a theme-led story**, all the subplots (strands) explore and are connected to the same theme, as there is no main plot (no plot significantly more important than the others). For example, in *Game of Thrones*, all the subplots explore the same theme (power). While all the strands converge towards the same goal – the families, houses, tribes and clans in the Seven Kingdoms are either protecting or plotting to seize the Iron Throne – none of the main strands is significantly more important than the others, even if one might be more in the spotlight than others over a few episodes.

## Sheriff Buster Subplot in *Misery*

While subplots often carry most of the meaning in plot-led stories and are frequently character-led, it's not the case in *Misery* and that's why I'd like to look at it here. You'll find a detailed analysis of *Misery* at the end of the chapter, but for now let's take some time to study its only subplot, which is designed around Buster, the sheriff.

As soon as Sheriff Buster hears about Sheldon's disappearance, he starts to investigate. He goes to the lodge that Sheldon uses to write, gets close to discovering the wreck of Sheldon's car when he notices traces of a possible car accident, tries to learn about Sheldon's work to see if it leads to anything and finally is rewarded when he notices Annie's altercation in town and starts investigating her. Of course, Buster is the victim of a strong dramatic irony: we know what happened to Paul, but he doesn't.

So while Buster's action is not as important as the main plot, it is connected to it. In fact, it even becomes the main plot in the last sequence of the subplot, when Buster goes to Annie's house, reaches his goal – finding out that Sheldon is there – but pays for this discovery with his life.

The Buster subplot is there to give us hope for some kind of external help, as well as to justify why this help doesn't arrive earlier. It doesn't convey much meaning, as most of the theme and meaning in *Misery* is carried through the main plot, and is related to creativity and captivity.

Like the main plot, the Buster subplot in *Misery* is structured in three dramatic acts. The inciting event is Sheldon's agent's call. The dramatic question it raises is: "Will Buster find out what happened to Sheldon?". Dramatic Act 2 lasts over most of the movie. The climax is when Buster searches Annie's house and finds Sheldon. The answer to the dramatic question of the subplot is *yes*, Buster finds out what happened to Sheldon. Dramatic Act 3, very short, shows the main consequence of his action: Buster gets killed by Annie.

This subplot is divided into dramatic sequences and scenes as Buster explores various subgoals to reach his goal: investigating the lodge (fails), investigating a possible car crash scene (fails), investigating Sheldon's work (fails) then investigating Annie (succeeds).

Again, not all subplots are structured that way. The main subplot in many plot-led movies is often character-led, as we'll see in the detailed analysis of *Gravity* or *Billy Elliot* at the end of the chapter.

However, this shows how we can use the dramatic three-act structure to shape not only the main plot and dramatic sequences in Act 2 of the movie, but also the subplots and sequences within each subplot. We can structure each part, and then weave them together in a seamless construction. While the audience will only see a succession of scenes, we'll be able to track the progress of main plot and subplot(s) separately, until the point where they connect.

This is the way theme-led movies – multi-stranded narratives – are structured. They don't have a main plot so there is no overall protagonist, but each strand, each subplot, is structured around a main action or an evolution, connected to the same theme. We'll see how this works in detail in the chapter about developing a theme-led story, but it's also very relevant to plot-led and character-led stories, so keep working on your subplot structuring skills.

# Hands-On: Designing a Sequence

Now that we've seen a few examples, let's put all this into practice and move to the next stage: structuring sequences.

I'd like you either to identify a dramatic sequence in a feature film screenplay you're developing or write a short film (less than thirty minutes) featuring a single dramatic sequence.

This dramatic sequence should be at least ten minutes long and contain at least three dramatic scenes structured in three dramatic acts. This means you should define a clear protagonist for the sequence, with a clear dramatic goal (three-act structure over the whole sequence), and then do the same for at least three scenes.

You can have a few more locations and characters than in the *Behind the Scenes* exercises, but I suggest you focus on the drama rather than logistics, so try to keep things as simple as possible. Look at the examples from *The Apartment* or *Misery*. We don't need many characters or locations to create an exciting dramatic sequence.

Aside from these constraints, you can use as many tools as you want. Try to use visual storytelling as much as possible, planting and pay-off as well, and of course play with managing information. Mystery, surprise, dramatic irony, suspense should all be part of the sequence in some way.

While you should work on character design and try to show relevant traits using conflict and visual storytelling, don't try to handle too much of an evolution for the protagonist. Character development needs time, and it's difficult to pull that off in less than thirty minutes. So make sure the sequence is plot-led rather than character-led. The main problem should be external to the protagonist (other characters or nature), not internal. If you feel like it, try to handle some form of character growth for your protagonist, but that's optional.

Even if you're not a writer, you should try to design a sequence and the dramatic engine of the scenes. You don't need to write a single line of dialogue if you don't want to. What's important at this stage is how you're going to unify a series of scenes under the same dramatic action and develop this mini-story using various dramatic tools.

When you're done, please come back to see how we might be able to improve your sequence.

\* \* \*

Okay, so you've got a sequence. Let's see how we can try to make it better.

1.  **Is there a crescendo in the sequence?** If the protagonist faces a few obstacles, do they get stronger and stronger in each scene, so that we have more conflict as the sequence unfolds, culminating in the climax of the sequence?

2.  **Is there enough causality in the sequence?** Does what happens in each scene happen because of what took place earlier, in the former scenes? Or does it feel episodic? A good way to check for causality is to try to swap scenes around. If you can, it means that there is not enough causality in your story. Planting and pay-off is a great way to add causality, so check you have at least one significant plant and pay-off.

3.  **Is the three-act structure of the sequence clear?** When do we understand the goal and motivations of the protagonist (Who wants what and why)? When do we get an answer to the dramatic question (*Yes*, the protagonist reaches the goal; *no*, the protagonist fails)? Do we see consequences of the protagonist's action in Act 3? If you look at the length of dramatic acts, are your first and third acts fairly short compared to your second act? Does each scene in Act 2 explore a clear subgoal (practical way for the protagonist to reach the overall goal in the sequence)?

4.  **Do you play with managing information as well?** Who knows what and when? Do you exploit at least one strong dramatic irony in the sequence? At least one surprise? Do

you have some mystery as well? Did you make sure not to use mystery over the whole sequence, just to create a surprise in the end? Many short films are designed like this, and it's fine for up to ten minutes, but for a sequence longer than fifteen minutes it's probably a bit boring. Play with all the tools at your disposal to manage information.

5. **You can, if you want to, shape the sequence using a dramatic irony** and an ironic question (How and when will the victim find out?) rather than the three-act structure and a dramatic question (Will the protagonist reach the goal or not?). If you do this, make sure your structure is clear, for example check that you set up, properly exploit and resolve the dramatic irony.

If any of the above improves your sequence, why not go over the whole screenplay and see if you have a) clear dramatic sequences exploring various subgoals in your second act and b) if these dramatic sequences have a strong enough structure.

If you do this with all your sequences and most of your scenes, you should improve the readability of your screenplay, both from a clarity point of view – we'll know what's at stake in each scene and sequence – and from a reader involvement point of view. Knowing what's at stake in the story and playing with the management of information is the best way to get the audience itching to know what's going to happen next. It's also the best way to avoid the sagging middle of Act 2 syndrome.

# 2.3 Craft the Draft

Crafting the draft encompasses everything we have to do to deliver an effective story that makes sense. It doesn't matter if we start with this design or if we prefer to start with an intuitive draft zero before making structural decisions. At some point in the development process, we have to think about the way the story works as a whole.

Of course, one of the most important things is to identify the story-type of the project, and develop it accordingly. But what other elements can we look at to improve the chances of our story working, i.e. to be meaningful, entertaining and moving?

## Genre

While not all stories have to sit in a genre, clarifying the genre of your story – or knowing how to deal with a story which doesn't fit a single genre – is a crucial aspect of the development process.

If you're developing a project in a specific genre, you have to know that genre inside out, not necessarily to follow its conventions, but to know the rules you're breaking or the expectations you might fail to meet. *Scream* was original because it made fun of the rules of the genre yet delivered a great slasher movie. *Se7en* was an original thriller, had a challenging and unique ending, yet it delivered a true thriller. The Zucker, Abrahams and Zucker trio, Farrelly brothers, Apatow gang all renewed the comedy genre with their own distinctive style, yet they delivered very funny movies.

There is nothing wrong with breaking the conventions of a genre, as long as you know it well. Also, be aware that while genre mixing can be fun, some genres don't mix well. Comedy and horror go well together, but comedy and thrillers less so (the hilariously scary *Mute Witness* being an exception).

Once you're set on your genre, make sure the chosen story-type allows you to deliver the goods. It's difficult to write a disaster movie or thriller which isn't plot-led. This doesn't prevent you from making it more interesting with a strong character-led element, but the definition of the genre requires an external main problem, hence a plot-led movie.

We don't have the space here to discuss the specifics of each genre – we'd need to dedicate a chapter or even a whole book to each genre to do that – but here is some generic advice:

- If your story doesn't have a clearly identified genre, it's not necessarily a problem, but if your aim is to reach as large an audience as possible, try to see if a genre – or a combination of genres – could serve your story without compromising its intention. Comedy is a very difficult genre to write, but there are few themes it can't explore successfully.

- If your story has a clearly identified genre, make sure you know this genre inside out, have studied many movies in that genre and are aware of audience expectations. If you sell a movie as a specific genre, you have to deliver on that. Some sell a movie as a thriller when it's a mystery or chiller. That's bound to disappoint. Others sell a film as a comedy, but it's not funny. So know your genre, be as original as you want, but if you break with the conventions, make sure you still deliver the promised genre to the audience.

## A Good Set-Up

Along with the ending, the first ten to fifteen pages are the most important in a screenplay. If they are not good enough, they are the only pages that are going to be read before the script is tossed away.

They are also the most important minutes in a film, because this is when we set up the world of the movie, its rules, characters, tone, genre, theme... Fifteen pages in, we're either hooked or bored.

There is a lot to do in a small amount of time. So what makes a good set-up?

A good set-up is an opening to the story that makes you feel the filmmaker is in control of the narrative. That you are in safe hands. That the journey is going to be exciting and rewarding. If it's a genre movie, that the genre is mastered with efficiency and originality.

By page fifteen, we're expecting to understand what's at stake in a story, why we should want to know what's going to happen next, what we should fear or hope for.

We can find dozens of exceptions, because screenwriting isn't a science, but here are a few things that can help to create a good set-up:

- Introducing the main characters visually, in a way that tells us about their personality (*The Breakfast Club* or *Rio Bravo*).

- If we're dealing with a **plot-led story**, establishing who wants what and why. If we have an inciting action rather than an inciting incident, the first part of this inciting action should have taken place (the car crash in *Misery*). In other words, we should know what the main dramatic action is going to be.

- If we're dealing with a **character-led story**, we should know – consciously or not – what the character needs so the main evolution is defined.

- If we're dealing with a **theme-led story**, we should understand what the story is about, which theme unites all these various strands and characters.

- If the world of the story is not well-known, we should be introduced to this world. This could be a fantasy world like *Lord of the Rings* or *Avatar*, but it could also be an unusual real-world setting, like the Amish community in *Witness*. We'll discuss this in the next section as it's a key element to get right.

- Something that really helps to create a good set-up is coming up with the right opening image. Michael Dorsey (Dustin Hoffman) putting on some make-up in *Tootsie*. The scorpion fighting the ants in *The Wild Bunch*. Can you find something which, without being obvious or clichéd, encapsulates the essence of your story, plants a key element or introduces the main problem in a visual, exciting and/or intriguing way?

Overall, a good set-up defines and introduces the elements of plot, character and theme which are going to matter in the story. Depending on the story-type of the project, the main focus will be different, but all three elements should be clear within about fifteen minutes.

The 2007 remake of the western classic *3:10 to Yuma* has a very effective set-up. Please watch the first five minutes of the film before reading what follows.

In this opening sequence (without the opening credits, we're talking less than three minutes), we are introduced to the main characters in a very visual and conflictual way. What's at stake – the survival of the protagonist's family – is made very clear. Dan (Christian Bale) has a week to pay his debts, or he loses everything. The theme of the story is set up, as is the main character-led element.

Towards the end of the sequence, William picks up his father's rifle, aims, but Dan stops him before he can shoot, saying: "I'll take care of this". His son replies with the most significant line of dialogue in the whole scene: "No you won't".

This sets up the main character-led element of the story, which is the relationship between father and son. Will takes his father's lack of action as cowardice, while we know it's more complex than that. The character who changes most in the film isn't Dan, the protagonist, but his son, Will, who needs to realise that the way he judges his father is wrong.

This opening sequence also clearly sets up the theme. The story is about a man regaining his self-esteem and winning his son's respect.

While *3:10 to Yuma* is a plot-led story, with a main problem anchored right at the bottom of Maslow's Hierarchy of Needs as it's about safety / survival, the character-led and thematic elements give it more depth, as they are about love, belonging, family, esteem and respect from others.

All of this is set up in less than three minutes, using mostly action and visual storytelling rather than dialogue. As a result, the few lines of dialogue at the end of the sequence carry significant weight and really stand out. Overall, a great set-up.

## Story World

The story world defines the setting, the environment in which the story takes place.

For some stories, it's our everyday world so we don't need that much research to define it. We're in a "write what you know" situation.

For other stories, especially those set in the past or future, in a different country or even in a different world altogether, a lot more work is needed to make the story world believable, with consistent rules, even if invented.

For example, in a fantasy or sci-fi movie, some rules of physics might change, but they must be well-defined and consistent.

In a historical drama or biopic, the way people dress, behave and even talk has to be researched.

If the world is invented, we need to define clear sociological, geo-graphical, astronomical and many other rules so that the fictional world feels real.

This is what J.R.R. Tolkien, George Lucas or J.K. Rowling achieve so brilliantly in *The Lord of the Rings*, *Star Wars* or the *Harry Potter* sagas.

This is also what James Cameron achieves in *Avatar*, in which he creates a world from scratch on Pandora, with its own botanical and animal species, as well as a mythology, a religion, a way of life for the Na'vi, even if he borrows a lot from Native Americans. All these inventions are needed to give the fictional world some believability, and the rules need to be consistent. If things don't add up, we can't suspend our disbelief.

But less fantastical pieces also need work on their story world. For example, *Witness* was set in contemporary Pennsylvania (at the time of its release), but the way the Amish community is depicted clearly required a significant amount of research.

Same thing with *Apocalypto*, which is set centuries ago in ancient Mayan territory, and needed to define a language, various tribes and the way they lived at the time.

I highly recommend reading the chapter *Building Your Story World* in *Writing Fiction for Dummies* by Randy Ingermanson and Peter Economy. Don't let the title mislead you, while it's primarily aimed at novelists, the book is cleverly written and I found this section – which applies equally to screenwriting – very useful.

# Characterisation

Developing a plot-led story doesn't mean that we can forgo strong characters. It just means that the main problem in the story lies outside the protagonist, in other characters or nature. We can design a brilliant plot, but if our characters aren't interesting, if the audience can't relate to them, care about them, root for them, all this effort is pointless. We have to work on characters – and on theme – in a plot-led story just as much as in a character-led or theme-led story. So let's dig in!

Characterisation is the art of designing characters. It's one of the most important aspects of story structure. In *Juno* or *Young Adults*, Diablo Cody doesn't only write great dialogue, she *designs* original, touching characters who move us because of who they are and what they do as much as they make us laugh because of what they say. This talent relies heavily on the writer's life experience and ability to create characters who come across as real human beings which, unfortunately, can't be taught.

However, we can discuss a few things that might help with characterisation when we struggle, feel stuck or suspect something is amiss with our characters.

First, there are some old school elements which are useful but not as important as one might think. We can all write pages on the physiology (what they look like), sociology (where they come from) and psychology (how they behave) of our characters, nail their backstory down to the kind of underwear they buy and what they eat for breakfast, but we end up with a lot of information, and not necessarily what we need to keep in mind as we write each character in each scene.

You can find this classic approach in just about every screenwriting book, so I'm not going to spend much time discussing this. Going through these long lists of questions often leads writers to fill them in with random answers. Most of the points are irrelevant to the character, or to the story. For me, this approach is similar to underlining everything in a text. It's exactly as if you had not underlined anything. Nothing stands out and often you have no idea who your characters are, except in a very superficial way.

Instead I'd like to look at some essential elements which will only take up half a page per character (at most) and will help you hold a clear picture of each character as you write them in each scene.

These elements are: the character's conscious goal (*want*), unconscious goal (*need*), motivations, internal obstacle(s), main characteristic, secondary characteristics and evolution (change or growth) or lack of (steadfast).

Let's take these one by one.

In a plot-led story, the protagonist's **conscious goal** is related to the main problem. It's what the character *wants*. It defines the plot (the character's dramatic action) as well as what's at stake in the story, the dramatic question: Will the character reach the goal or not?

The character doesn't have to have an **unconscious need**, because we're not developing a character-led story. The protagonist doesn't have to change, because the main problem lies outside the protagonist, not within. But we can still have an unconscious need, as a secondary problem, possibly as a source of internal obstacles for the protagonist, or to create a dilemma. Very often in a plot-led story, the protagonist doesn't need to change. There is nothing so wrong within the character that it would define what's primarily at stake in the story. The character simply needs to overcome an internal flaw in order to reach the goal (solve the main problem); or the dramatic action will cause the protagonist to grow, to evolve, usually in a positive way. For example, Luke Skywalker in *Star Wars* needs to believe in himself and in the power of the Force before he can blow up the Death Star. Sometimes, as in *Billy Elliot*, it's the antagonist – Billy's father – who needs to change in order for the protagonist to reach the goal.

Characters' **motivations** can be obvious, but when they're not, it helps to clarify them so that we can be with the protagonist trying to reach the goal, or understand why other characters oppose the protagonist. It's not only the logic of the story which is at stake here, it's also our emotional involvement. If we don't understand why a character wants to do something, we can add as much conflict as we want, but the audience won't root for the character.

Characterisation can be a great source of conflict in plot-led movies. For example, we can design **internal obstacles** for the character so that reaching the goal becomes even more difficult. Chief Brody's fear of the sea in *Jaws* is a perfect example of that. It's more difficult for him to go after a great white shark – and to get into the water for a final confrontation when the boat sinks – than for anyone else. Characterisation is used to create more conflict for the protagonist, hence increase our emotional identification with the character. Chief Brody needs to control his fear in order to blow up the shark and survive.

Defining a **main characteristic** for each character helps us create clearly identifiable archetypes. For example, a brave fighter, a jealous husband, a fearful soldier, a brainy woman, a seductive man. These are archetypes, clichés, but they help us draw a very clear picture of the character.

To go beyond the cliché or the archetype, we define a few **secondary characteristics** that make this character unique. For example, Salieri in *Amadeus* is jealous (that's his main characteristic), but he's very different to Othello. A few secondary characteristics, like his love of food, his abstinence, the way his faith evolves are significant elements which help make this archetypal jealous man a unique and memorable character. The key here is to be clear about what the main characteristic is (define an archetype) and what the secondary ones are (make the character unique).

Finally, the **evolution** (change or growth) of the character is one of the most neglected elements in characterisation. Static, steadfast characters are often two-dimensional. It's fine for James Bond, Indiana Jones or secondary characters, but usually we want to design main characters who change or grow because of what happens to them in the story, or who have to change or grow to move the plot forward. This helps us define some character turning points in the story, which means going beyond: "This is my character's backstory, and this is who my character is now" to: "This is who my character is at the beginning of the story, who the character is at the end and here is how this evolution happens (main psychological/emotional changes)". We'll study this in detail in the section about developing a character-led story, as it's the backbone of the structure in that case, but even in a plot-led story it's a good idea to define the evolution of each character and of the key relationships (protagonist/love interest, protagonist/antagonist, love interest/rival, co-protagonists, etc). We'll study more practical tools for working on characters in the last section, *Bringing It All Together*, where we'll look at the difference between selling documents and story design tools.

We still need to flesh out the characters when developing a plot-led story. B movies are often plot-led stories with weak characterisation.

Also, we need to design all the characters, not only the protagonist. For example, we don't want a cardboard villain or antagonist. Understanding the motivation of each character will make the story more involving.

A protagonist's action is determined by their decisions. If we question these choices, if we don't understand the protagonist, if we don't care about the characters, the story will probably leave the audience cold.

As mentioned earlier, having a plot-led main action doesn't mean that we can't have one or more character-led subplot(s). Sometimes, an internal problem within the protagonist provides the most important subplot in the story; resolving this internal problem will be closely tied to the resolution of the main plot. The protagonist either needs to grow to solve the external problem, or grows as a result of the dramatic action.

This often creates near-*hybrids*. The main plot defines the story-type of the movie (what's primarily at stake), but it's the character-led subplot that makes it interesting to watch as it adds depth to the story and causes an internal obstacle or dilemma for the protagonist.

Examples: *Midnight Run*; *Bourne Identity*.

Similarly, many character-led stories are disguised as plot-led, because they introduce a seemingly very important plot problem while what's really at stake lies with the characters.

Examples: *Silver Linings Playbook*; *Little Miss Sunshine*; *Two Days, One Night*.

It's crucial to identify these near-hybrids because they can easily be mistaken for plot-led stories. It's almost impossible to design a satisfying ending if we don't identify what's most important in these stories, which is not what the character *wants* but what the character *needs*. The protagonist might fail to reach the goal yet manage to change, as in the above examples. So failure on the dramatic action/plot can still mean success on the character/evolution side of the story. More on this in *Happy Ending vs Satisfying Ending*.

**Deciding on the story-type doesn't mean that we should neglect the other aspects of a story**. In plot-led stories, we need to define strong characters. We can even develop character-led subplots, up to the point when the story becomes a hybrid. Of course it doesn't hurt if there is a strong theme as well. This is what an action-comedy such as *Midnight Run* achieves brilliantly.

**The story-type only defines the main problem in the story** to help us clearly define what's at stake so we can introduce, develop and answer a main dramatic question. One of the worst mistakes one can make is to think that plot-led stories don't need strong characters, or that character-led stories don't need a strong plot. Having weak characters in an eventful plot or great characters in a weak plot rarely makes fascinating drama.

## Theme

In a story, the theme is linked to the premise. It answers a simple question: What is the story about? It can be something as simple as "Good triumphs over Evil" (the premise of 99% of action movies and thrillers), or it can be something subtler like the difficulty of becoming a *Mensch* or choosing between a career and love (*The Apartment*), whether the end justifies the means (*Ridicule*) or racial tension in L.A. (*Crash*).

You don't *have* to be aware of your theme and it certainly shouldn't feel like the writer is standing on a soapbox hammering the theme into the audience's head. However, identifying the theme can help in a plot-led story, is usually important in a character-led story and is clearly vital in a theme-led story.

In theme-led stories – multi-stranded narratives – the theme is so important that it takes over plot or characters and becomes the main structural component.

This doesn't mean that character-led or plot-led stories can't have a strong theme. Stories are only character-led or plot-led because the main problem lies within the protagonist or in other characters and nature. The theme remains an essential part of the structure and can still be woven into character design or one or more subplots. The writer's point of view regarding the theme is usually expressed through the ending of the story.

We'll have a chance to explore theme further in character-led and theme-led movies in the next two chapters, but for now let's take a look at theme in a plot-led movie: *The Dark Knight*.

Thematically, *The Dark Knight* builds on the elements explored in the first part of Christopher Nolan's trilogy, *Batman Begins*, which was all about the difference between revenge and justice. In the sequel, there's not just one but many connected themes which contribute to raising the film far above the average super-hero movie.

The first theme is related to **order versus chaos,** and sets Bruce Wayne/ Batman (Christian Bale) and Commissioner Gordon (Gary Oldman) against the Joker (Heath Ledger). Batman doesn't seek criminals to kill them but to bring them to justice. He proves this repeatedly, as when the Joker, prior to his arrest, invites him to run him over and Batman doesn't, or towards the end when Batman unwillingly throws his enemy to a certain death only to catch him before he hits the ground.

The Joker, as an agent of chaos, tries to turn Gotham City against Batman by killing innocent people until the Dark Knight reveals his identity. His backstory is irrelevant – he even gives different stories for the origins of his scars – because anarchy doesn't have to be motivated. The Joker represents a force that can't be controlled. Wayne's butler, Alfred (Michael Caine), explains that: "Some men aren't looking for anything logical, like money. They can't be bought, bullied, reasoned, or negotiated with. Some men just want to watch the world burn."

Like fanatics, terminators and great white sharks, mad characters are terrifying because they can't be reasoned with. This makes the story very relevant to a real world threatened by enemies who, like the Joker, can't be bought, bullied, reasoned or negotiated with.

Then there is a parallel theme, which is related to **good versus evil.** This strand is explored through Harvey Dent (Aaron Eckhart) – referred to semi-jokingly as The White Knight in the film – who journeys from good to evil through the story under the Joker's influence, which suggests that the title could just as well refer to him.

While Batman is able to resist his urge to avenge Rachel's death, Dent isn't and ends up consumed by his negative feelings, threatening to destroy all the work that has been achieved by the trio – Batman, Gordon and Dent himself – up to that point and wipe out any hope for change in Gotham City.

Harvey Dent's journey illustrates what Bruce Wayne would have become had he not been able to resist his thirst for vengeance, following the assassination first of his parents, then of Rachel, the woman he loved.

One more important thematic strand is about **who we really are,** what we would do if pushed to the limits by extreme circumstances. When do we bypass social boundaries? This is explored throughout the whole film, for example when people are pushed to kill accountant Reese as the Joker threatens to blow up a hospital if he lives. Will normal citizens kill each other to protect their loved ones? Or to save themselves, as in the river boat bomb situation, when the passengers of each boat have to decide whether they will blow up the other boat, or let the others blow them up first. It's interesting to see how this situation is resolved, because it's one of the only moments of hope in the film. While most individuals fail to resist the Joker's manipulation, neither set of passengers can bring themselves to blow up the other one. It's important because they represent Gotham's population and doing the right thing against all odds means that Batman's efforts to protect them and give them a better future is justified. Difficult situations can reveal the worst, but also the best of human nature, and this episode was necessary to balance the rest of the movie, which is overall pretty bleak.

As always, most of the meaning is expressed through the ending of the movie. While Batman manages to get the Joker arrested and saves Gordon and his family from Harvey Dent's blind revenge, he can't prevent Dent's death. Although he's not done anything wrong, he decides to take the blame for Dent's crimes, so that the people of Gotham can remain hopeful. This is the personal price he has to pay to defeat the Joker's plans. While he turns down the opportunity to be a public hero, which wouldn't help his cause, he becomes one in our eyes by sacrificing himself for the greater good.

Earlier in the film, Dent says: "You either die a hero, or live long enough to see yourself become the villain". While this is a fairly grim statement, it encapsulates the theme of *The Dark Knight*. While order triumphs over chaos when Batman captures the Joker, Evil has triumphed over Good when Dent loses his sanity and starts his revenge killing spree. Even saving Gordon and his family can't stop that. The only way for Batman to turn this defeat into a victory after Dent's death is to sacrifice himself so that Dent's memory remains untarnished. Batman becomes a villain so that Dent can remain a hero. It's all about what Gotham needs – knowing clearly who to admire and who to hate so they remain hopeful for a brighter future – and truth or justice have nothing to do with it.

Bruce Wayne's powers as a man are limited, but Batman's power as a symbol are limitless, whether he stands for Good or Evil. Thanks to dramatic irony – we know what really happened – we can still root for Batman, probably even more so thanks to his sacrifice.

So while *The Dark Knight*, like most super-hero movies, is plot-led (the main problem in the story is rampant crime in Gotham City, personified by characters like Moroni, Gambler and of course the Joker), it explores strong themes which gives the story more depth and makes it intellectually more rewarding. This doesn't prevent great action scenes but gives them context and texture and makes them all the more thrilling.

# Protagonist vs Antagonist

Usually, in a story, we can easily identify the protagonist (the character experiencing the most conflict) and the antagonist (main source of opposition). That's assuming there *is* a protagonist and an antagonist of course, as both are optional. So let's clarify this.

First, and this is very common, some stories have a protagonist, but no antagonist because there is no single source of conflict and obstacles for the protagonist. For example, in *Thelma and Louise* or *Midnight Run* there isn't a character or a group of characters sharing the same goal and representing the main source of conflict for the protagonist. Just various characters or groups of characters with different goals and motivations causing conflict for the protagonist, and that's fine. What matters is that the protagonist experiences a lot of conflict on the road to the goal. It's not necessary for all the conflict to come from a single source.

Some stories have neither a protagonist nor an antagonist because there is no main plot; therefore, there isn't a single character (or group of characters sharing the same goal) experiencing more conflict than the others, or representing the main source of conflict and obstacles. Most theme-led movies – multi-stranded narratives – for example *Crash* or *Cloud Atlas*, and many TV series like *Game of Thrones* fall into this category.

Finally, some stories combine both in the same character: in character-led movies, the antagonist *is* the protagonist, because most of the conflict comes from within the protagonist, who tries to overcome an internal problem and resists change.

We'll discuss theme-led and character-led movies in the next chapters, so let's focus on plot-led movies for now.

If we go back to the definition of *protagonist* (the character – or group of characters sharing the same goal – who experiences the most conflict in a story) and *antagonist* (the character – or group of characters sharing the same goal – who represents the main source of conflict and obstacles for the protagonist), it's usually pretty easy to decide which is which.

For example, in a movie like *The Night of the Hunter*, in which the children are trying to escape from preacher Robert Mitchum after he's killed their mother, the children clearly experience more conflict than the hunter. They are the (co)protagonists of the story and he's the antagonist. Both from a moral and dramatic standpoint, there is no doubt.

However, sometimes, the protagonist and antagonist in the story experience the same amount of conflict, becoming interchangeable. In that case, we'll tend to identify with the character we feel closer to from a conceptual or moral point of view, which is subjective of course. But not everyone in the audience needs to identify with the same character. As long as the structure makes it possible for everyone to find an emotional way into the story, that's fine. It's not even necessary to be able to pick a side. We can also enjoy being pushed back and forth between two opposing sides, two different ways to see the world. We can empathise with both protagonist and antagonist, and that can be a rewarding emotional experience, as in *Amadeus* or *Billy Elliot*.

Let's take a closer look at a movie like *Heat* (1995) to see how Michael Mann manages to create such a powerful exception.

*Heat* tells the story of professional thief Neil McCauley (Robert De Niro) and his gang, chased relentlessly by Lt. Vincent Hanna (Al Pacino), a veteran L.A.P.D. robbery-homicide detective. It's a fascinating movie because though it starts with a clear protagonist/antagonist situation, it quickly blurs the lines between protagonist and antagonist, yet it doesn't prevent full emotional involvement in the story. We care equally for both characters, which soon creates a dilemma for the audience. Knowing that one of them has to defeat the other, which one is it going to be? This is extremely hard to pull off, but Michael Mann does it brilliantly. As always, it's a good idea to watch the film before reading what follows.

We start with McCauley who is the first to experience conflict when Waingro, a new recruit, needlessly kills a guard in cold blood during their first heist, forcing them to execute all the other guards.

Waingro introduces a scale of morality to the story. There are "good" bank robbers (McCauley and his gang) and bad ones, who kill gratuitously (Waingro). This is also the function of money launderer Van Zant: to give us real villains in the story so that the bank robber protagonists, by contrast, can be seen as the good guys.

When the character of Vincent Hanna is introduced, he's more of an antagonist to McCauley and his gang. However, due to the way he's characterised, the insight we have into his private life and the amount of conflict he experiences – McCauley is very good at his job – it soon becomes a two-hander and there is no longer a clear protagonist. That is, unless your own moral values lead you to lean more to one side (be it the cops or robbers). Besides this conceptual identification, there is no clear protagonist/antagonist, because both experience an equal amount of conflict trying to reach their respective goals, in their professional and personal life. Each of them becomes a protagonist in their own right, and an antagonist for the other character.

We end up rooting for two characters instead of one. Dramatic irony is used all along, as we get to see both sides. Sometimes we're ahead; sometimes we're surprised and realise we've been misled. An example of this is when McCauley leads Hanna and his men to the docks to take their picture and show them that they know they're being tailed. It's scenes like this that blur the lines, because they show the antagonist experiencing conflict, making him more of a protagonist and leading us to empathise with him as well.

*Heat* is very different to a film like *The Fugitive*, which also develops a protagonist / antagonist situation, but where the protagonist Richard Kimble (Harrison Ford) always experiences more conflict than antagonist Samuel Gerard (Tommy Lee Jones). First because we know that Kimble – a conceptually nice protagonist, unlike violent thief McCauley – is innocent of the murder of his wife, and injustice combined with under-served punishment creates a strong initial identification. Then, because Kimble experiences a lot more conflict than Gerard, there is never any ambiguity regarding the protagonist / antagonist roles as there is in *Heat*.

McCauley and Hanna only meet twice in the entire film: during the famous café scene and the climax at the hotel / airport. They are nevertheless constantly aware of each other's moves. As they remind each other during the café scene, this is a fight to death. Neither of them will hesitate to pull the trigger, despite the respect they have for each other. The absence of any direct physical confrontation – until the climax – makes it even more gripping.

Even during the climax at the airport, it's very difficult to take sides. We would like them both to survive, but we know it's not possible. McCauley's death is the only possible outcome, as he has to pay for the consequences of his actions, especially for the last decision he makes, which is to go after Waingro instead of driving to the airport with his girlfriend and boarding a plane to a new life. His inability to let go, his decision to avenge the death of his friends, is what leads him to pay the ultimate price.

*Heat* provides a great example of an unhappy yet satisfying ending. If McCauley was to board that plane without dealing with Waingro, it would be a happy – he makes it alive, with the money and the girl – but unsatisfying ending as Waingro has to be punished. It would feel as if Waingro had won, as if a wrong was left uncorrected in the story world. If we were to reverse this and get McCauley to kill Hanna after dispatching Waingro, it would be both unhappy and unsatisfying as Hanna doesn't deserve to die. He's only doing his job as a cop, playing by the rules, even giving McCauley a fair warning. There would be no gratification or catharsis in his death. In a way McCauley deserves to die, as a consequence of the wrong decisions he's made, both in his life – from a moral point of view – and at the end of the movie, from a character choice point of view.

It's the inevitability of McCauley's death that makes the climax so gripping. We know it's the only possible outcome, yet we still want to hope there will be a way out for both of them. We'll come back to this crucial notion of happy versus satisfying ending because it's an essential element of story design.

*Heat* also shows that we shouldn't get too hung up on the notion of protagonist versus antagonist, and that conceptual identification (who is nice; who isn't) doesn't really matter. There is no nice guy in *Heat*. There are cops and robbers, and all have good and bad sides, which is what makes them human. McCauley and Hanna are both flawed, but we can root for both of them. They oppose each other because they have to, though underneath they are very similar. They need each other – at least what they represent.

While it's important to have a clear structure, and identifying a clear protagonist and antagonist can help achieve this, what really counts is to provide the ability for the audience to get emotionally involved in the story. *Heat* provides this. We feel for McCauley as much as for Hanna, just like we can feel for Salieri as much as for Mozart in *Amadeus*. If we're talented enough to design a story in which the audience can root for more than one character, as we can in *Heat* or *Crash* (Paul Haggis), that's great. What we want to avoid is creating a story in which the audience would be unable to root for any character. That would be boring.

In other words, sticking to a clear protagonist / antagonist structure might be a safer bet and can produce great movies such as *The Fugitive, Terminator 2* or *Misery*, but successfully straying from it can lead to a gem like *Heat*.

## Protagonist vs Main Character

This is another important distinction. Main character and protagonist are often used interchangeably, and in most situations rightly so.

Usually, at least in plot-led and character-led stories, the protagonist (the character who moves the plot forward and experiences the most conflict) is also the main character (the most important and most interesting character, the character the story is about).

However, in some stories and for various reasons, the protagonist is *not* the main character.

For example, in *There's Something about Mary*, the protagonist is Ted (Ben Stiller) but the main character is Mary (Cameron Diaz).

**When the protagonist is a group of characters sharing the same goal,** as in *Little Miss Sunshine* or *Saving Private Ryan*, the main character is often one of the characters within the protagonist, one of the co-protagonists, the character we'll feel the closest to emotionally, often the character who changes most in the story or experiences the most conflict within the protagonist group. So the main character will be the father (Greg Kinnear) in *Little Miss Sunshine* or Captain Miller (Tom Hanks) in *Saving Private Ryan*.

This is also common **in stories in which the protagonist has to deal with an extreme internal problem,** a problem so acute that it's difficult to see what can be done about it. A problem that prevents the main character from making choices or taking action.

*Shine* is an interesting example because its past storyline is plot-led, with David Helfgott (Geoffrey Rush) being the protagonist and main character as a child. His main problem, his main source of conflict, is external (his father not wanting him to become a pianist) rather than internal (his talent hasn't turned into a disability yet). But in the present, after his breakdown, he's facing an internal problem, so the storyline is character-led (Can he live with his mental disability?) and other characters like his wife or friends become co-protagonists, with the goal of helping him overcome or live with his problem. David remains the main character, but other characters inherit at least some of his protagonist attributes.

Whenever a protagonist has an internal problem so strong that it might lead the audience to feel there is no hope, it might be a good idea to offer an alternate, more accessible protagonist who is actively trying to help the main character, so that the dramatic situation doesn't feel alienating. We have drama when a character tries to solve a problem, consciously or not. If a character isn't doing anything about a problem, or if it feels like there is nothing to be done about the problem, there is no drama because nothing is at stake. We can already answer the dramatic question with a negative.

This is the case in a movie like *Leaving Las Vegas*, in which the main character, screenwriter Ben Sanderson, (Nicolas Cage) is dealing with an internal problem (alcohol abuse and depression leading to suicidal behaviour) and where co-protagonist Sera (Elisabeth Shue) tries to help the main character to get better. Ben has a goal (to drink himself to death in Vegas) and we start the story with him, but as we understand that there isn't much he can do about his problem, we see him increasingly as an antagonist to himself. While they initially agree not to interfere with each other (Ben's drinking and Sera's prostitution), Sera breaks their pact first and begs Ben to see a doctor.

Without the co-protagonist bringing hope that the main character might be saved from himself, the story would feel static. In this case, the co-protagonist offers an emotional way in for the audience, someone who is less destructive, someone we can empathise with while the main character is stuck in a self-harming spiral. The main character becomes the problem that another character – the protagonist – is trying to solve.

**In many horror / monster movies**, the main character is the antagonist, not the protagonist. We identify emotionally with the protagonist, but the most interesting, the most fascinating character in the story – in other words, the main character – is the monster, the antagonist. The story is really about the alien, the shark, nurse Annie Wilkes, Freddy Krueger, Norman Bates, etc.

Annie Wilkes (Kathy Bates) is more fascinating than Paul Sheldon (James Caan), even if we identify with him as a protagonist. It's her story, a study of her character, more than his even if the film is designed around his dramatic action.

In these movies, the antagonist is often the character who evolves, changes the most (as in *Alien* or *The Shining*) or if the monster doesn't change, it's our perception or understanding of the antagonist which changes (as in *Misery* or *Jaws*), and that's another form of evolution.

Usually, the protagonists don't need to change much in horror / monster movies, as the main problem isn't in them but outside them. However, they often need to become stronger or to overcome an inner fear (like Chief Brody's phobia of the sea in *Jaws*) in order to succeed. They don't need to *change* (there is nothing wrong with them, at least not wrong enough to be the main problem in the story), but they need to *grow*.

If we have a group of co-protagonists in a monster / slasher / horror movie, the main character is often the monster / serial killer. Although the protagonist is the whole group, we usually identify more closely with a central character who ends up being the last one standing. In *Alien*, Ripley is the only surviving central protagonist of a larger group of people who are killed one by one.

In *The Silence of the Lambs*, Clarice Starling (Jodie Foster) is the protagonist. The main character is her *quid pro quo* mentor and co-protagonist, Hannibal Lecter (Anthony Hopkins), one of the two monsters in the film, the other one being antagonist James Gumb, a.k.a. Buffalo Bill (Ted Levine).

*The Shining* is a notable exception, because main character Jack Torrance (Jack Nicholson) is introduced as the protagonist and only gradually revealed as the antagonist. It takes about half an hour before we start to identify more with his family, and in the climax we're definitely rooting for them trying to save their lives more than for him trying to axe-murder them. So the main character is first protagonist, then antagonist. That's not common, but as it's handled skilfully it doesn't prevent the film from working.

We have something similar in *Psycho*, where the main character, Norman Bates (Anthony Perkins) becomes the protagonist for a while. This occurs after the first protagonist, Marion Crane (Janet Leigh), is killed, and before her sister and lover come to the motel to investigate her disappearance and become the co-protagonists of the last sequence and climax of the movie. This other exception works because Hitchcock and his writer always make sure that we have a protagonist we can empathise with, a character – or group of characters – who experience more conflict than the others. This is another working exception. We have more than one protagonist but one main character, Norman Bates, who is the real antagonist of the movie (even if we only find out in the very end). When we identify with him as a protagonist, we don't know he's the killer. We only think he's the son of the killer, trying to cover up for his mother's action. It would have been much more difficult to identify with him for such a significant portion of the film if we knew at the time that he had just killed Marion Crane.

## Hero vs Protagonist

The notion of hero, while interesting and relevant for some stories, especially those with a mythical element like *Star Wars, Lord of the Rings* or *Jaws*, is quite limiting compared to the notion of protagonist.

Having heroes leads us to the notion of anti-hero, which still suggests a world in black and white (good and anti-good).

A hero – or heroine – is a character who is generally positive, and often sacrifices himself/herself for the greater good. Many plot-led stories follow this pattern, but not all.

A tragic hero – or heroine – is a character with an internal flaw. The failure of the character to change, to deal with this internal problem, causes a tragedy leading to a negative but meaningful ending. Some character-led stories follow this structure, but again, not all.

What happens if my central character is conceptually negative? Isn't nice? But isn't necessarily bad either? And yet behaves heroically? Can we call this an anti-hero?

Or if a character with an internal flaw manages to change, correct the internal flaw, leading to a positive ending. That's not a tragic hero anymore, as there is no tragedy.

Or if the central force in the story isn't a single character but a group of characters sharing the same goal, as in *Alien* or *Little Miss Sunshine*?

So the notion of hero, tragic hero and anti-hero may work well for some stories, but clearly not for others. While it applies to some stories, it can be confusing or misleading.

The notion of protagonist has greater scope and embraces any type of character – good, bad or ugly – and any story. A protagonist is simply defined as the character who experiences the most conflict in a story (or in each strand in a multi-stranded narrative).

Phil Connors in *Groundhog Day* or Melvin Udall in *As Good As It Gets* or Wall-E can be protagonists as well as Indiana Jones, Jason Bourne, Bruce Wayne, Maleficent or James Bond.

It's not who they are conceptually – or whether they look like us – that makes them protagonists. They are the character in the story who experiences the most conflict; therefore, the character we will empathise most with. We won't necessarily find them nice or sympathetic, but we'll understand their conflict and we'll feel for them.

This difference between hero and protagonist is crucial, because it allows us to move from conceptual identification (sympathy, we like the character and the character's action) towards emotional identification (empathy, we understand, feel for the character, even if we disapprove of the character's action).

It's also what's going to help us design a satisfying ending for the story, even if it's not a happy one.

So if your protagonist is on a mythical quest and if *The Writer's Journey* helps you to map it, it's fine to call your protagonist the hero and populate your story with other archetypes – as long as you avoid clichés. If the notion of tragic hero or anti-hero helps you because you feel it applies to your story, then make the most of it.

Otherwise, it might be safer to stick to protagonist, especially if you like stories where things are not black and white, good versus evil, etc.

To illustrate this, let's take a look at *Maleficent* which forces us to experience the story from the point of view of a character who would, in any other story, be the antagonist or villain. Yet because of the way conflict is managed and motivations are explained, the story allows us to feel strong empathy for a conceptually negative character.

*Maleficent* shows how limiting the notion of hero is, and how there isn't necessarily a hero, or even an anti-hero in a good screenplay.

It also shows that no antagonist (as Maleficent is the antagonist in the original tale) is born an antagonist. Usually events happen in the character's life that fuel their motivation to behave in an antagonistic way.

In this original adaptation of *Sleeping Beauty*, writer Linda Wolverton manages to tell the story from the emotional point of view of the antagonist (with some key changes of course).

This approach divided the critics more than the audience. For those who enjoyed the movie, it shows that if you manage conflict properly and work on explaining the motivation of a negative character, you can get the audience to root for almost anyone, including one of the most emblematic villains in the repertoire. This is similar to what is achieved in *Dracula Untold*. Count Dracula becomes the protagonist because the story is told from his point of view and he's the character who experiences most of the conflict.

Instead of relying on the conceptual design of a character – good or bad, nice or not nice, hero or villain – the story is designed to help us understand the conflict of a character who will go as far as cursing an infant to get revenge on the man who mutilated and betrayed her.

The old King and Stefan himself are more antagonistic than in the original tale, which helps. The King attacks the Moors and Stefan betrays Maleficent's love and trust. They cause an injustice as well as a physical and emotional wound, which leads us to see Maleficent as the protagonist, despite the pain she causes to her enemy and his family when she curses Princess Aurora. We feel for her. For example, when she wakes up and discovers her precious wings have been ripped off her body, or when her growing affection for Aurora takes her by surprise.

If, like the original tale, the only motivation for Maleficent was jealousy, making her a one-dimensional evil character, and if the King and Stefan had done nothing wrong, it wouldn't be possible to see her as the protagonist because the other characters would experience more conflict. If you haven't done anything to deserve it, having your baby cursed by an evil fairy represents more conflict than not being invited to a christening party.

However, jealousy and revenge remain at the core of the story. Maleficent needs to control these two negative feelings, which she manages to do by the end of the movie.

It's Maleficent, betrayed by Stefan, the man she loved, who changes the curse so that only true love's kiss can awaken Aurora. This is significant thematically. In the original tale, it was one of the fairies who changed death into eternal sleep. Here it's Maleficent herself, the betrayed woman who doesn't believe in love anymore, who puts this condition on the curse, as she believes it will never be met.

Once her wings are taken, Maleficent's goal is to get revenge on Stefan. The affection she starts to feel for Aurora as the princess grows up away from her parents is a strong internal conflict and an essential addition to the story. This is the key element that allows Maleficent to remain the protagonist. She's getting revenge for a true injustice, but it's difficult for her to see it through, and when she tries to revoke her curse, she realises that even she can't undo what she's done. Also, Stefan and his wife are mostly out of the picture after the curse and because Aurora is blessed with eternal happiness, we can go on identifying with Maleficent because she remains the character experiencing the most conflict.

During the climax of the movie, while Stefan might deserve to die, Maleficent doesn't kill him, and gives up on her vengeance, probably because despite all he's done to her she doesn't want to kill Aurora's father. It's Stefan who doesn't let go and causes his own death (a classic trick at the end of a movie to avoid turning the protagonist into a villain and still dispatch the antagonist in style).

In dramatic Act 3, after Aurora is made Queen of the Moors by Maleficent uniting the two kingdoms, the voice of the former princess tells us:

"And I should know. For I was the one they called Sleeping Beauty.

In the end, my kingdom was united. Not by a hero or a villain as legend had predicted. But one who was both hero and villain. And her name was Maleficent".

Maleficent, indeed, is neither a hero nor a villain in this adaptation. She's simply the protagonist.

So leaving aside heroes and villains, simplistic notions of good or bad, can help to design more interesting characters – both protagonists and antagonists – and bring about a strong identification link irrespective of their conceptual nature.

While this is used in *Maleficent* to create a conflicted protagonist, the same approach could help shape a motivated antagonist. A character who isn't simply bad or evil, but who has reasons to behave the way he or she does. This is what we'll discuss next.

# Villain vs Antagonist

We can't discuss the difference between a hero and a protagonist without doing the same for villains and antagonists. A villain is a negative character who opposes the hero. If we discard the notion of hero as limiting for most stories, then villains go the same way.

First of all, let's state again that there isn't an antagonist or a villain in every story. We only have an antagonist if there is a character – or a group of characters sharing the same goal – in direct opposition to the protagonist and representing the main source of obstacles and conflict for the protagonist. For example, in *Misery*, nurse Annie Wilkes is the antagonist to protagonist Paul Sheldon. But in *Midnight Run*, there isn't just one antagonist because there is more than one source of conflict for protagonist Jack Walsh (Robert De Niro): the FBI led by Alonzo Mosley (Yaphet Kotto); rival bounty hunter Marvin Dorfler (John Ashton); the Duke himself (Charles Grodin); mafia boss Serrano (Dennis Farina) and his goons. Serrano would be the villain of the story, because he's the root of all of the protagonist's problems, but he isn't the antagonist. He's one of the antagonistic forces in the story, or one antagonistic character, but he isn't the main source of conflict for Walsh.

Finally, in most if not all character-led movies, the protagonist *is* the antagonist, because most of the conflict in the story comes from the protagonist's resistance to change, to evolve. The other characters in the story, often causing the conflict that is going to force the protagonist to change, are rarely antagonists. Even if they oppose the protagonist, they are usually catalyst characters (characters who trigger the change) or even co-protagonists. For example, in *As Good as it Gets*, waitress Carol (Helen Hunt) or neighbour Simon (Greg Kinnear) are not antagonists or villains, even if they are the source of most of the external conflict that is going to cause internal conflict for protagonist Melvin Udall (Jack Nicholson) and force him to change.

While we do need a protagonist in most plot-led and character-led stories (theme-led stories are different and we'll see this in detail in the chapter dedicated to them), there is no need for an antagonist.

However, when we do have an antagonist opposing the protagonist in a plot-led story, that character doesn't have to be a villain like Cruella De Ville in *101 Dalmatians*, Mr Potter the evil banker in *It's a Wonderful Life*, Hans Gruber the bond thief in *Die Hard or* Voldemort in the *Harry Potter* saga.

An antagonist can be a positive or neutral/ambivalent character, who simply has a valid motivation for opposing the protagonist. For example, in Michael Mann's *Heat*, we can identify primarily with criminal McCauley (De Niro) or with detective Hanna (Pacino) or even with both of them at the same time. While each character is the antagonist of the other, neither is a villain. Even McCauley, who is a criminal, isn't the worst character from a conceptual point of view. He wants out, which puts him halfway to redemption, and unlike Waingro (Kevin Cage) or Van Zant (Fitchner), he doesn't commit gratuitous murder. He's no saint, but he's not evil either. Both McCauley and Hanna can be seen as protagonists; both are each other's antagonist, but neither are villains. If there are any villains in the story, it's Waingro and Van Zant.

In *Dawn of the Planet of the Apes*, Koba makes a great antagonist because he isn't all bad, at least not to start with. He used to be Caesar's best friend and saved his life, risking his own. His hatred of men just turned him from co-protagonist to antagonist.

Let's take another example, from *Finding Nemo*, in which there is no villain or antagonist. As the movie is quite episodic, there is no single source of conflict for Marvin, Nemo's father, as he looks for his son with co-protagonist Dory. Sure, there are local antagonists like the sharks, the jelly-fish and so on, but there is no character – or group of characters – who opposes the protagonist over the whole story and causes most of the conflict.

In disaster movies and monster movies involving forces that can't be reasoned with like *Jaws*, *The Terminator*, *Duel* or *Alien* there are no villains, only antagonists or antagonistic forces. A volcano, an earthquake, outer space, an avalanche or a tornado, a shark, a robot, a truck or an alien can't be called villains, which would imply evil or conceptually negative anthropomorphic traits. They are simply antagonistic forces.

Sometimes, the antagonist is a conceptually positive character. For example, the antagonist in *Billy Elliot* is Billy's father (along with his brother). They aren't bad people; they just need to realise they have the wrong values.

Making a distinction between an antagonist and a villain, or an antagonist and antagonistic forces, can clarify the structure of your story and also create more interesting, less conventional, more original, multi-dimensional characters.

Working on the antagonist's motivation, the reasons why someone opposes the protagonist, means we can give antagonistic characters more depth and leave cardboard villains aside.

It's often said that antagonists are characters we love to hate, and that's definitely true for nurse Annie Wilkes in *Misery*, Shere Khan in *Jungle Book* or the Joker in *The Dark Knight*. Neither of these are cardboard villains. They have motivations and more than one layer. They are not evil simply to be evil.

Beware, not all evil characters are antagonists or villains. For example, Hannibal Lecter (Anthony Hopkins) in *The Silence of the Lambs* isn't an antagonist or a villain because he doesn't stand in the way of Clarice Sterling (Jodie Foster) in her attempts to catch serial killer Buffalo Bill (Ted Levine). On the contrary, he helps her to find him. Clarice has to pay a price for this and each encounter with Lecter takes a psychological and emotional toll, so he's a source of conflict for her, but the real antagonist of the story, the main source of conflict, is Buffalo Bill. Sure, Lecter is a negative character from a conceptual point of view being a serial killer himself, but he's more of a co-protagonist / mentor than a villain.

Occasionally, villains or antagonists start out as the protagonists of a story, either because we only understand later who they really are, like Norman Bates (Anthony Perkins) in *Psycho*, or because they slowly evolve towards evil like Jack Torrance (Jack Nicholson) in *The Shining*. They are the main characters all along, but they shift from protagonist to antagonist and are replaced by other characters as protagonists – characters who experience more conflict than they do – towards the end of the movie (Marion Crane's sister and boyfriend in *Psycho*; Jack Torrance's wife and child in *The Shining*).

Sometimes, we don't even hate the antagonist. We understand why they are who they are, why they do what they do, and we can even feel some compassion for them, like we do for Darth Vader at the end of *Return of the Jedi*. An antagonist can even occasionally become the protagonist – or at least the co-protagonist – like Gerd Wiesler (Uhlrich Muhe) in *The Lives of Others* or Billy's father (Gary Lewis) in *Billy Elliot*.

So let's leave aside the notion of villain which, like that of hero, is mostly relevant in some plot-led movies. Instead, let's use – when necessary – antagonists or antagonistic forces.

Here are a few tips to improve your antagonist, when you have one in your story:

1) Treat all your characters – including the antagonist – with compassion. Understand them, empathise with them, even if you don't approve of their actions. You should care about all your characters, not only the protagonist.

2) Give all your characters – including the antagonist – a backstory. An explanation isn't an excuse. We can still disapprove of an antagonist's

behaviour if we know why the character behaves that way, but that understanding of the antagonist's motivation will make the character more human, more real.

3) Consider giving the antagonist a journey. It's not because the antagonist opposes the protagonist, and because the protagonist experiences more conflict, that the antagonist doesn't experience conflict. The evolution of an antagonist, like *Billy Elliot*'s father, can be very moving. The protagonist isn't always the character who changes the most. This is usually true in character-led stories, but it isn't necessarily the case in plot-led stories.

4) Look at the story from the point of view of each character, including the antagonist. This will not only bring more coherence to the story, it will also help you to find obstacles you didn't think of. If you think like the antagonist, you'll make the antagonist more resourceful, smarter, and that will create more conflict for the protagonist, making the story more fun. You'll find surprises, twists that you'd never think of otherwise.

## Inciting Incident vs Inciting Action

In many movies, a single event triggers the goal of the protagonist. A girl is killed by a shark at the beginning of *Jaws*, which sets Chief Brody on his quest to protect Amity's population and get rid of the threat. Or Billy Elliot discovers dancing and decides to become a ballet dancer. Or Nemo is taken and Marvin embarks on a quest to find his son. Or a boulder falls on Aron Ralston's arm in *127 Hours* and starts his ordeal.

In all of these plot-led movies, we have a clearly defined inciting incident, or inciting event, and this event takes place during the movie, usually towards the end of dramatic Act 1, as it's the event that triggers the protagonist's goal, that starts the main dramatic action.

There is also an inciting event in many character-led movies. In fact, we often find two: one that triggers the protagonist's unconscious need and one that triggers the protagonist's conscious goal. For example, in *Groundhog Day*, Phil Connors (Bill Murray) needs to become a better person as soon as he meets Rita (Andy McDowell). This is the inciting event for the character-led part of the story, which is why I call this the *character* inciting event. However, it's when he realises that he's stuck in a time-loop that his conscious goal – finding a way to deal with the situation – is triggered.

Sometimes, the protagonist already has his or her goal at the beginning of the story, and the inciting incident has already taken place when the film starts. For example, in *Once Upon a Time in the West*, Harmonica (Charles Bronson) already has his goal – to get revenge on Frank (Henry Fonda) – at the beginning of the movie. Although we understand his goal as the movie unfolds, we only understand his motivations at the very end of the film, when a flashback reveals that Frank killed Harmonica's brother (which is the inciting incident of the movie). So while Harmonica is in his Act 2 right away, we – the audience – only enter Act 2 when we understand what he wants. For some, this only happens at the end of the film. This explains why many people don't get the film, despite its qualities.

Often though, there is no single event that triggers the protagonist's goal, but a series of events. For example, at the beginning of *Misery*, the car accident is only part of the inciting event. We also need Paul Sheldon to realise that nurse Annie is crazy before his goal to escape and survive is triggered. The car accident is an important plot point. It sets up the main dramatic situation, but it doesn't in itself trigger the protagonist's goal. So in *Misery*, instead of an inciting incident (or inciting event), we have an inciting action.

It's similar in *Alien*. When Mother – the ship computer – wakes the crew of the Nostromo and they are sent to investigate what is perceived as a call for help on LV426, we're still in Act 1 because the main problem (the alien) hasn't been introduced yet, at least to the audience and most of the characters. The wake-up call is an important plot point, but it's not the inciting event or incident of the main dramatic action. It's only the inciting event of the first dramatic sequence, which happens to be in Act 1. The real inciting event, the one that triggers the problem of the movie, is when the *facehugger* embraces Kane (John Hurt). So in *Alien* we also have an inciting action rather than a single event that triggers the protagonist's goal.

While an inciting event can be very useful, especially to clarify the goal or motivation of the protagonist, it's not always shown in the film. Sometimes, as we've just seen, it can be an inciting action rather than an inciting event. Remember, the definition of an inciting event is *a plot point that triggers the protagonist's goal*. Nothing prevents this decision from arising from more than one plot point, as in the examples above.

Also, depending on our project's story-type, we can have more than one inciting event. We've already mentioned character-led stories, in which we often have two inciting events, one for the protagonist's unconscious need and one for the conscious goal. In theme-led stories, each subplot or strand will usually have its own protagonist and its own plot-led main action or character-led main evolution, so we'll have one inciting event per strand, and just as many climaxes. For example, the beginning of *Crash* (Paul Haggis) is a succession of inciting events, one for most of the eight strands, and the last thirty minutes is a succession of climaxes, again one per strand. One advantage of multi-stranded narratives is they can have very exciting beginnings and endings because of the many dramatic actions being introduced / resolved.

Similarly, each subplot in a plot-led or character-led story will often have its own protagonist, its own main action or evolution and usually its own three-act structure, with an optional inciting event – or inciting action – and a climax.

When developing a story, make a distinction between inciting event and inciting action, taking into account the narrative's story-type so you know what to look for, and where. Don't be surprised if there is no inciting event or incident, but always consider if showing one – possibly in a flashback – could clarify the protagonist's goal or motivation and facilitate a stronger identification with that character.

## *Encore Twist*

The *Encore Twist* is frequently used in genre movies, especially action/ adventure, horror and thrillers, but it's also used in comedies and almost expected in romantic comedies, in which we're led to believe that the two characters won't end up together, that all is lost, and finally they do after a last *Encore*.

Here's how it works.

In a standard three-act structure, the protagonist tries to solve a problem / reach a goal over dramatic Act 2, then either succeeds or fails during the climax, leading to a usually short third act showing the consequences of the action. The *Encore Twist* introduces a surprise at the beginning of Act 3, just after the climax. This surprise leads the protagonist to try to reach the same goal, as it reopens the dramatic question that we thought had been answered at the climax.

This pursuit of the same dramatic action creates a mini three-act structure in Act 3.

- Act 3.1, what happens at the beginning of Act 3, before the action starts again;

- a surprise, the *Encore Twist*, which is the inciting incident leading the protagonist to try to reach the same goal again;

- Act 3.2, the main dramatic action resumes;

- a second climax at the end of 3.2 providing a second answer to the main dramatic question;

- Act 3.3, showing the consequences of the action once it's really over.

Here is an illustration to visualise the difference to a standard three-act structure:

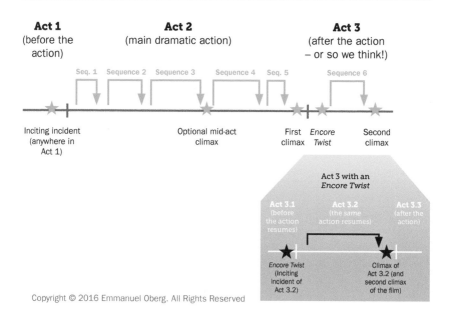

# The *Fractal* Aspect of Structure

## The *Dramatic* 3-Act Structure with an *Encore Twist*

So when we have an *Encore Twist*, it makes dramatic Act 3 longer than usual, sometimes as long as fifteen minutes or more. Used like this, the *Encore Twist* is similar to what Lavandier calls a "modified structure" in *Writing Drama*.

Of course, with hindsight, we could consider that Act 3.3 is the "real" Act 3 and that 3.2 is still part of Act 2, but from the audience point of view, as long as we believe that the action is over – because the protagonist seems to have either reached the goal and started celebrating or failed and given up – we enter Act 3.

Another way to look at this would be to say that when we use an *Encore Twist*, there is a mini three-act structure in Act 3 for the audience, but for the writer, who knows that the action isn't really over, Acts 3.1 and 3.2 are still part of Act 2, and Act 3.3 *is* Act 3.

What's important isn't how we name these sections, but how the *Encore Twist* can help us to design the last sequence or scene in the story, should we decide to use it.

Let's look at a few examples.

In *Alien*, Ripley (Sigourney Weaver) escapes in the shuttle just before the Nostromo blows up. This is a first climax at the end of Act 2, which provides a first answer to the dramatic question: *Yes*, Ripley has managed to escape from the alien and survive. For a while it seems like she has succeeded, so we enter dramatic Act 3. In 3.1, Ripley is stroking Jonesy, her cat, getting ready to hibernate for the journey back to Earth. We all breathe in relief. When, surprise, she finds out that the alien was hiding inside the shuttle! This surprise / inciting incident at the beginning of Act 3 leads her to try to reach the same goal as before (escape from the alien / survive), which means we enter 3.2. When she manages to flush the alien out of the shuttle at the end of 3.2, this is the climax of the sequence. It's also the second climax of the film, providing a second answer to the main dramatic question: *Yes*, Ripley has managed to escape and survive. We then enter 3.3, a short dramatic third act for the sequence (and for the film, as the action is now really over). So in *Alien*, because of this *Encore Twist*, dramatic Act 3 is longer than usual.

In this example, the two answers to the dramatic question are the same. The first one is *yes*, Ripley has reached her goal, then surprise, maybe not, and the second answer is *yes* again. If you'd like to see an illustration, please look at *Subgoals in Alien* in *Sequence the Action*.

There are other possible combinations, some more prevalent than others. A frequent one is *no*, then *yes*, which embeds the positive, hopeful message that even when everything seems to be lost, we can still succeed. For example, in *E.T.*, the kids led by Elliott spend the whole film trying to help E.T. go home. Then, about two-thirds into the movie, E.T. dies. They could still try to send his dead body home, but it would be significantly less interesting, so Elliott and his siblings give up. They have failed to reach their goal (first answer to the dramatic question). Then, surprise, E.T. isn't dead! They can try to send him home again, and this time, they succeed (second answer to the dramatic question).

*No* and *no* (the protagonist seems to have failed, wait, maybe not... no, it's definitely a failure) can be a bit depressing and *yes* but *no* (the protagonist seems to have succeeded, maybe not... no, the protagonist has failed) a bit sadistic, but these are other possible variations. What's important is to have a satisfying ending, not a happy or an unhappy one. An ending can be sad and satisfying, or happy and feel wrong, more on this in *Happy Ending vs Satisfying Ending.*

A few important things to keep in mind. We only have an *Encore Twist* if the protagonist gives up or succeeds for good, then a surprise starts the same action again. If the audience isn't surprised, if the surprise starts a different dramatic action or if the protagonist doesn't give up or behave as if the goal is reached, there is no *Encore Twist*. In most plot-led movies, the protagonist fails, tries something else and fails, tries another way and fails again, until a success or failure provides a final answer to the dramatic question. For example, in *Terminator 2*, when the T1000 is frozen solid by leaking liquid nitrogen, breaks down into pieces and then starts re-assembling itself, it's not a surprise as he's done this a few times already and the protagonists never really drop their guard, so there is no *Encore Twist* there.

Similarly, if the protagonist doesn't give up, for example if the protagonist only has a moment of doubt or despair but resumes the dramatic action without any surprise, there is no *Encore Twist*. It might be obvious, but we need a twist to have an *Encore Twist*.

Funnily enough, structure can be subjective. For example, watching the same movie, some of the audience could be convinced the action is over, then be surprised to see the action resume. For them, there is an *Encore Twist*. Others might not be surprised. They might be expecting the action to go on because they never thought it was over. For them, there is no *Encore Twist*.

Finally, this has become such a convention in action/horror/thriller movies that the audience familiar with these genres expects the surprise at the beginning of Act 3. It's not necessarily a problem if it's handled well, because it's a form of dramatic irony. We know the action is not really over. We still fear for the protagonist, and bam! a surprise proves us right. It's not really a surprise; it's the resolution of a dramatic irony over the protagonist (we know the action isn't over because we know the convention of the genre, but the protagonist doesn't). Still, if the writer manages to make the *Encore Twist* exciting, it can be effective.

The *Encore Twist* works best about ten to fifteen minutes before the end of the movie. It has to feel believable that this could be the end of the story. Do it earlier and we'll know it's too early for the film to end.

As always though, there are no rules, so doing it early isn't necessarily a problem. For example, in *Gravity,* the *Encore Twist* happens about two-thirds into the movie, when Ryan Stone loses hope and switches the oxygen supply off. It looks like the story is over, until a surprise at 01:02 gives her another way to reach the goal and re-launches the same dramatic action. It just leads to a longer than usual dramatic Act 3 (twenty-eight minutes), with a last dramatic sequence in 3.2 made of two sub-goals (or two sequences, depending on how you look at it). See the full analysis of *Gravity* at the end of the chapter for more details.

In *Alien,* we have in fact two *Encore Twists.* One in the usual place towards the end of the movie, at 01:46, when we realise that the alien has sneaked into the shuttle, as discussed earlier. But there is another one around the middle of the film. When the *facehugger* dies at 00:49, it looks like the problem has solved itself. The crew is ready to go back to Earth, so it feels like we're in Act 3. Except it's too early, so we know the film can't be over. Still, when the *chestburster* leaps out of Kane's ribcage at 00:57, it's a huge surprise, which leads the same protagonist to resume the same goal (finding a way to deal with a shapeshifting alien). Although some might see this scene as a late inciting event or as a midpoint, for me it's an early *Encore Twist.*

Finally, the dramatic question is sometimes simply reversed in a last surprise. It seems like the protagonist has failed or succeeded, and surprise! It's the other way around. For example, we think that the protagonist at the end of a thriller is dead, but in fact the protagonist is alive and has succeeded, and the movie ends. Or at the end of *There's Something about Mary,* we think Ted has lost her, but then she walks up to him and tells him she wants him. This isn't an *Encore Twist* either; it's a final surprise, a reversal of the apparent and temporary answer to the dramatic question. If the surprise doesn't lead the protagonist to try to reach the same goal until we get a second answer to the same dramatic question, we're not dealing with an *Encore Twist,* just with a final twist / reversal of the answer to the dramatic question.

## Midpoint vs Mid-Act Climax

The hazy notion of a midpoint often leaves even experienced writers confused, so I thought it might help to clarify what they are and why they are not very useful, at least from a structural point of view.

A midpoint simply marks the middle of the script. The only justification for midpoints is that the 30–60–30 logistical approach to the three-act structure leaves a longer chunk in the middle.

So some theoreticians came up with the idea of a midpoint, around the middle of every script. This made it possible to have four logistical units of an equal length of thirty minutes (Act 1, Act 2.1, Act 2.2 and Act 3).

Of course we can find an important plot point or turning point in the middle of most stories, and call it the midpoint. The problem is, in most good movies, there are important plot points every five minutes, so you're bound to find one around minute sixty, just like you would find one around minute fifty-five or sixty-five.

In some stories, there is a kind of break or pause in the action in the middle, and some call this the midpoint too. I'm not sure how it helps to say that in all stories we need to have the same thing happen at the same point. If it helps you, great; otherwise, don't fret about it. There is no dramatic reason or structural justification for it.

Like the rest of the logistical 30–60–30 approach to story structure, a midpoint defined like this doesn't mean anything structurally. It has no theoretical foundation, and has nothing to do with the dramatic three-act structure, so feel free to forget about it.

However, from a methodology point of view, it can help writers using a superficial approach to story structure to cut a long logistical Act II into two more manageable units of thirty minutes, called Act 2.1 and Act 2.2.

While this logistical approach allows you to cut down a screenplay into smaller units, it's much less efficient structurally than using dramatic acts and cutting them into more manageable dramatic units – sequences – usually defined by subgoals or tasks, ways for the protagonist to try to reach the goal. This defines the dramatic approach to story structure which lies at the heart of the *Story-Type Method*.

So for most stories, I would suggest you forget the midpoint, just as I would suggest you forget about logistical acts.

This being said, there is a structural tool which *can* actually be useful around the middle of dramatic Act 2, and that's the mid-act climax.

The big difference between the two is that while a midpoint supposedly marks the middle of every script, with no structural justification, a mid-act climax only happens in some stories, in which for some reason the protagonist's goal needs to evolve in the second half.

For example, in many heist movies, the first part of dramatic Act 2 would be about preparing the heist (assembling the crew, getting insider information, finding the right equipment, etc) then a mid-act climax will be the heist itself, which will provide an answer to the first dramatic question (*Yes*, the heist is successful, or *no*, the gang fails to get the money/diamonds, etc).

Then a second half of Act 2 deals with a logical consequence of the first half, with the same protagonist having to reach a different goal, connected to the first one (otherwise it might lead to a structural issue as we might feel we have two unconnected stories). In a heist movie, the goal over the second half could become dealing with the consequences of the heist: escaping from the police, resolving internal conflict as the gang members fight over the money, etc.

So we have a first half of Act 2 structured around a first goal (Will they pull the heist off?), a mid-act climax answering that first dramatic question (*Yes,* they do; *no,* they don't), and a second half of Act 2 structured around a second goal, connected to the first one (Will they get away with it?), with a second climax answering it towards the end of the story (*Yes,* they will; *no,* they won't).

Of course this isn't only used in heist movies, and all heist movies aren't structured with a mid-act climax. For example, there is a mid-act climax in *Heat*, although it's not exactly in the middle of the movie. It's the bank heist that goes terribly wrong, even though they do get the money. This legendary mid-act climax sequence starts at 01:41 and ends 01:54, for a movie that lasts almost three hours overall. However, there is no mid-act climax in *Ocean's Eleven* because the heist takes place towards the end of the movie and is the climax itself.

Though I don't find the midpoint a useful structural tool – like the rest of the logistical approach to the three-act structure – a mid-act climax might help when you can't find a single goal to unify the whole of dramatic Act 2.

Also, because it has a dramatic justification, the mid-act climax doesn't have to take place exactly in the middle of the script, as we've seen in *Heat*. Unlike a midpoint, which is determined by a page count, a mid-act climax is where we need it to be. It allows us to shape the story with two successive dramatic goals, one being the logical consequence of the other. It doesn't tell us that we have to have a specific plot point in the middle of every story.

Be careful, though, because most of the time we don't have mid-act climaxes, we only have a succession of climaxes at the end of each dramatic sequence (subgoals). If one of these happens to be around the middle of the script, it's not a mid-act climax. We only have a mid-act climax if, around the middle of dramatic Act 2, a climax answers a first dramatic question, before another one – a logical consequence of the first one – is raised and explored until the end of the film. In other words, if the story explores two successive problems connected to each other, not just one.

Also, don't mistake an *Encore Twist* for a mid-act climax. A mid-act climax answers a dramatic question around the middle of the story before a *different* problem is raised and explored over the second half. As discussed earlier, an *Encore Twist* provides a first answer to the dramatic question towards the end of the story, before a surprise raises the *same* dramatic question and a second climax brings a new answer to that *same* dramatic question, so a *new* solution to the *same* problem. This is why we have an *Encore Twist* in *Alien* or *Gravity* (a new solution to the *same* problem towards the end of the film) but a mid-act climax in *Heat* or *Avatar* (a *different* problem, connected to the first one, is raised and explored in the second half).

You could have both a mid-act climax and an *Encore Twist* in the same story, but most stories have neither a mid-act climax nor an *Encore Twist*.

There is a mid-act climax in Roberto Benigni's *La Vita E Bella* (*Life Is Beautiful*) though. Guido (Benigni), the protagonist of the film, spends the first half of the movie trying to seduce Principessa (Nicoletta Braschi). In the middle of the story, he reaches this goal. He abducts her – with her consent – during the climactic dinner scene, preventing her from having to marry a man she doesn't love, which brings an answer to the dramatic action that shapes the first half of the movie: *Yes*, Guido does succeed in seducing Principessa.

We then ellipse a few years and find the married couple with a five-year-old son, Giosue (which is both the third act of the first part of the movie and the first act of the second part). When the family is taken to a concentration camp, Guido's goal becomes to protect his family, and especially his son. This goal is different from his goal in the first half, but it's a logical consequence of it (having seduced his wife, he now has a child and has to protect them).

The change in tone though (the first half is a comedy; the second half much darker) and the use of a mid-act climax led some to feel this was almost two different movies. This is a potential danger of using mid-act climaxes, especially when the change of tone is so extreme. For those who enjoyed the movie, it worked because the second half is seeded in the first. The main subplot in the first half of the movie is the rise of fascism in Italy at the time, and is illustrated by many things: the anti-Semitic insults painted on the horse; the aggression towards Jewish citizens; the ironic speech on the supposed superiority of the Aryan race. All these thematic elements seed the events in the second half. The subplot in the first half of the movie becomes the main plot in the second half.

We can also find another example of a mid-act climax in *North by Northwest*. Roger Thornhill (Cary Grant) spends the first half of the movie trying to find out who "Kaplan" is and who wants to kill him. Once he finds out – after the auction, the Professor tells him that Kaplan never existed – his goal becomes to get Eve Kendall (Eva Marie-Saint) out of trouble, as he's put her life in danger. This mid-act climax – the auction sequence – doesn't sit exactly in the middle of the screenplay, but structurally it does work as a mid-act climax. We have an answer to the first dramatic question, then another dramatic question is raised, as a consequence of the first action, leading to a second climax (the famous chase and fight sequence on Mount Rushmore).

So think of a mid-act climax when you can't find a way to design the story around a single main dramatic action or evolution. As long as the second half is logically connected to the first and the successive goals allow you to tell the same story, the mid-act climax can be a handy structural tool, much more useful than a vague, logistical midpoint supposedly in every screenplay around page sixty.

## *Cold Start*

A *Cold Start* is an efficient technique to use when a story opens in an unknown environment, but you don't want to slow down the beginning with a long piece of exposition – things that happened before the story starts – or distance us from the protagonist, if the protagonist knows more than we do about something important.

It allows us to start the story as late as possible without having to front-load it with exposition. It also gives us the added benefit of a very short dramatic Act 1: the main problem is introduced right away. It often goes hand in hand with flashbacks, which give us fragments of the forgotten backstory during the film until the protagonist remembers what happened.

It's been successfully used in movies like *Predators*, *Cowboys vs Aliens*, *The Maze Runner*, *Memento*, *The Bourne Identity* or *Before I Go to Sleep*.

It works like this:

1.  We start the story as late as possible, which means closer to the most exciting, most conflictual, most interesting part.

2.  We give some form of amnesia to the protagonist so when the protagonist wakes up in a new or an unknown environment, we feel close to the character. They have no idea what they are doing there, so it's easy for us to identify with them. We can imagine how it would feel to be in the same situation. It increases both anxiety and identification.

3.  We exploit what happened in the past and caused the situation as a mystery.

4.  We give the protagonist the goal (or subgoal) of solving the mystery.

5.  Gradually, we provide information to resolve the mystery in the backstory. This information comes from the protagonist trying to find out what happened, usually with a lot of conflict to make the exposition more palatable. Often, one significant chunk is revealed as a surprise, either in the course of the story or at the end.

We can thus avoid two equally undesirable storytelling problems:

A.  Having to front-load the movie with exposition so we can catch up with the protagonist and share the same emotional point of view.

B.  Being asked to identify with a protagonist who knows more than we do, over a long period of time, which prevents us from being close to the character. This can work in some stories, but it's usually an issue in a thriller or horror movie.

The *Cold Start* isn't the only way to solve these problems. We can also start the story earlier. This is what was decided during the development of *Groundhog Day*. Initially the screenplay started with Phil Connors already stuck in the time loop, as screenwriter Danny Rubin explains in his excellent *How to Write Groundhog Day*.

We can also try to find a clever, non-boring way to deliver some of the exposition upfront. A movie like *Oblivion* just pulls it off by using stunning visuals and a decent voiceover, but you'll notice that some of the backstory (the fragmented glimpses of the unknown woman) is kept as a mystery through partial amnesia due to the mandatory memory wipe and only revealed – to both protagonist and audience – later in the movie.

Be careful, a *Cold Start* only works if the protagonist knows as little as we do. If the protagonist knows more and there is a mystery over the backstory or the motivations, it can go against the identification process.

In many scripts, the writers decide to hold some information back to try to make the protagonist more interesting. While this can be an effective hook for a while, it can cause an identification problem if we understand that the protagonist is hiding something crucial, say, regarding his or her motivations. It creates a distance between the audience and the protagonist and prevents a full emotional identification with the character.

For example, in *Cake* it takes a long time before we understand why Claire Simmons (Jennifer Aniston) is so depressed. It's only when we find out that she has lost her son in a car accident that we can fully identify and empathise with her.

It's not always a problem, at least not for everyone. In *Once Upon a Time in the West*, we only understand why Harmonica (Charles Bronson) wants revenge on Frank (Henry Fonda) at the very end, when we realise that he forced him to kill his brother. Some of us are fine with that, but others find the movie boring because they don't have enough information about Harmonica's motivations and can't empathise with him.

Overall, the *Cold Start* is a useful tool to consider, especially with high concept sci-fi and thrillers. It allows us to start right in the action and create a strong identification with the protagonist.

Let's take a closer look at one of the most famous and effective examples, *The Bourne Identity*, to see how it works.

When Jason Bourne wakes up at the beginning of the movie, he's been pulled from the sea by fishermen, unconscious and wounded. He finds himself in an unknown environment (the boat) surrounded by strangers, having no recollection of who he is or where he comes from.

This triggers his goal which is first to find out who he is and what happened to him, and once his life is threatened, to survive. Finding out about his past becomes a way to stay alive and defeat those who want him dead.

We can identify with him straight away both because he experiences an intense amount of conflict, and because we know as little as he does. He isn't hiding anything from us about his past. We can be with him emotionally because we share the same level of information.

This is crucial in a thriller. We can't have a thriller if the protagonist knows more than we do over a long period of time, because we can't be the protagonist anymore. We can have a crime story or murder mystery, a whodunit of some sort, but not a thriller. The opposite is fine. For example, we know more than the protagonist in *The Apartment*, *The Truman Show* or *Bolt*, but these are not thrillers.

To generate suspense, we need to know where the danger is coming from, and to create a strong identification, we need to know at least as much as the protagonist, not less.

As Bourne pulls the clues together, we get closer to finding the truth and climb the information ladder with him. While he'll overcome Treadstone (the organisation trying to kill him) by the end of the first movie (so the problem of the movie is solved), it will take him until the end of the third movie to put together the last piece of the puzzle regarding his past, which is why the trilogy has to end there.

The *Cold Start* makes Bourne more interesting than the average action/thriller protagonist because of the internal conflict he experiences. He can't remember who he is, which makes it more difficult for him to survive and defeat his enemies.

So with a *Cold Start*, we hit three birds with one stone. We make the protagonist more interesting emotionally through internal conflict (amnesia), we hook the audience intellectually with mystery and we start the story late without the need for upfront exposition.

Triple whammy!

## Flashbacks: To FB or Not to FB?

Some people have a problem with flashbacks. Howard Hawks, for example, when asked what was wrong with flashbacks, replied: "What's good? If you're not good enough to tell a story without having flashbacks, why the hell do you try to tell them?". Most anti-flashback activists stop the quote here, conveniently forgetting that Hawks then added: "Oh, I think some extraordinarily good writer can figure out some way of telling a story with flashbacks, but I hate them". This becomes a more balanced quote – assuming Hawks meant he hated the flashbacks, not the writers – because it makes it clear that it's a very subjective thing. Some people don't like flashbacks, and Hawks was one of them. However, he also makes it clear that an effective use of flashbacks requires a lot of talent, and he was objectively right on that point.

Personally, I have nothing against flashbacks. Many great movies and TV shows use flashbacks very effectively, in many different ways: *Amadeus*, *Goodfellas*, *Saving Private Ryan*, *Titanic*, *Memento*, *The Intouchables*, *Ordinary People*, *Unbroken*, *The Secret in Their Eyes*, *Little Big Man*, *Pulp*

2.3 CRAFT THE DRAFT

*Fiction, Gone Girl, Shine, Serpico, The Usual Suspects, It's a Wonderful Life, True Detective, Breaking Bad...* so flashbacks are clearly not a bad thing, at least in my book.

The problem with flashbacks is that they are often used for the wrong reasons. Flashbacks are a bit like voiceover. 99% of the time, they are a tell-tale sign of a poor screenplay, using an artificial literary device to prop up an ill-designed story. And then, you have the 1%, the successful exceptions to that rule (many of them directed by Martin Scorsese: *Goodfellas, Casino*, etc).

My take on flashbacks is quite simple: Use them if it makes the story better, or if it's the only way to tell the story. Most importantly, if you use them, use them well. Otherwise, just don't.

Before we take a look at the various ways to use flashbacks in a movie, let's consider the potential issues with flashbacks and good reasons for *not* using them.

1. **Making emotional identification more difficult.**

   If a flashback structure isn't handled properly – as it is in *Citizen Kane, Amadeus, The Secret in Their Eyes* or *True Detective* – the danger is that we won't be able to identify emotionally with any character, because we won't know what's at stake in the story. If we go back and forth between present and past, not knowing what's at stake in the present or what's at stake in the past, we are likely to get bored quickly, because we won't care about any of the characters.

2. **Giving an answer to the dramatic question too early.**

   If a movie is about the survival of the protagonist, and if we see the protagonist alive at the beginning of the movie, before the flashbacks start, it can lower the effectiveness of the dramatic question. So when we use a flashback structure, we have to be careful not to answer the main dramatic question too early because of the information provided to the audience in the present time. See teaser flash-back below.

3. **Confusing the audience.**

   Yes, flashbacks can make the story confusing, especially if it's not clear whether we are in the present or the past. One of the positive aspects of flashbacks is that using them can make the story more stimulating intellectually, because it sets up a mystery, or raises interesting questions. The danger is that the story becomes so challenging and confusing that it works against any emotional involvement. It becomes purely an intellectual puzzle. This might get the critics raving, but it will often have the audience confused. Find the right balance though and you can actually increase the emotional involvement of the audience along with an intense intellectual gratification.

Now that we've listed some of the possible dangers of using flashbacks, let's discuss a few ways of using them effectively.

**Exposition-killer flashback**
What's more boring than a character telling us what happened in the past? There are techniques to make this more bearable – like using conflict to disguise exposition, which is done brilliantly in the first fifteen minutes of *Silver Linings Playbook* for example – but using flashbacks is a nice alternative. Instead of being told through dialogue what happened in the past, we go back in time and see what happened, before coming back to present time. Although this can be clumsy, when done elegantly, it's effective. Examples of this can be found in many movies, from *Frenzy* to *Misery* to *Silver Linings Playbook* again, which uses a short flashback to *show* us a key past event rather than *tell* us about it. This is one of the most legitimate reasons for using flashback: as a brief alternative to exposition.

**Book-end flashback**
A book-end flashback frames the whole story. We start in present time, then we have a long and unique flashback into the past, until we come back to present time at the end.

Let's take a look at some examples illustrating a few reasons to use a book-end flashback.

*Titanic*
There are two main reasons for a book-end flashback. First, to anchor the story in the present to try to make it more relevant to the younger audience, who might not be drawn or ready to jump into a story set so far into the past; second, to set up a hook, the precious necklace, which gives a kind of mystery / investigation frame to the story. Something at stake beyond the love story and the disaster plot.

*Saving Private Ryan* (spoiler warning)
While it's also a way to anchor the story in the present time to make it

more relevant to a younger audience, it's also used to create a very effective final surprise. When we meet the WWII veteran at the beginning of the movie visiting a military cemetery, we know that he survived the war, but we don't know who he is. When we dissolve to Miller (Tom Hanks), the leader of the unit that is going to try to save Private Ryan, we assume it's him, remembering his actions, drawing this assumption from classical examples like *Little Big Man*. So when Miller dies in the end, it's a huge shock because we thought he was the veteran we saw alive at the beginning. And then we realise that the old man from the beginning is Ryan himself (Matt Damon), in front of Miller's grave, paying respect to the man who saved his life. A very moving visual pay-off, planted with clever storytelling. It's pure manipulation – good storytelling often is – but it's effective and honest. We've not been lied to as in *Stage Fright* or *The Usual Suspects*; we've just made a wrong assumption, which caused a powerful surprise. A great use of flashback.

### Teaser flashback

The teaser flashback is a variation on the book-end flashback in which we start in present time and have a long flashback. Instead of coming back to present time right at the end, as in *Little Big Man* or *Saving Private Ryan*, we come back to present time earlier – sometimes much earlier, sometimes during the climax of the story – and then go on in present time without any further flashbacks. Like the book-end flashback, this is often used when a story needs time to set up the characters, their relationships and/or the story-world. The teaser flashback allows us to start right in the action, hook the audience, often set up some kind of dramatic irony or mystery and then take the time to unfold our slow beginning, without the risk of losing the audience early on.

For example, movies like *Fallen*, *Goodfellas*, *The Hangover*, *Walk the Line* or *The Intouchables* all chose an important turning point in the story to start the movie, then go back in time until we return to this point and continue on.

In a movie like *Run All Night*, the teaser flashback is a brief moment taken from the climax of the movie, so we start the movie with the protagonist (Liam Neeson) shot in the woods but still alive. We then go back sixteen hours and it's only at the very end that we return to the situation teased at the beginning, closing the flashback loop to find out whether he survives or not and whether he reaches his goal or not (which is to protect his son and his family). At the end of the movie, while everyone relaxes in the forest lodge waiting for the police, we know that something will happen because the teaser flashback sets up a nice dramatic irony. The protagonist is shown wounded in the woods, so we're waiting for this to pay off, here and now. The way and the moment the hitman strikes are surprising for the protagonist, but not for us. We were expecting it so we don't have an *Encore Twist* in this case.

We have a similar use of a teaser flashback in *John Wick*. We start the movie with our protagonist (Keanu Reeves) crawling out of the wreck of a car, badly hurt. Is he going to die? Then we go back a few days, watch the whole film mostly chronologically, and right at the end we get to the same point with John badly hurt to find out whether he makes it or not. While the flashback is in no way necessary (in fact it might even be counter-productive as it tells us that John will survive at least until we get back to that moment), it starts the movie at a very intense, conflictual moment so that we can then take a bit of time for a fairly slow set-up.

It's slightly less efficient than *Run All Night* because it doesn't set up a dramatic irony and also because the moment shown at the beginning takes place after the climax, not during or before it. So when we get back to it, there is little at stake as he's already reached his goal, while in *Run All Night* we're still in dramatic Act 2 and have no way of knowing whether the protagonist manages to save his son and his family.

This is not really an issue in *John Wick* as the movie is very entertaining. But if you have a choice, try to pick a teaser opening from the climax, or slightly before, rather than after, when the dramatic question is already answered; otherwise, it can take some tension away from the climax as we already know the outcome. Of course, there are always exceptions. The teaser opening for *Lone Survivor* comes from after the climax, but the main dramatic question hasn't been answered, as we still don't know if Marcus Luttrell (Mark Wahlberg) will make it or not.

**Flashback Structure**

Sometimes, the whole movie is built around flashbacks. We keep jumping between a present and past (with sometimes more than one storyline in the past). Done lazily, for the wrong reasons, in the wrong way, it can produce the most boring movies, in which we have no idea of what's at stake and are unable to identify with any character.

But done skilfully, the creative and structural use of flashbacks can produce memorable stories: *Amadeus*, *Citizen Kane*, *Shine*, *Slumdog Millionaire*, *The Secret in Their Eyes*, *The Usual Suspects*, *True Detective* and many more.

Let's have a quick look at *Citizen Kane* as it illustrates perfectly how a flashback structure can shape an effective, original story and turn it into a classic masterpiece.

*Citizen Kane* is a fascinating movie because the story is at the same time plot-led, character-led and theme-led, and as such is quite an exception. It also jumps back and forth between present and past, creating an intricate flashback structure.

**The present-time story is plot-led**, and the protagonist is Thomson, the journalist, who tries – like the audience – to solve a mystery, to find the meaning of the last word uttered by Kane on his death bed: Rosebud. He fails, but we do get the answer thanks to a final visual twist which also sets up an unresolved dramatic irony. The audience is shown what Rosebud means, but the other characters, especially Thomson, never find out.

**The past-time story is character-led**, with Kane as a protagonist who needs to stop controlling the ones he loves – or rather the ones he thinks he loves. He needs to learn to love again after the childhood trauma of being taken away from his mother. This inciting event, over which he had no control, is both a defining moment regarding his character development – this lack of control triggered his increasingly abusive, controlling behaviour as an adult – and the starting point of the story itself. There would be no *Citizen Kane* without this inciting event, which is why Rosebud is associated to it: the sleigh represents the last time he was with his mother, free of the problem that is going to define and ruin his entire life. Kane fails to get what he needs, but we gain a better understanding of his character by the end of the film, and we can learn from his failure.

**The whole movie is a biopic and as such explores one theme (Kane) through different strands, which makes it theme-led overall.** Like *Cloud Atlas*, it's not only multi-stranded but also non-linear. Each flashback offers a way to explore a different aspect of Kane's life and personality, through his relationships with various characters: his legal guardian, his best friend, his wives, etc. It's quite dark, but the ending is emotionally and intellectually satisfying because we get to understand both the reason why Kane behaved the way he did and the meaning of the word Rosebud. Kane made the wrong choices, failed to change and paid the price. It's a great example of an unhappy, yet satisfying ending.

While flashbacks in a screenplay can point to a poor dramatic structure, it's certainly not the case in *Citizen Kane*.

Each flashback moves the character-led, plot-led and theme-led aspects of the story forward. By the end of the film, we've been told one story using three different story-types.

It's a fantastic exception which shows that if you know what you're doing – and are blessed with Orson Welles' and Herman J. Mankiewicz's talent – well, you can really do anything you like.

# Time-Locks

A time-lock – a limited amount of time to reach a goal or solve a problem – in a story is not necessary, but it can add suspense and both enhance the emotional impact and the tension of a narrative.

A time-lock can be used at scene level, for example we only have a few minutes to convince the person we love to marry us (or not to leave us) because a train / plane is about to leave. It can also be used at sequence level. Often, a time-lock is introduced in the second half of the movie or during the climax as a way to raise the stakes. For instance, we only have until the sun rises to kill the vampire or escape from jail.

Let's look at a few examples of movies which use a strong time-lock over the whole story to increase dramatic tension and the emotional involvement of the audience:

- In many *James Bond* movies, there is a ticking bomb. Bond has to find it and deactivate it before it explodes. This is the most classical example of a time-lock. As such, it has become a cliché – so make sure the audience knows you know it's a cliché if you use it, and do something clever with it.

There are subtler and more original uses of a time-lock. Some of the following examples span almost the entire film.

- In *Apocalypto*, Jaguar Paw (Rudy Youngblood) has to get back to his pregnant wife and young son before they die of hunger or drown in water. The exact amount of time isn't known, but it's clear the protagonist doesn't have much time to achieve his goal. Once rain starts to fall during the climax and the water starts to rise, the time-lock becomes visual: his wife and child will soon die if he doesn't reach them.

- *In Back to the Future*, a similar visual pressure is put on Marty McFly (Michael J. Fox): If his parents don't make up during the ball, the protagonist and his siblings won't be born. We see their image fading on a family photograph he carries with him. He only has moments to get his parents to kiss before it's too late. Later, during the climax at the clock tower with Doc (Christopher Lloyd), Marty has to strike a cable with his car at exactly the right moment – when lightning strikes the old clock – in order to power his energy-hungry time machine. So when the DeLorean doesn't start, or when the cable detaches itself, it causes a lot more tension than if there were no time-lock. This is their only chance, because this is the only time they know when and where lightning will strike. If Marty misses it, there is no way back to the future for him.

- In *High Noon*, Marshall Will Kane (Gary Cooper) has until noon – when the antagonist's train is expected to arrive in town – to find help and prepare to face the gangster and his posse.

- In another Western, the 2007 remake of *3:10 to Yuma*, protagonist Dan Evans (Christian Bale) only has a couple of days to get outlaw Ben Wade (Russel Crowe) to the town of Contention, and once there he has to get him on the train to Yuma before it leaves at 3:10. There was a similar time-lock in the 1957 original movie.

All these examples come from plot-led stories, but we can also find examples in character-led stories or plot-led stories with a strong character element:

- In *Groundhog Day*, Phil Connors (Bill Murray) has both an infinite amount of time to become a better person and less than twenty-four hours to seduce Rita, as she will forget everything once each day is over.

- In *Midnight Run*, Jack Walsh (De Niro) has only until Friday at midnight (five days) to bring the Duke (Charles Grodin) from N.Y.C. back to L.A. It's an action movie with a strong character element. The main subplot is about Walsh's need to change, to move on which will lead him to make the right decision about the Duke. So Walsh also has a limited amount of time to change before it's too late, especially once he's got Serrano, the villain of the movie, arrested.

- In *Two Days, One Night* (by the Dardenne brothers), the protagonist Sandra (Marion Cotillard), a young woman who comes out of a long hospital stay following depression, has only – yes, you guessed it – two days and one night to convince her colleagues to give up their bonuses so she can get her job back. Although this one seems plot-led, it's a character-led movie because what's really at stake is her psychological and emotional state, her ability to be happy again, rather than getting the job back.

While we don't need a time-lock in every story, it's often useful to think about ways to use one or more – in scenes, sequences or over the whole story – to increase the tension. When we feel we have a limited time to achieve something, we tend to pay more attention and it becomes more interesting and suspenseful. It also pushes characters to take more extreme action, because time is running out. And that's usually good for drama...

So if you can find a clever, original way to add a time-lock to your overall story, some of its dramatic scenes or sequences, or at least your climax, consider doing so. It doesn't suit every story, but there are few stories which won't benefit from one, as we've seen in the examples above.

# Climax vs Ending

Just as the first ten to fifteen pages of a screenplay are crucial, the last ten to fifteen pages of the screenplay are essential because they determine what we leave the reader/audience with, hence playing a huge part in word of mouth.

In the last ten to fifteen pages of the screenplay, we need to bring an answer to the dramatic or thematic question we have raised in the first pages, and make sure that this answer conveys our point of view.

Usually, when we have a problem at the end of a screenplay, it's because the whole story structure is unclear. We're not sure what's at stake, we're not sure what the movie is about or we haven't defined a clear protagonist or a strong evolution.

What's the difference between the climax and the ending then? Let's discuss the first, then we'll clarify the second.

One of the many practical aspects of the *Story-Type Method* is that once you've identified your story-type, you have a much clearer idea of what the climax of a specific project should achieve, which is the first step to a satisfying ending.

From a structural point of view, the climax is the moment when you answer the dramatic question(s).

**In a plot-led movie**, it's when you show whether the protagonist succeeds or fails to reach the conscious, overall goal. It's the final step of the main dramatic *action*. We know from the beginning who wants what and why. We've been wondering whether that goal will be reached over the whole movie, whether that external problem will be solved. During the climax, towards the end of the story, we get our answer. It usually happens as the protagonist faces the strongest obstacle. The climax is often related to growth rather than change, either before the climax in order to make success possible, or afterwards as a consequence of the success/failure of the protagonist.

**In a character-led movie**, the climax shows whether the protagonist succeeds or fails to reach an unconscious goal. We know from the beginning that besides what the protagonist wants consciously, the protagonist needs to change. The climax shows the moment when the main dramatic *evolution* is confirmed or not. This character-led climax – answering the dramatic question related to the unconscious *need* of the character – can take place before or after a plot-led climax, which answers the dramatic question related to the conscious *want* of the protagonist. Often, the protagonist of a character-led story will give up the conscious goal because reaching the *need* makes the character realise the *want* was pointless.

**In a theme-led movie**, because there isn't one main action or one main evolution, but many different strands united by the same theme, we don't have one but many climaxes. When this is well-handled, it can be very satisfying because it adds intensity to the last third of the movie. Depending on the story-type of each strand (usually character-led or plot-led), we get an answer to the dramatic question raised in each strand / subplot. Each individual climax can be exciting, funny or moving. Sometimes, all the subplots converge into a thematic united climax in which all the characters get together. For example, in *Parenthood*, as Steve Martin's new baby is born, the whole family – all generations – is brought together in a thematic conclusion to the movie. But in a movie like *Crash*, we see how all the various plot-led or character-led subplots conclude each storyline through a succession of independent or combined climaxes during the last third of the movie.

Overall, in non-theme-led movies, the climax marks the end of dramatic Act 2, the end of the main *action* or main *evolution* of the protagonist. What happens after the climax, once the protagonist has succeeded or failed to reach a conscious or an unconscious goal, is Act 3, which shows the consequences of the action/evolution of the protagonist. Because a logistical approach to structure doesn't lead you to define what the main action of the protagonist is, and doesn't connect the climax with the end of dramatic Act 2, it can make it more difficult to find the right ending. If you've not defined the main dramatic action or evolution, if your structure doesn't reflect this, how would you know which question you are expected to answer, and when you're supposed to do so? This lack of clarity can lead to confusing, unsatisfying endings.

Now that we've defined the climax, what's the ending? Usually the ending will be the last significant plot point of the movie and its consequences. Most of the time, it's the climax and its consequences in dramatic Act 3. The way in which filmmakers decide to answer the dramatic question usually conveys most of the meaning of the movie, at least in a plot-led or character-led story. But sometimes, a final surprise brings in a reversal which constitutes the proper ending (in movies like *The Sting*, *The Usual Suspects* or *Don't Look Now*).

We can also have an *Encore Twist*, which adds a mini three-act structure in dramatic Act 3, as discussed earlier.

The most important thing to remember is that if you have a problem with your ending, start by looking at the climax. Have you defined a main dramatic action or evolution? Does the climax answer the dramatic question you have raised and played with over dramatic Act 2? Does this answer convey a satisfying meaning? Does it convey the point of view of the filmmaker? Does it fit the genre of the story? Or does it simply go against the expected without paying off the whole story? Are you dealing with an *Encore Twist*? All these questions are part of the STM Framework, one of the story design tools we'll discuss in *Bringing It All Together*.

One last thing to keep in mind is that for an ending to be moving, it needs to be a pay-off for what's come before. Add the resolution of a dramatic irony through visual storytelling and you get a pure moment of cinema as in *Cyrano de Bergerac*, *City Lights* or *Tootsie*. Add a strong surprise instead and you get *The Usual Suspects*, *The Sixth Sense*, *Se7en* or *The Intouchables*.

It's easy to surprise the audience at the end of the movie, but it's even easier to disappoint as well. What's hard is to surprise in a satisfying way, which can be happy or unhappy. For example, the surprising ending of *Se7en* is both unhappy and satisfying.

Often we keep rewriting the ending. It doesn't work, so we keep changing it, focusing on the last pages of the screenplay. This is usually a symptom of a deeper structural problem. In a plot-led or character-led story, identifying the climax, checking whether it answers a clear dramatic question – regarding a main dramatic action or evolution – and whether it conveys a satisfying meaning is the first step to finding the right ending, whether it's happy or not. In a theme-led story, try doing this for each strand and check if the overall ending of the movie – this succession of climaxes – expresses the filmmaker's point of view and is satisfying or not.

Let's discuss further the notion of happy ending versus satisfying ending because it's a crucial one.

## Happy Ending vs Satisfying Ending

Just as the misguided way to reform an unsympathetic protagonist is to "make the protagonist nicer", a simplistic approach to an ending is to believe that a happy ending is more "commercial" than an unhappy one.

Of course this isn't true, and has sadly led to the common belief among arthouse filmmakers that if a happy ending is more commercial, then an unhappy ending must be more artistic.

I couldn't think of a worse way to approach the ending of a movie. An unhappy ending can be just as commercially successful as a happy one, as proved by *Titanic, Cyrano de Bergerac, West Side Story, Romeo+Juliet, Planet of the Apes, Birdman* and many other stories not exactly famous for their cheerful endings.

Forcing a happy ending on a story that should end tragically is just as flawed as forcing a depressing ending on a story that should end happily.

Much more interesting is the notion of a satisfying ending.

In a character-led movie, if the only way for a character to change is to fail, or if the only way for the audience to learn something is from the mistakes – sometimes even the death – of a protagonist, then we might find an unhappy ending very satisfying.

In a plot-led movie, if the only way for a protagonist to succeed is to sacrifice his or her life for the greater good, we might find such a heroic ending satisfying too.

Similarly, if we've truly identified with a protagonist, if they have made the right choices despite adversity, then killing them off at the end doesn't make a movie more artistic. It only makes the story depressing and the ending unsatisfying.

We can't predict the commercial success or failure of a movie, or even judge its artistic merit before it's made, so why don't we focus instead on the story and whether its ending is satisfying or not?

An audience has an inner, acute sense of justice. If a protagonist deserves to die or fail, we can deal with it.

If the failure or death of a protagonist is meaningful, we'll be sad, even devastated, but we can take it. We might even learn from it. We've discussed this in *Flashbacks: To FB or Not to FB?* in our analysis of *Citizen Kane* and in our analysis of *Heat* in *Protagonist vs Antagonist*.

However, if a protagonist should succeed or survive but doesn't, then you'd better have a good reason, beyond simply surprising the audience, "being less commercial" or "breaking the rules".

The *Story-Type Method* can help here, because it forces us to define what's at stake. For example, defining precisely what the goal is in the story means that if reaching the goal is more important than surviving, as in a war movie, then the protagonist's death can be an option because this sacrifice might be the only way to succeed, as in *Saving Private Ryan*.

If, however, the goal is to survive as in a thriller, then killing the protagonist not only goes against the genre, it also makes the story pointless. A thriller is a story of survival against all odds. Killing the protagonist simply shows a misunderstanding of the genre. So it's surprising, but not in a good way. An interesting example was the debate within the creative team during the development of *Misery* regarding the "hobbling" of the protagonist. In Stephen King's novel, Paul Sheldon's legs are amputated. Screenwriter William Goldman wanted to keep the scene as it was while director Rob Reiner couldn't imagine shooting it (you can read the whole story in William Goldman's *Adventures in the Screen Trade* or *Four Screenplays with Essays*, both highly recommended). In the end, the amputation was turned into extreme hobbling. Breaking Paul Sheldon's legs is painful and horrible, but this allows Paul to emerge mostly unscathed physically at the end of the movie. His scars are primarily psychological – he still has visions of Annie – and that feels like the right balance. This is because *Misery* is a psychological thriller, and Paul Sheldon ending up in a wheelchair didn't feel satisfying, simply because he didn't deserve it. There was nothing we could learn from such an ending – we already know that bad things happen to people who don't deserve it – so the audience would most likely have rejected it.

In character-led stories, the protagonist's failure can be the only meaningful way to end the story. For example, most tragedies are character-led stories in which the protagonist fails to correct a fatal flaw, and this often leads to death. The negative ending is the penalty for failing to change. The story is meaningful because it teaches us – the audience – that jealousy (*Othello*), iniquity (*King Lear*), thirst for power (*Macbeth*) or procrastination (*Hamlet*) is a bad thing.

In many character-led stories the protagonist gives up the conscious goal – what the protagonist wants – which allows them to get what they need. For example, in *Silver Linings Playbook*, protagonist Pat Solitano (Bradley Cooper) gives up his goal – to get his ex-wife back – which allows him to get what he needs: to move on from a failed relationship and end up with Tiffany (Jennifer Lawrence), the right woman for him. In *Two Days, One Night*, protagonist Sandra declines the job she's spent the whole film fighting to get back, but she's found her self-esteem in the process, which means she can move on and be happier. So failing to reach the conscious *want* can mean a satisfying ending if the unconscious *need* is fulfilled.

For various reasons, there are few true tragedies made today, but an unhappy ending can still be meaningful and satisfying.

For example, *Heat* doesn't end well for protagonist Neil McCauley (De Niro) as he dies, shot by antagonist detective Vincent Hanna (Al Pacino). While this is an unhappy ending, McCauley's death is the consequence of his inability to change, to let go. He could drive to the airport and take a plane to a new life with the woman he loves, instead he chooses to seek out Waingro (Kevin Cage) in his hotel to get revenge. It's this wrong decision that makes McCauley's death inevitable. He doesn't die because he was on the wrong side of the law. He dies because he fails to change, and pays the price. This inevitable, tragic ending is nevertheless satisfying because it's meaningful.

In order to design a satisfying ending, try to make a distinction between the goal (conscious or not) of the protagonist, and the survival/death of the protagonist. Try to assess whether the ending is meaningful or not. In a heroic story ending with the hero's death, is this sacrifice truly the only way to reach the goal? In a character-led story, when the protagonist ends up failing, is it a logical consequence of all the decisions made, of the protagonist's inability to change? Or is it simply a way to force a darker ending onto a story that should have ended positively?

At the end of the 2007 remake of *3:10 to Yuma*, protagonist Dan Evans (Christian Bale) dies as he gets outlaw Ben Wade onto the train and reaches his goal. While the ending is darker than in the original movie, it's more satisfying, at least for a modern audience. Here, Evans dies for the greater good. This is a classic hero's sacrifice. His death is sad but realistic. The ending feels satisfying because he's reached his goal (which was to provide for his family), and he's mended his relationship with his son. The two main problems in the story have been solved. Death is the price to pay for this positive resolution.

Focus on providing a satisfying ending, whether the ending is happy or not, and you will stand a better chance of reaching a wider audience. We'll be moved by a happy ending or a sad ending if it's the right one for the story.

Tack on an unsatisfying ending – happy or not – to the end of your story for the wrong reasons, and the audience is unlikely to forgive you. If we root for a character over two hours, we become the character. We want what the character deserves because we would like to get what we feel we deserve in life, even if that rarely happens in reality.

If the character doesn't get what they deserve, there has to be some meaning, or a value in their death or failure. For example, at the end of *Thelma and Louise*, the two protagonists die. While they don't deserve it, they have made the choice to die free rather than survive in captivity. Also, cleverly, Ridley Scott doesn't show them dead; he freezes the picture when they are exulting, their car mid-air, free as the wind. If you think about it, because of what happened in the story, this was the only satisfying ending. Thelma and Louise have gone too far to go back.

This "don't show them dead; show them free" trick is also used by Luc

Besson in *The Big Blue*, when we see Jacques Mayol (Jean-Marc Barr) swimming at the end of the film to a certain subaquatic death: free and happy with his dolphin friends, at last.

Similarly, at the end of the thriller *Run All Night*, Jimmy Conlon (Liam Neeson) reaches his goal – which isn't to survive but to protect his son – yet pays the price with his life. While Jimmy hasn't done anything in the movie to deserve this death, what he's done in the past – the many people he's killed – justifies it. So his death is at the same time a sacrifice to save his son's life, and a path to redemption as he releases the list of his victims, to allow their loved ones to move on. Also, he's managed to mend his relationship with his son, so while the ending is sad, it also feels satisfying. The protagonist isn't killed just to make the film "less commercial". The protagonist dies because given what's happened before, it provides a satisfying ending to the story.

# 2.4 Hands-On: What's at Stake?

This simple question makes or breaks a majority of movies. Some genres are easier than others, because what's at stake is meaningful for everyone.

For example, in a thriller, the life of one or more characters is at stake. In a horror/slasher movie, the life of a group of characters, of a small community is at stake. In a disaster movie, when it's not the passengers of a boat or the residents of a tower, it's the population of a whole city or region, sometimes the survival of the whole world – or an entire galaxy – which is at stake.

Even in smaller movies, like *Bicycle Thieves* or *Billy Elliot*, in which the stakes might be subtler, it really pays to clarify them.

The best way to work on this is to ask the question: What happens if the protagonist fails? If the answer doesn't describe something that fills you with dread, pity, fear or sadness, there might be a need to clarify the protagonist's motivations and/or the consequences of failure.

For example, in *Goodbye Lenin*, we know that the protagonist's mother will probably die if she finds out that Communism is over. That's great! It really helps us to be with the protagonist because we know exactly what the consequence of his failure would be. Now imagine if we had the same movie, but he just didn't want his mother to be upset. It might still be funny thanks to the dramatic irony, but it wouldn't be as gripping and moving.

Let's go back to the initial examples in *Hands-On: What's Your Type?*

In *North by Northwest*, Roger Thornhill's life is at stake, as well as Eve Kendall's. However, there is a strong love element in the story through the relationship between Roger and Eve. Finally, there is a threat regarding what would happen if the microfilms end up in the wrong hands, which is a matter of national security.

In *Two Days, One Night*, what's at stake on the surface is Sandra's job and her ability to keep her house, as the couple won't be able to pay their mortgage on a single salary. What's truly at stake, though, is Sandra's ability to be happy again, to regain her self-worth, her confidence in the future. This is what she achieves in the end, despite the fact that she loses her job.

Now let's go through the list of movies and define what's at stake in each story.

*Jaws*
*Silver Linings Playbook*
*Parenthood*
*Game of Thrones*
*Billy Elliot*
*Saving Mr Banks*
*Traffic*
*Interstellar*
*Little Miss Sunshine*
*Finding Nemo*

You'll find my answers at the end of the book, in the *Hands-On Solutions* section.

**Hands-on**

Now, look at your story, at a project you're developing, and try to define as precisely as possible what's at stake. Is it clear for the audience? Do we care about the consequences of the protagonist's failure? Do we care about the protagonist and the other characters who might suffer from this failure?

If not, you might want to clarify or raise the stakes in your story and work on your characters, especially during the set-up of the story: we need to care early on in the process.

To illustrate this and the other points developed in this chapter, here's a detailed look at three memorable plot-led stories: *Misery*, *Billy Elliot* and *Gravity*.

# 2.5 Case Studies

## *Gravity*

**Screenplay by Alfonso and Jonás Cuarón**

**Directed by Alfonso Cuarón**

Detailed Analysis

**Note: As usual, it's best to watch the film just before reading the analysis.**

*Gravity*, released in 2013, was met with near universal critical acclaim and regarded as one of the best films that year. Great cinematography, musical score, sound design, editing, visual effects, direction, first-class performances by both Bullock and Clooney as well as its ground-breaking use of 3D stereo photography and immersive sound made it a widely applauded technical and artistic achievement.

According to Wikipedia, *Gravity* also became the eighth highest grossing film of 2013 with a worldwide aggregate of over US$716 million (US$274 million in North America and US$442 million abroad, for a net profit estimated around US$209 million). It was nominated for ten Academy Awards and won seven: Best Director, Best Cinematography, Best Original Score, Best Film Editing, Best Sound Editing, Best Sound Mixing and Best Visual Effects.

*Gravity* perfectly illustrates how clarity and simplicity are the two most difficult – as well as underrated – qualities to achieve in screenwriting, and why they are not exclusive of meaning or depth. So let's take a look at the design of its screenplay.

To help visualise the following analysis, here is the overall dramatic three-act structure of *Gravity*:

# The *Fractal* Aspect of Structure

## *Dramatic* 3-Act Structure of *Gravity*

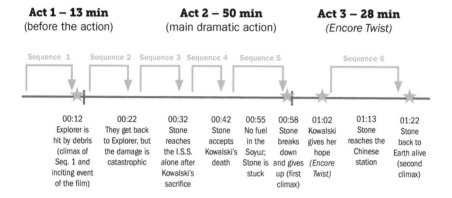

**Act 1 – 13 min**
(before the action)

**Act 2 – 50 min**
(main dramatic action)

**Act 3 – 28 min**
*(Encore Twist)*

Sequence 1    Sequence 2    Sequence 3    Sequence 4    Sequence 5                Sequence 6

| 00:12 | 00:22 | 00:32 | 00:42 | 00:55 | 00:58 | 01:02 | 01:13 | 01:22 |
|---|---|---|---|---|---|---|---|---|
| Explorer is hit by debris (climax of Seq. 1 and inciting event of the film) | They get back to Explorer, but the damage is catastrophic | Stone reaches the I.S.S. alone after Kowalski's sacrifice | Stone accepts Kowalski's death | No fuel in the Soyuz; Stone is stuck | Stone breaks down and gives up (first climax) | Kowalski gives her hope *(Encore Twist)* | Stone reaches the Chinese station | Stone back to Earth alive (second climax) |

Sequence 1 (12 min): Installing Stone's prototype in Hubble
Sequence 2 (9 min): Getting back to Explorer
Sequence 3 (9 min): Reaching the I.S.S. to use the Soyuz pod
Sequence 4 (7 min): Using the Soyuz pod to rescue Kowalski
Sequence 5 (12 min): Using the Soyuz pod to reach the Chinese station
Sequence 6 (16 min): Using the Chinese pod to get back to Earth

The perfectly choreographed first shot of the movie is thirteen minutes long – the entirety of dramatic Act 1, until the cloud of satellite debris hits Explorer and Ryan Stone (Sandra Bullock) is forced to untether herself from the severed mechanical arm and starts drifting away into outer space. That's quite a flamboyant beginning!

This opening sequence first sets up the astronauts – mission specialist Stone, mission commander Matt Kowalski (George Clooney), flight engineer Shariff (Phaldut Sharma) and Houston mission control (Ed Harris's voice) – doing their job on a routine mission: installing Dr Stone's prototype board into the Hubble telescope, using the Explorer shuttle as a base. This defines the only dramatic sequence in Act 1. Enjoyable banter and anecdotes between the astronauts and mission control makes them look like people we can relate to. It also plants that Kowalski has around 30% of power left in his jetpack after five hours, which means there is a limited supply.

The first out-of-the-ordinary event takes place at 00:07, when Houston announces that a NORAD satellite has incurred a missile strike creating a cloud of debris. While there doesn't seem to be any reason to worry yet, this had to be foreshadowed. It would have made Houston look pretty incompetent if they only found out about it when it was already heading towards the astronauts, about to strike them.

The other technical reason for this plant is to provide an explanation for what happens and why, before we're in the heat of the action (when the cloud of satellite debris hits Explorer later). We'll then only have to explain why it suddenly becomes a threat. It's a clever way to split exposition into a few palatable chunks, instead of trying to convey it all at once during a set piece which would inevitably slow down the pace.

For now, though, the current debris orbit isn't overlapping Explorer's trajectory. "Should we be worried?" asks Stone. "Let them worry for us," answers Kowalski.

However, for the audience, it sets up a diffused dramatic irony, especially when Houston mentions they'll keep them posted on any development. We kind of know that this is going to pay off later, that the cloud of satellite debris is going to find its way to them one way or another, so we start to worry for them. This isn't a telegraphed pay-off, something we'd try to avoid technically if the audience was able to foresee some future help for the protagonist. It brings in an anticipation of conflict: something bad is going to happen, and we know about it before the protagonist, simply because we're watching a movie. We know – or rather hope – that things will get worse.

One interesting thing to notice is that Stone is a scientist, a civilian, who is there as a trained "guest" (we learn here that she only had six months' training). This makes her very much like us. She isn't an expert astronaut like Kowalski. She's no super-hero, just an ordinary person. She's a fish out of water (a human thrown into space), and that really helps us to empathise with her, as she will experience a lot more conflict than someone already familiar with this environment. She's nauseous due to the lack of gravity; she'll make mistakes; she'll panic, all things unlikely to happen with Kowalski. The contrast between them leads us to identify with Stone more than Kowalski, which is essential for the rest of the story. Kowalski is a co-protagonist and mentor. Stone is the protagonist and main character of *Gravity*. The way they are designed and introduced to us already establishes this.

Another important point to notice: Stone needed to have enough training to stand a chance of surviving, but not so much as to make the outcome predictable. She's somewhere between us and Kowalski, from a competence point of view. In all stories, we have to find the right balance between the strength of the protagonist and the strength of the obstacles. This difference is what generates actual conflict for the protagonist and makes a strong identification possible. It's also what keeps the dramatic question alive. We have to feel, until the very end, that it's going to be difficult yet possible for the protagonist to reach the goal.

When Stone's life is in danger later, especially when she's left on her own, we do wonder if she'll survive. If it were us, completely untrained, we know we'd die. If we saw just Kowalski experiencing the same situation, we'd have to up the ante regarding obstacles to generate enough conflict. In fact, Stone's inexperience is an obstacle for Kowalski, who would likely fare better on his own.

The inciting event is re-introduced ten minutes into the story, when Houston announces "Mission abort" and the astronauts learn that the cloud of debris is headed towards them due to a chain reaction caused by the Russians striking one of their own satellites. This is when the main problem of the story (the satellite debris hitting Explorer and the consequences of that incident) is properly introduced, after a first plant three minutes earlier.

**Note:** We're still in dramatic Act 1, though, because the co-protagonists (the astronauts and mission control) are going to spend the next few minutes trying to avoid the inciting event: the satellite cloud hitting them and Explorer, while Stone keeps trying for a short while to fix her board. So we have a dramatic sequence (more of a scene as it's very short) at the end of Act 1: trying to avoid the oncoming disaster. Note that the whole movie could have been about this, in which case we'd already be in Act 2. However, because they fail to prevent it, the entire movie is going to be about dealing with the consequence of this disaster. The debris hitting Explorer is an inciting event for the movie and the climax of the only sequence of dramatic Act 1 which forces Stone to give up her goal.

The main consequence of this sequence is that Stone doesn't immediately stop what she's doing, which is going to make her feel guilty about what happened. As Kowalski tells her later, though, they would have been hit anyway; there is nothing she could have done that would have changed that. This is important because we don't want the audience to feel that everything happened because she goofed up. It's clearly not the case here. In fact, preventing them from getting into Explorer earlier might very well have saved their lives, given the damage to the shuttle (no survivors there).

Back to the end of Act 1, they fail to prevent the oncoming disaster and are hit by the cloud of debris around 00:12. This triggers the goal for co-protagonists Stone and Kowalski over the rest of the movie: to survive the catastrophic consequences of the cloud of debris hitting Explorer and find a way to get back to Earth.

At 00:13, the opening shot ends abruptly when she untethers – like cutting an umbilical cord – giving a formal end to dramatic Act 1 and releasing our main protagonist into outer space, completely on her own, helpless.

**Note:** In *Gravity*, as in most movies, the first dramatic act is much shorter than the artificial, logistical first act (thirty minutes in a two-hour movie theoretically, so as *Gravity* is ninety minutes long, this would give us a logistical first act of roughly twenty-two minutes). We're significantly shorter than that here, and that's the way it should be. We really want the main dramatic action (or evolution) to be launched by minute fifteen, unless there is a good reason to delay it further, for example if we have a longer inciting action, as in *Misery*.

From a storytelling point of view, this one-shot opening is a clever, subtle way to give us the feeling that what we're watching is real, as if a single camera was just filming events unfolding in front of it, as they happen, including when the cloud of debris actually strikes and all hell breaks loose. This really adds to the realism of the movie and the visceral feeling we have when Stone detaches herself. At that point, we are Ryan Stone, lost in space, panicking as she does, almost suffocating.

So thirteen minutes into the movie, Stone is forced to untether from Explorer's mechanical arm and ends up drifting in outer space – hard to imagine anything more terrifying – which starts the **first dramatic sequence of Act 2**: She's going to try to control her panic, help Kowalski locate her and attempt to get back to Explorer.

At 00:16, it looks like all is lost as she gets no reply, until finally Kowalski is back on line and instructs her to guide him to her. There is some humour when Kowalski asks Stone: "Give me your status" and she answers: "I'm fine". Otherwise, the sequence is very tense, especially as Stone is running low on oxygen (which starts a nice time-lock; they have a limited amount of time to get back to relative safety). The nearby I.S.S. (International Space Station) and Chinese station are also planted, which is important as both are going to pay off later, as possible rescue resources once Explorer is proven to be non-viable.

Just short of 00:18, they are reunited, which marks the end of the first half of the sequence (her first sub-subgoal was to be reunited with

Kowalski) and starts the second half of the sequence: getting back to Explorer. One interesting thing to note, Kowalski insists they have to keep talking to "Houston in the blind" despite the fact that they get no answer. When Stone says: "They can't hear us" – which is an objection the audience might have, so it's a good idea to answer it now – Kowalski replies that they don't know that. Houston might still hear them, which could save their lives. This is important because it allows Kowalski and Stone to convey important information about what they are doing – this will become even more important when Stone is on her own later – without feeling like they are talking to themselves, just for the benefit of the audience.

They have to recover Shariff's drifting body on the way, which mainly serves the purpose of showing what they risk if the integrity of their space suit is compromised. This scene shows us visually what happens when an astronaut's helmet is smashed, although in this case the satellite debris also took half his brain, making the lack of oxygen a minor contributing factor to Shariff's death.

By 00:22, **they get back to Explorer, which is the climax of the sequence,** and witness the catastrophic damage. Kowalski reports that they are the sole survivors and announces their next subgoal, as Explorer is now useless. They are going to try to reach the I.S.S. The plan is to use the escape pod – the Soyuz – to get back to Earth.

So **the second sequence of dramatic Act 2** starts at 00:23. As Kowalski is trying to save the limited remaining power in his jetpack, they are drifting more than speeding to the station, which gives time to convey some of Stone's backstory. Kowalski tries to get her to relax to save oxygen and as they talk we learn about her daughter's death. This starts the character-led subplot, which is Stone's need to move on from this loss. It gives some depth to her character, and will pay off later, when she's tempted to give up and so be reunited with her daughter. Stone is running out of oxygen as they reach the I.S.S., and Kowalski has almost no thrust left in his jetpack.

This explains why he has to propel them towards the station and can't slow down their approach. Stone manages to grab the station but is hit by Kowalski. They both drift until Stone's feet get caught in a deployed parachute. She misses his hand but just manages to grab Kowalski's tether. Unfortunately, gravity is pulling him away, and Kowalski has to convince her to let him go.

00:32 **marks the end of the second sequence in Act 2.** Only one of them has reached the station; the other is drifting away, so it's only a partial success. As Kowalski is Stone's main chance of survival – she needs him – it's a double blow: she's lost a co-protagonist and we've lost a character we really liked. Stone is now on her own, though still guided by Kowalski's voice. Some will see here the classic disappearance of the mentor before the disciple is ready, and they wouldn't be wrong as long as they don't look for this in every story.

Sacrificing his life to save Stone's makes Kowalski a hero, although one who keeps his sense of humour in adversity. The way Kowalski enjoys the view as he drifts to certain death gives us the feeling that it's the perfect way to go for a family-less astronaut on his last mission.

At 00:35, **Stone announces her next subgoal for the third sequence in Act 2**: to get into the station and use the Soyuz to rescue Kowalski. Interestingly, he tells her she has to learn to let go, which reflects her emotional journey in the film. Kowalski also tells her what she has to do next, which is to use one of the Soyuz pods – they are too damaged to get her to Earth, but they should be usable for a shorter journey – to reach the Chinese station; then use one of the Chinese pods, a Shenzhou, for re-entry to Earth. Kowalski reckons Stone should be able to handle them. Once again, it's about finding the right balance between the strength of the protagonist and the strength of the obstacles. She has to be able to handle the pods (she learnt on a simulator), but we have to wonder if she'll be able to do it (she crashed every time).

Stone, guided by Kowalski, finds a way to get into the I.S.S. just before running out of oxygen around 00:38. There is a moment which is symmetrical to the moment when she has to figuratively cut the umbilical cord. For the first time, she's back to relative safety, and as she gets out of her space suit she briefly curls up in a foetal position, floating in the womb-like gravity-free station.

She then moves through the space station looking for a way to communicate with Kowalski and at 00:40, the fire is planted so that it doesn't feel as though it comes out of the blue later.

Stone finds a radio, but she can't communicate with Kowalski and therefore locate him. By 00:42, she has to give up her goal of saving him and focus on her own survival instead. **This is the end of the third sequence in Act 2**. This isn't a mid-act climax, as Stone has the same goal over the whole film, but it might be when a midpoint would be found by those looking for one. It's close to the middle of the movie and an important plot point as it's the first time Stone is really on her own, with no one to help her. However, such a midpoint has no real structural significance or justification.

00:43, a fire alarm pushes Stone back into action, giving her little time to mourn the loss of her mentor. **It also triggers the fourth sequence in Act 2,** which is about reaching the Chinese station using the Soyuz pod. Stone has to overcome the fire planted at 00:40, which itself helps to plant, at 00:44, the fire extinguisher needed by Stone later, when she uses it as a portable jetpack to reach the Chinese station.

It's not only the object itself which is planted, but also its possible use in a gravity-free environment: it works like a jetpack, pushing Stone backwards and almost knocking her out when she tries to use it to put the fire out. It makes sense to try to use a fire extinguisher to stop a fire, and to take it with you if it blocks the airlock. The future help is planted, but conflict is used – the fire, the knocking out, the blocking of the airlock – to disguise the plant and distract the audience so that the help isn't telegraphed. If Stone found a fire extinguisher in the Soyuz just as she needed one and suddenly had the idea to use it as a jetpack, it would feel like a *deus ex machina* (an unplanted help). Planting it skilfully like this – before it's needed, using conflict to disguise it – makes it possible for the audience to accept the help when it's needed, during the pay-off.

00:45, Stone has managed to reach the Soyuz, and tries to escape in it once she finds a way to undock it, but she discovers it's entangled in cables from the parachute. We have a new time-lock as she knows the satellites will come around again in about seven minutes (Kowalski had predicted shortly after the first strike it would take about ninety minutes for the cloud of debris to return and they both set a timer on their watches).

00:49, she gets out to try to free the pod. A few minutes later, the cloud of debris strikes again while she's desperately trying to free the Soyuz, finally destroying the I.S.S. at 00:53. Stone does manage to free the Soyuz and gets back on board to try to reach the Chinese station (after a funny line, "I hate space"). She sets her watch to ninety minutes again, knowing that's when the debris will be back.

00:55, Stone aims the Soyuz at the Chinese station, but she realises there is no fuel left in the main engine. It's a huge setback because it looks like she has no way to escape her predicament and is now drifting again. **This is the end of the fourth sequence in Act 2.**

It seems for a while like all is lost. She has a false hope of being able to communicate with someone, but it turns out to be a Chinese radio amateur who doesn't understand her.

00:58, Stone breaks down. She realises she's going to die today. She hears a baby on the radio, in the background. This makes Stone think of her own daughter, of the possibility of being reunited with her. She switches her oxygen supply off and prepares to die, sent to sleep by the radio amateur's lullaby. She's given up on her goal to survive and find a way to get back to Earth, so we enter dramatic Act 3.

But at 01:02, someone knocks on the window. Is it really Kowalski? Thankfully not – that would have been hard to accept – it's only a dream or vision, probably induced by the lack of oxygen as she drifts out of consciousness. But it's one that gives her the idea of how to get out, using the soft landing jets as a propulsion engine. Kowalski asks her to choose, going back or staying here. Will she move on and start to live again? Of course she will. Time to go home!

Kowalski's sudden appearance introduces an *Encore Twist*. We had entered dramatic Act 3 as Stone had given up, and Kowalski is the surprise – inciting event at the beginning of Act 3 – that provides her with a new way to reach her goal, and leads her to resume the same dramatic action. This defines a mini 3-act structure in Act 3 with an Act 3.1 (before the action resumes), 3.2 (as the same action resumes) and 3.3 (consequences of the action once it's really over). It's a bit early in the movie as we're barely past the hour mark, but we're two-thirds into the story, as *Gravity* is only eighty-four minutes long, excluding credits. We might not really believe that it's going to be the end of the story when we see Stone apparently about to die, yet structurally it's an *Encore Twist*. Please see *Encore Twist* in *Craft the Draft* for more details.

01:06, Stone comes round – Kowalski is gone of course – switches the oxygen back on and gets the Soyuz ready, **starting Act 3.2 and the last sequence of the movie**, which is about using the Chinese pod to get back to Earth. The first half of the sequence is about using the Soyuz to get to the Chinese station (first sub-goal); the second half, using the Shenzhou to get back to Earth (second sub-goal).

01:09, as Stone is getting the Soyuz ready for the one-hundred-mile journey to the Chinese station, she asks Kowalski to say hello for her to her little girl, Sarah, and to tell her that Stone isn't quitting and loves her. We understand that Stone is moving on. She didn't die, but it's a kind of emotional rebirth, triggered by her traumatic experience. It's a moving moment because she's chosen life over death. Since her daughter's death, she's only been functioning. Now she's going to live again. If she survives the last leg of the journey, that is.

01:10, she launches the Soyuz and is on her way to the Chinese station. We sense a new purpose, a new energy in her. She isn't a victim anymore; she's in control. Just before launching herself out of the Soyuz, she grabs the fire extinguisher planted earlier, using it as a rudimentary jetpack.

**Note:** While the help was planted, she's active in using it and still experiences conflict, as it's far from a smooth landing, especially because just as she reaches the Chinese station the cloud of debris strikes again, threatening to destroy her last hope for a ride back to Earth. A planted help should make the resolution possible for the protagonist, but not easy.

01:13, she reaches the station (climax for the first sub-goal), right when the cloud of debris strikes again, and now she has to get to the pod.

01:15, she's in the pod and we start the second half of this last sequence, which is also the climax of the movie. She's finally on her way back to Earth. Fearless. Enjoying the ride despite the chaos surrounding her and the constant threat of going up in smoke. Transformed by her ordeal.

01:17, she manages to detach her capsule from the rest of the pod, starting the last leg of the journey, as everything seems to burn and disintegrate around her. The parachute deploys and she lands in a lake. Houston has detected her and is sending a rescue mission to retrieve her.

01:19, she still has to survive one last ordeal. The lake water gets into the capsule and threatens to drown her. She finally manages to slip out of her heavy suit, get back to the surface and crawl onto firm land. Dramatically, it's a last obstacle. Symbolically, it's a way to strip her – almost – naked, showing her rebirth.

01:22, she's made it. She survived against all odds. **This is the end of the last sequence and of Act 3.2.** We enter Act 3.3, which shows the consequences of the dramatic action once it's really over.

Like dramatic Act 3 in most movies, Act 3.3 here is very short. A few minutes showing Stone finally back on Earth, elated, grateful, transformed.

Just as the first dramatic act was a single shot, Act 3.3 is a single shot which starts at 01:21, when she breaks the surface of the lake, up to the end credits, just shy of 01:24. A one-shot, very short conclusion similar to Spielberg's *Duel*, showing the elated protagonist having escaped death by truck. Here, Stone has escaped death by outer space. And as in *Duel*, *Jaws* or *The Terminator*, well, what doesn't kill you makes you stronger.

* * *

Thematically, *Gravity* explores many ideas, from the evolution of life to its very meaning or purpose, but the main themes are probably resilience – how human beings can fight for survival against all odds – and transformation, rebirth – how an ordeal can lead someone in emotional pain to move on and value life again.

I love the fact that *Gravity*, while deeply anchored in the lowest levels of Maslow's Hierarchy of Needs (safety of the body, breathing, homeo-stasis) as a good thriller / disaster movie should be, also provides elements in the story that reach higher levels, from love/belonging/relationships in the protagonist's backstory up to the spiritual and existential themes it explores. I give it a high M-Factor because it's such a universal, visceral experience, spanning all levels of Maslow's pyramid and its budget tallies with its story-type, genre and intended audience.

Apart from being a rewarding, suspenseful, intense movie to watch, *Gravity* is also an ideal case study because of the simplicity, clarity and efficiency of its story structure. There is a lot to learn from a craft point of view.

It's a plot-led story, yet the characters are well-designed so we can root for them and care about what happens to them. While the main problem in the story is resolved in the end, the journey has also led the protagonist to grow. Her internal problem – moving on from the death of her daugh-ter – could have been handled as a main problem in a character-led story had she been stuck in a less life-threatening environment, but her survival being what's primarily at stake makes *Gravity* a plot-led story.

The character-led element, as in most plot-led stories, is a subplot which adds depth to the character, increases identification and provides meaning to the story. Her growth is both a consequence of her ordeal, and what allows her to survive, as she chooses life over death during a key turning point.

*Gravity* also makes an ideal case study because like *Misery*, it illustrates perfectly the notion of tasks – as defined by screenwriter Terry Rossio – or subgoals which break up a long Act 2 into dramatic sequences. We know *who wants what and why*, and what's at stake in every scene or sequence, as well as for the whole story. While not all movies have such clear successive sequences, their presence in *Gravity* make it possible to explain the principle of tasks or subgoals with crystal-clear clarity.

Let's take a look now at the STM (*Story-Type Method*) framework of *Gravity*. You'll find more information on this key development tool as well as a link to download a template in the *Story Design Tools* section of *Bringing It All Together*. Please note that for most case studies there will be some repetitions between the analysis and the STM Framework. This is so that each part of the case study can be read independently.

# STM Framework for *Gravity*

## STORY-TYPE, M-FACTOR AND THEME

**Story-Type**: Plot-Led, like most thrillers / disaster movies.

**Main Problem in the Story**: The main problem in *Gravity* lies outside of the protagonist, in nature. It's about surviving in outer space, following the satellite debris strike and its catastrophic consequences, and finding a way to get back to Earth.

**M-Factor**: *Gravity*'s main problem is firmly rooted at the lowest levels of Maslow's pyramid, making it possible to reach a wide audience and cross borders. It explores universal needs such as safety (of the body) and even physiology (breathing, homeostasis). Not being able to breathe is one of the most fundamental fears for any human being. Beyond these classic thriller / disaster movie needs, the dead daughter subplot provides more emotional depth as it's about relationships (love/belonging). Several thematic elements – see below – go all the way up to the top of Maslow's pyramid, exploring spiritual and existential issues. This widens *Gravity*'s potential even further, without losing its core audience. Its genre, story-type and intended audience all tally with its substantial budget, so I'd give it a high M-Factor.

**Theme**: The main theme in *Gravity* is resilience, fighting to survive against all odds. A perfect illustration that "what doesn't kill you makes you stronger" – a classic theme in thrillers – it also explores transformation and rebirth (how an ordeal can lead us to move on and overcome grief) and even the origin, meaning and value of life. *Gravity* develops a very positive, optimistic, humanist point of view on human nature, which probably helped it to reach such a wide audience.

## MANAGING CONFLICT

**Protagonist**: Ryan Stone is the protagonist; Kowalski, a co-protagonist/mentor for the first third of the story (with a spirited comeback two-thirds in).

**Conscious Goal**: To survive in outer space following a catastrophic incident and find a way to get back to Earth.

**Motivation**: While it's not necessary to explain why someone would want to survive, it's interesting that in *Gravity*, due to her grief, Stone could be tempted to give up as well.

**Unconscious Need**: Stone needs to move on from the meaning-less death of her daughter, Sarah. She needs to learn to live again. Her instinctive fight for survival will lead her to value life again.

**Main Characteristic**: Stone is resilient. She doesn't quit. She's not super human and she has moments of doubt, fear, panic or weak-ness like any of us, but she ultimately controls herself and finds a way to go on, not to give up. That's often the key characteristic of a good protagonist in a plot-led story, especially in a thriller / disaster movie.

**Secondary Characteristics**: Stone is clever, resourceful, has a sense of humour. She's also vulnerable. First, because she isn't a professional astronaut; second, because her young daughter died recently and she's still grieving her loss.

**Evolution (growth, change or steadfast)**: Stone doesn't need to change because there is nothing fundamentally wrong with her at the beginning of the story. She's struggling to cope with the death of her daughter, as any parent would. The difference between change and growth is that you need to change when you're going in the wrong direction (something is wrong with you), while you need to grow when you need to move to the next stage, in the same direction.

So here, Stone needs to grow, not change. In a different story, if her physical survival wasn't at stake, her unconscious need could be the main problem if her grief was preventing her from function-ing – emotionally, professionally – making the story character-led. In *Gravity*, Stone functions. She's just grieving, normally, until an external ordeal leads her to grow out of her grief and choose to live. Her growth is visible and gratifying. She goes from being caught in her grief to being free and alive. The story gives her a chance to be reborn and move on.

**Main Character**: The main character is Stone, the protagonist. Not that we have much of a choice, but it's her story. Not only her dramatic action, but also her transformation / evolution.

**Main Plot**: Stone's attempts to survive the consequences of the satellite debris hitting Explorer and her attempts to get back to Earth.

**What's at Stake**: Stone's life is at stake, both quantitatively (dead or alive) and qualitatively (captive of her past, or free to live again).

**External Obstacles / Antagonist**: There is no thinking, scheming antagonist in the story. As in most disaster movies, the antagonist is nature, specifically outer space here (you can't survive in space without functioning equipment/protection) and causality (every-thing happens because of the initial strike by the satellite debris).

**Internal Obstacles**: Stone's inexperience is the main source of internal conflict for her: she isn't a seasoned astronaut like Kowalski. She isn't really responsible for what happened – it would have happened anyway – but she feels responsible for not having obeyed Kowalski's orders more quickly. Her fear, which can lead her to panic at times, is another big internal obstacle, fuelled by her inexperience. Her grief tempts her to commit suicide, when she thinks there is no hope and sees death as a way to be reunited with her daughter.

**Subplots**: The dead daughter related to Stone's unconscious need is the only subplot, introduced in her conversation with Kowalski as they are on the way to the I.S.S. The moment she contemplates suicide as a way to be reunited with her daughter is when the subplot becomes part of the main plot, as her will to live – linked to her survival – is directly connected to her ability to move on and embrace life again. We understand she's moved on when she asks Kowalski to tell her daughter that she loves her and she's not giving up.

**Comedy:** Not much comedy except the early banter between the astronauts and Mission Control, and also from Kowalski who uses humour to defuse Stone's panic. A few comedic moments linked to Stone's inexperience and some of her reactions ("I hate space").

## DRAMATIC THREE-ACT STRUCTURE

**First Act / Set-Up:** The first shot of the movie, which is thirteen minutes long, sets up the main characters, their various levels of experience, their respective roles in the mission and the reason for the oncoming catastrophe, up to the moment when it strikes and separates Stone from Explorer, sending her drifting away into outer space. This set-up efficiently tells us the minimum we need to know to understand the situation and care about the characters. Very good first act, short and to the point, yet a visual *tour de force*.

**Inciting Event / Inciting Action:** The inciting event is when the cloud of satellite debris strikes Explorer and its crew. This is what triggers Stone and Kowalski's conscious goal to survive and get back to Earth. They spend the last few minutes of dramatic Act 1 trying to avoid the inciting event (prevent the catastrophic damage to Explorer and its crew), but they fail.

**Beginning of Dramatic Act 2**: We enter Act 2 as soon as the cloud of debris strikes Explorer, and Stone and Kowalski try to survive the consequences and get back to Earth. We were in a kind of pre-Act 2 before, as they were trying to prevent this from happening, although Stone was still stuck in her previous goal (to install her experimental module in Hubble), which shows that she had not really clocked the extent of the upcoming danger.

**Sequences in Act 2**: There are six dramatic sequences in *Gravity*, one in Act 1, four in Act 2 and one in Act 3 due to the presence of an *Encore Twist:*

1.  **The first sequence of Act 2** is nine minutes long. It lasts from 00:13 until 00:22. Protagonist: Stone, with co-protagonist Kowalski. Subgoal: To get back to Explorer after she's forced to untether from the severed mechanical arm – inciting event of the sequence – and starts drifting away into outer space. The sequence is structured in two halves. She first has to be reunited with Kowalski (first sub-subgoal, which she reaches at 00:18), then they have to go back to Explorer together (second sub-subgoal), picking up Shariff's body on the way. They succeed, but Explorer is completely destroyed, so they have to find another way to get back to Earth.

2.  **The second sequence of Act 2** is nine minutes long. It starts at 00:23 when Kowalski, having witnessed the damage to Explorer (inciting incident of the sequence) declares their next subgoal: to reach the I.S.S. and use the Soyuz Pod to get back to Earth. They are co-protagonists of this sequence, which ends at 00:32, when only one of them – Stone – has reached the I.S.S., Kowalski having sacrificed himself to save her. Plus, the Soyuz is damaged, which makes it impossible to use it for Earth re-entry.

3.  **The third sequence of Act 2** is seven minutes long. It starts at 00:35, when Stone announces her next subgoal: to get into the I.S.S. and use the Soyuz to rescue Kowalski. She reaches the first sub-subgoal when she gets into the station at 00:38 then tries to communicate with Kowalski to locate him but fails. He's most likely dead and there is nothing she

can do to save him. At 00:42, she gives up her announced subgoal, which was to try to rescue her mentor with the Soyuz. Kowalski isn't her co-protagonist during the first half of this sequence because he doesn't believe she should risk her life trying to rescue him: "This boat has sailed". However, he's still her co-protagonist and mentor regarding her overall goal, to survive and get back to Earth. This is why he helps her get into the I.S.S. and tells her what she should do next: use the Soyuz to reach the Chinese station and use one of their pods to get back to Earth.

4.  **The fourth sequence of Act 2** is twelve minutes long. It starts at 00:43, when a fire alarm forces Stone to spring back into action, not leaving her much time to mourn the loss of her co-protagonist and mentor. She's going back to the initial plan, suggested earlier by Kowalski: using the Soyuz to reach the Chinese Space station, about one hundred miles away in order to use one of their pods. Stone manages to survive a fire, untangle the Soyuz from an accidentally deployed parachute, dodge the returning cloud of debris, only to realise, at 00:55, that there is no fuel and that the Soyuz is useless. This is the climax of the sequence, and also the first climax of Act 2, as she realises she's going to die and gives up her goal at 00:58. She shuts off her oxygen supply, ready to die in her sleep.

We enter Act 3, but we have an *Encore Twist* – Kowalski's return, a surprise at the beginning of Act 3 – which leads Stone to resume the same dramatic action (to survive and get back to Earth).

Act 3.2 is sixteen minutes long, in two parts, because she first has to reach the Chinese station using the damaged Soyuz (first subgoal) in order to use its Shenzhou pod to get back to Earth (second subgoal). Feel free to split it into two distinct sequences if it makes more sense to you, but for me reaching the Chinese station is only a way to get a Shenzhou in order to return to Earth, which is why I see it as one sequence with two subgoals.

**The last sequence starts** at 01:06, when Stone restores her oxygen supply and starts trying to use the soft landing jets of the Soyuz, as suggested by Kowalski, to boost her away from the I.S.S.

towards the Chinese station. Stone reaches the station at 01:13 (success for the first subgoal) just as the cloud of debris strikes again. The second half of the sequence in the Chinese pod is the second climax of the movie (the first one was when she failed to use the out-of-fuel Soyuz and gave up). When she reaches the ground at 01:22, we have a second answer to the dramatic question: *Yes*, she survives and finds a way to get back to Earth. This is the end of 3.2 and the beginning of 3.3.

**Mid-Act Climax**: There is no mid-act climax in *Gravity* as Stone has the same goal over the whole movie, but there is an *Encore Twist*.

**Climax of Dramatic Act 2**: The first climax at the end of dramatic Act 2 is when Stone fails to start the engine of the Soyuz at 01:02 and gives up hope. The second climax – at the end of Act 3.2, due to the *Encore Twist* – is when she successfully lands the pod and reaches firm ground, at 01:22.

**Answer to the Dramatic Question**: The first answer to the dramatic question at 01:02 is *no*, Stone has failed, there is nothing she can do, and she's going to die. The second answer to the dramatic question at 01:22 is *yes*, Stone has succeeded. She's survived her ordeal against all odds.

**When Do We Enter Dramatic Act 3?** We enter dramatic Act 3 at 01:02, when Stone realises that she's going to die today and switches off her oxygen supply. She's given up her goal, which was to survive and get back to Earth.

*Encore Twist*: Kowalski's spirit/delirious vision knocking on the window, providing her with a new solution, is a surprise which leads her to resume the same action – surviving the consequences of the satellite debris hitting Explorer and finding a way to get back to Earth. So we do have an *Encore Twist* in *Gravity*, a surprise at the beginning of Act 3 which triggers the same goal for the protagonist.

**Does the Answer to the Dramatic Question Convey the Point of View of the Filmmaker(s)?** Definitely. *Gravity* is about resilience and transformation. Stone failing to survive or move on would go against the substance of the film. This is why we first have a negative answer (all is lost; the protagonist gives up) and then a final, positive one (the protagonist succeeds, transformed). This embeds a very optimistic message (even when all seems to be lost, don't give up; you can still succeed) which explains why the *Encore Twist* with a *no/yes* combination is still as popular today as it was in the 90s.

**Does the Answer to the Dramatic Question Fit the Genre of the Story?** *Gravity* is a thriller / disaster movie: the life of the protagonist is at stake. There is little value in a thriller if it shows that by facing an ordeal, you die, according to the odds. We already know that. The protagonist of a thriller (or disaster movie) usually survives, shows resilience and often grows in the process, as the ordeal transforms him, her or them. This is precisely what happens in *Gravity*. There are exceptions to this principle, but it tends to apply to horror movies and even thrillers told from the point of view of the antagonist (like *The Shining* or *The Hand That Rocks the Cradle*) in which the main character (the antagonist) dies, but the protagonist survives.

**Is the Ending Satisfying?** *Gravity*'s ending is satisfying because it's optimistic and meaningful. It shows us how resilience can lead to survival, and how an ordeal can have a positive, transformative effect. It doesn't show life as it is, unfair and meaningless. It shows life as we would like it to be, fair and meaningful. Even Kowalski's death isn't pointless: his sacrifice is what allows Stone to survive.

**Duration of Dramatic Acts**: The first act of *Gravity* is thirteen minutes long. Act 2 is fifty minutes long and Act 3 is twenty-eight minutes long (with an *Encore Twist*). Act 3.3 is only three minutes long. Both Act 1 and Act 3.3 are a single shot, which is quite rare. However, the duration of Act 1 (thirteen minutes) and Act 3.3 (three minutes) are typical for the first and third dramatic acts in a movie, quite far from the logistical 30–60–30.

## MANAGING INFORMATION
### Main Dramatic Ironies:
There is little dramatic irony in *Gravity*. We have a small diffused dramatic irony at the beginning, because as soon as the cloud of debris is mentioned by Mission Control we know they should worry about it more than they do (we're watching a disaster movie and we know this planting of an impending conflict is going to pay off).

Other than that, a few minor dramatic ironies, like the fact that we notice the fire starting in the I.S.S. before Stone sees it – once it's too late and it's got much stronger. We also guess – or hope – that Kowalski's return can't be real before she realises it, that he is a lack-of-oxygen-induced vision simply because it doesn't make sense otherwise.

Overall, dramatic irony doesn't play a large part in the structure of *Gravity*.

**Main Surprises:**

Primarily the dead astronaut's head popping up in the damaged Explorer; the Soyuz's empty tank; the imagined return of Kowalski and the idea of using the soft landing jets for propulsion. There are a few other minor ones, but these are the biggies.

**Main Elements of Mystery:**

There is very little mystery in *Gravity*. In fact, I can't find any. Everything we need to know is told to us upfront, or as the story unfolds.

**Main Elements of Suspense:**

*Gravity* generates a lot of suspense, primarily because we know exactly where the danger is coming from. A title even reminds us at the very beginning of the movie: Life is not possible in space. So every time the integrity of a space suit, a helmet, a shuttle or pod is compromised or threatens to be, we know the penalty would be instant death. This generates most of the suspense in the film. We also know that if Kowalski doesn't find Stone, or if Stone doesn't catch Kowalski, the penalty is slow death and eternal drift in outer space. Suspense always comes from the near constant threat of oxygen deprivation or lack of gravity. Both are visceral, primal needs lying at the very bottom of Maslow's pyramid. Every human being knows that if you can't breathe, you die. More locally, there are threats such as the fire in the I.S.S., or the cloud of debris striking, which can add fatal physical injuries – as shown with Shariff – making the oxygen deprivation a secondary problem. The fact that the antagonist is nature – in this case, outer space and man-made objects which become lethal through circumstance – is what makes *Gravity* a disaster movie.

## VISUAL STORYTELLING, PLANTING/PAY-OFF, EXPOSITION

### Planting/Pay-Off and Visual Storytelling:

There is a lot of planting and pay-off in *Gravity*. The first plant is related to the main source of conflict in the story: the threat of death related to their presence in space and the lack of oxygen is planted by our knowledge of biology and physics. It's re-stated for the forgetful in the titles at the beginning of the movie. The cloud of satellite debris is planted before it strikes the first time, so that it doesn't feel like a *diabolicus ex machina* (a terrible accident coming out of the blue). The first strike plants the next one, every ninety minutes like clockwork, as calculated by Kowalski. Everything that happens is planted by what happened before, and most of the big problems – catastrophic damage to Explorer; damaged Soyuz in the I.S.S.; fire in the Soyuz; deployed parachute in which the Soyuz is entangled; every strike from the cloud of debris – come from the accidental satellite destruction that started a chain reaction. Even the vision/ghost of Kowalski is planted by the fact that Stone has been deprived of oxygen and we know that oxygen deprivation can lead to hallucinations.

The biggest plant is of course the fire extinguisher, which has to be used as a jetpack during the climax to reach the Chinese station. Planting it during the fire – and planting the fire itself – is necessary to avoid a *deus ex machina*.

From a visual storytelling point of view, *Gravity* is a masterclass. From the long opening shot to the last shot evoking the evolution of life on Earth in a few seconds, most of the story is told visually, leading to its universal appeal. A non-English speaking audience would only need a few subtitles to grasp the essence of the story.

From a visual storytelling point of view, one of the most significant moments is when Stone drifts after Explorer is hit, suffocating, showing her panic in a visceral way. Later on, the way she looks and behaves during the climax: re-energised, fearless, finally grateful and relieved as she reaches firm ground. The contrast with the frightened, emotionally-wounded Stone at the beginning of the story couldn't be more striking, and is done with very few words.

**Exposition:**

There is little exposition in the movie. The short titles at the very beginning, laying down the scientific facts, are a good example of written exposition (only acceptable in a modern story if brief and at the very beginning of the film). The last line: *Life isn't possible in space* is mostly there to make sure that absolutely everyone realises where the danger comes from and is fully emotionally involved during the whole movie.

We then have some exposition through dialogue in Act 1, when we learn about the characters and their respective roles in the mission, as well as the impending source of conflict, the cloud of debris. Humour – the astronauts' enjoyable banter – and the contrast between experienced Shariff or Kowalski really enjoying the ride and rookie Stone fighting every inch of it give us the conflict we need to make this exposition palatable.

The first bit of dialogue when Stone talks about her daughter's death is welcome as we need the breathing space after the intense beginning. Learning about her backstory adds depth and makes us care more about her – because of the conflict related to her grief. The second part, however, when she talks about her daughter in the I.S.S. before switching off her oxygen supply, is possibly the only place in the movie with too much dialogue and exposition. The third part, when she decides to embrace life and tells Kowalski about her daughter, asking him to say hello, is more palatable because she's energetic and positive, so there is no pathos involved. But she's still telling us something we don't need to be told. We can see for ourselves that she has decided to live and isn't giving up. This commenting of her own actions feels a bit clunky because it's primarily for the benefit of the audience.

Other than that, there are a few technical elements briefly explained by Kowalski or Mission Control, but overall we have little exposition in *Gravity*. When there is some, it's mostly handled skilfully using conflict – primarily humour or tension – to disguise it.

# Billy Elliot

### Screenplay by Lee Hall

### Directed by Stephen Daldry

Detailed Analysis

**Note: As usual, it's best is to watch the film just before reading the analysis.**

*Billy Elliot* was written by Lee Hall, adapted from his stage play *Dancer* and influenced by photographer Sirkka-Liisa Konttinen's book, *Step by Step*, about a dancing school in North Shields. It became one of the most successful British movies ever made. It pleased critics and was a massive commercial success at home and abroad (close to US$110 million worldwide for an estimated budget of around US$5 million, according to Wikipedia). Hall was nominated for a 2001 Academy Award for his screenplay (along with director Stephen Daldry and actress Julie Walters). Hall and Daldry won a BAFTA that year (Best Screenplay; Best Director), along with actor Jamie Bell (Best Newcomer). In 2001, author Melvin Burgess was commissioned to write the novelisation of the film based on Hall's screenplay. The story was adapted for the West End stage as *Billy Elliot the Musical* in 2005; it opened in Australia in 2007 and on Broadway in 2008.

There are many reasons why *Billy Elliot* makes a great case study.

First, although it's plot-led – there is nothing wrong in Billy; the problem lies primarily in his father – it's the strength of its characters and theme that makes the story so funny and touching. These elements remain essential, irrespective of story-type.

It also breaks the supposed rule stating that the protagonist of a story is the character who changes most. This is true in character-led movies, but mostly nonsense otherwise. In many plot-led stories, the protagonist doesn't change at all. Sometimes, as in *Billy Elliot*, the protagonist needs to grow to stand a chance of reaching the goal, but here it's Jackie, Billy's father and antagonist of the movie who changes most. He needs to accept Billy for who he is, to overcome his prejudice and move on from his wife's death. Jackie's transformation is so drastic that he moves from antagonist to co-protagonist. Yet, this doesn't make him the protagonist of the movie.

*Billy Elliot* illustrates perfectly the difference between the need for a protagonist to *grow* in a plot-led movie, and the need for a character to *change* in a character-led movie. There is nothing wrong with Billy, who is coping fairly well with the recent death of his mother and just wants to become a ballet dancer. Billy only needs to *grow* and stand up to his father in order to reach his goal. Jackie, however, needs to *change* because he's the one who is prejudiced. He is the protagonist of an important character-led subplot, which is about Billy and his father mending their relationship. It's only when Jackie changes, resolves his internal problem, that their relationship can improve and Billy can succeed. If the father was the protagonist of the main plot, if his inability to cope with the death of his wife or his prejudice were the main problem in the story, we would have a character-led story, as the film would be about his unconscious need to change, to resolve that problem. But as the main plot is about Billy's struggle to become a ballet dancer, and because his father stands in his way as an antagonist, we have a plot-led movie.

Also, while *Billy Elliot* is a coming of age story – the protagonist is eleven years old and about to face a life-changing transformation which will mark the end of his childhood – it also has a very strong goal which makes it a triumph over adversity story. So unlike some coming of age stories in which we have a powerless young protagonist drifting through an aimless plot, here we have a strong character with a clear conscious goal driving the story forward.

Finally, *Billy Elliot* wasn't only a successful movie in its home country. It also travelled very well across the world. Some of this success is due to the universality of a great music track, wonderful acting and directing, but this ability to cross borders owes a lot to Hall's excellent screenplay, which explores universal themes and uses dramatic tools to tell a story in a very visual way, allowing it to reach a wide audience at home and abroad. Like another British hit from around the same time, *The Full Monty*, the story is set in a very specific place in the world, at a very specific time, yet top-notch storytelling gives it a universal appeal. It provides meaning, entertainment and emotion and reaches a wide audience without losing its cultural or intellectual integrity. So let's see how it's done!

To help visualise the following analysis, here is the overall dramatic three-act structure of *Billy Elliot*:

# The *Fractal* Aspect of Structure

## *Dramatic* 3-Act Structure of *Billy Elliot*

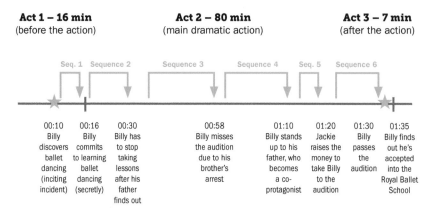

**Act 1 – 16 min**
(before the action)

**Act 2 – 80 min**
(main dramatic action)

**Act 3 – 7 min**
(after the action)

Seq. 1  Sequence 2  Sequence 3  Sequence 4  Seq. 5  Sequence 6

| 00:10 | 00:16 | 00:30 | 00:58 | 01:10 | 01:20 | 01:30 | 01:35 |
|---|---|---|---|---|---|---|---|
| Billy discovers ballet dancing (inciting incident) | Billy commits to learning ballet dancing (secretly) | Billy has to stop taking lessons after his father finds out | Billy misses the audition due to his brother's arrest | Billy stands up to his father, who becomes a co-protagonist | Jackie raises the money to take Billy to the audition | Billy passes the audition | Billy finds out he's accepted into the Royal Ballet School |

Sequence 1 (6 min): Billy fighting his own prejudice
Sequence 2 (13 min): Getting better – secretly – at ballet dancing
Sequence 3 (24 min): Getting ready for the Royal Ballet School audition
Sequence 4 (20 min): Trying to overcome Jackie's prejudice
Sequence 5 (7 min): Jackie helping Billy to achieve his goal
Sequence 6 (15 min): Passing the Royal Ballet School audition

The movie starts with a title telling us where we are, and when: Durham coalfield, northeast England, 1984.

Over the opening credits, we have a wonderful music sequence showing Billy jumping on his bed playing *Cosmic Dancer* by T-Rex. This tells us almost everything we need to know about Billy: his energy, his feistiness, and the words of the song tell us about his love of dancing: "I was dancing when I was twelve, I danced myself out of the womb". Perfect opening, which sets the tone of the movie. Billy is an energetic, cheeky child who loves music. He isn't a dancer yet, but he has what it takes to become one.

00:03, Billy's preparing breakfast, still full of energy, realises Grandma's missing.

00:04, Billy's now looking for Grandma – who has dementia – and bringing her back home. This introduces Billy as a caring, gentle boy. The miners' strike is also visually planted with the presence of the police.

We introduce Billy's older brother, Tony, angry that Billy played his record. This sets up a fairly standard relationship between two brothers and plants the fact that Billy can lie if needed.

00:05, the miners' strike is planted further: the mine is running out of coal, Tony – a union leader – is more hopeful than Jackie, Billy's father, regarding the outcome of the strike. We get a sense that for Jackie, the fight is already over, even if he's still on the strikers' side.

00:06, the piano playing introduces the theme of Billy's mum. Music is a connection to her. Her absence stands between Billy and Jackie (who isn't a bad person, just a grieving husband struggling to cope with feelings he's unable to control or express). The character-led element of the story is introduced: Billy and his father need to mend their relationship.

00:07, the miners' strike, full on. This – along with a few other moments – plants what it means to break the picket line and be labelled a scab: hate from the other miners and humiliation.

00:08, Billy's taking boxing lessons with George, one of Jackie's friends. Billy's friend Michael makes fun of him: he sucks at boxing. His dad watches him, hopeful that he's going to improve, but it doesn't look like boxing is for Billy – who is already kind of dancing in the ring instead of fighting, and gets knocked out. Because downstairs is being used as a kitchen for striking minors, half of the boxing hall will be used by Mrs Wilkinson for her ballet dancing class. This plants the inciting event. It's not Billy who goes to ballet dancing; it's ballet dancing that comes to him, which is much more believable given Billy's background.

00:09, Billy told by his boxing teacher to practice until he can do it. He's left with the keys, alone except for the ballet dancing class. Billy looks at the girls dancing, fascinated. This is the inciting event: Billy discovers ballet dancing. He tentatively joins them. Seems to have the legs for it, according to the teacher.

00:12, after the class, Mrs Wilkinson asks Billy to pay for the lesson: "You owe me 50p". Billy doesn't have the money as he's paid for his boxing lesson already. "Bring it along next week". Billy weakly protests that he has boxing. "But you're crap at boxing!" says Debbie, Mrs Wilkinson's daughter. **This starts the only sequence in Act 1**, showing Billy struggling with his attraction to dancing.

00:13, Fred Astaire was Billy's mum's favourite, according to Grandma. They used to dance together like lunatics. In fact, Grandma might have become a professional dancer. Now dancing is connected to Billy's mother, along with music.

00:14, Billy at his mother's grave. Now we know she died recently (one or two years earlier).

00:15: Billy with Debbie. He's concerned all dancers are gay. Debbie, like Michael, helps Billy to overcome his own prejudice against ballet dancing. Great visual presence of the strike via the police in the background.

00:16, Billy skipping boxing for his second ballet class. He's still concerned he looks gay. "Don't act like it then". He pays for the class and commits to coming back next week. He's on! **Beginning of the first sequence of Act 2**: learning to dance without anyone – especially his father – finding out.

00:17, Billy at home, hiding his ballet shoes under his mattress. His dad almost catches him, but Billy pretends he's looking for his boxing gloves (which belonged to his grandfather). This sets up a strong dramatic irony: Jackie doesn't know that Billy is dancing instead of boxing. He's the victim of this dramatic irony, and becomes the antagonist (main source or potential source of conflict for the protagonist). We fear Jackie's reaction if he finds out. This is a classic way to generate suspense when the victim of a dramatic irony is the antagonist.

00:18, Michael knows that Billy is going every week. Billy makes him swear not to tell anyone. We understand that Michael is more interested in wearing a tutu than in dancing. Billy explains his motivations as if they were obvious: he simply goes to get better at it.

00:19, Billy steals a book on ballet dancing from the library (he's too young to borrow it). Again, the confrontation between the strikers and the police is very much present.

00:20 to 00:22, Billy practicing, getting better.

00:23, Billy dancing, full of joy and energy. Happy. Dancing clearly helps him express his feelings, release his energy.

00:24, during a strike demonstration, George breaks it to Jackie: Billy hasn't been boxing for weeks. This is the beginning of the resolution of the dramatic irony. Jackie doesn't know yet what Billy is doing, but he knows he isn't boxing. This starts Jackie's subgoal of finding out what Billy is up to. We see him yelling "scab" along with the others at those who break the strike (planting his humiliation and pain when he's about to break the strike later to help Billy). This alternates with a montage of Billy dancing.

00:25, Billy leaves for his lesson before his father can talk to him.

00:26, Jackie barges into the dance lesson, furious. Mrs Wilkinson tries to help, but Billy leaves.

00:27, Billy tries to convince his father that it's fine for a boy to do ballet dancing. Jackie's prejudice becomes clear. He tells Billy to forget about dancing or boxing, and to stay home to look after his grandma. Billy hates him, calls him a bastard, runs away when his father tries to hit him.

00:30, Billy goes to see Mrs Wilkinson and tells her he has to stop the lessons. "You should stand up to him". "You don't know what he's like". **This is the end of the first sequence of Act 2**: Billy has failed, his father has found out and he's giving up dancing.

00:32, Debbie wants to kiss him. Billy is mildly confused but has to go home before anything happens – bar a pillow fight. Billy is still a child.

00:34, Mrs Wilkinson is thinking about Billy for the Royal Ballet School. There will be an audition soon in Newcastle. She offers to teach Billy privately, for free, so his father doesn't have to know about it. **This is the beginning of the second sequence of Act 2**: getting ready for the Newcastle audition. The dramatic irony resumes; Jackie is still the victim and we fear the consequences of him finding out even more.

00:37, Michael, wearing his mother's clothes, asks about a tutu again, which plants the reason for Billy to be found dancing with him wearing one later. Billy talks about the ballet school. Michael is worried that Billy might move away, that he will lose his friend.

00:38, Billy having his first private lesson with Mrs Wilkinson. She's asked him to bring things that are special to him, to get ideas for a dance routine for the audition. Billy asks her to read a letter his mum wrote for him for when he'd be eighteen, but he's already read it. He knows it by heart. Very touching moment. The key part of the letter is Billy's mother last wish for him: "Always be yourself". This is what the story is about. He's also brought a tape: "I Love to Boogie" by T-Rex.

00:43, energetic dance montage to the song.

00:45, one night, Jackie tries to stop Tony from leaving the house, as he suspects he's up to something sinister regarding the strike. When Tony insults him, telling him he's been useless since their mother died, Jackie punches his son, who then leaves. Billy witnesses all this, upset to see his father in such pain, humiliated.

00:46, Mrs Wilkinson tells Billy off; he hasn't been practising. Billy says he can't do it. He rebels and runs away. She apologises. He tells her off for picking on him because she messed up her life. They make up.

00:49, Mrs Wilkinson tells Billy about *Swan Lake* as they listen to the music. Planting of the final scene when Billy, aged twenty-six, dances the lead part of the ballet.

00:51, Billy talks with his mother in the kitchen. He clearly misses her.

00:52, another dancing lesson. Billy is progressing.

00:54, scene with Debbie. The audition is the next day. "If you want, I'll show you my fanny". "No, you're all right". Billy is still a child; he isn't interested in sex yet.

00:55 to 00:57, strike demonstration montage; Tony running away from police; getting arrested, all this witnessed by a powerless Billy.

00:58, Billy tries to call Mrs Wilkinson to tell her he has a problem for the audition, but Debbie hangs up the phone. Mrs Wilkinson, waiting on her own at the boxing hall. Billy doesn't show up. **This is the end of the second sequence of Act 2**: Billy has failed to pass the audition and is forced to give up again.

00:59, Mrs Wilkinson comes to Billy's house, meets Billy, Tony and his father as they come back from the police station. She confronts them. **This is the beginning of the third sequence of Act 2**, trying to overcome Jackie and Tony's prejudice against ballet dancing. She tells them about the audition Billy missed for the Royal Ballet School. Tony dares Billy to dance, joining the father as a prejudiced antagonist. Mrs Wilkinson has failed.

01:00 to 00:63, Billy runs away, dancing with rage to escape confrontation and vent his frustration.

01:04, time has passed; it's Christmas. The strike is still going on. Billy's father has to tear Billy's mother's piano to pieces to feed the fire. They are clearly running out of money.

01:05, the family celebrates a grim Christmas. Billy's father breaks into tears.

01:06, Billy and Michael playing in town. Michael has brought one of his dad's bottles to celebrate. He makes a move on Billy, who gently declines ("It's not because I like ballet dancing that I'm a poof") and promises not to tell anyone.

01:08, Billy takes Michael to the boxing hall, lends him a tutu, starts teaching him how to dance.

01:09, George notices there is someone in the club, sees Billy and Michael dancing together, goes to fetch Jackie.

01:10, Billy's father catches them dancing. He can't believe his eyes. This is his worst fear come true: his son dancing ballet with another boy dressed like a girl. Billy, for the first time, stands up to him, starts dancing, showing him what he can do. Jackie leaves, impressed and overwhelmed. Michael claps. Billy calls after his dad, who tells him to go home. **This is the end of the third sequence of Act 2**: Billy has stood up to his father, forcing him to overcome his prejudice.

01:12, Jackie goes to see Mrs. Wilkinson. Finds out it will cost £2,000 for the school, but he's likely to get financial support. The only immediate cost is the fare to London for the audition. She offers to pay for it. Jackie thanks her for everything she's done for Billy, but says he'll handle it himself.

01:13, Jackie comes to see Billy in his bedroom. Doesn't say anything. He still can't communicate his feelings to his son, but we sense that he's trying to get closer to him.

01:14, **this is the beginning of the fourth sequence of Act 2**: Jackie trying to raise the money to help Billy go to the RBS audition. Heartbroken, he crosses the picket line and joins the scabs in a coach heading to the mine, receiving the same abuse he used to give out.

01:15 to 01:17, Tony notices his dad inside the coach, goes after him, confronts him. Jackie explains it's for Billy, to give him a chance. Tony stops his father from going into the mine. They'll find another way.

01:18 to 01:19, Tony is on board now. "You're right. Mum would have let him". Boxing teacher George will organise a raffle and a concert. Jackie sells his wife's jewellery.

01:20, Jackie and Billy are on the way to the Royal Ballet School for the audition. **This is the end of the fourth sequence of Act 2: Jackie has succeeded in raising the money for the audition**. It's the first time in London for both of them. "There's no mines in London". "Is that all you think about?"

01:21, they arrive at the Royal Ballet School. **This is the beginning of the fifth and last sequence of Act 2**, which is also the climax of the movie: passing the audition. Billy first passes medical tests while Jackie watches classes. Billy, suffering from stage fright or fear of failure, wants to leave, but Jackie sends him back.

01:23, the audition starts in front of a panel of judges. **This is the climax of the sequence and of the movie**. Billy dances, a very unconventional routine, full of energy. Feels rubbish afterwards, convinced he's failed. Punches a boy who tries to cheer him up, out of frustration.

01:27 to 01:30, Billy and his dad facing the panel, concerned about Billy's violent behaviour. Then Billy and Jackie answer questions from the panel. Jackie confirms that Billy's family is 100% behind him. One of the judges asks Billy one last question: What does it feel like when you're dancing? Billy struggles, then manages to convey how special dancing makes him feel. It's like electricity. He forgets about everything else when he's dancing. This gives us a bit of hope.

01:31, they're all waiting for the school's decision. Finally, the postman delivers the letter.

01:32, Billy, back from school, first can't bring himself to open it in front of the whole family, waiting anxiously.

01:33, Billy isolates himself. Opens the letter and starts to read it.

01:35, Jackie can't wait any longer, finds him crying: he got in. Jackie runs to tell the good news to his friends, finds out that the union caved and they are going back to work the next day. It's the end of the strike. **This is the end of the last sequence of Act 2.**

01:36, Billy and Jackie, discussing Billy's future. He worries about leaving. Can he come back if he doesn't like it? His dad jokes that he's already rented his room. Billy gets the joke and for the first time they both laugh together. Billy and Jackie have got what they both needed: their relationship is mended. This is the end of the character-led subplot.

01:37, Billy and Mrs Wilkinson. "I'll miss you". "No you won't".

01:38, Billy says bye to his grandmother, gives his friend Michael a kiss on the cheek. Time to hug his father and get on the bus to London. Tony says: "I'll miss you", but Billy can't hear him.

01:41, the miners resume work. Mrs Wilkinson, on her own in the boxing hall.

01:42, Jackie and Tony in London, fourteen years later. About to watch Billy's first performance in *Swan Lake*. They notice Michael in the audience, with his boyfriend.

01:43, Billy, twenty-five years old now, is told off stage that his family is in the audience. He springs onto stage, powerful, athletic, watched by his father who is overwhelmed with emotion.

\* \* \*

What's striking in *Billy Elliot* is how intricately the character-led subplot is mixed with the plot-led main plot. It's all about the characters. The antagonist struggling with his feelings and his prejudice creates the main source of conflict for Billy. Once Billy grows and manages to stand up to him, Jackie becomes a help rather than an obstacle. Billy experiences the most conflict in the main plot; his father, in both subplots. It's really a two-hander. If Billy's aspiration to become a ballet dancer were not so clearly what's at stake in the film, it would be a character-led movie. It's Billy's action – through his persistence and dedication – that causes the antagonist's evolution.

Hall also skilfully alternates highs and lows, funny and sad, exciting and touching. This emotional workout prevents linearity and boredom and helps create a moving piece. If we were to draw a line showing how the tone shifts during the story, it would be full of spikes and dips. Never flat. Each setback, each success, generating opposite emotions. This is exactly what we should try to achieve in a screenplay.

It might be clearer here who the protagonist/antagonist is than in a movie like *Heat*, in which the roles can more easily be switched. Yet *Billy Elliot* also allows us to empathise with both characters. If we feel more conflict for Billy and identify more with him than his father, we see it as a plot-led movie, but anyone who identifies more with the father would see it as a character-led movie. Remember, story structure is subjective. The way we perceive a story – and therefore its structure – can change not only between two individuals, but also depending on who we are at a specific time in our lives, even how we feel on the specific day we see a film. The same person could watch *Billy Elliot* aged twelve and identify with Billy, and watch it again aged fifty and identify with his father. What counts is whichever way you experience it, it works emotionally. This is the case in *Billy Elliot*, as it is in *Heat* or *Amadeus*. This delicate balance isn't easy to achieve, but when you have Hall's talent, well, you can write *Billy Elliot*.

*Billy Elliot* is an encouraging case study for non-Hollywood filmmakers because it proves it's possible to write a story set in a very specific place in the world, with a limited budget, no special effects or action sequences, and yet reach a wide audience worldwide. Not to underestimate the quality of everything else in the movie, especially the directing and acting, but to me a large part of this success is down to the story, its design, the way it uses visual storytelling – and music of course – to explore truly universal themes. Although what's primarily at stake is about self-actualisation and esteem (becoming a ballet dancer; overcoming prejudice), so hangs quite high in Maslow's pyramid, the subplots are all about love/belonging (Billy's relationship with his father) and survival of the family and community (miners' strike). Thus the story reaches almost all the way down to the bottom of the pyramid, which helps the film to widen its potential audience. Overall, I would give *Billy Elliot* a medium-high M-factor.

Let's take a look now at the STM (*Story-Type Method*) framework of *Billy Elliot*. You'll find more information on this key development tool as well as a link to download a template in the *Story Design Tools* section of *Bringing It All Together*. Again, there will be some repetitions between the analysis and the STM Framework. This is so that each part of the case study can be read independently.

# STM Framework for *Billy Elliot*

## STORY-TYPE, MASLOW FACTOR AND THEME

**Story-Type**: Plot-led.

**Main Problem in the Story**: The negative stereotype of the male ballet dancer is what's standing in Billy's way. This is the main source of conflict for Billy in his struggle to become a ballet dancer. He has to overcome it first in himself, then in his father, Jackie, and brother, Tony.

**M-Factor**: Billy's main problem sits right at the top of Maslow's pyramid. It's about self-actualisation (creativity, lack of prejudice, acceptance of facts) and esteem (respect to others and from others), which doesn't bode well for a large potential audience at first sight. Fortunately, two subplots in *Billy Elliot* reach down to more universal layers. The miners' strike subplot is entirely about survival – security of resources, employment, the community itself. The other subplot regarding Billy's relationship with his father is about love and belonging. This contributes to making the film relevant to a wider audience, because these are needs almost everyone can relate to. Overall I'd give *Billy Elliot* a medium-high M-Factor.

**Theme**: The main theme in *Billy Elliot* is simply to "be yourself", which is truly universal. Then of course the story explores the themes of prejudice against homosexuality and the male ballet dancer, how father and son deal with the grief of a deceased wife and mother, as well as the nature of the English class system in the eighties. It's a triumph over adversity story: the protagonist is struggling to be true to who he really is against family and social pressure to conform and become someone else, someone he doesn't want to be. This is what makes *Billy Elliot* such a universal, uplifting story, and helps it to cross borders. That, and the music track of course.

## MANAGING CONFLICT

**Protagonist**: Billy.

**Conscious Goal**: To become a ballet dancer.

**Motivation**: He loves dancing. As he explains to the school panel at the end, dancing makes him forget everything; it's like electricity. Subconsciously, it's also a way to be close to his late mother, who was a musician and loved Fred Astaire. His love of dancing, music and creativity no doubt comes from his mother's influence.

**Unconscious Need**: Billy needs to mend his relationship with his father. They both miss Billy's mother; they struggle to express their feelings and communicate with each other. In relation to his conscious goal, Billy needs to stand up to his father, which defines a growth rather than a change.

**Main Characteristic**: Billy is full of energy. It can be positive or negative, but he's always energetic.

**Secondary Characteristics**: Billy is talented, good-natured, non-judgemental. He has a sense of humour. He sucks at boxing and he loves dancing. Billy is also stubborn, hard-headed. This is the first thing we see, when he head-butts things in the kitchen or uses his head to open doors. It's both an asset and a liability.

**Evolution (growth, change or steadfast)**: Billy doesn't need to change because there is nothing wrong with him. However, he needs to grow; he has to stand up to his father in order to reach his goal. This happens gradually through the movie and climaxes when Billy dances in front of him. This is the first time he defies his father, and this is what Jackie needs to see to trigger a change in himself, to start supporting Billy, to let go of his prejudice. So Billy's growth triggers his father's change.

**Main Character**: Although the movie is about Billy, his father comes a close second. That's because although he behaves as an antagonist over most of the movie, he's not a bad person, only a grieving husband and prejudiced – but loving – father. His evolution – he's clearly the character who changes most in the movie – makes him the main character and protagonist of the character-led subplot. As a result, we feel a lot of empathy for him during the film. We don't approve of his actions, but we feel his pain. We identify with Billy, but we empathise a lot with Jackie.

**Main Plot**: Billy's struggle to become a ballet dancer.

**What's at Stake**: Will Billy be himself, as encouraged by his mother in her letter, or will he give in to family and society's pressure to conform?

**External Obstacles / Antagonist**: Jackie, the father – later joined by Tony, the older brother – represents the main source of conflict and obstacles for Billy. Jackie is the antagonist of the movie, but the protagonist of the character-led subplot, see below.

**Internal Obstacles**: Once Billy overcomes his own prejudiced view of the male ballet dancer, Billy's love and respect for his father, his attachment to his older brother become his main internal obstacles. It is, for example, what leads Billy to miss the first audition when he goes with his father to pick up Tony from the police station. No one forces him; he's simply supporting his family in a time of need. His fear of failure is another internal obstacle, which leads him to want to give up or argue with his dance teacher. It even tempts him to run away before the final audition. We know he has a natural talent for dancing, so we always believe he'll make it as long as he finds a way to overcome his internal and external obstacles.

**Catalyst**: Mrs Wilkinson is not only Billy's ally and co-protagonist, like all mentors and good teachers she also pushes him to *grow*, to develop his potential. She's Billy's catalyst. If *Billy Elliot* was a character-led story with Jackie as a protagonist, Billy would be his father's catalyst, forcing him to *change*, like Tiffany forces Pat to change in *Silver Linings Playbook*. We'll discuss the catalyst character in more detail in *Developing a Character-Led Story*.

**Subplots**: There are two main subplots in *Billy Elliot*.

The first is related to **the miners' strike**. It's about the survival of the mining community. The protagonists are the strikers (Will they get what they are fighting for?) and the supporting community. Tony is a leading figure in this fight, which provides a very strong socio-economical background and context to the story. It's really part of the texture of the film. Jackie, the father, is stuck in the middle. He doesn't believe they stand a chance. For him, it's already over. The subplot connects with the main plot when Tony's arrest leads Billy to miss the first audition, or when Jackie considers breaking the picket line in order to make money to help Billy achieve his dream. We know what it means for Jackie, the pain, shame and humiliation of being labelled a scab, which makes his sacrifice very moving. The subplot ends when the miners lose their fight, just as Billy is accepted into the Royal Ballet School. It feels like the end of an era, both for the community (the strike is over; they have lost their fight) and for Billy's family (Billy is going away; they have found a way out for him through his passion for ballet dancing).

The second subplot is related to **Billy's relationship with his**

**father**. They need to mend their relationship, which broke down when Billy's mother died. The problem is apparent right from the beginning of the movie, when Jackie asks Billy to stop playing the piano (his mother's piano). They are exploring opposite ways to cope with the mother's absence. Billy is happy to keep a connection with her through music and dancing; Jackie is trying to forget, to block anything that reminds him of her. This is resolved when Billy's father changes and starts supporting Billy, accepting him for who he is, and culminates in the touching scene when Billy and his father can joke and laugh together again. For the first time, they are connected, able to communicate and show affection to each other. This is the emotional, character-led climax of the movie, right after the plot-led climax (when Billy finds out he's accepted into the Royal Ballet School).

The protagonist of this subplot is Billy's father, because he's the one who needs to change and the one who experiences the most conflict in that subplot, even if it's also what causes a lot of conflict for Billy in the main plot.

This subplot is connected to the main plot as it feeds the motivations of the antagonist. Only when his father fully supports him – like his mother would have – does Billy stand a chance of making it. The subplot becomes the main plot when Jackie decides to help Billy and becomes a co-protagonist, after having spent most of the movie being the antagonist.

**Comedy:** There is a lot of comedy, even if it's not always the laugh out loud type. Billy's energetic nature makes us smile: he's so full of life that it's contagious. When he's dancing because he's happy or frustrated or furious (dancing is how he expresses his feelings), it's funny because it's extreme, yet truthful. His relationship with Mrs Wilkinson, with Michael, his gay friend, and with Debbie, Mrs Wilkinson's daughter, are also quite funny, in a touching way. Jackie's prejudice, his reaction to Billy's aspiration is funny too, at times.

## DRAMATIC THREE-ACT STRUCTURE

**First Act / Set-Up:** In about ten minutes, Billy is set up as a good-natured, caring, energetic boy who looks after his grandma. He misses his mother – he's drawn to music, a connection with her – and has a not-so-great relationship with his father and a classic relationship with his older brother. The miners' strike context is set up mostly visually. The first song over the opening credits works brilliantly ("Cosmic Dancer" by T-Rex) as it tells us almost everything we need to know about Billy in a visual way: his energy, his cheekiness. Very efficient set-up overall.

Right after the inciting event – when Billy discovers ballet dancing by chance in the boxing hall – at the end of Act 1, Billy first fights his own prejudice: he's concerned that ballet dancing is for "poofs". Debbie and Michael help him through that stage. This is the only dramatic sequence in Act 1. It lasts six minutes. Billy is not fully committed to his goal yet, so he's still in Act 1, but we are already in Act 2 because we're giving him the goal to overcome this and go for it.

**Inciting Event / Inciting Action:** Billy discovers ballet dancing at 00:10 when Mrs Wilkinson has to use half of the boxing hall for her dancing class. This is the event that will trigger Billy's conscious goal to become a ballet dancer. It's cleverly done, as it's ballet which crashes into his life. Billy is hooked straight away, but he has to overcome his initial reluctance before allowing himself to go for it. First he wants to leave the class but isn't allowed to, then he struggles for a while at the end of Act 1 before committing fully to his goal. Given his background, it makes it much more believable – and interesting – than if he had looked for ballet dancing and had instantly wanted to do it.

**Beginning of Dramatic Act 2**: We enter Act 2 as soon as Billy goes back to the dancing class and commits to learning ballet dancing, at 00:16.

**Sequences in Act 2**: There are five main sequences in the second act of *Billy Elliot*:

1. **The first sequence of Act 2 is thirteen minutes long**. It starts at 00:16, when Billy pays for the class and commits to coming back the next week. Subgoal: Getting better at ballet dancing without his father finding out. Protagonist: Billy. Antagonist: His father, victim of a strong dramatic irony which generates most of the conflict in the sequence: We fear the consequences of the resolution, the father's reaction when he finds out what Billy is up to. This happens at 00:26, when Jackie barges into a dance lesson and takes

Billy away, leading to the climax of the sequence. Billy tries to convince Jackie that it's fine to become a ballet dancer, but fails, telling him he hates him and calling him a bastard. The sequence ends at 00:30, when Billy goes to see Mrs Wilkinson and tells her he has to stop taking lessons. Billy has failed and gives up.

2. **The second sequence of Act 2 is twenty-four minutes long**. It starts at 00:34, when Mrs Wilkinson tells Billy that she's thinking of him for the Royal Ballet School and offers to give him free private lessons. The same dramatic irony is resumed: Billy's father still doesn't know, and we fear his reaction when he'll find out. Protagonist: Billy (and Mrs Wilkinson as co-protagonist). Subgoal: To get ready for the audition with the Royal Ballet School. The sequence ends at 00:58, when Billy doesn't show up to go to the audition due to his brother's arrest. Until now, Billy was drawn to dancing because it made him feel a connection with his mother. But when he sees his father suffer during his fight with Tony, Billy doesn't feel like hurting his father and deserting him for an audition right when his father needs him most. It's an internal obstacle – Billy's love for his father and attachment to his brother – that leads him to give up on that subgoal.

3. **The third sequence of Act 2 is twenty minutes long**. It starts at 00:59, when Mrs Wilkinson tries to convince Billy's father and brother to let Billy do what he's good at, but fails. The sequence is about overcoming Billy's father's and brother's prejudice. After Mrs Wilkinson's failure and Billy's inability to stand up to his father initially, Billy is offered another opportunity at Christmas, when his father finds him dancing with Michael in the boxing hall, at 01:10. The scene exploits and resolves the same dramatic irony (Jackie doesn't know that Billy is still dancing). Although the situation confirms Jackie's worst homophobic fears – he finds his son dancing ballet with a boy in a tutu – this time, Billy stands up to his father. He shows him what he can do, which leads Jackie to change his attitude and overcome his prejudice. This time, Billy succeeds.

4.  **The fourth sequence of Act 2 is only seven minutes long.**
    It starts at 01:12, when Jackie goes to see Mrs Wilkinson,
    thanks her for what she's done for Billy and tells her he's
    taking it from there. He's too proud to accept her financial
    help, so the sequence is about helping Billy achieve his goal,
    primarily to find the money to pay for the fare to London.
    The protagonist is Billy's father. Tony, first an antagonist
    when he tries to stop him from breaking the strike, joins
    him when he agrees that: "He's right. Mum would have let
    him" and says that they'll find another way. The community
    helps them, and the sequence ends when we understand
    that Jackie is going to sell his wife's jewellery.

5.  **The fifth sequence of Act 2 is fifteen minutes long,** and is
    the climax of the movie. The protagonist is Billy; his father
    is a co-protagonist. Subgoal: Passing the audition at the
    Royal Ballet School. It starts at 01:20, when Billy and his
    father are on the way to London, and it ends 01:35, when
    we find out that Billy is accepted, which is the answer to the
    dramatic question of the film: *Yes*, Billy will become a ballet
    dancer. However, the actual climax of the sequence is when
    Billy dances in front of the panel and answers their ques-
    tions. The answer to the dramatic question is just delayed
    from the climax of the sequence itself.

**Mid-Act Climax:** There is no mid-act climax in *Billy Elliot* as
Billy has the same goal (to become a ballet dancer) over the whole
movie, but the no-show at the end of sequence 2 at 00:58 would
probably be seen as a midpoint for those looking for one. It has
little structural significance, apart from being the end of a dramatic
sequence. Alternatively, Billy dancing with rage and frustration
from 01:00 to 01:03, after Mrs Wilkinson fails to convince Billy's
father and brother to let him do what he is talented at, and before
the time ellipse, could be another candidate. As there is no dramatic
justification for a midpoint, it's always a guessing game to find one
as it simply marks the middle of the screenplay.

**Climax of Dramatic Act 2:** The audition in front of the Royal
Ballet School panel from 01:20 to 01:30 is the climax of the film. It's
the last, strongest obstacle to overcome, both external, regarding the
decision of the panel, and internal, as Billy almost gives up before

the audition. We only get the answer to the dramatic question a few minutes later, when Billy finally receives the letter.

**Answer to the Dramatic Question**: We get the answer to the dramatic question when Billy's father finds out about the contents of the letter at 01:35. For Billy, it's a few minutes earlier, when he reads the letter but is too overwhelmed to share it with anyone else. The answer is *yes*: Billy is accepted into the Royal Ballet School. He will become a ballet dancer.

**When Do We Enter Dramatic Act 3?** We enter Act 3 at 01:36, right after we find out that Billy is accepted into the Royal Ballet School. Act 3 shows the consequences of the protagonist's action, mainly that the relationship between Billy and his father is healed. Billy also says goodbye to all those who matter in his life: Mrs Wilkinson; his grandma; his friend Michael; his father and brother. Finally, we see him as a grown up, being the ballet dancer that he wanted to be: athletic, powerful. We also see Michael and his boyfriend, and we see Jackie's emotion as he watches Billy dance.

*Encore Twist*: There is no *Encore Twist* in *Billy Elliot*, but there are many reversals. Billy keeps giving up for various reasons, but there is no final surprise in Act 3 relaunching the same action.

**Does the Answer to the Dramatic Question Convey the Point of View of the Filmmaker(s):** Yes, *Billy Elliot* is about the ability to be yourself, to stand up to family and social pressure to conform. Having Billy fail would go against the story entirely.

**Does the Answer to the Dramatic Question Fit the Genre of the Story:** Yes, *Billy Elliot* is not only a coming of age story; it's a triumph over adversity story, so it has to end in triumph, which it does.

**Is the Ending Satisfying?** The ending is satisfying on many levels.

First, Billy triumphs over adversity and does become a ballet dancer. That's the main point, full of optimism. Yes, we can be ourselves if we try hard enough and don't give up.

Then, Billy and his father mend their relationship, which is very satisfying emotionally and a big part of the story.

Finally, Billy's father overcomes his prejudice about ballet dancing, which makes us feel that anyone can change, can become a better person.

Overall, the ending of *Billy Elliot* might not show life as it is

– although it's a very truthful story – but it certainly shows it as we would like it to be.

**Duration of Dramatic Acts**: The first act is ten minutes long for the audience, sixteen minutes long for Billy, who has to overcome his own fears and prejudice before fully committing to ballet dancing. The second act is eighty minutes long, split into five dramatic sequences. The third act is seven minutes long. These act lengths (fairly short first act, a second act lasting most of the film and a very short third act) are typical for dramatic acts.

## MANAGING INFORMATION

### Main Dramatic Ironies:

There is a lot of dramatic irony in *Billy Elliot*. First, Jackie doesn't know that Billy is ballet dancing instead of boxing. Then, he doesn't know that Billy is getting private lessons to prepare for the RBS audition. Finally, he doesn't know that Billy is still dancing, with his gay friend Michael. These are variations of the same dramatic irony. As in a thriller, the victim is the antagonist and this generates suspense, because we fear the reaction of the antagonist when the resolution happens and the victim finds out.

### Main Surprises:

Mrs Wilkinson's offer to teach Billy privately and prepare him for the Royal Ballet School and Jackie's decision to go back to work are the biggest surprises. Otherwise, there are a few smaller ones, like Debbie's kind offer to show her fanny to Billy, and Billy matter-of-factly declining.

### Main Elements of Mystery:

There is very little mystery, except at the beginning when we understand that the mother isn't there anymore, but we don't know yet if she's dead or she's left them. It's minor and doesn't last very long.

### Main Elements of Suspense:

As discussed, the main element of suspense comes from the dramatic irony the father is victim of, as we fear his reaction when he finds out. There is also a strong suspense in the last, climactic audition sequence, as we wait to find out if Billy is accepted or not at the school. We know that his passion, his whole life, hangs on this decision. It first seems like he failed the audition, but what he says about dancing just before leaving gives us hope. The suspense remains until we find out.

# VISUAL STORYTELLING, PLANTING/PAY-OFF, EXPOSITION

## Planting/Pay-Off and Visual Storytelling:

Because of the importance of music in *Billy Elliot*, the story-telling is very visual. We have many dance sequences efficiently showing how Billy feels – happy, frustrated or angry. The most moving moments in the movie – when Jackie crosses the picket line and goes back to work; Billy stands up to his father and dances in front of him for the first time; Billy and his father laugh together in the end; Jackie sees Billy dancing during his first performance – all pay off an earlier plant. For example, what it means to be a scab is planted many times, so when Jackie goes back to work, we feel his shame, his humiliation, with no need for words. So there is a lot of planting and pay-off in the film both to generate an emotion and allow visual storytelling.

## Exposition:

There isn't much exposition in the movie. We learn through small, well-dramatised moments some key elements about the mother and the strike. There are no large chunks of exposition that would require special handling. The only significant bit of exposition is Billy's mother's letter. This is done skilfully as Mrs Wilkinson asks Billy to bring along things that are special to him. The content of the letter is moving, but there is no melodrama or pathos. Also it's not about past events, but about the way his mother still influences him and gives him the strength to be himself. Very well-handled overall.

# *Misery*

## Screenplay by William Goldman from a novel by Stephen King

## Directed by Rob Reiner

Detailed Analysis

**Note: As usual, it's best to watch the film – and, if possible, read the screenplay – just before reading the analysis.**

*Misery* is a 1990 American psychological thriller/horror based on Stephen King's 1987 novel. Directed by Rob Reiner, the film was critically acclaimed and Kathy Bates won the 1990 Academy Award for Best Actress. According to Wikipedia, the film grossed a total of US$61.3 million for a budget of US$20 million.

The following case study is based on the Blu-ray of the movie. The screenplay of *Misery* is available in *William Goldman, Four Screenplays with Essays* (Applause), along with notes about the development, casting and production of the movie. These notes can also be found in *Adventures in the Screen Trade* (Abacus), by Goldman as well. Both are highly recommended reading.

*Misery* is a brilliant example of a plot-led story. The protagonist, writer Paul Sheldon, has no need to change because the main problem lies outside of him, in the form of crazy nurse Annie Wilkes (the antagonist).

For this analysis we're going to go through the story in detail, discussing each significant plot point and looking at the way each dramatic tool is used. We'll also analyse a sixteen-minute sequence in the middle of the film to illustrate the fractal aspect of the dramatic three-act structure.

To help visualise the following analysis, here is the overall dramatic three-act structure of *Misery*:

# The *Fractal* Aspect of Structure

## *Dramatic* 3-Act Structure of *Misery*

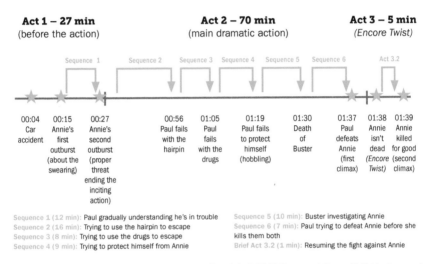

**Act 1 – 27 min**
(before the action)

**Act 2 – 70 min**
(main dramatic action)

**Act 3 – 5 min**
*(Encore Twist)*

Sequence 1    Sequence 2    Sequence 3    Sequence 4    Sequence 5    Sequence 6    Act 3.2

| 00:04 | 00:15 | 00:27 | 00:56 | 01:05 | 01:19 | 01:30 | 01:37 | 01:38 | 01:39 |
|---|---|---|---|---|---|---|---|---|---|
| Car accident | Annie's first outburst (about the swearing) | Annie's second outburst (proper threat ending the inciting action) | Paul fails with the hairpin | Paul fails with the drugs | Paul fails to protect himself (hobbling) | Death of Buster | Paul defeats Annie (first climax) | Annie isn't dead *(Encore Twist)* | Annie killed for good (second climax) |

Sequence 1 (12 min): Paul gradually understanding he's in trouble
Sequence 2 (16 min): Trying to use the hairpin to escape
Sequence 3 (8 min): Trying to use the drugs to escape
Sequence 4 (9 min): Trying to protect himself from Annie

Sequence 5 (10 min): Buster investigating Annie
Sequence 6 (7 min): Paul trying to defeat Annie before she kills them both
Brief Act 3.2 (1 min): Resuming the fight against Annie

The film starts with writer Paul Sheldon (James Caan) finishing his novel in an isolated mountain lodge and setting off back to civilisation. After four minutes, he has a car accident. Although it doesn't trigger a goal yet, it's an important plot point as it establishes the main dramatic situation: Paul in the hands of nurse Annie. In *Misery* we have an *inciting action* which unfolds over most of Act 1 – a few cumulative plot points which together trigger the protagonist's goal – rather than an isolated, well-defined inciting event or inciting incident. The car accident is the first part of the inciting event. The second part is the realisation that the protagonist is in the hands of a mad nurse. Take away one part – a mentally healthy nurse rescues Paul Sheldon after the accident, or Paul Sheldon can get away from a deranged nurse because he isn't paralysed by the accident and locked in her house – and you don't have a movie (well, at least not this one).

A quick flashback to a meeting with his agent Marcia Sindell (Lauren Bacall) tells us that Paul wants to "kill" Misery Chastain, the main character in his successful series of romance novels. He's not written anything else since he started the *Misery* series, and he's tired of it. He would like critical recognition, not just commercial success. He's going to Colorado to write a new book. This sets up an important dramatic irony: we know that the next volume of *Misery* (about to be published) will be the last of the series.

**Note:** This also makes Paul partially responsible for what happens to him, as things might not have gone so wrong with Annie if he hadn't decided to kill Misery in the first place. This is what helps avoid the melodrama present in less satisfying thrillers, when something bad happens to entirely innocent protagonists. While this can happen in life, it's usually more satisfying – and believable – if the protagonist is at least partially responsible for what happens in the story. Annie becomes an external obstacle with an internal origin, which makes the story more interesting.

00:06, Paul is rescued by someone who pulls him out of the car. Just after that, we meet his saviour when he comes to, in her house: Annie Wilkes (Kathy Bates), a nurse and his number one fan. Paul asks about hospital and is told that it's impossible because of the blizzard, plus the phone lines are down. It's important in a thriller to rule out the obvious options that anyone would try in this situation, so that we don't question the story and can empathise with the protagonist.

00:10, Paul's agent calls Buster, the local sheriff (Richard Farnsworth). She's worried because no one has heard from Paul since last Tuesday. He reassures her that Paul is probably fine.

00:12, we find out that Annie had "luckily" followed Paul, as she knows where he writes. This is why she was there to save him when he had his accident. She comes across as a bit of a stalker, but nothing too spooky at this stage. She asks Paul if she can read his new manuscript. Paul accepts; after all, she saved his life. Annie is grateful.

00:13, at the Lodge, Buster doesn't find anything out of the ordinary. Paul finished his book, paid and left, as usual.

00:15, in the meantime, Annie has read forty pages of his manuscript and she doesn't like the swearing. For the first time, she's verbally violent. Paul is shocked. She says she loves him (as a writer), but that's no comfort. This is the first indication that the situation could be worse than it seems. It's another key point in the inciting action.

00:18, on the way back, Buster spots a broken branch at the scene of the accident, but he can't find Paul's car because of the amount of snow. This exploits a dramatic irony (we know the car is there / Paul is alive, but Buster doesn't).

00:21, Annie sees the Sheriff but doesn't say anything about Paul. This strengthens the anticipation of conflict and the fact that she's not "right".

00:22, Annie has brought Paul's latest book from town. The last of the *Misery* series. Paul wants to talk to his daughter; Annie pretends she's called his agent and told her to call his daughter. A bit later, she's already read seventy-five pages. She loves the book. It's perfect. Further exploitation of the dramatic irony set up in the scene with the agent. We know Annie's unlikely to appreciate the ending and we fear her reaction.

00:24, we're introduced to Misery the pig. Another indication that Annie is not "right". Annie is about to finish the *Misery* book and find out about the ending. She still loves it. We learn that she was married once.

00:27, Annie has found out that Paul has killed Misery. She's mad with anger. First sign of physical violence (she looks like she's going to hit Paul with a chair but smashes it against the wall). She reveals that she hasn't told anyone about Paul. No one knows he's here. If she dies, he dies. She leaves. This is the last part of the **inciting action** that is going to finally trigger **Paul's goal: to escape, protect himself and survive**. What's interesting is that Paul will constantly have to find a balance between escaping / protecting himself / surviving. He could easily stay alive as a captive, or escape and die. But he has to escape *and* survive. This is what makes *Misery* such a great psychological thriller. It's not only about physical survival/escape, it's also about trying to handle a deranged antagonist.

**Note:** This is when we enter dramatic Act 2 as Paul now has a conscious goal, but we already knew that he was in more trouble than he thought. This dramatic irony generates a lot of conflict in what would otherwise be a long first dramatic act. Thanks to this irony, we lend Paul the goal of finding out what his true situation is. This happens in this scene, so the resolution of the dramatic irony coincides with the beginning of Act 2. We've given Paul the unconscious goal of finding out what we already knew, and when he does, he becomes an active protagonist. So while it looks like dramatic Act 1 is the recommended length for a first logistical act (thirty minutes in a two-hour movie), the audience was already in Act 2 thanks to the dramatic irony from Annie's first outburst minute fifteen (probably even earlier thanks to the poster and title). This is why it's so important to look at the way information is managed, and not only at the way conflict is managed using the protagonist–goal–obstacles device. Both elements are part of the story's structure.

00:30, Paul tries for the first time to get out of his room. Despite the horrible pain in his broken legs and arm, he manages to crawl to the door, which is locked.

00:31, Buster talking to his wife and Paul's agent. Paul hasn't used his credit card since the day he left the Lodge. Looks like he's clearly missing.

00:33, God has shown Annie the way. She wants Paul to burn his untitled manuscript. Paul tries every possible way to avoid burning his only copy, but she makes it clear she'll kill him if he doesn't do it. Gutted, Paul burns his book.

**Note:** This is a well-structured scene and a great example of the fractal aspect of story structure with a clear dramatic three-act structure at scene level. The protagonist of the scene is Paul, as soon as Annie explains what she wants him to do (inciting incident), his local goal is to avoid having to destroy the only copy of his manuscript. He tries everything he can think of to achieve this, but fails. This local goal goes against his overall goal of staying alive. It's only when he realises that she will set him on fire if he doesn't burn the manuscript that he gives up and destroys his work (climax of the scene). More on this in *Behind the Scenes*.

00:38, Paul understands that people are looking for him, but there is no way for him to signal his presence to the helicopter. He stops taking the pills Annie gives him, and starts hiding them.

## DETAILED ANALYSIS OF A SIXTEEN-MINUTE DRAMATIC SEQUENCE (Fractal Aspect of Story Structure):

**Note:** If you've already read this in *Sequence the Action*, feel free to skip this detailed analysis of the sequence.

00:40, Annie gives Paul a table, a chair and a typewriter, as well as a wheelchair. She expects him to write a new book for the series, in order to bring Misery back to life: *Misery's Return*.

00:41, Paul spots a hairpin on the floor. This inciting event for the sequence triggers a new subgoal which shapes the dramatic action of the next sixteen minutes: **using the pin to escape**. We enter the second dramatic act of the sequence. Annie is the victim of a dramatic irony: she doesn't know that Paul has potentially found a way to escape.

00:42, the *first sub-subgoal* from here is *to get Annie out of the house*. Paul uses the paper excuse and manages to convince Annie, but he pays a price (more pain!). First success for Paul.

00:45, Paul now has *to get out of the room (second sub-subgoal)*. He first needs to get the pin, then to open the door.

00:46, new success: he's out of the room. Paul can now *try to find a way out of the house (third sub-subgoal)*. But the front door is closed. The phone is a fake.

00:47, Annie is on her way back. Because she's a victim of a dramatic irony (she doesn't know that Paul is trying to escape) and she's the antagonist, we fear the resolution of that dramatic irony (How is she going to react when she finds out?). Paul is also victim of a dramatic irony: we know Annie is on her way back, but Paul doesn't. These two elements generate a lot of suspense and tension in the sequence.

00:48, Paul manages to catch the falling penguin, but he puts it back facing the wrong direction. This foreshadows the way Annie will find out about his escape attempts (and sets up a minor dramatic irony).

00:49, Paul visits the "pharmacy" and gets more pills.

In the kitchen, Paul has to give up the wheelchair (more pain), but the back door is locked too. It feels like the end of his sub-subgoal (he's giving up on finding a way out). This is in fact the mid-act climax of the sequence. The answer to the local dramatic question is *no*, the hairpin won't allow him to escape. Just as he spots a knife, which would trigger a new sub-subgoal (*to get a weapon*), he hears that Annie is back on the farm. We then enter the second half of the second act of the sequence. Paul has to deal with the consequences of his attempts to escape in the first half.

00:51, Annie's return triggers his *fourth sub-subgoal in the sequence: getting back to his room before Annie finds out.* There is a strong time-lock, which adds to the tension of the end of the sequence. He has to get back in the wheelchair, make his way back, close all the doors and lock his bedroom door, in just a few minutes. Success on this sub-subgoal, but...

Small local dramatic irony: we see that the pills are visible, but he doesn't. Just as Annie comes into the room, Paul realises that the pills are visible, which triggers his last sub-subgoal: *preventing Annie from finding out he's tried to escape.* He manages to cover the pills with his hands and send her away before she puts him back to bed, which allows him to hide the pills better. Success on this sub-subgoal. We enter the third act of the sequence.

00:54, Annie apologises about her bad temper; Paul jokes about it. This is linked to the drama of pretending all is fine in order to keep as good a relationship as possible with Annie and prevent one of her bad-tempered outbursts.

00:56, Paul is back in his bed. **This is the end of the "hairpin" sequence.** He's failed on the subgoal "using the pin to find a way to escape", but his exploration of the house has allowed him to get more pills, and he's managed not to get caught.

### END OF THE SIXTEEN-MINUTE HAIRPIN SEQUENCE

00:56, Buster in the helicopter spots the car. Everyone believes Sheldon is dead, except Buster who sees that someone has forced the car open.

00:57, Paul puts all the drugs into a paper sachet. He tastes the drug and swallows the shells of the pills to get rid of them. We understand he's going to try to use the drugs to get out, and this is going to shape the next **seven-minute sequence: using the drugs to escape**.

00:58, Paul starts writing. Annie's not happy. It's not good enough, and Paul realises she has a point. His plot is weak.

01:00, Paul has made changes. She likes it now.

01:02, Paul asks her to join him for dinner, to celebrate Misery's return. Touched, Annie accepts. We know he has something in mind with the drugs, but she doesn't (dramatic irony), and we don't know how he's going to do it (bit of mystery).

01:03, Buster starts to read Sheldon's books to see if they give him any clues.

01:04, it's dinner time. Paul suggests a toast to Misery. Asks for candles to get Annie away from her glass. This gives him enough time to pour the drug into her glass (and exploits the dramatic irony further: Annie doesn't know her drink has been spiked). This is the climax of the sequence. Not much conflict for Paul in this sequence. It comes mostly from the dramatic irony (Will she find out he's trying to drug her?).

01:05, Annie spills the wine. Paul's plan has failed. He's gutted. **This is the end of the "using the drug" sequence.**

01:07, beginning of a montage sequence showing the change of time/season: Paul writes on. Buster reads on.

01:08, Annie loves the new *Misery* novel. Paul goes on writing. Starts exercising, lifting the typewriter.

01:09, Annie is depressed, suicidal: she loves him, knows he doesn't love her. The book is almost over. His legs are getting better. He's about to leave.

01:10, she's got a gun. She's thinking about using it. This triggers a new subgoal for Paul in the **following nine-minute sequence: protecting himself from Annie's announced violence.**

01:11, Paul gets the kitchen knife (planted during the hairpin sequence).

01:12, Paul finds the "memory lane" book, and learns that Annie committed murders following her father's death, to get her job at the hospital and a promotion. She was arrested for killing babies, and put in jail. This is one of the main bits of exposition in the film and it's delivered visually.

01:14, Paul, back in his bedroom, rehearses how to use the knife.

01:15: Annie comes back to the house, but she doesn't come into his room. Paul relaxes.

01:17, Paul wakes up. Annie stands next to him, injects him with some drug. The climax of the sequence begins.

01:18, Annie knows he's been out of his room twice (pay-off for the penguin and resolution of the dramatic irony of Paul not knowing he made this mistake). She's found his knife and hairpin key. He's defence-less. Note that we don't see the resolution of the dramatic irony she was a victim of (Paul getting out of his room twice). She found out off screen.

01:19, Annie has found the solution to him leaving: she disables both his legs in the hobbling scene. Paul is in agony. **This is the end of the "trying to protect himself from Annie" sequence**: he's failed.

01:20, Buster witnesses Annie's verbal violence in town. This is **the inciting event for the following ten-minute sequence: Buster, protag-onist of the sequence, investigates Annie**.

01:21, Buster finds out about Annie's past in the library. His suspicion is strengthened. She knows Paul's work very well; she's his number one fan and has bought lots of paper recently.

01:24, Paul sees the Sheriff's car approaching. Before he can do any-thing, Annie enters his room and injects him again. She hides him in the cellar.

01:25, Buster visits the house; Annie provides an explanation for everything. The sequence exploits the dramatic irony (we know Paul is in the cellar, but Buster doesn't).

01:28, just as Buster is leaving (he's not found anything conclusive), Paul comes to and manages to attract his attention.

01:29, Buster comes back into the house and finds Paul in the cellar. Annie kills him. **This is the end of the sequence**. Buster has found out the truth about Annie, at the cost of his life.

01:30, Annie announces that this was unavoidable. More people are to come. She is going to kill them both. This triggers Paul's subgoal in **the last sequence: defeating Annie before she kills them both**.

01:31, his first sub-subgoal, when she comes back with the gun and a syringe, is to buy some time. He uses her fascination for the *Misery* book he's writing for her and asks her to give him the night to finish it. In the morning, they will have brought Misery back to the world and they will kill themselves. He manages to steal a small can of petrol.

Paul asks Annie for the three things he needs to celebrate the comple-tion of a book: one cigarette, a match and a glass of Champagne. This was planted at the beginning at the lodge.

01:37, **this is the climax of the last sequence and of the film**. Paul asks for a second glass, and uses the time to prepare to set fire to the manuscript. When Annie comes back, he sets the book alight, and as she tries to stop the fire, he smashes her head with the typewriter.

They fight. Annie falls on the typewriter and lies still. **This is the end of Act 2 and the beginning of Act 3: Paul has apparently succeeded in defeating her...**

01:38, **surprise**, Annie's not dead and attacks him. This *Encore Twist*, a surprise at the beginning of Act 3, leads Paul to resume the same dramatic action and starts Act 3.2, which is a single scene, not a long sequence as in *Gravity*. They fight again, and Pauls kills her for good this time with one of her pig statues (second climax). This is the end of Act 3.2. Please see *Encore Twist* in *Craft the Draft* for more details.

01:39, Epilogue (Act 3.3). Eighteen months later, Paul can walk to a meal with his agent. He confesses that in a way, this ordeal has helped him to become a better writer. We think for a moment that Annie may be back, as a waitress, but we realise that it's just a psychological consequence of his ordeal. He still sees her from time to time...

\* \* \*

As we can see, *Misery* is clearly plot-led: the main problem in the story, nurse Annie, is external. Paul, the protagonist, doesn't need to change. The main character is Annie, the antagonist. We're fascinated by her. We progressively realise the extent of her madness. We're shocked and surprised by every one of her fits of violence. Annie doesn't evolve much until the end, but our perception of her changes as the story unfolds. Overall she changes more than the protagonist, proving wrong the rule stating that the protagonist is the character who changes most in a story. This can be true for character-led stories but isn't necessarily the case for plot-led stories.

The simplicity of the structure, especially the way dramatic sequences are so clearly designed, makes it an ideal film to study the fractal aspect of story structure. Many scenes (for example when Annie forces Paul to burn his manuscript) or sequences (the hairpin and Buster sequences) show how the dramatic three-act structure can be used to shape scenes or sequences, with a local protagonist, local goal or subgoal, and local inciting events or climaxes.

*Misery* uses dramatic irony a lot, mainly to create suspense because we fear the resolution (we know Paul is trying to escape, but Annie doesn't) and we fear the consequences of the resolution, which is a classic way to generate tension in a thriller/action film, when the victim of the dramatic irony is the antagonist.

Also it has a classic protagonist/antagonist structure, Annie being the main source of obstacles and conflict in the story. One could even think that she engineered the whole situation. After all, she was following Paul, so couldn't she have provoked the accident?

One important point already discussed in *Happy Ending vs Satisfying Ending* is that in order to be satisfying, thrillers have to restore a stable situation. This is why Paul is seen walking at the end. After all he's been through, it would feel only partly satisfying if he was alive but disabled, because he doesn't deserve it. This is the reason why he doesn't have his feet cut off, as in the Stephen King novel. As discussed earlier, this was the subject of an intense discussion between the writer, William Goldman, and the director, Rob Reiner. Goldman was adamant Paul's feet should be cut off. Reiner thought it was too much and couldn't see how he could film the scene. He was right and Goldman later acknowledged it (see his *Adventures in the Screen Trade*).

Often a "happy ending" isn't about what's commercial versus what's artistic, but what's fair to the protagonist (i.e. ourselves, thanks to the identification process) versus what's unfair and undeserved. If the protagonist has a problem, and needs to learn a lesson, it's fine. But that's rarely the case with thriller/horror movies in which the antagonist/problem tends to be external. It's definitely not the case in *Misery*, as Paul's main problem is Annie. "Killing" Misery, which is the internal root of the problem he's trying to solve in the film, isn't serious enough (from our point of view) to justify losing his legs. It's interesting to compare it in that respect to a film like Cronenberg's *The Fly*. Seth Brundle (Jeff Goldblum) is much more responsible for what is happening to him in the film, and therefore may "deserve" to die, given what he's become through his own doing. We know he's doing something "wrong" with his experimentation, so we expect him to learn a lesson in the end.

Same thing in *Se7en*. Mills (Brad Pitt) fails to control his anger, which allows antagonist John Doe (Kevin Spacey) to complete his work.

If we look at Maslow's Hierarchy of Needs, *Misery*, like most good thrillers, has its main problem anchored right at the bottom of the pyramid: the movie is primarily about survival, so it can reach anyone. It explores lower needs such as safety of the body and homeostasis thanks to scenes like the hobbling. However, *Misery* also explores very interesting themes in relation to creativity, fandom and captivity. There are elements higher in the pyramid which trigger interest for a more sophisticated audience. This is why it works so well as a psychological thriller. It's mainstream, but with substance. Overall, I'd give it a high M-Factor.

*Misery* was made for $20M, with probably a good chunk of it above the line given the talent involved. From a below the line point of view, it's not a very expensive movie: no special effects; very few stunts; limited number of locations; a handful of characters.

The film made over $60M domestically and much more worldwide, so while not a blockbuster it was a very profitable movie. It was also turned into a play by William Goldman in 2012. The fact that it was an adaptation of a Stephen King novel written by one of the best screenwriters of his generation, directed by Rob Reiner and played by two fantastic actors certainly helped, but a contained horror/psychological thriller like this is achievable for an independent producer... with the right script!

Let's take a look now at the STM (*Story-Type Method* ) framework of *Misery*. You'll find more information on this key development tool as well as a link to download a template in the *Story Design Tools* section of *Bringing It All Together*. As usual, there will be some repetitions between the analysis and the STM Framework. This is so that each part of the case study can be read independently.

# STM Framework for *Misery*

## STORY-TYPE, M-FACTOR AND THEME

**Story-Type**: Plot-Led (PL), the main problem lies outside the protagonist.

**Main Problem in the Story**: Annie Wilkes, the antagonist.

**M-Factor:** The main problem explores universal layers such as safety of the body and homeostasis. It's Paul Sheldon's life that's at stake, and both his physical and psychological integrity that are threatened. This is where the main problem should be in good thriller/horror movies. However, there are thematic elements in *Misery* that explore higher levels in Maslow's pyramid, mostly in relation to creativity and self-actualisation. This opens up the story and gives it more depth, but it's not so abstract or cryptic that it would restrict the potential audience. Overall, I'd give *Misery* a high M-Factor.

**Theme**: On the surface, *Misery* explores issues around creativity, in connection with the dark side of fandom, personified by nurse Annie. Can a deranged number one fan dictate what you should write or not write? Is it possible to write under constraint? Can a mad fan's critique sometimes be right? Can creativity save a writer from a life-threatening situation? Can a writer recover creatively from such an ordeal? But behind all that, the main theme explores what happens to a writer who cares too much about the critics, who seeks critical recognition. So in a way, *Misery* is about a writer reconnecting with himself, instead of writing for the audience (the *Misery* series) or for the critics (his burnt untitled manuscript). All these fascinating elements exploring creativity, fandom and captivity contribute to making *Misery* more than a simple survival story. It's the substance under the brilliance of the writing, which permeates every sequence and every scene.

## MANAGING CONFLICT

**Protagonist**: Paul Sheldon.

**Conscious Goal**: To survive, protect himself and escape from Annie.

**Motivation**: He doesn't want to die, or have to spend the rest of his life with a crazy nurse.

**Unconscious Need**: There is no strong unconscious need for

Paul, and that's not a problem at all as we're dealing with a plot-led story. The only unconscious need we might identify is that Paul needs to care less about external validation, which he seems to reach at the end when he says he's written his latest book for himself and doesn't care about the critics anymore. But it's very subtle and not really explored during the movie; it's more a consequence of it. However, it's what triggers the whole situation, because that's what leads him to kill Misery and write a new book, both of which elicit Annie's anger.

**Main Characteristic**: Paul is first and foremost a writer. So being creative is his main characteristic.

**Secondary Characteristics**: Paul is resourceful, clever, determined, resilient. He doesn't give up easily. All these attributes make for a great protagonist in a plot-led thriller/horror.

**Evolution (growth, change or steadfast)**: Paul doesn't need to change because there is nothing wrong with him. The problem, Annie, is external. However, Paul *grows* as a result of surviving this ordeal. Apart from being less interested in external validation – he wrote his new book for himself – he becomes a better writer.

**Antagonist**: Annie Wilkes.

**Conscious Goal**: To nurse Paul back to health, to protect himself from his own failures, to keep him for herself.

**Motivations**: She loves Paul, first as a writer, then as a man. She wants to be with him forever.

**Unconscious Need**: There is no strong unconscious need for Annie in the movie, at least one that would be exploited dramatically. She needs to be loved, but we know that's unlikely to happen, so it's never a real question.

**Main Characteristic**: Annie is barking mad.

**Secondary Characteristics**: She isn't a two-dimensional maniac; she's also caring, sadistic, violent, romantic, religious, unpredictable. And she doesn't like swearing.

**Evolution (growth, change or steadfast)**: Annie doesn't evolve much until the end. It's mainly our perception of her which changes as the story unfolds. However, towards the end, she becomes depressive, suicidal when she realises that Paul is going to leave. This leads Paul to pretend they have to finish the book, to buy some time and find a way out.

**Main Character**: Annie (we gradually learn about her over the course of the film, mostly from Paul's point of view). We identify with Paul as a protagonist (he's the one experiencing most conflict in the film), but we are fascinated by Annie as a character. In other words, *Misery* shows Paul's dramatic action, we share his emotional point of view, but it's a study of Annie's character. As in many horror movies, the main character is the "monster", the antagonist; although it's not the case here, it often gives its name to the movie: *Jaws*, *Alien*, *The Terminator*, *Godzilla*, *Monsters*, *etc...*

**Main Plot**: Paul's attempts to escape, protect himself and survive (to consciously resolve the problem).

**Subplot**: Buster's attempts to find out what happened to Paul. The main plot and subplot are obviously related, and the connection happens when Buster investigates Annie and finds Paul in her cellar. The subplot briefly becomes the main plot in the fourth sequence of Act 2, when Buster starts to investigate Annie and ends up at her farm.

**What's at Stake**: Paul's survival and his physical/emotional/psychological integrity. Like all good thriller/horror movies, *Misery* tells a life or death story.

**External Obstacles / Antagonist**: Annie is the antagonist and main source of conflict for Paul. She's an external obstacle with an internal origin though. Who knows what would have happened if Paul hadn't killed Misery in his last book? Paul's physical condition (can't walk; in pain), following the accident, is an important external obstacle. Although this temporary disability is part of Paul, it's considered an external obstacle because it's physical, not psychological. The snow that prevents communications and slows down Buster's action is another one.

**Internal Obstacles**: None. Paul Sheldon has no internal source of conflict, except maybe when he tries to protect the manuscript that Annie wants him to burn. However, he's partly responsible for what happens to him as he's the one who decided to "kill" Misery in the first place. This makes the story more interesting, as he's not just the random victim of a psychopath.

**Comedy**: There is more irony than comedy, coming primarily from the contrast between Annie's actions and the way she forgets or minimises what she's done to Paul. Misery the pig is quite funny.

Paul's reaction to Annie's requests (for example when she wants him to write a new book after having forced him to burn his manuscript, or when she asks him to rewrite the beginning of the new Misery novel, are quite funny). Buster's relationship with his wife is also light in tone. This is a psychological thriller / horror; there is no need for a huge amount of comedy.

## DRAMATIC THREE-ACT STRUCTURE

**First Act / Set-Up:** As detailed below, *Misery* has a fairly long first act (around twenty-seven minutes). This is quite common with horror (and disaster) movies, in which the audience is frequently aware of an upcoming danger before the protagonist. However, the set-up is much shorter (see below, beginning of Act 2) as the main dramatic situation is established and the audience is hooked by minute fifteen, at the latest.

**Inciting Event / Inciting Action:** The car accident is the first part of the inciting event. It doesn't trigger the goal of the protagonist (to survive and escape) by itself; however, it creates the main dramatic situation. The second part of the inciting event is Annie's first outburst after fifteen minutes (the swearing). This triggers Paul's first active goal (he stops trusting her blindly and tries to get in touch with his agent/daughter/outside world). This is reinforced by Annie's second outburst, when she finds out he's killed Misery at 00:27. For the first time, she is threatening his life directly (if I die, you die) and he realises what his situation really is. This last outburst is the final part of the inciting incident, as it fully triggers Paul's conscious goal. Such a "late" start to the action could make Act 1 feel a bit long, but it's compensated for by 1) the anticipation of conflict and 2) the dramatic irony (we know something isn't right before he does). *Misery* illustrates why it's often more relevant to think of the first act as being the inciting action, rather than trying to pinpoint a single plot point as being the inciting incident. In *Misery*, we need three successive plot points to fully trigger the conscious goal of the protagonist.

**Beginning of Dramatic Act 2**: We enter Act 2 "proper" around 00:30, when Paul tries for the first time to get out of his room (and fails as the door is locked), because this is when Paul starts to do something about the problem. But we give Paul the goal of realising that his situation is worse than he thinks earlier than that, when we understand there is something wrong with Annie. This happens as early as 00:15 when she has her first outburst, or 00:21 when Annie sees the Sheriff but doesn't say anything about Paul. This dramatic irony means that we enter dramatic Act 2 before Paul, because we know more than the protagonist does, until 00:30 when Paul joins us and becomes proactive. In fact, because of the title, the poster and the genre, we know he's in trouble right from the beginning. It's just a case of the protagonist catching up with us.

**Sequences in Act 2**:

There are five main dramatic sequences in the second act of *Misery*:

1. The first starts around 00:40 and lasts until 00:56 (Protagonist: Paul. Subgoal: Using the hairpin to escape). He fails.

2. The second starts around 00:57 and lasts until 01:05 (Protagonist: Paul. Subgoal: Using the drugs to escape). He fails.

3. The third starts around 01:10 and lasts until 01:19 (Protagonist: Paul. Subgoal: Protecting himself from Annie's violence). He fails and is disabled again.

4. The fourth starts around 01:20 and lasts until 01:30 (Protagonist: Buster. Subgoal: Investigating Annie). He succeeds (Buster discovers Paul but is killed before he can help him). Note: Buster's goal in the film is to find what happened to Paul Sheldon. This sequence is a subgoal for him. So Buster reaches his goal just before he dies.

5. The fifth and last sequence in Act 2 starts around 01:31 and lasts until 01:37 (Protagonist: Paul. Subgoal: Defeating Annie before she kills them both). He succeeds this time.

**Mid-Act Climax**: There is no mid-act climax in *Misery* as Paul has the same goal over the whole movie.

**Climax of Dramatic Act 2**: Paul hits Annie with the typewriter, they fight and she falls (01:37). As long as we believe that Annie is really dead when her head hits the blunt object, we enter Act 3 and there is an *Encore Twist*. If we suspect she's still alive, we're still in Act 2 and there is no *Encore Twist*.

**Answer to the Dramatic Question**: This first climax brings a first answer to the dramatic question (of the last dramatic sequence of dramatic Act 2 and of the film): *Yes*, he's managed to survive and escape from Annie.

**Beginning of Dramatic Act 3**: We enter Act 3 when Annie's head hits the typewriter following her fight with Paul (01:37) and she collapses, apparently dead. We believe the action is over because Paul seems to have reached his goal and defeated Annie.

*Encore Twist*: Provided we believe her to be dead the first time, there is an *Encore Twist* in *Misery*; Annie isn't dead – surprise – she comes back for Paul at 01:38. This defines a mini three-act structure in Act 3 with an Act 3.1 (before the action resumes), 3.2 (as the same action resumes) and 3.3 (consequences of the action once it's really over). In a brief Act 3.2, Paul tries to reach the same goal again (defeating Annie), until he kills Annie for good with the pig statue. This second climax brings a second, final answer to the dramatic question: *Yes*, Paul manages to survive and escape. A short epilogue shows the consequences of the action once it's really over, mainly that Paul is a better writer now (creative gain) but is still haunted by Annie's memory (psychological scar). This brief Act 3.3 is the equivalent of dramatic Act 3 in a story without an *Encore Twist*. More on this in *Craft the Draft*.

**Does the Answer to the Dramatic Question Convey the Point of View of the Filmmaker(s)?** This one is for the filmmakers to answer, but there is no apparent contradiction between the meaning of the movie and the chosen ending. Yes, creativity and resourcefulness might get you out of such an extreme situation, but you will probably be scarred by the experience.

**Does the Answer to the Dramatic Question Fit the Genre of the Story?** Yes, it does. A horror/thriller usually shows how we can survive a terrible ordeal against all odds, mostly unscathed. The protagonist survives the situation, and the audience survives the experience. Showing that we can't survive a terrible ordeal is likely to be rejected by the audience if it feels unfair. That's why it's rarely the outcome of a satisfying thriller/horror, unless the protagonist deserves to die or achieves something through their death.

**Is the Ending Satisfying?** In *Misery*, the right balance is found so that Paul Sheldon survives mostly unscathed – he's able to walk at the end; his feet aren't cut off as in the original novel. There was nothing wrong in him, so he didn't deserve any stronger punishment. However, he suffers some psychological scars – after all, he was partially responsible, having killed Misery – but he's also become a better writer. So he pays a price for his "mistake", but he has grown as a human being. As a result, the ending of *Misery* is satisfying, especially with the last twist, when the waitress turns into Annie, which is an efficient and chilling way to show that Paul is psychologically scarred.

**Duration of Dramatic Acts**: Act 1 is twenty-seven minutes long; Act 2 is seventy minutes long; Act 3 is five minutes long (with an *Encore Twist*). However, as we've said, while the protagonist only starts to be active in the resolution of the problem after almost thirty minutes, the problem is clear to the audience earlier because we have more information, so the audience is in Act 2 before the protagonist, waiting for the protagonist to catch up.

## MANAGING INFORMATION
### Main Dramatic Ironies:
Most dramatic ironies in the film fall into one of the following three categories:

1.  We know that there is something wrong with Annie before Paul does. This generates a lot of expectation of conflict in Act 1, before Paul becomes a proactive protagonist.

2.  We know that Paul is trying to escape, but Annie doesn't. The antagonist being the victim of the dramatic irony, we fear the resolution (What will she do if/when she finds out?). We were right to be fearful because when she does find out, she hobbles him.

3.  We know what happened to Paul, but Buster (and his agent) don't. This means conflict for Paul. If they knew where he was, or what was happening to him, they would try harder / come for him earlier etc... We want them to find out so they can help him. Every minute lost by Buster may cost Paul's life (Of course, we don't want the film to end too quickly, so we don't *really* want him to find out too early).

**Main Surprises:**

The car accident is a surprise.

The fact that Annie is a woman is a surprise. When we see her stocky silhouette leave the scene of the accident carrying Paul effortlessly, we assume Paul's saviour is a man.

The fact that Annie is a nutter is half a surprise (we're kind of expecting it). But the extent and originality of her madness is a surprise.

For example, her first burst of anger when she doesn't like the swearing in Paul's new book, or the fit she throws when she finds out he's killed Misery in the latest volume of the series, are both surprising in their intensity.

Annie forcing Paul to burn his book is a surprise.

Annie asking Paul to write a new book – *Misery's Return* – is a surprise.

Discovering Annie standing next to Paul's bed is a surprise.

Discovering that Annie knew about Paul's escape attempts is a surprise.

The "hobbling" is a surprise. We were definitely not expecting that!

The death of Buster is a surprise, a shock even. Just when we thought Paul would be saved, all our hopes are dashed.

Annie's comeback after her apparent death is a surprise at the beginning of Act 3, which defines an *Encore Twist*.

The final vision of Annie as the waitress during the epilogue is a surprise we can't explain, until we realise it's in Paul's mind.

**Main Elements of Mystery:**

We know that there is something weird about Annie, but we only discover the extent of her madness gradually. We understand it fully when Paul finds the "memory lane" album and reads its contents.

We don't know exactly what Paul is planning to do with the drugs but we soon find out.

Same with the typewriter at the end. We only find out about his exact plan when it happens.

In general, less mystery than dramatic irony and surprises in *Misery*.

**Main Elements of Suspense:**

Most of the suspense at the beginning comes from us knowing more about Annie than Paul does. We know, for example, that she doesn't speak to the Sheriff. We know we're watching a thriller called *Misery*, but Paul doesn't. This dramatic irony increases the tension and makes us want to shout a warning to Paul.

Then there is suspense because we know about Paul's attempts to escape and Annie doesn't, at least for a while. This is commonly used in thrillers to create tension, because we fear the resolution: What will the antagonist do when this dramatic irony is resolved, when Annie finds out?

Finally, there is tension in the fight(s) during the climax(es) at the end because the strength of both opponents is matched: Paul is recovering physically, but he's still hobbled; Annie is a strong, crazy woman. There is also suspense because there is no way to know for sure who will win, and the source of danger for Paul – Annie, armed with a gun – is clear.

## VISUAL STORYTELLING, PLANTING/PAY-OFF, EXPOSITION

### Planting/Pay-Off and Visual Storytelling:

There is quite a lot of planting/pay-off in *Misery*. Everything happens for a reason and is caused by what's taken place before. From Paul's ritual which is planted at the beginning and pays off in the climax, to the penguin, which allows Annie to find out about Paul's escape attempts, to the presence of the knife in the kitchen, to the use of the drug. The burning of Paul's manuscript at the beginning of Act 2 also plants the way he will get his revenge and distract Annie during the climax, to avoid a *deus ex machina*. The storytelling style is very visual. The dialogue is excellent, but as much as possible is shown visually.

### Exposition:

There is very little exposition in *Misery*. Most of it is related to Annie's backstory and is handled mostly visually, through the Memory Lane album. There are a few lines of dialogue, for example when she talks about being married or about the trial in Denver. The other bit of exposition is the short flashback with Paul and his agent, which tells us that Paul wants to be taken seriously as a writer, and sets up the dramatic irony related to the fact that he's killed Misery in the last book of the series (which Annie isn't aware of initially).

# 3. Developing a Character-Led Story

## First Up

**We're going to use *Groundhog Day*, *Silver Linings Playbook* and *The Intouchables* as examples during this chapter, so it's highly recommended you watch these films before reading on.**

Character-led stories are less prevalent than plot-led stories, but they can be very rewarding. They can also be a little trickier to develop, as what's primarily at stake isn't what the protagonist consciously *wants*, but what the protagonist unconsciously *needs*.

This means that you can't really follow the classical paradigm, because what holds the story together isn't a main dramatic action but the character's evolution. Being aware of the difference between plot-led and character-led movies and using the *Story-Type Method* accordingly can help a lot. Here is how our initial definition of drama changes when we're dealing with a character-led story, as it becomes the *evolved* form of drama:

# Structure (Character-Led Story)

## Protagonist – Goal – Obstacles – Conflict – Emotion

The *evolved* form of drama:

- A character, the **protagonist,**
- tries to reach a **goal** (connected to an unconscious *need*);
- meets **obstacles** and
- experiences **conflict** and **emotion,**
- which force the character to *change.*

Even if you're mostly interested in plot-led stories, it's essential to understand how character-led stories work because that's the way you'll design the character-led element of a plot-led story, which is usually related to the protagonist growing rather than changing – although it can also be the antagonist, as in *Billy Elliot.*

Because this evolution often concerns one character, the protagonist of a character-led movie is usually a single protagonist, as in *Groundhog Day* or *As Good As It Gets.*

However, there are a few situations in which the evolution might concern a group of characters.

Romantic comedies can be plot-led, like *There's Something about Mary,* but very often they are character-led. The protagonist is the couple, and their problem is that they aren't aware yet that they're meant for each other. As long as there is enough chemistry between the two lead characters, we, the audience, will want them to end up together. This is what we identify as their need, which plays as a dramatic irony they are victim of over the whole film. If we don't identify that need, the romantic comedy is dead in the water, which is why finding the right cast is essential. So even if they spend the whole film arguing with each other (as in *You've Got Mail* or *The Shop around the Corner*), or choosing other partners (as in *When Harry Met Sally*), or being kept apart by an obsession for a former partner (as in *Silver Linings Playbook*), we watch how they evolve, how the conflict they experience forces them to change, how their relationship evolves, until they finally realise they are meant for each other. Of course we're not sure they are going to end up with each other, and the question has to remain open over most of the movie, but that's what we hope for.

If a romantic comedy doesn't end up like this, it might be a good idea to warn the audience right from the beginning, as in *500 Days of Summer*, and find a satisfying ending which doesn't involve the two main characters hooking up for good.

Another example will be movies in which the evolution of a larger group is at stake. For example, in *Little Miss Sunshine*, the apparent, conscious goal of the whole family is to get nine-year-old Olive (Abigail Breslin) to a mini-miss beauty pageant in time, but the real need for the family is to stop being so dysfunctional: a complete loser of a father obsessed with winning; a suicidal uncle; a brother who has stopped talking. While getting to the beauty pageant in time provides an external goal – and a strong time-lock – what's really at stake in the story is the evolution of the whole family, especially those who need to change: the father, the uncle, the brother. The conflict and emotions they experience on the road to the conscious goal is what forces them to change. And by the end of the movie, they are closer, more united. The family is healed. *Little Miss Sunshine* is a good example of a character-led movie disguised as a plot-led movie (like *Silver Linings Playbook* or *Two Days, One Night*).

So the three-act structure of a character-led movie plays differently, because it's shaped around the dramatic evolution of the protagonist rather than the dramatic action.

While in a plot-led movie we have a single protagonist trying to pursue a single conscious goal, in a character-led movie we have a single protagonist who needs to experience a single evolution. This evolution defines the main plot, which is why the protagonist can have more than one conscious goal, as in *Groundhog Day*, without this being a structural problem for the story.

The dramatic three-act structure is used, but it's based around a single *evolution*, not a single dramatic *action*:

# Structure (Character-Led Story)

## Why Three Acts?

1. The first act lasts until the audience understands the protagonist's need.

2. The second act shows the protagonist's evolution.

3. The third act shows the consequences of that evolution.

The fact that character-led stories are structured around a single *evolution* rather than a single dramatic *action* explains why they are difficult to develop using plot-led paradigms and are often crushed by the development process if not handled properly.

So how do we approach character-led stories? Well, first we *Map the Change*, then we *Sequence the Evolution*, and finally we *Grow the Draft*. As always, this isn't defining a methodology that's supposed to work for everyone. It just suggests elements of design which can be applied in any order and at any stage, consciously or not, depending on what works for each writer.

Let's discuss these techniques in the next few sections, drawing many examples from *Groundhog Day*, then we'll look at two case studies, *Silver Linings Playbook* and *The Intouchables*.

# 3.1 Map the Change

Just as we can split a dramatic *action* in dramatic Act 2 of a plot-led story, we can split a dramatic *evolution* in Act 2 of a character-led movie.

The main difference is that while in a plot-led story, the subgoals defining each dramatic sequence will be triggered by a conscious want related to the conscious goal, in a character-led story each dramatic sequence will be there to lead the protagonist to experience the conflict that's going to force the character to change.

If there is a unique conscious goal over the whole story, the subgoals will be ways to reach that goal, but underneath they are the means to force the character to go through the various steps of their evolution.

The character has an unconscious need, tries to reach a conscious goal, experiences conflict and emotion that force the character to change (or not).

Therefore the most important thing to do in a character-led story is define the way the character needs to change. What is the evolution the character has to go through? Not only what causes it – we'll get to that later – but what are the main emotional or psychological steps – usually around four to six – that make such an evolution possible and believable?

This is what I call *mapping the change:* defining a start point and an end point for the main evolution, as well as the main steps connecting these two stages:

# Structure (Character-Led Story)

## Map the Change

- Define the **start point** for the protagonist (usually struggling with a character flaw).
- Define the **end point** for the protagonist (failure or success at overcoming the flaw).
- Define **four to six psychological or emotional steps** to map this *evolution*.

For example, here is how we could map the change of Phil Connors (Bill Murray) in *Groundhog Day*.

Phil *needs* to become a better person to get Rita (Andie MacDowell), the woman he's fallen in love with. This defines his evolution in the story. Problem is, in life, this almost never happens, and when it does, it takes either a very long time or a huge trauma. So in *Groundhog Day*, Phil gets both. He's trapped in the same day – the worst one possible – repeating itself over and over again. This gives him both a traumatic experience and an almost infinite amount of time.

With this in place, here is how we can map his change:

**A** (start point in the story): Phil is an arrogant, selfish TV star (Rita tells him in the diner: "Egocentric is your defining characteristic"), unable to love anyone apart from himself (actually including himself, but he doesn't know that at this stage). He clearly needs to change and become a better person. This is the unconscious goal that the audience gives him at the beginning of the film. That's what we're hoping for. We see someone suffer, someone unhappy (even if he's not aware of it), and we hope he will get better.

**B** (end point in the story): Phil is generous and able to love other people. He is able to love himself. He has changed. He's got what he needed (he's become a better person) and as a result he gets what he wants (a way out of the situation and the girl he loves). It's a satisfying ending for him and us.

As we can see, this is a significant evolution. If we don't find a way to map how, psychologically and emotionally, this change is made possible by what happens in the story, the ending would feel artificial, especially if it's positive. Sadly, it's usually easier to get the audience to accept a negative evolution, because we see this more often. Many people become bitter, pessimistic, lose passion and enthusiasm; that's what "life" does to them. The opposite is less common, therefore more interesting as long as we can show it in a convincing, entertaining and moving way.

So, here is how we might break down Phil's evolution:

1. Phil is trapped in a nightmarish situation. He's stuck in time, the same awful day repeats over and over again and there is apparently nothing he can do about it. **He realises that he doesn't control his life as much as he thought he did, and is not all-powerful (step 1).**

2. Phil tries to deal with the situation without changing. He first tries to adapt, then to make the most of the situation, in a childish, selfish, manipulative, self-centred way. **When he fails to seduce Rita, it leads him to despair (step 2).**

3. Phil tries to commit suicide. He fails, but is "reborn" in some way. His old, arrogant self is dead. He starts to open up to others, and to make the most of the situation in a positive way. He begins to change, tries to make the most of every day. **He discovers compassion (step 3).**

4. The new Phil changes inside. He's not selfish anymore and is finally able to love. **He can reveal his true self, and as a result becomes lovable (step 4).** He seduces Rita (without trying this time) and is released from the situation.

Breaking down the evolution is more convincing – there are steps and causality in the evolution – but it would still be corny without lots of conflict.

This is why, once we have defined these psychological and emotional steps, we need to start thinking about the best way to make each one of them happen.

For each step in the evolution, what's the conflict, the emotion, the trauma, the discovery, the realisation that's going to make this change happen, that's going to move the character closer to – or further away from – their unconscious need?

This is when we can start *sequencing the evolution*: finding the various conscious goals – or subgoals if there is one conscious goal over the whole story – which are going to lead the character to experience the conflict and emotions that will cause the character to change, one step at a time.

Before we discuss this, let's take a look at the way you can map a change in your story, whether it's character-led, plot-led or theme-led.

## Tips: Mapping the Change in Your Story

**If you're developing a character-led story,** can you map the change, the evolution of the protagonist? Can you define the start point for the character, the end point – success or failure at solving the main problem – and the main steps making this change, this evolution, possible – and believable – or not?

To make sure you get a satisfying ending, especially if the protagonist fails to change, can the audience understand the mistakes the character has made, the wrong decisions that explain this failure?

If the protagonist succeeds, finds a way to change in the end, is it because of what happened in the story, because of the conflict experienced by the protagonist, the emotions the character has gone through, the choices – right or wrong – made by the character, or is it simply because the writer wanted the change to happen?

Mapping the protagonist's change in a character-led story is the best way to avoid an unsatisfying ending, one that feels artificial. It will bring causality to the story. The evolution, the change will happen because of what came before, because of the conflict and emotion experienced by the character, and not simply because the writer wants to make a statement. Or it won't happen because it's not meant to happen, because the protagonist is unable to change.

This has nothing to do with a happy ending or reaching the conscious goal. For example, in *Leaving Las Vegas*, Ben Sanderson (Nicolas Cage) reaches his goal of drinking himself to death, which is what he wants, but fails to change, to get better, which is what he needs and what we and Sera (Elisabeth Shue) wish for him as we care about him. We never really have a hope that he can change or that his determination to kill himself could falter. It's clearly not a happy ending, but it's a satisfying one because we understand how Ben's death brings him closure. It's moving, sad and depressing, yet strangely hopeful at the same time. Sharing Ben's last days has a positive impact on Sera's life, so the story isn't pointless.

**If you're developing a plot-led story**, can you define the growth of your protagonist, like the way Ryan Stone learns to cope with the death of her daughter in *Gravity*, or the way Jack Walsh moves on from the separation from his ex-wife in *Midnight Run*? This growth could stem from an unconscious need to resolve an internal problem, which will allow the protagonist to reach the goal. Make sure this flaw isn't so strong that it becomes the main problem, as this would make the story character-led. This growth could also be an evolution that happens as a consequence of the protagonist's action.

Can you define an evolution in another character, using the same principles, like the change in *Billy Elliot*'s father turning him from an antagonist into a co-protagonist, or the way Marty's parents are transformed by his action in the past when he comes *Back to the Future*?

The evolution of one or more characters is often what adds depth to a story. It can even be what the story is really about, what conveys most of its meaning. In buddy movies, the evolution, the change is centred on the relationship between the two main characters. This is often an important part of the story, if not the main part. Even if they have a strong goal and a clear protagonist, as in *Planes, Trains and Automobiles*, *Lethal Weapon* or *Midnight Run*, mapping this change, mapping this evolution will help you plot the story.

So if you don't want your plot-led story to lack depth, meaning or warmth, think about a change, an evolution – possibly more than one – that you could define, and map it! Be careful not to have too many, or you might end up with a theme-led story. That's no bad thing, just something to be aware of.

Important note: Try to avoid the clichés, especially in action movies, like the dead wife (*Lethal Weapon*), the ex-wife (*Die Hard*), the estranged daughter (*Taken*), etc. They did well in the past – before they became clichés – but they are getting a bit long in the tooth now, which is why *John Wick* kind of makes fun of it. Not only does the wife die, but the dog she sends him from beyond the grave is killed too. That's backstory and motivation for you! Remember that the protagonists of a plot-led movie don't have to change because the main problem isn't within them, but outside them. So make the most of that, give your protagonist a more original, subtler way to grow.

The supposed rule that a protagonist is the character who changes most isn't based on anything solid and doesn't apply to plot-led stories. Remember that identification is linked to the amount of conflict the protagonist experiences, and forget about a heavy backstory if you can. If you have to have one, at least make it fresh and either avoid the clichés or make sure the audience knows you know it's a cliché and play with that.

**If you're developing a theme-led story**, a multi-stranded narrative, look at each strand and decide whether it's plot-led or character-led (sometimes it might be both). Look for a growth or change in one or more characters, and map that change or evolution within the strand, making sure that it's triggered by conflict and emotion experienced by the characters as they try to reach their respective goals.

All the strands in a theme-led story explore the same theme, but the only way to get the audience to relate to the characters is if they are actually trying to solve – consciously or not – a problem connected to that theme. Otherwise, it will feel as if we're standing on a soap box with a megaphone, using the characters to explain the theme to the audience.

There are a few theme-led stories which have only plot-led strands, but they tend to be in the minority. Most theme-led stories are about characters, human beings facing the same problem in society. If you want the story to be moving, entertaining and meaningful despite the lack of an overall three-act structure, get some of the characters to change or fail to change to illustrate your point and explore your theme. More details on this in the next chapter, *Developing a Theme-Led Story*.

# 3.2 Sequence the Evolution

Okay, now we've defined the main steps mapping the change, making it possible, believable and leading to a satisfying ending, let's sequence this evolution.

This means defining clear dramatic sequences in dramatic Act 2 so that in trying to reach a conscious goal or subgoal, the protagonist is forced to change. Experiencing conflict in the story because of what the character consciously *wants* makes each step towards the unconscious *need* happen (or not). Clear as mud? Let's try again.

When do we change in life? Usually, when we have to, when we are forced to. Otherwise we tend to resist change because we know it's difficult; change is painful. So what forces us to change? Yes, you guessed it. Conflict. The bigger the conflict, the bigger the change. A near-death experience or losing a relative can lead you to reconsider all your priorities and what you value in life, but even smaller events like getting a divorce, losing a job, a friend, winning the lottery, being the victim of a crime can cause major changes in someone's life.

A good way to generate comedy is to show a character not changing when experiencing a massive conflict. It's funny because it doesn't feel real. Likewise, a change happening without conflict for the character doesn't feel true or meaningful, but arbitrary and superficial. Simply because we know that in life, we resist change. As a result, if you want to make a character change believable in a story, you need to define the conflict that causes it.

So what we're going to do in a character-led movie is take each emotional step and find the conflict or emotion that would make it happen. Then we'll try to find the conscious goal or subgoal that will lead the character to experience this conflict or emotion, forcing the character to change, one step at a time, and develop each sequence accordingly:

## Structure (Character-Led Story)

### Sequence the Evolution

- For each emotional or psychological step, **define the conflict that might cause it.**
- Then decide which **conscious subgoal** could lead to this conflict (as a result of the **character's action**).
- **Develop each dramatic sequence accordingly**, so that by trying to reach each conscious subgoal, the protagonist experiences the conflict that forces a *change*.

Again, this isn't defining a methodology. Writers rarely do it this way. They end up with something like this, often having not realised consciously how they got there. If the screenplay works, great. If it doesn't, mapping the change to try to see if some steps are wrong or missing or checking if dramatic sequences are actually generating the right conflict to make each step happen can be a good way to diagnose and fix character-led stories (or a character-led subplot in a plot-led story).

If we go back to our *Groundhog Day* example, here is how we can sequence Phil Connors' evolution once we've mapped his change, by defining which conscious subgoal causes each step to happen in relation to Phil's unconscious need:

1.  Phil first starts dealing with the situation by **trying to find a way out (conscious subgoal 1)**. This defines the first dramatic sequence of Act 2 and quite a few sub-subgoals. He tries to get help from Rita, then from a neurologist (Harold Ramis himself), finally from a shrink. **He fails (conflict)**, and as a result **starts to realise that he is not all-powerful** (emotional/psychological **step 1** on the road to his change). He ends up in a bar, drowning his sorrows, where he discovers the positive side of the situation: the absence of consequences. What if there were no tomorrow? We could do anything we want! This triggers the next sequence:

2.  Phil decides to **make the most of the situation, in a negative way (conscious subgoal 2).** This defines the second dramatic sequence of Act 2, full of various sub-subgoals. First a warm up: he punches Ned Ryerson, stuffs his face with food, quits his job, seduces Nancy Taylor, robs a bank and lives his wildest fantasies. He enjoys the power that comes from knowing what is going to happen (dramatic irony offers a similar kind of control and power to the audience, by the way). He has no worries. But he ends up feeling empty inside ("If you had only one day to live, what would you do?"), and decides to move on to what really matters to him: Phil tries to seduce Rita. It first looks like it's working, but he's manipulating her; she senses it and he fails (Rita: "I'll never love you because you'll never love anyone but yourself". Phil: "That's not true. I don't even love myself!"). The situation may give him some power, but he nevertheless experiences **conflict.** Phil realises **he's still powerless regarding things that really matter** (seducing Rita and getting out of the situation). **He ends up exhausted and depressed (step 2),** which triggers the next sequence:

3.  Phil comes to the conclusion that there is an extreme way to deal with the situation: **committing suicide (conscious subgoal 3).** After numerous unsuccessful attempts (and as many sub-sub-goals), he fails to kill himself and as a result **realises that he has no power, not even the power to take his own life (conflict).** So, even if he doesn't die, the old, arrogant Phil dies. A new Phil is born. He stops doing things for himself, and starts doing things for others: **Having failed to get what he wants forces him to look outside, to turn to other people (step 3).** This triggers the last sequence:

4.  Phil then starts to **make the most of the situation, in a positive way (subgoal 4).** He first spends some time with Rita, trying to understand the situation. He's mistaken as he seems to think he's some sort of God, but he's honest with Rita. He's no longer attempting to seduce her. His love for her is genuine. For the first time he's sincere, and tries to get her to spend the day with him. He's not trying too hard. He's not controlling. Rita tells him she loves him, and we hope it may mean he's on his way out of the spell. But it's not the case. In the next few scenes, Phil is not concentrating on Rita anymore. He tries to do as much good as he can in one day, which starts to change him internally.

**He still experiences conflict even with this positive goal,** for example from failing to save the old man. Phil becomes less and less selfish. As a result, people start to love him. **He starts to love himself (step 4).** He's confident and peaceful: "Whatever happens tomorrow, I'm happy because I love you". Rita sees that and loves him even more. This is the climax of the subplot – same as his unconscious goal (to become a better person) – and also of the main plot: Now that he deserves her, he gets Rita and is allowed out of the situation.

This is how conflict and causality are used to get the audience to accept Phil's extreme evolution and feel satisfied by it. The conflict experienced by Phil trying to reach each conscious subgoal generates the conflict that triggers an internal change. The character tries to do something (dramatic action) and experiences conflict and emotion that cause one small change towards an unconscious need (dramatic evolution). The protagonist can have different conscious goals, because what holds the story together isn't one single conscious goal but one single evolution.

Now that we've defined the main dramatic sequences breaking down dramatic Act 2 into more manageable units, we can show what the dramatic three-act structure of *Groundhog Day* looks like:

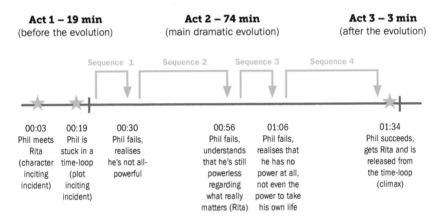

# The *Fractal* Aspect of Structure

## *Dramatic* 3-Act Structure of *Groundhog Day*

**Act 1 – 19 min**
(before the evolution)

**Act 2 – 74 min**
(main dramatic evolution)

**Act 3 – 3 min**
(after the evolution)

Sequence 1   Sequence 2   Sequence 3   Sequence 4

| 00:03 | 00:19 | 00:30 | 00:56 | 01:06 | 01:34 |
|---|---|---|---|---|---|
| Phil meets Rita (character inciting incident) | Phil is stuck in a time-loop (plot inciting incident) | Phil fails, realises he's not all-powerful | Phil fails, understands that he's still powerless regarding what really matters (Rita) | Phil fails, realises that he has no power at all, not even the power to take his own life | Phil succeeds, gets Rita and is released from the time-loop (climax) |

Sequence 1 (10 min): Trying to find a way out of the situation
Sequence 2 (25 min): Making the most of the situation in a negative way
Sequence 3 (10 min): Trying to commit suicide
Sequence 4 (28 min): Making the most of the situation in a positive way

Note that while we have only four main dramatic sequences, sequence two and four are split into many scenes with a clear protagonist / goal. However, they all fall within the main subgoal defining the sequence. There is no fixed magic number regarding how many sequences we should have or how many minutes each sequence should last for. This is the beauty of the fractal aspect of story structure and of using dramatic acts and sequences instead of logistical ones. You can still cut down your acts into more manageable sequences, but they don't have to fit an arbitrary, one-size-fits-all paradigm.

Of course, a lot of foreshadowing and pay-offs, plus plenty of dramatic irony, help make the story very enjoyable, moving and entertaining. But Phil's extreme evolution is accepted because it shows a believable metaphor of everyone's struggle to deal with life (looking helplessly for answers;

taking advantage of others; contemplating suicide; helping others). The positive ending gives us hope, even if we know that it's unlikely we'll ever manage to achieve a transformation as extreme as Phil's. Well, not in just one life, but he had eternity!

Now that *mapping the change* and *sequencing the evolution* are hopefully clearer concepts, we're going to discuss how we can *grow the draft*. But before that, let's take another look at your project and share a few more tips.

## Tips: Sequencing the Evolution in Your Story

So, we're back to your project.

You've mapped the change and have identified any missing steps, any wrong steps, any steps that don't make sense or go against the evolution of your character, or any steps that run in the wrong order.

Here are a few key elements which can help you sequence the evolution:

**If you're developing a character-led story:**

- First make sure that the change in your protagonist represents the biggest problem in the story. If it's not – use Maslow to try to assess which problem might be seen as most important by the majority of the audience – you might be dealing with a plot-led story with a strong character-led element or subplot, like *Midnight Run* or *Billy Elliot*. This is why it's difficult to make character-led disaster movies or thrillers: in these stories the main problem lies outside the protagonist. So identify this before going forward, or you might end up with a structural problem (or a successful hybrid/exception if you find a way to handle this well). Once you've checked you're actually developing a character-led movie, ask yourself the following questions:

- Would your story benefit from an overall conscious goal which would be the same for your protagonist over the whole film?

Like Pat (Bradley Cooper) trying to get his ex-wife back in *Silver Linings Playbook*. This means that your story will look like it's plot-led, but will be in fact a character-led story disguised as plot-led. The audience will be aware very early in the story that what's at stake isn't: "Will the protagonist reach the conscious goal?" but: "Will the protagonist reach the unconscious need?". In *Silver Linings Playbook*, we don't spend the whole film wondering if Pat will get his ex-wife back. We know he shouldn't and probably won't. We know he's wrong to want that. Instead, we wonder if he'll find a way to get better, which is what he needs, and we hope he'll end up with Tiffany, who is the right woman for him. The main problem is internal (Pat *needs* to get better and realise that Tiffany is the right woman for him) rather than external (Pat *wants* to get his ex-wife back). This is what defines the story as being character-led. This is crucial because very often, in a character-led story structured in such a way, the protagonist will realise in the end that he or she was wrong, and will give up the conscious goal. Giving up what they want so they can get what they need is a common ending for character-led stories structured around a single conscious goal, like *Silver Linings Playbook* or *Two Days, One Night*.

 - Would your story benefit from various conscious goals not necessarily connected to each other, as in *Groundhog Day*? A main conscious goal could start the story after a strong inciting event, like finding a way out of the situation in *Groundhog Day*, but that conscious goal can be abandoned, replaced by another (seducing Rita for example) not directly connected. This would be a problem – or possibly an exception – in a plot-led story, but in a character-led story it's fine as long as you make it clear to the audience that what's at stake is what the character needs, not what the character wants. In *Groundhog Day* or *As Good As It Gets*, the structural backbone of the story isn't a single, apparent, strong, conscious goal, it's a single evolution linked to an unconscious need. So you can sequence this evolution using subgoals which aren't directly connected, as long as the conflict created by these subgoals causes steps, minor changes on the same, unique evolution.

**If you're developing a plot-led story:**

In this case, the evolution – usually a *growth* rather than a *change* in the protagonist, sometimes a change in the antagonist or any other character – doesn't define the main problem. It might be what adds depth, possibly conveys most of the meaning, even what we're most interested in, but it's not what's at stake, or you'd be developing a character-led story.

Very often, your protagonist will need to change in order to stand a chance of reaching the goal, or will change as a result of having experienced the story. You need to be clear about that so your movie engine fires on all cylinders. For example, in *Midnight Run*, the characterisation is very strong and we have two main evolutions in the story: one is Jack Walsh (De Niro) moving on from the separation with his ex-wife; the other is the evolution of his relationship with Jonathan "The Duke" Mardukas (Charles Grodin). These are the two evolutions that you would want to map in this story. You wouldn't sequence them, because the main plot is about the external problem, not either evolution. Instead, you'll define the key moments which map these changes and find a way to connect them with the plot. The plot makes the changes happen, and the changes make the plot happen. But you have to get your priorities right. In a plot-led story, you're sequencing the *action*, not the *evolution*. It's the protagonist's single conscious goal that breaks dramatic Act 2 into sequences, not any change or evolution. You can sequence a character-led subplot, especially if the protagonist of that subplot isn't the protagonist of the main plot, but often it will be just one sequence (one subgoal) with a few sub-subgoals.

**If you're developing a theme-led story:**

Let's say that there is no single protagonist in your story, that you have many characters who don't share the same goal. You're dealing with a multi-stranded narrative, a story with only subplots connected by the same theme and no main plot. In this case, you're first going to look at each strand (parallel subplot) and identify if it's plot-led or character-led. Then, you're going to sequence each one according to its story-type. You'll first map the change of each character-led strand. Then you'll sequence each strand, sequencing the dramatic *action* of plot-led ones and sequencing the dramatic *evolution* of character-led ones. You'll deal with them exactly as if they were mini-movies, just not as complex as you don't have the space to develop each strand the way you could if you were developing a plot-led or character-led story. For example, in *Crash*, we have eight different strands, some are plot-led, some character-led, some both, and each strand is developed accordingly. All strands are connected to the same theme, and each strand is connected to at least one other strand, sometimes more than one. Again, more details on theme-led stories in the next chapter, but this is the general idea.

Now, ready? Steady? Grow!

# 3.3 Grow the Draft

Once we've mapped a change and sequenced a main evolution – whether it's the main plot in a character led-story or a character-led subplot in a plot-led or theme-led story – we need to grow the draft around it.

This simply means that we want to make sure that the plot and evolution are linked, from the beginning of the story until the end.

We want the protagonist's evolution to be caused by what happened in the story. We don't want it to be something that just happens at the end. We also want the ending to be a consequence of the action.

What's tricky in character-led movies is that we tend to have two inciting events that are not necessarily connected. For example, in *Groundhog Day*, Phil (Bill Murray) being stuck in time is the inciting event that causes the external story, starts the situation and triggers his first conscious goal (finding a way out). But the true inciting incident, the event that actually causes the story to happen, is when he first meets Rita (Andie McDowell) three minutes into the film. Everything else happens because of that. Unconsciously, he knows he doesn't deserve her; therefore, he has to become a better person.

Also, in character-led stories, there is often a character who triggers the change or makes the change necessary. This catalyst character is Rita in *Groundhog Day*, Carol (Helen Hunt) in *As Good As It Gets*, Driss (Omar Sy) in *The Intouchables* or Tiffany (Jennifer Lawrence) in *Silver Linings Playbook*. Not all romantic comedies are character-led stories, but when they are, they often work this way: for the protagonist, changing becomes a way – the only way – to get the girl (or the boy).

It's similar for the character-led element in a plot-led story. Jonathan Mardukas (Charles Grodin) is the catalyst who forces Jack Walsh to change in *Midnight Run*, allowing him to get what he needs in the end: to move on from the separation with his wife.

So defining the true inciting event, the one that triggers the unconscious need, as well as finding the best catalyst to make this change happen, is a crucial part of growing the draft in a character-led story.

Another very important point to remember is that in a character-led story, the protagonist *is* the antagonist. Most of the conflict and obstacles come from the protagonist (which makes sense, as the main problem in the story lies within the protagonist). The protagonist is fighting against an internal flaw, internal demons. There might be antagonistic characters, but they are not true antagonists. They tend to be catalysts, people – or situations – who force the protagonist to change. The protagonist's main action in a character-led story is to resist change, or experience pain as a result of the changes caused by the story. It's crucial to keep this in mind because it's almost the opposite of what happens with a plot-led story, in which by definition most of the conflict comes from outside the protagonist, from other characters – sometimes a true antagonist – or nature.

Because we are more aware of the protagonist's need to change than the protagonist, this sets up a strong dramatic irony which is exploited over most of the story. However, the resolution is frequently not shown. Instead, we often have what I call a reveal scene, in which the protagonist reveals that he was aware from the beginning, just not consciously. This scene is present, for example, in *Groundhog Day*, when Phil Connors tells Rita that he knew he had to become a better person the moment he met her to stand a chance to deserve her. In *As Good As It Gets*, this is the scene in the restaurant when Melvin Udall tells Carol he realised, when she came to see him at his flat, that she made him want to become a better man. In *Silver Linings Playbook*, this happens right at the end when Pat tells Tiffany that he fell in love with her the minute he met her, but he just got stuck. This device is interesting because it's almost a reversal of the dramatic irony. It makes the protagonist smarter by suggesting that even if they didn't act that way, they knew all along. It's a way to get even with the audience, who have enjoyed thinking they were ahead over most of the movie, only to realise that the protagonist wasn't that stupid or deluded. Of course we don't need a reveal scene in every character-led screenplay, but it's an interesting option to consider. Well-handled, it can be effective and rewarding as a final surprise / pay-off.

Another thing to keep in mind: In a character-led story, the theme is often connected to the evolution of the character rather than to the dramatic action. This is why a character-led subplot in a plot-led movie often conveys more meaning than the main plot.

Finally, we have to find a satisfying ending and this is directly connected to what causes the protagonist to succeed and change, or to fail and remain flawed. The ending doesn't have to be happy, and the protagonist doesn't have to change, but for the ending to be satisfying we have to understand what makes the evolution possible or not, and in which way this ending is meaningful. In a character-led movie, we have to separate the conscious goal from the unconscious need, because often giving up the former is what will lead the protagonist to reach the latter.

To sum it up, here is how we can grow the draft of a character-led movie:

## Structure (Character-Led Story)

### Grow the Draft

- Look for **two potential inciting events** (one related to the conscious want, the other to the unconscious need).
- Find the right **catalyst** to provoke the change.
- Remember that in a character-led story **the protagonist *is* the antagonist.**
- Consider a *reveal* scene to reverse the dramatic irony and offer a final surprise / pay-off.
- The *theme* is usually **connected to the evolution.**
- Find a **satisfying ending.**

We're going to look at a few case studies to clarify all this, but before we do that let's see how we can apply all this to your character-led story, if you are developing one.

## Tips: Growing Your Draft

Hands-on

All right, you've *mapped the change* and *sequenced the evolution* of your character-led story – or the character-led subplot(s) of a plot-led or theme-led story – so what's next?

Again, this isn't a methodology or a conscious task for most writers. *Growing the draft* is an organic process, not a step-by-step recipe.

However, there are a few things we can do to check key aspects of your project's structure.

First, much of what we've discussed in *Craft the Draft* for plot-led movies also applies to character-led movies, so going back and taking another look at this section might be helpful. There are differences, like the need to define/locate two possible inciting events (an internal one *and* an external one), but overall most of the content of the previous chapter will help develop a character-led story.

While *Sequencing the Action* becomes *Sequencing the Evolution*, all the tools explored in *Behind the Scenes* are also used in character-led stories, not only in scenes but at sequence and script level, so if you skipped the whole chapter about plot-led stories, I'm afraid it's time to go back.

In fact, character-led stories are a bit like advanced plot-led stories. Mastering plot-led stories will definitely help you to handle character-led ones, and in turn understanding how character-led stories work will help make plot-led ones more complex and interesting. Understanding how both work will also be crucial when developing theme-led stories, which we'll get to in the next chapter.

The main thing to bear in mind is that the border between the two story-types isn't like the Great Wall of China. Very often, you'll be dealing with a hybrid or an exception, so the most important thing is to understand the principles and relax about the perceived rules. There aren't any!

Movies like *Billy Elliot, Edge of Tomorrow* or *Midnight Run* are very close to being character-led stories. What you want is a story that works, that gets the reader or the audience wanting to know what's going to happen next. If you're starting out in screenwriting, sticking to a clear story-type can help, but what counts isn't the theory or the way we label story-types to try to make the theory clearer, it's what we end up with. Clear story-type, hybrid or exception, no one really cares as long as the story works and delivers meaning, entertainment and emotion.

This is important because while writers developing plot-led stories tend to be quite comfortable with structure and theory, writers developing character-led stories – like those developing theme-led stories – tend to be more intuitive. Writers with a natural inclination for plot-led stories tend to be ascending writers, as suggested in *Are You (or Are You Working With) an Ascending or a Descending Writer?* They start with an idea and develop the story by expanding it into more and more detailed stages – beat sheet, step outline, scene breakdown – until they get to a first draft. Writers developing character-led stories – and even more theme-led stories – tend to be descending writers, who first write an intuitive draft zero before digging their way down structurally and doing most of the design work on the screenplay itself.

For these more intuitive writers and those working with them, it's probably best not to put the tools at the forefront of the writing process or the development meeting. Use the tools to try to pinpoint a weakness if the story doesn't work, use them to fix possible issues once you have a draft, but don't try to follow the various stages outlined in this chapter as a fail-safe recipe, as it's very unlikely to work. *Map the Change, Sequence the Evolution* and *Grow the Draft* describe principles that are applied unconsciously by talented writers. They provide guidelines and troubleshooting tools for a rewrite, but they are not intended to be step-by-step instructions for a first draft.

# 3.4 Hands-On: Growth, Change or Steadfast?

Understanding the difference between *growth* and *change* is crucial when assessing the story-type of your project (or of each strand in a theme-led story). Get it wrong and you might think you're dealing with a character-led story when you're in fact dealing with a plot-led story, or vice-versa. If you're dogmatic about it, you might fail to identify that you're dealing with a hybrid or an exception.

So let's recap:

A **change** is when something is wrong with the protagonist and needs to be corrected; in other words, the protagonist is going in the wrong direction and has to change. For example, grieving the death of a loved one isn't wrong. Grief is painful, but it's not an internal problem. However, not being able to move on years after that death would be seen as a problem and would define a need to change. Depending on the other problems present in the story, this need to change can define the story-type. For example, if what's missing or what's wrong in the character is the biggest problem in the story, it will be character-led.

A **growth** is when there is nothing fundamentally wrong with the protagonist – the character functions as most human beings would in the same circumstances – but the character needs to learn something or move on in order to reach their goal, or they learn something or move on as a consequence of reaching the goal. The character doesn't need to change direction, only needs to get stronger to go on in the same direction. In a plot-led movie, a growth is often more appropriate than a change because it's not competing with what's primarily at stake. However, in some stories, especially thrillers or disaster movies, a character might need to change, yet we're still dealing with a plot-led story. This is because the character's need to change remains less important than the larger external problem in the story.

A character remains **steadfast** when there is nothing wrong with them and they don't learn that much from the story. For example, in most instalments of *Indiana Jones, Mission Impossible, The Avengers* or *James Bond*, Indy, Ethan Hunt, Tony Stark and 007 don't change much and that's fine. It's not expected from the genre. In fact, those who enjoy these movie franchises like these characters just as they are and don't want them to change. We'll have some form of evolution in the story, but it will be minor. For example, a relationship with another character rather than the evolution – change or growth – of the protagonist.

Of course, a steadfast character could also be evil and remain evil. Many antagonists, from Mr. Potter (Lionel Barrymore) in *It's a Wonderful Life* to Gordon Gecko (Michael Douglas) in *Wall Street* or The Joker (Heath Ledger) in *The Dark Knight* are steadfast characters. They don't change. As a result, they are often punished in the end, at least when the filmmaker has a clear moral stance. Sometimes even a protagonist can remain negative, as in *American Psycho* or *Scarface*.

Let's take a look at our two initial examples in *Hands-On: What's Your Type?*

Roger Thornhill in *North by Northwest* doesn't really change – there is nothing drastically wrong with him – but getting married will hopefully lead him to finally separate from his mother, which could be seen as a *growth*.

In *Two Days, One Night*, Sandra *changes*. She was depressive, suicidal, with low self-esteem. She comes out of her fight standing on her own two feet, smiling, looking to the future with hope and confidence. She's lost the job, but that's fine. After all, she was depressed while she had it, so keeping it was clearly not a long-term solution to becoming happier. She hasn't got what she wanted, but she has got what she needed, which is much more important. She was heading in the wrong direction (trying to keep her job) and she realises that by the end of the film.

So let's go back to the list of movies in *What's Your Type*, and for each film let's work out whether the protagonist grows, changes or remains steadfast. If the movie involves co-protagonists, or if the movie is multi-stranded, we'll define the evolution of each co-protagonist, or of the protagonist of each strand.

Then, let's see if this is consistent with the story-type we defined earlier for each of these.

*Jaws*
*Silver Linings Playbook*
*Parenthood*

*Game of Thrones*
*Billy Elliot*
*Saving Mr Banks*
*Traffic*
*Interstellar*
*Little Miss Sunshine*
*Finding Nemo*

You'll find the answers – well, my answers! – at the end of the book, in the
*Hands-On Solutions* section.

Hands-on

Look at your story, at a project you're developing, and define, for
the most important characters – protagonist, antagonist if present,
catalyst – whether they change, grow or remain steadfast. Then,
assess whether this is consistent with your story-type.

If you're developing a plot-led story, your protagonist doesn't
need to change most of the time, only to grow. It's fine if your
protagonist remains steadfast as long as the character doesn't feel
two-dimensional.

If you're developing a character-led story, your protagonist
needs to change but might fail to do so, as in *Birdman*.

If you're developing a theme-led story, feel free to do this for
each strand, checking that each action and evolution – or lack of –
is connected with the theme in some way.

# 3.5 Case Studies

## *Silver Linings Playbook*

**Written and Directed by David O. Russell**

**From a novel by Matthew Quick**

Detailed Analysis

**Note: As usual, it's best to watch the film just before reading the analysis.**

David O. Russell's *Silver Linings Playbook* was first screened at the 2012 Toronto International Film Festival and was released in the United States in November that year. The film opened to major critical success and won many awards. It was nominated for eight Academy Awards, including Best Picture, Best Director and Best Adapted Screenplay and became the first film since 2004's *Million Dollar Baby* to be nominated for the Big Five Oscars, with Lawrence winning for Best Actress. It was also nominated for four Golden Globe Awards, with Lawrence also winning Best Actress; three BAFTA nominations, with Russell winning for Best Adapted Screenplay; and five Independent Spirit Award nominations, winning in four categories, including Best Film. The film was a huge commercial success, grossing over US$236 million worldwide according to Wikipedia, which is more than eleven times its budget of US$21 million.

Although it's disguised as a plot-led story, *Silver Linings Playbook* is a complex character-led story which makes it an ideal candidate for a first case study. Character-led movies tend to be more difficult to analyse than plot-led ones, so let's start with a detailed breakdown of the story.

To help visualise the following analysis, here is the overall dramatic three-act structure of *Silver Linings Playbook*:

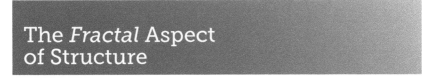

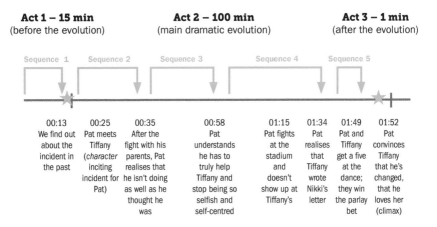

Sequence 1 (14 min): Resolving the mystery about Pat's past
Sequence 2 (20 min): Getting back with Nikki his way, in denial
Sequence 3 (21 min): Helping Tiffany in order to impress Nikki
Sequence 4 (30 min): Helping Tiffany with the dancing to communicate with Nikki
Sequence 5 (9 min): Winning the parlay bet

The film opens on Pat Solitano Jr. (Bradley Cooper) telling us about some regrets he has about the past. He was negative towards his wife, Nikki. They both blew it, but he feels better now. He announces a clear goal, to get back what they had together: true love. We also see his new motto, Excelsior, tacked on the wall. We realise he's in a psychiatric hospital. One minute into the film, we already know his conscious goal: to get his wife back. If this was a plot-led movie, we'd be in dramatic Act 2 already.

However, we soon understand that what's really at stake in the movie isn't whether Pat is going to get Nikki back. What's at stake is whether he's going to get better, to move on, because that's what he unconsciously needs and we perceive this *need* as being more important than his *want*. In fact, in order to get what he needs, he'll probably have to realise that he has to give up what he wants, which is often the case in a character-led story. So let's see how the story is designed to get him through this intense emotional journey.

As we get to know more about him over the next ten to fifteen minutes, we start to suspect he might not be as well as he thinks he is. He doesn't take his medication, which could be a good or a bad thing depending on our take on chemical drugs. Still, he seems determined to be positive about life, to fight negativity. This makes him very endearing. He might be deluded, but his energy is contagious.

00:02, Pat's mother, Dolores (Jacky Weaver) takes him out of the hospital against his doctor's advice. Eight months is long enough. She doesn't want him to "get used to the routine". This mystery is a great hook into the story at this stage as it triggers a question for the audience which shapes the **first and only dramatic sequence in Act 1**: Who is Pat and what has he done to end up in psychiatric hospital?

00:03, Pat asks his mum to give his friend Danny a lift too, assuring her it will be fine. They set off to Philadelphia, but she soon gets a phone call from the hospital telling her that Danny didn't have permission to leave. She's upset that Pat lied to her, starts having doubts about taking him out. Danny reassures her that it was his idea; Pat didn't know. He asks her to take him back to hospital but to take Pat back home: he's fine.

Before arriving home, Pat asks his mum to stop at the library. He wants to read Nikki's syllabus. She seems worried, but he reassures her: It's a good thing; he's remaking himself.

00:04, we meet Pat's father, Pat Solitano Sr. (Robert De Niro), with his friend Randy (Paul Herman) as they argue about their common passion: American football. Pat Sr. supports the Philadelphia Eagles, while Randy supports the Dallas Cowboys, two teams with a long history of rivalry.

00:06, Pat Sr. is surprised to see his son as Dolores didn't tell him that she was taking him out of the hospital. He wants to be sure Pat is fine. Dolores tells him not to worry. The court said yes, but Pat Sr. wants to know about the doctor, because the court listens to the doctor. Pat reassures him that he's fine. That was the plea bargain he made with the court: serve eight months and get out. All is under control. Here, a dramatic irony is being exploited. We guess it's not that fine and we're waiting to see it go wrong.

00:08, Pat asks his dad if he's going to pay for the restaurant he's planning to buy with his bookmaking, which he heard Pat Sr. started when he lost his job. We realise that Pat just says everything that goes through his head, even things his mum told him in confidence. It's Pat Sr.'s turn to reassure him that everything is fine. What is Pat going to do? Pat tells him about his plan of reading Nikki's syllabus, getting fit and getting her back. We realise that he's in denial: she's sold the house and she's left. But he doesn't want to see this. He's going to take all this negativity and use it as fuel, find a silver lining. Excelsior.

00:09, that night, Pat starts reading Nikki's syllabus with Hemingway's *A Farewell to Arms* and ends up throwing the book out the window. In a 4am rant at his parents, he explains why he's so gutted that the writer didn't stick to a happy ending. Pat's outburst confirms that he's not entirely done with his bipolar disorder: his attitude swings from confident and positive to obsessive and angry. It's both worrying and endearing (not to his parents who'd rather get some sleep).

00:11, the next morning. Pat would like to go running instead of fixing his broken window as his father asks, but his mother reminds him he has to go to therapy: that's part of the deal with the court. If he doesn't go, he goes back to hospital.

At therapy, Pat is unable to control himself when he hears Stevie Wonder's song, "Ma Cherie Amour", playing in the waiting room. He trashes a stack of magazines while looking for the speakers, desperately trying to stop the song. When his therapist, Dr Patel, takes him into his office, we realise that the song is a trigger. It's the song that played at his wedding with Nikki, and also the song that played as he found her in his home, naked, having sex with her lover. A short flashback shows how he snapped and physically assaulted his rival, leading to Pat ending up in front of a judge and Nikki obtaining a restraining order on him. This scene is crucial because along with all we've learnt in the first act, it tells us everything we need to know about Pat's past to be able to fully identify with him. We know what he's done, why he's done it, and how he sees both the past and the present. **It's both the climax of the only sequence in Act 1** (now we have the answer to the mystery) and the confirmation we need to give Pat the unconscious goal of getting better and moving on.

Without this scene, if the mystery about what happened in the past regarding key events in the story had gone on any longer, it would have been much more difficult to be close to Pat. We might have felt sorry for him, but we wouldn't have been able to "be" him. An example of this can be found in *Cake* with Jennifer Aniston. The protagonist knows what happened in the recent past – her son died in a car accident, which explains her depression, pain and apathy – but we don't find out until much later in the film, which prevents us from being able to fully empathise with her. This is brilliantly avoided in *Silver Linings Playbook*. The first fifteen minutes of the film are a masterclass in exposition: how to use conflict and humour to tell us what we need to know about past events without spoon-feeding the audience with information.

This scene also clarifies the main subplot, which is about Pat's relationship with his father, who he sees as the explosion guy and doesn't like to be compared to. These two need to mend their relationship, which might be connected to Pat's disorder, in order for Pat to get better. Dr Patel also suggests that Pat take his medication, which Pat refuses to do at this stage. By the way, if we saw the main action as Pat trying to get his wife back, Dr Patel could be a subplot, but because what's at stake is the need for Pat to get better, Dr Patel is part of the main plot. Like Tiffany, he is a co-protagonist trying to help Pat to move on, while Pat resists change (and is his own antagonist).

Fifteen minutes into the film, we start to see the difference between what Pat consciously wants (to get Nikki back) and what he needs: to get better, to accept that his relationship with Nikki is over, to stop his delusion. Now that we know enough about his past to be able to fully identify with him as a protagonist, we start to give him the unconscious goal to move on. We know what he *needs*, which defines more clearly what's at stake in the story than what he *wants*. The main problem is inside him, which is why we are dealing with a character-led story. The structural backbone of the film is Pat's *evolution* rather than his dramatic *action*. So this is when dramatic Act 2 actually starts, because we know who *needs* what and why (Pat needs to get better in order to move on), as well as what stands in the way (himself and his bipolar disorder).

This is the beginning of the **first sequence in dramatic Act 2**. Pat, in denial, refusing to take advice from his therapist, refusing to take his medication, convinced he's fine, is going to try to get Nikki back his own way, pretending all is well. Most of the conflict in this sequence comes from the fact that we know he's wrong, that he's not fine. It's a strong dramatic irony, present in most character-led stories due to the awareness we have over the protagonist regarding what the main problem in the story really is.

00:16, Pat Sr. asks Pat to watch a game with him, for good luck. He's convinced that when Pat is around, his team scores – which happens right then. He's very superstitious, in fact completely OCD as far as football is concerned.

00:17, Pat goes jogging – his parents begging him not to go looking for Nikki – and stops by his old school, giving his ex-colleague Nancy a fright. He claims he's fine now and ready to start work, any work, whenever they want, but he freaks her out. Nancy notices that Pat has lost lots of weight which pleases him. Then she gets rid of him by vaguely agreeing that he might come back to work later, which he takes as a silver lining despite the fact that she clearly – at least to us – doesn't mean any of it. This is an example of a scene in which the dramatic irony – we know he needs to move on, but he doesn't – is well-exploited. We lend him a lot of conflict despite the fact that he doesn't seem to be experiencing any himself as he's so optimistic about the future. This contrast makes the scene very funny.

00:18, Pat meets his friend Ronnie outside his house. Unlike Nancy, Ronnie is very glad that Pat's back: he needs someone to talk to. His wife Veronica, who seems to have him on a tight leash, invites Pat for dinner. Pat initially refuses, as he believes Veronica hates him, but he finally accepts when Ronnie confirms his wife is still seeing Nikki.

00:19, as Pat comes home, his dad complains that his team started losing as soon as Pat left and asks him to show some respect, which means to be there when the team plays. Pat Sr. pretends to want to spend time with him, to keep him out of trouble, but we guess it's mostly about the game and his superstition that Pat's presence means a win. Pat is cheerful because he believes Nikki will be at Ronnie and Veronica's dinner. They start to argue as Pat wants to make a phone call – which he isn't allowed to do – just as a cop rings the bell. He's been assigned Pat's case and he's not happy about the complaints he's received following Pat's visits to his old house and school. The restraining order is five hundred feet from his wife; he has to abide by it or he goes back to jail or hospital.

00:21, Dr Patel tells Pat that to avoid going back to jail or hospital, the best thing is to take his medication. He also tries to get Pat to accept that he might not get back together with his wife. True love is letting her go, and seeing if she comes back. Pat dodges the issue and tells him that what he learnt at hospital is that if he stays positive, he'll get a shot at a silver lining. Again he mentions the dinner. He's clearly hoping that Nikki will be there. They agree he should wear his DeSean Jackson jersey: he's the man, says Dr Patel. This plants Dr Patel as another football fan, so that his presence at the Giants match later doesn't look like it's come out of the blue.

00:22, Pat arrives at Ronnie's house for dinner. He's so nervous he almost chickens out, but Ronnie catches him and convinces him to come in. Ronnie is clearly under a lot of pressure from work, family, the baby... He's not happy and believes he has no choice. Pat disagrees, just as another guest arrives. It's not Nikki, it's Tiffany, Veronica's younger sister, whose husband Tommy – a cop – recently died.

00:25, meet Tiffany. She's gorgeous, with a gothic slant. As always, Pat says exactly what he thinks and asks her how Tommy died, despite Ronnie having just asked him not to mention this. There is immediate chemistry between the two, which introduces a nice source of conflict for Pat on his conscious goal. From that moment, he's going to be torn between his goal to get back with Nikki and his attraction to Tiffany. This is also the *character* inciting event of the film, because this meeting with Tiffany is what's going to trigger Pat's unconscious need to change. Up to this point, we had given him this goal, but it hasn't been clear that he wanted this himself, even if unconsciously. As he tells Tiffany at the end, he falls in love with her the minute he sees her. He's just going to spend a long time battling this attraction because it goes against what he consciously wants: Nikki. Pat is going to spend the rest of the film fighting himself. He is his own antagonist. Tiffany, as a catalyst, is going to force him to change, and as a co-protagonist will try to help the part of him that wants her, that wants to move on, to overcome the part of him that still wants Nikki. In fact, in an attempt to remind himself what he wants, Pat immediately starts talking about Nikki and how he's determined to be nice to his wife when they get back together. They go on a tour of the house as Veronica shows off the latest improvements. Pat still wants to call Nikki.

00:26, dinner time. Tiffany and Pat share their experience of anti-depressants – they're both very knowledgeable. Both of them stopped taking medication because it made them feel foggy. The fact that Tiffany likes dancing and is preparing for a local competition is planted. Tiffany, who doesn't have a great relationship with her sister, decides to go home early before the end of dinner and asks Pat to walk her home. He agrees.

00:30, Tiffany lives outside her parents' house, in a separate bungalow. She's very direct and invites him in. She felt the attraction, he felt the attraction, why lie? They are not like them. She didn't like the fact that he wore a football jersey but "He can fuck her if they turn the lights off". Pat says thanks but no thanks: he's married. "So am I", replies Tiffany. Pat finds this confusing: her husband is dead. Tiffany breaks down in tears in Pat's arms, and when he still doesn't give in, she slaps him and walks into her house. Now that's a catalyst!

00:31, clearly troubled by his encounter with Tiffany, Pat starts looking for his wedding video at home, and wakes up his parents at 3am. The situation spirals out of control as Pat gets more and more frustrated, starts shouting and refuses to calm down, waking up the whole neighbourhood. Pat loses it, having flashbacks of "the incident" and accidentally hits his mother. A full-scale, messy bipolar episode. A fight ensues with Pat Sr. who starts hitting his son while a confused Pat apologises and tries not to return the blows. The fight is stopped when the cop in charge of Pat knocks on the door. Things calm down as the cop leaves. This is the **climax of the first sequence of dramatic Act 2**: Pat was trying to ignore the problem, and he realises he's not doing as well as he thought he was. He's not fine. He was in denial, and we get a sense that some of this denial is over. The dramatic irony he was a victim of is at least partially resolved.

00:35, in the morning, Pat starts taking his medication and repairs the broken window (consequences of the first sequence). This is also a visual way to *show* the beginning of a change.

00:36, Pat jogs past Tiffany's house just as she runs past him and attempts to engage him in conversation. He tries to shake her off, but as she follows him he ends up insulting her and hurting her feelings, which he immediately regrets. Refusing his apology, she confronts him. Yes, there is a part of her that's sloppy and dirty, but she likes that, like every other part of herself. Can he say the same? Can he forgive? Tiffany here is playing her role as a catalyst, pushing Pat to ask himself the right questions. The tone shifts seamlessly from funny to moving. We also start, with this scene, to empathise with Tiffany as well, as we can feel and understand her conflict (she's been dealing with the death of her husband, probably not very well). Although the film started with Pat as a clear protagonist, we are slowly shifting to a two-hander. We start to want both of them to get better, and we also want them to end up together (provided one senses the chemistry between them) because we feel they would be a good match. Tiffany offers an alternative to Nikki, and that's when the romantic comedy part of the film kicks in. Beyond the question about Pat's ability to move on, we start to wonder whether they will end up together or not. Of course, Pat needs to move on to be able to end up with Tiffany, so we're still telling the same story. It's just moved to a higher level of complexity. Tiffany wants Pat from the beginning, but Pat still wants Nikki, so there is conflict. She has to help him to move on if she is to stand a chance of getting him. So she becomes a co-protagonist on Pat's unconscious goal, while remaining an obstacle on his conscious goal despite pretending to be helping him. Phew!

00:37, Dr Patel is aware of the fight Pat had with his father the night before. Pat sets the record straight: hitting his mother was an accident, he hates himself for it, he hates his illness and he wants to control it. But his father has no shame for beating him up. Dr Patel remarks that his father was probably scared. Pat agrees that last night was a mess. Dr Patel tells him again that he needs a strategy to control his feelings, to find a quiet place in himself when they rise. Pat asks him to give a letter to Nikki, but Dr Patel refuses: Pat is under a restraining order. Instead, he suggests that spending time with Tiffany might be a good way for Pat to stop thinking of Nikki. If Pat helps Tiffany, Nikki will think he's a kind, generous, large-hearted person, who helps people in need, who is thriving. So if he helps Tiffany, it will be good for him. This is the inciting event that triggers Pat's conscious subgoal for the **second sequence of Act 2: helping Tiffany in order to impress Nikki**.

00:40, Pat, jogging past Tiffany's house, bumps into her running again, wondering how she knows where he runs. She tells him she just wants them to be friends. Pat invites her to have dinner at a diner. Tiffany accepts.

00:41, Pat picks Tiffany up that night – it's Halloween – and they walk to the diner. He doesn't want it to look like it's a date, so he orders cereal. They start talking and when Pat tells Tiffany that he wishes he could get a letter to Nikki to explain that he's not out of control, that the incident with his parents the other night was a minor thing, she offers to help. She could get a letter to Nikki, but she'd have to be careful. She tells him how she lost her job by having sex with everybody at the office. We get a sense that Pat is more and more attracted to Tiffany, despite still resisting it. He wants to leave and write the letter, but when he finds out that Veronica told Nikki about the dinner and realises it might have been a kind of test, he sits down, excited. Then he blows it when Tiffany says they are kind of the same. From his reaction, Tiffany realises that Pat thinks she's crazier than him, which she finds appalling. She tells him she won't help with the letter and leaves in an exaggerated crazy fit.

00:49, Pat catches up with her, tries to explain why he didn't want Nikki to associate him with the kind of sexual behaviour Tiffany de-scribed earlier because he's never done that. Again, she confronts him and pushes him to look at himself: he's afraid to be alive. He's a hypocrite, a conformist and a liar. She opened up to him and he judged her. He's an asshole. He tries to get her to calm down, but she yells he's harassing her, leading some kids in the crowd to step in. Pat hears the trigger song play and might have another episode when the cop in charge of his case takes him away, threatening to send him back to hospital. Tiffany realises it's gone too far and rescues Pat, blaming the kids. She helps him to control himself, to realise that the song is only playing in his head. They apologise to each other. The cop realises she's Tommy's widow and offers to have a drink with her sometime. Tiffany leaves, upset, and Pat tells the cop she doesn't do this anymore. We get a sense that they are starting to look after each other. Pat walks Tiffany home and she tells him she'll give the letter to Nikki. Pat is grateful. He'll bring it tomorrow.

00:52, in the morning, Pat has written his letter to Nikki; he's upbeat. His father wants him to stay for the game, but Pat refuses. He can't wait to see Tiffany and give her the letter.

00:54, Tiffany isn't at home so Pat calls at her parents' looking for her. Just as he tries to convince them that he isn't one of the "creeps", one of them – an ex-colleague from work – shows up. Pat defends Tiffany, explains that she's vulnerable, she needs some space to heal and he's getting in the way of that. As Pat walks the guy back to his car, we realise that Tiffany has overheard what he said. She's clearly touched. She had texted the guy and Pat just saved her from going back to her old, self-damaging ways.

00:55, Tiffany catches up with Pat and tells him she won't help with the letter. She can't do it. She always does stuff for other people and she never gets anything in return which makes her feel empty. Pat understands, asks what he can do for her, and she mentions the dance competition at the Franklin hotel. Her husband never wanted to do it; she needs a dancing partner. Pat refuses. He isn't going to dance, so she leaves. Pat mentions he's just done something for her, dealing with the jerk at her house. He believes he's his best self today, that Nikki is her best self today and that their love will be amazing. Tiffany takes this on the chin but doesn't flinch. If he wants her to give the letter to Nikki, he'll have to dance with her. This is the **end of the second sequence of dramatic Act 2** because it triggers a new subgoal for Pat. To get his letter to Nikki, he has to help Tiffany with the dancing.

00:59, back at home, Pat realises that Danny is out of hospital and being used by his father as a next-best lucky charm, which seems to be working. He makes up with his brother Jake (Shea Whigham), just as the cop in charge of his case comes to take Danny back to the hospital, despite Pat Sr.'s plea to leave him until the end of the game.

01:04, **beginning of the third sequence of dramatic Act 2**. Pat meets Tiffany at her place for his first dance practice. He gives her the letter, which she says she's going to give to Nikki that night as she should see her at Ronnie and Veronica's. She tries to get Pat to feel something for her, asking him during their dance practice to walk to her as if she were Nikki. When Pat tells her he feels nothing, she tells him how Tommy died. She loved her husband, but she was depressed, and they hadn't had sex for a while. One night after work he went to buy some underwear for her to get something going. On the way back, he helped a motorist with a flat tire, and got killed by another car, with the lingerie box still on the front seat. "That's a feeling". On that note, they start training. This is the last significant bit of exposition regarding Tiffany's backstory. From this point on, we know enough about her and her past to fully identify with her as a co-protagonist.

01:08, montage sequence showing Pat going to bed exhausted, then back to Tiffany's for more training. They watch old musicals and seem to be having fun. Pat's attraction to her becomes more obvious, even if he tries to fight it and let off some steam with his running.

01:10, Pat Sr. expects Pat to spend time with him, always in relation to his OCD superstition with the football games. He gives him a newspaper with the dates of upcoming games, but when Pat shows this to Tiffany, she throws it out: football and Nikki's syllabus stay out of her place. Just then, Danny pays them an unexpected visit. He's been released – again – and suggests a few changes to their moves before leaving to see a girl on the other side of town. He brings a nice craziness to their dance routine.

01:13, in the morning, Pat Sr. wakes his son with both a request and confession. He wants to spend more time with him, as the Eagles have a big game coming up against the Giants. He also touchingly admits that he might have spent too much time with his brother Jake and not enough with Pat when they were kids. He didn't know how to deal with his condition, and might have made it worse. He's determined to help Pat get back on his feet. And he hopes that their spending time together will make up for the past. Pat agrees. Downstairs, Randy tells him that Pat Sr. has bet all his restaurant money on that big game. Pat Sr. believes in Pat, and wants him to go to the game with Jake. He can't go himself as he's banned. Pat is torn because he has an important training session with Tiffany that day. The dancing is important for him. It makes him disciplined, focused. It's a good thing.

01:17, Pat asks Tiffany if he can spend half the day with her tomorrow and half the day at the Eagles game. She refuses as they have two days left to nail the big move. Pat tries to convince her. His father opened up to him. It was beautiful. Now he would like to help him, as he believes his presence will help to win the game. Tiffany counter-strikes: Nikki has replied to his letter, but he can't read it until they have nailed the big move. They make a few comical attempts, but Pat's mind is on the letter; he can't concentrate. Tiffany gives in and allows him to read it. Although Nikki's answer is positive, she suggests that if it's her reading the signs, she needs to see something to prove he's ready to resume their marriage; otherwise, maybe they are better going their separate ways. Gutted, Pat is about to leave, but Tiffany tells him that their dance could be that something. It shows he's different. It's romantic. It's for Nikki. Pat leaves, promising he'll be there the next day.

01:21, Pat Sr. drops Pat at the Stadium without letting him use his phone to let Tiffany know he'll be late. We can sense that Pat Sr. doesn't like her. He gives Pat some last minute advice: no drinking, no fighting, and he'll be fine. Once there, Pat meets his brother Jake and his friends. He also bumps into Dr Patel, who came with a group of Asian supporters of the Eagles. Here, he's not his therapist; he's a fan. Everything starts well but ends badly when Pat is drawn into a fight to help Jake, who himself was trying to defend his new Asian friends from racist hooligans. They all end up in jail, and Pat doesn't show up at Tiffany's. This is the **end of the third sequence of dramatic Act 2**. Pat has succeeded in getting his letter to Nikki, but he's failed Tiffany because of his dad.

01:26, they all get back to the house and find a furious Pat Sr. who has lost a fortune to Randy as the Eagles lost the game. Pat's father blames Pat, accusing his son of being a loser. This is when Tiffany walks in, not happy with Pat's no-show. Pat Sr. immediately blames her for messing up the Eagle's juju. It all went wrong when Pat started to spend time with her. She brilliantly counters, giving many examples of recent Eagles wins, which took place when she was with Pat. If he had been with her today, Pat wouldn't have got into trouble and maybe the Eagles would have won against the Giants. Pat Sr. is impressed, ready to reconsider his judgement. He does like Tiffany now. They manage to talk Randy into making another bet: a parlay, double or nothing, the Eagles have to win against the Cowboys the day of the Franklin dance competition, and Pat and Tiffany have to score at least a five out of ten. Pat doesn't want to be part of this and responsible for his father losing everything. He leaves the house while Tiffany convinces his parents that the only way to get him to do the dance competition is to lie to Pat and tell him that Nikki will be there. We find out that Pat's mother is the one who told Tiffany when Pat was running. They all agree on what they call a white lie.

01:34, outside the house, Pat thinks about something that Tiffany just said twice in the heat of the argument: "If it's me reading the signs", and he connects it with a sentence in Nikki's letter. He understands that Tiffany's the one who wrote the letter, not Nikki.

01:36, they resume the training for the competition. This is the **beginning of the fourth and last sequence of dramatic Act 2**, which is about winning the parlay bet. This is the way Tiffany managed to get Pat's parents on her side. Pat has to show up for his dad, and also because he hopes Nikki will be there. For now, we don't know what Pat is doing with his realisation that Tiffany wrote the letter, as he's not confronting her, so she doesn't know he knows, which exploits a dramatic irony she is a victim of.

01:37, Christmas time and the evening of the competition. Tiffany helps Pat to get dressed. She's nervous. He pockets a letter in his jacket, looking very smart. Pat seems calm, composed: Nikki's going to be there. What's meant to happen will happen. This exploits more than one dramatic irony and a mystery. We know that Nikki isn't supposed to be there, that it's a lie, and Pat doesn't. But we're also not sure of Pat's agenda as he's still not told Tiffany that he knows about the letter. In this last sequence, we're closer to Tiffany than to him, because we feel he's hiding something from us. It's not a problem at all structurally because they are co-protagonists. She's going to experience more conflict anyway during the whole sequence and the climax, so we don't mind too much that Pat is a step ahead of us.

01:38, they get to the hotel, meet Pat Sr. and the rest of the family, as well as Danny and his girlfriend. The other dancers look impressive; Randy believes he's already won his bet. The Eagles are drawing against the Cowboys, so anything is possible. Pat Sr. reminds Pat that the only thing they have to do is get a five out of ten.

01:40, Tiffany asks Pat to register them while she goes looking for Veronica, when she has a shock: Nikki is here, with Ronnie and her sister! That's a huge blow for Tiffany and it doesn't help when Ronnie and Veronica tell her that she has to give Pat a chance to save his marriage. She loses it, goes to the bar and starts drinking and chatting up a random guy.

01:42, Pat sees Nikki with Ronnie and Veronica but goes on looking for Tiffany, while watching an amazing couple dancing and getting 7.3. This is not going to be easy!

01:43, the Eagles beat the Cowboys! Now the only thing the family needs to win their bet is Pat and Tiffany scoring a five or better at the competition.

01:44, Pat finds Tiffany at the bar and rescues her. She's had two vodkas, and she's not in a good mood. Pat ignores it and takes her to the dance floor just as they are announced.

01:45, they start dancing as Pat Sr., Randy and Danny join the rest of the audience. Their dance is beautiful, messy, energetic, sensual, unconventional. It's impossible to say how they are going to score. Technically, they are way below the other dancers, but there is something special in their performance. They are clearly enjoying it and having fun. They almost pull off the big move, in a *could be intentional even if it looks super messy* kind of way.

01:49, when they get a five, no one understands why they all erupt in joy and celebration. Pat finds out that the Eagles have defeated the Cowboys: They have won the parlay and Randy has lost his bet. It's a big moment for all the family and friends. Tiffany falls into Pat's arms: he was amazing. This is the **climax of the last sequence of dramatic Act 2**: against all odds, they have won the bet. But Pat leaves Tiffany and walks to Ronnie and Veronica's table to talk to Nikki, reminding us that the main questions are still open: Has Pat moved on? Will Pat and Tiffany end up together? So we're still in dramatic Act 2 as we need an answer to these two questions.

01:50, gutted, Tiffany sees Pat talking to Nikki. When he leans closer to tell her something, Tiffany's convinced she has lost him and she leaves, upset.

01:51, Pat leaves Nikki, looking for Tiffany. He was just saying goodbye to his wife. Pat Sr. tells his son Tiffany has left and gives him a pep talk. He doesn't know if Nikki ever loved him, but she sure doesn't love him now. Unlike Tiffany. Pat hugs his father and tells him he loves him. At least these two have moved on... Pat's goal is now to get Tiffany. It's achieved over one scene so this new goal doesn't trigger a new sequence.

01:52, Pat finds Tiffany in the street, tries to catch up with her, but she runs away, asking him to leave her alone. Pat asks her to read one last letter for him, then if she doesn't want to see him ever again, she won't have to. Tiffany complies reluctantly and finds out the letter is addressed to her. In it, Pat tells her he knows she's written Nikki's letter. He loves her. He knew it the minute he met her, but he got stuck. He's sorry it took him so long to catch up. He confesses he wrote the letter a week ago. Tiffany doesn't understand why he let her lie to him for a week, so he explains that he was trying to be romantic. They kiss. This is the **climax of the movie**, which provides the **answer to the main dramatic question(s)**: *Yes*, Pat has moved on, and *yes*, these two will end up together. As often in a character-led movie, Pat doesn't get what he *wants* (to get back together with Nikki), but after resisting change for most of the film, he finally gets what he *needs* (to move on). As a result, he is rewarded and ends up with Tiffany.

01:55, the film ends on Pat's voiceover, as it started. He can't explain the craziness in him and around him, but when he thinks of everything everyone did for him, he feels like a very lucky guy. We see a montage of happy moments with the family (parents, Jake), friends (Danny, Ronnie) and the new couple.

* * *

As *Silver Linings Playbook* is a character-led story, let's first see if we can define the start point and end point in Pat's evolution.

> **A** (start point in the story): Pat is deluded. He's full of anger and resentment – for his wife, his father, and above all himself – buried under his positive attitude. He has changed superficially but deep inside, he's the same. He believes he's in control of his condition when he isn't. And he isn't aware that his relationship with his wife, Nikki, is over. He's self-obsessed and self-centred. He needs to get better and move on.

> **B** (end point in the story): Pat is at peace with others and himself. He's realised that he needed help to control his condition, and he has taken action. He's also realised that his relationship with Nikki is over; he's let her go, so he has moved on. He's also more generous and caring, less self-obsessed. As a result of this change, he gets Tiffany, his true love.

As always, when described like this, the main evolution in a character-led story sounds both unbelievable and corny. This is because we haven't yet defined the intermediary steps, or sequenced the evolution to find the conflict that is going to force the character to change.

So let's first *map the change* and find the key four to six psychological / emotional steps that make this evolution possible.

1.  **The first step** for Pat is to realise that he isn't as well as he thinks he is. This happens after the fight with his father, when he starts taking his medication and accepting advice from others, especially Dr Patel.

2.  **The second step** is to be less self-centred, less judgemental about others. He needs to see Tiffany for who she really is and stop seeing her as a "crazy slut". He achieves this when he helps

Tiffany get rid of her former colleague from work, yet he is still deluded about his relationship with his wife.

3.  **The third step** is to lose hope regarding Nikki. This happens when he reads the answer to his letter, written by Tiffany.

4.  **The fourth step** is to recognise that Tiffany is the right woman for him. This happens when he understands that she has written Nikki's answer to his letter, because this is when he realises how much she loves him, and the extent of his own feelings for her.

5.  **The fifth step** is to mend his relationship with his father. This happens after they win the parlay bet and he's able to hug his father and tell him he loves him.

All these steps combined lead him to be able to get better, move on and end up with Tiffany.

This evolution becomes more believable because it's broken down into a few key steps, but it still sounds corny. This is because while we know the steps, we haven't defined the conflict which is going to lead to these changes, to force the character to change.

This is when *sequencing the evolution* kicks in. We're going to define the conscious subgoals which will lead Pat to experience the conflict that forces him to change. Each conscious subgoal defines a dramatic sequence which is going to lead Pat to experience, because of what he *wants* consciously, the conflict that will provoke an internal change in relation to his unconscious *need*.

- So **Pat's first subgoal** is to get Nikki back in his own way, pretending everything is fine. This ends up in the fight scene with his father after he's accidentally hurt his mother (conflict) which leads him to realise he's not doing as well as he thought (realisation). As a result, he starts taking his medication (change).

- Then **Pat's second subgoal** is to help Tiffany in order to impress Nikki. Pat has not really changed; he's still self-centred and obsessed with Nikki. This ends up with Tiffany telling him that he is a hypocrite, a conformist and a liar (conflict) which leads him to realise he's not better than her (realisation). As a result, he starts to understand her better and be less self-centred (change).

- **Pat's third subgoal** is to help Tiffany with the dancing so that she will help him to communicate with Nikki. While he's still obsessed with Nikki, we get a sense that he's more and more attracted to Tiffany, and genuinely cares for her. This ends up with him reading what he thinks is Nikki's answer to his letter (conflict) which leads him to realise that she doesn't believe in them being together (realisation). Spending time with Tiffany also leads his father to open up to him (realisation), which introduces a dilemma (conflict) as Pat tries to help his dad (change). This ends up with him having disappointed both his father and Tiffany (conflict) and discovering that Tiffany has written Nikki's letter (conflict). This is when he understands she is the right woman for him, because he becomes aware of how much she loves him and of his own feelings for her (realisation), although we only find out for sure later. In the meantime, he's going to concentrate on the next subgoal.

- **Pat's fourth subgoal** is to do the best he can with Tiffany at the dance competition, not only for Tiffany but also to win the bet for his father and prove his worth to him. We think he's doing this for Nikki, although as we'll find out later he's genuinely doing this for Tiffany (trying to be romantic), as well as his father (trying to be a good son). The main change in this sequence is related to his father, as the subplot has merged with the main plot. When they win after a tense number (conflict), he's able to hug his father and tell him he loves him (change).

- **Finally**, in the last scene between Tiffany and Pat, it's Tiffany who experiences the most conflict and changes the most when she realises that Pat loves her. This gives her back her self-esteem. They have healed each other.

It's more difficult to *sequence the evolution* in a character-led story than it is to *sequence the action* in a plot-led one, because it's of course more complex and subtle than the brief summary above. There are other minor steps and changes, but hopefully this shows how structuring the conscious action of the protagonist leads the character to experience the conflict that is going to cause internal changes, the sum of which will lead to the bigger change (or in some stories, especially tragedies, a failure to change).

In character-led stories, we often have to look for two inciting events: one for the conscious goal; one for the unconscious need. In *Silver Linings*

*Playbook*, there is no inciting event for Pat's conscious goal (he already has his goal when the story starts), but his meeting with Tiffany is the *character* inciting event, an event that triggers his internal change.

As a catalyst, she's going to force him to change, so she becomes a co-protagonist on his unconscious goal. As Pat tells her at the end of the film, he falls in love with her as soon as he meets her, but he gets stuck. This means that he spends most of the film rejecting his attraction for her because of his obsession with Nikki. So Tiffany is also an obstacle for Pat on his wrong, conscious goal (getting Nikki back) because she doesn't want him to get Nikki; she wants him for herself.

As soon as they meet, because of the chemistry between the characters – if you don't feel it, the film probably doesn't work for you – there is another very strong dramatic irony, common to most romantic comedies: We want them to end up together because we feel they are right for each other and at least one of them isn't aware of that, or rejects it. Note that Tiffany also has a strong goal – to get Pat – and a strong need – to move on from the death of her husband. While she helps/forces Pat to change, he also helps her to get better, for example when he stands up for her and sends away one of the men she sleeps with. Or when he chooses her over Nikki in the end, which helps restore her self-esteem.

As we saw earlier, it's important to define *conscious* subgoals so that we know what's at stake on the surface, what the protagonist is trying to achieve consciously while all this conflict and change happens under the surface. For example, the motivation for helping Tiffany comes from the scene with Dr Patel and leads to the idea of the letter. We give the protagonist a conscious goal so that by trying to get what he wants – getting a letter to Nikki – he experiences the conflict that's going to force him to change and get what he needs – move on from Nikki, get better and get Tiffany.

Interestingly, in *Silver Linings Playbook*, Pat changes – reaches his unconscious need – and gives up his conscious goal before we fully realise it. When we discover with Pat that Tiffany wrote Nikki's answer, he realises how much she loves him and the extent of his own feelings for her. However, we won't know for sure how he feels about her, whether he's chosen Nikki or her, until the climax. We don't know, during the last sequence, if he's doing the competition because Nikki will be there – the fact that she shows up is a huge obstacle for Tiffany – or because of his feelings for Tiffany. The main dramatic questions are still alive: Will Pat change? Will he give up trying to get Nikki back? Will Tiffany and Pat end up together? When Tiffany sees Pat talking to Nikki, she thinks she's lost him and runs away. We still have hope, but we can see the situation from her point of view and believe she's lost him.

Just as managing information was crucial at the beginning of the story to make it possible for us to fully identify with Pat, towards the end we feel closer to Tiffany because she experiences more conflict, both because of the obstacles she faces and the dramatic irony she is a victim of. Pat, on the other hand, doesn't share his intentions with us, so he is more distant. This would be a problem if they were not co-protagonists, but at this stage in the movie we identify with both of them, so it's absolutely fine and keeps the suspense until the very end.

The *reveal* scene during the climax is moving because we realise that Pat was more aware of his problem and his feelings for Tiffany than we thought. Sure, it's a happy ending, but more importantly, it's a *satisfying* one. They end up together for a reason. They both helped each other to change and are now ready to embrace a new part of their lives. There is meaning in this positive outcome: people can change, get happier, even when the odds seem to be stacked against them.

Let's take a look now at the STM (*Story-Type Method*) framework of *Silver Linings Playbook*. You'll find more information on this key development tool as well as a link to download a template in the *Story Design Tools* section of *Bringing It All Together*. As usual, there will be some repetitions between the analysis and the STM Framework. This is so that each part of the case study can be read independently.

# STM Framework for *Silver Linings Playbook*

## STORY-TYPE, M-FACTOR AND THEME

**Main Problem in the Story**: Pat's inability to acknowledge and control his condition (he's bipolar) and his need to move on from his failed marriage. This is dramatised through his main dilemma in the film: Will he choose Nikki, his estranged wife, or Tiffany, the woman we know is right for him?

**Story-Type**: Because the main problem lies within the protagonist, we're dealing with a character-led story.

**M-Factor**: The need to move on and get better suggests that the main problem sits quite high in Maslow's Hierarchy of Needs (self-actualisation as in problem solving, lack of prejudice, acceptance of fact). However, what's at stake lies lower, as it's also about esteem (respect from others, to others) and love/belonging, thanks to the addition of the romantic comedy element, as well as the subplot connected to Pat's relationship with his father. Also, if Pat doesn't get better, he will be sent back to jail or a psychiatric hospital, which significantly raises the stakes. Finally, his condition has physiological consequences on his sex life, his sleep and even the clarity of his mind due to his medication. All this helps explore a wide range of needs and open up the potential audience. Overall, I'd give *Silver Linings Playbook* a medium-high M-Factor.

**Theme**: The story is about love, life and happiness. Can a positive, proactive attitude lead to a better life? This theme is embedded in the title and the motto of the protagonist: Excelsior. It's introduced right away, with Pat's voiceover telling us about his positive attitude, and it's dramatised in the scene about Hemingway's ending in *A Farewell to Arms*: Life is hard enough, can't we get a happy ending? The solution lies in his ability to change more profoundly than he believes he has, showing that the positive attitude might be part of the solution, but isn't enough. Another important theme is how to deal with being different. Pat and Tiffany illustrate two opposite ways to deal with their singularity: Tiffany is ready to embrace hers (and his), while Pat is trying to conform, to pretend he's "normal" and is embarrassed by her.

## MANAGING CONFLICT

**Protagonist**: **Pat** is a clear protagonist at the beginning of the movie, but **Tiffany** gradually becomes a co-protagonist, because she

312 DEVELOPING A CHARACTER-LED STORY

ends up experiencing a lot of conflict too. As the story progresses, we identify with her as much as we do with him. We want them to end up together, to overcome what's separating them.

**Conscious Goal: Pat** clearly defines his conscious goal in his first monologue: I *want* what we had – true love. Unfortunately, he's obsessed with his estranged wife Nikki, so getting her back becomes his main goal for most of the film. It's only when he realises his feelings for Tiffany that he can move on, forget about Nikki and find true love with Tiffany. **Tiffany**'s goal is to get Pat because unlike him, she immediately knows they are right for each other.

**Unconscious Need: Pat** *needs* to get better and move on. He needs to realise that his ex-wife Nikki isn't his true love, that Tiffany is the right girl for him. Although we understand his conscious goal (getting Nikki back to reclaim his true love) right away, we give him the unconscious goal of realising he's wrong and his need to change about fifteen minutes into the film, once we know enough about him to make an assessment about what he needs versus what he wants. This creates a dramatic irony (we know more than he does) which is gradually resolved over the course of the story. **Tiffany**'s need is to stop the negative way she's trying to deal with her grief and guilt in relation to the death of her husband Tommy. This is a character subplot for her, because her internal problem is less acute than Pat's. Her main problem is that Pat doesn't want her, but she also needs to change because the way she deals with Tommy's death isn't healthy. Mirroring her action towards Pat, Pat is her co-protagonist on her unconscious need. He's helping her get better in the same way she's helping him move on.

**Motivation: Pat** wants Nikki back because he still believes they are in love and he clings to his deluded version of the past. He's also in denial of his condition, and that's why we give him the unconscious goal to get better. We know that he'll only find true love and happiness if he gets better, if he stops thinking he doesn't have a problem and starts tackling it. **Tiffany** wants Pat because she fell in love with him right away.

**Main Characteristic: Pat** is bipolar, which gives him great potential for unpredictability. He can be explosive during an episode, but he also has the wonderful belief that if he remains positive, if he works hard to fight negativity, he will find his silver lining. **Tiffany** is slightly crazy, although this is more a posture than reality. In fact, she's determined and strong-willed. Her guilt following the death of Tommy led her to be promiscuous, but she's trying to break this behaviour.

**Secondary Characteristics: Pat** is intelligent, sensitive, caring, loving and generous even if initially he's too self-obsessed to let these qualities shine. He also has no filter when he speaks, which makes him a kind of social bomb as he has no social skills. His determination to be optimistic and positive makes him very endearing. He used to be overweight, but he's got himself back into shape (because that's something Nikki would have liked) so he is an avid runner. He struggles to control himself when he hears his trigger, Stevie Wonder's song, "Ma Cherie Amour". **Tiffany** is clever, vulnerable yet independent. She's direct and funny.

**Evolution (growth, change, steadfast): Pat** *changes* because initially, he's going in the wrong direction. It's not wrong to want to find true love, but it's wrong to believe you're fine when you're not. It's wrong to stalk your estranged wife when true love is a new woman in your life who you cannot see as such because you're still obsessed with the wrong woman. When he stops his delusions (that he's fine and that Nikki still loves him), starts taking his medication, manages to control his trigger, lets his wife go and sees Tiffany for who she really is, he has changed so he finds true love. **Tiffany** also *changes*, because her guilt and lack of self-esteem led her to self-damaging behaviour. By the end of the story, she's healed too.

**Main Character:** Pat and Tiffany are the main characters. They are the most interesting characters in the story, and we're telling their story. Although we start with Pat's point of view, it quickly becomes a two-hander.

**Main Plot:** The story is shaped by Pat's *evolution*, his *need* to get better and move on. While the plot is about getting his wife back, the real dramatic question is about his ability to change, to realise that Tiffany is the right girl for him. We want to know if Pat and Tiffany will end up together more than we want to know if Pat will get Nikki back.

**What's at Stake:** Pat's freedom, well-being and happiness. If he gets better and moves on, he gets true love with Tiffany. If he fails, at best he spends his life with a woman who doesn't love him (Nikki); at worst he goes back to jail or psychiatric hospital. As they become co-protagonists, it's their happiness that's at stake. The dance competition and the parlay bet add to the stakes nicely as Pat Sr. loses everything if they fail.

**External Obstacles / Antagonist**: Most of the conflict in the story comes from Pat himself. He's struggling against his inner demons, so he is his own antagonist. All the other characters (Tiffany, Dr Patel, Pat's mother, Ronnie, Danny, Jake, even the cop in charge of his case) are trying to help Pat in various ways in his fight against himself. The only external obstacles are Pat's father, when he stands in the way of him spending more time with Tiffany, and Tiffany herself, who schemes against Pat's conscious goal.

**Internal Obstacles**: Pat's delusion is his biggest obstacle, along with his bipolarity. He believes he's fine when we know he isn't. He believes Nikki still loves him when we know she doesn't. Because this prevents him from getting better and moving on, it's one of the biggest sources of conflict. Most importantly, he can do something about this delusion. Becoming aware of the problem is often half the solution.

**Catalyst:** Tiffany. She pretends to be helping Pat to get his wife back, in reality she's trying to get him to realise he has to move on because she's the one for him. She's the character forcing Pat to change, constantly pushing him to ask himself the right questions. As often in character-led stories, she's both the catalyst and a co-protagonist in relation to Pat's unconscious goal.

**Subplots**: The most important subplot explores Pat's relationship with his father. Protagonist: Pat Sr. Goal: To spend more time with Pat who supposedly brings him luck with his superstitious gambling. We get a sense that Pat's relationship with his father is connected to his condition, so healing it is one way to get better and move on. This is confirmed when Pat Sr. tells his son that he didn't know how to deal with his condition, that he's worried he might have spent too much time with his brother and not enough time with him when they were kids, that he might have contributed to making his condition worse. This subplot becomes the main plot in the last sequence of dramatic Act 2, which seems to be about winning the parlay bet but is really about Pat proving his love to Tiffany and his worth to his father. When they hug at the end, and Pat is able to tell his father he loves him, this closure marks the end of the subplot. The subplot with Danny, Pat's friend from the hospital, is more minor. Still, it's a nice thread in the story which brings humour and helps Pat to realise he's attracted to Tiffany (when he feels jealous seeing Danny dancing with her).

**Comedy:** There is a lot of comedy in *Silver Linings Playbook*. The characters are original, surprising and funny. This adds greatly to the screenplay, not only because it brings conflict, but also because it adds pace and energy to the story.

## FRACTAL ASPECT OF STORY STRUCTURE

**First Act / Set-Up:** The first act is a masterclass in exposition. The main characters – except Tiffany – are introduced, and in about fifteen minutes we learn everything we need to know to be able to fully identify with Pat and give him the unconscious goal to get better.

The following elements also contribute to a very enjoyable and entertaining set-up: the way conflict is used to make this exposition palatable; how we start with just enough mystery to raise our interest and ensure this mystery doesn't last too long, which would prevent a full identification with the protagonist; the pace and humour in this first act. There is a lot of information conveyed in a short amount of time, often visually (even using a brief flashback to show us the key incident in the past), and we never feel like we're being spoon-fed with information. Fantastic writing.

**Inciting Event / Inciting Action:** *Silver Linings Playbook* offers a very interesting example of how complex inciting events can be. First, there is no inciting event shown for Pat's conscious goal, because he already has his goal – to get back together with his wife Nikki – at the beginning of the story. However, there is an inciting action, which is everything that happens in the story until we know enough about Pat to give him the unconscious goal to get better and move on. This culminates with the scene with Dr Patel at 00:14 when we learn what happened in the past. The resolution of this mystery, which shapes the only dramatic sequence in Act 1, leads the audience to give Pat the unconscious goal of moving on, but it's not an inciting event because it doesn't trigger a goal for Pat, conscious or not.

The real inciting event for Pat is his meeting with Tiffany, twenty-five minutes into the movie. It triggers Pat's unconscious goal to realise that she's the right girl for him, that he needs to change. This makes it the *character* inciting event. This is when the romantic comedy element of *Silver Linings Playbook* kicks in. The main dramatic question becomes: "Will Pat and Tiffany end up together?". This question is deeply connected to Pat's ability to get better and move on. If he doesn't get better, he can't move on and if he doesn't move on, he can't get Tiffany. So to summarise, Pat has his conscious goal right away, then fifteen minutes in, the audience gives Pat the unconscious goal to change. At 00:25, the character inciting event brings this need to change into Pat's subconscious mind.

**Beginning of Dramatic Act 2**: In character-led stories, we enter Act 2 when we understand what the character needs, or when we realise that what the character needs is more important than what the character wants. This happens around 00:15, in Dr Patel's office, when we understand that Pat isn't as fine as he thinks he is, and when we find out what happened in the past. From this point, we know he's deluded about his condition and about his wife's feelings towards him, so we give him the unconscious goal to get better and move on.

**Sequences in Act 2**: There are four sequences in dramatic Act 2.

1. **The first sequence in Act 2** is twenty minutes long. It starts around 00:15 and lasts until 00:35. Protagonist: Pat. Goal: To get back with his wife Nikki his way, without acknowledging his condition. He's in denial, doesn't listen to his therapist's advice, refuses to take his medication. He pretends it's all fine, and we know it's not. The meeting with Tiffany around 00:25 introduces the biggest obstacle to his conscious goal. It's also the *character* inciting event that triggers Pat's unconscious need to change. His immediate attraction to Tiffany creates the dilemma that is going to be exploited over the rest of the movie: Will he choose Nikki or Tiffany? This sequence culminates around 00:34, in a climax during which Pat accidentally kicks his mother and has a fight with his father. The next morning (third act of the sequence), he starts taking his medication. This shows that he's starting to realise that he's not as well as he thinks he is. This is the first step in Pat's evolution; some of his delusion falls away. He's making a step towards getting better, but no apparent progress yet regarding moving on: he's still obsessed with Nikki. The scene with Tiffany at 00:36 shows this clearly. He rejects her and hurts her feelings one more time, which leads her to ask him a key question: Is he happy with himself? Can he forgive?

2.  **The second sequence in Act 2** is twenty-one minutes long. It starts at 00:37 when Dr Patel suggests that Pat help Tiffany to show Nikki that he's a kind, generous, large-hearted person who helps people in need, who is thriving. We understand that Dr Patel is trying to get him to spend more time with Tiffany, hoping that it will take his mind off Nikki. Protagonist: Pat. Goal: To help Tiffany in order to impress Nikki. Over the sequence, Pat is genuinely going to help Tiffany as he gets to know her better. However, she refuses to help him with the letter unless he does something for her in return. This is the climax of the sequence, around 00:58. The conflict in the sequence leads Pat to realise that he's been selfish, that he was taking rather than giving.

3.  **The third sequence in Act 2** is thirty minutes long. It starts at 01:04, when we realise that Pat has agreed to help Tiffany. Protagonist: Pat. Goal: To help Tiffany with her dancing so she'll help him communicate with his wife. The climax of the sequence is in two parts (because they have both promised something to each other). The first one is when Pat reads Nikki's answer to his letter 01:19. He has managed to communicate with his wife (or so he thinks), but he's gutted with the outcome. He still promises to spend some time with Tiffany the next day to fulfil his part of the bargain. Then during the big match he's drawn into a fight at 01:25 and ends up not showing up at Tiffany's. This second part of the climax brings a dual set-back: his father has drawn him away from Tiffany, and Pat has failed to control himself. Overall he's managed to communicate with Nikki (or so he thinks), but he's failed Tiffany with his no-show; his dad, with the fighting. The third act of the sequence is fairly long (almost ten minutes), as it includes the fight-off between Pat Sr. and Tiffany (a logical consequence of the action of the third sequence), which leads to the inciting event for the next sequence (the parlay bet). It's only because there is a lot of conflict during this confrontation that the third act of the sequence can be so long. In a way, Pat Sr. and Tiffany have been fighting over Pat during the whole sequence, so the third act of the sequence is the end of their second act, when their growing rivalry is finally resolved.

4. **The fourth sequence in Act 2** is nine minutes long. It starts at 01:36 when Pat and Tiffany resume training for the competition. Co-protagonists: Pat and Tiffany. Goal: Winning the parlay bet. Tiffany, because she hopes it will help her to win Pat when Nikki doesn't show up. Pat does it both for Tiffany and his dad. Although they are co-protagonists, Tiffany experiences more conflict than Pat during this sequence. First, because she's the victim of a strong dramatic irony (we know Pat has found out she wrote Nikki's answer, but she doesn't) and also because she faces a huge, unexpected obstacle when Nikki does show up with Ronnie and Veronica, which is a massive blow to her plan. Because Pat doesn't share with us what his intentions are regarding Nikki and Tiffany, we tend to empathise more with Tiffany than Pat over this sequence. As they are co-protagonists, this isn't a problem as it allows the main dramatic questions to remain open until the end.

**Mid-Act Climax**: There is no mid-act climax in *Silver Linings Playbook* as Pat has the same conscious goal and we give him the same unconscious need over the whole story. If someone was to look for a midpoint, it might be when Tiffany forces Pat to help her with the dancing in exchange for her help with the letter, because it introduces a very important element for the rest of the story (them dancing together). However, from a structural point of view, it's just a plot point because Pat's conscious goal and unconscious need remain the same.

**Climax of Dramatic Act 2**: There are two climaxes in short succession in the story. The first one is their dancing at the competition, when they win the parlay bet. This is the climax of the last dramatic sequence of Act 2, but the main questions are still open: Has Pat changed? Has he chosen Tiffany over Nikki? Will they end up together? Interestingly, Pat has already achieved his change, but we don't know this for sure because there is a small mystery over his intentions. For him, the climax of his evolution is probably when he finds out that Tiffany wrote Nikki's letter. But just like we gave him the unconscious goal to change before he became aware of it, we only enter Act 3 once we know he has changed (or failed to change). Structure is always from the point of view of the audience, not from the point of view of the character, which is why it's subjective. We enter Act 2 when *we* understand what the goal of the protagonist (conscious in a plot-led story; unconscious in a character-led story) is going to be, and we enter Act 3 when *we* get an answer to the dramatic question: *Yes*, the protagonist has changed, or *no*, he hasn't. This is why we have to wait until the last scene between Pat and Tiffany to get our answer and why it's the real climax of the story.

**Answer to the dramatic question**: *Yes*, Pat does manage to change and his internal problem is solved by the end of the story. He has given up trying to reach a wrong conscious goal (getting back with Nikki). As a result, he gets what he needed (to get better, to move on). And he also gets Tiffany, which ironically is what he wanted from the beginning: true love. Except it's not with a person he was infatuated with (his estranged wife, who possibly never really loved him), but with someone he truly loves and who truly loves him back.

**Beginning of Dramatic Act 3**: We enter Act 3 after the climax, when Pat and Tiffany kiss for the first time. We see the consequences of the evolution: a happier, closer family, friends reunited and a happy couple.

*Encore Twist*: There is no *Encore Twist* in *Silver Linings Playbook*.

**Does the Answer to the Dramatic Question Convey the Point of View of the Filmmaker(s):** The point of view of the filmmaker is clearly that we can have a happy ending if we take a positive look at life and find the courage to change. At least that's what the answer to the dramatic question suggests.

**Does the Answer to the Dramatic Question Fit the Genre of the Story:** *Silver Linings Playbook* is a romantic comedy even if it explores serious themes. It's both funny and romantic. Both characters deserve to get a better life. We want them to end up together. Therefore, the ending does fit the genre of the story. If the two main characters of a romantic comedy are not supposed to end up together, it's better to seed it early on, as with *500 Days of Summer*, in which a voiceover tells us right away that this isn't a love story. The main function of romantic comedies is to help us believe that finding true love is possible. It might not be realistic, but that's the value of the story. If you take it away, you'd better have either a good reason to do so, or be prepared to disappoint the audience.

**Is the Ending Satisfying?** The ending is satisfying because although Pat gives up on his conscious goal (to get his wife Nikki back) he does get what he needs (to move on, and get lovely Tiffany). Pat hasn't made any mistake that would justify that he failed to change. He hasn't done anything to deserve an unhappy ending. He's worked hard, first in the wrong direction, then in the right direction, to do the right thing. Depriving him (and Tiffany) of a happy ending would probably be unsatisfying. This has nothing to do with law or morality. We want what feels right for the characters, and in this case we want them rewarded because they both deserve it.

**Duration of Dramatic Acts**: It takes about fifteen minutes before we learn enough about Pat to know that he's going in the wrong direction, that he's deluded and needs to get better and move on. This is the length of Act 1, which is everything that happens before we understand what the story is about, what the main problem is (in this case, it's going to be about Pat's ability to solve his internal problem). Note that while Pat has his conscious goal before the story begins, and we understand it right away, it's only when we're able to assess whether it's the right or wrong goal that we can decide what the main problem is. If this was a plot-led story, Act 1 would be one-minute long as we understand right away what Pat's conscious goal is. Pat's evolution lasts for most of the movie. It's only at 01:52 that we get an answer to the main dramatic question: *Yes*, he has changed, and *yes*, he has chosen Tiffany over Nikki. So Act 2 is about one hundred minutes long. Dramatic Act 3 is very short. If we don't take the end credits into account, it takes about one minute to show the consequences of the evolution: a happier family, friends reunited and the happy couple.

## MANAGING INFORMATION

### Main Dramatic Ironies:

The main dramatic irony is that we know that Pat isn't doing as well as he thinks he is. Nikki isn't the right woman for him and getting her back isn't going to solve his problem. He doesn't know that. This strong dramatic irony – we know something about the protagonist that they are unaware of – creates a lot of conflict over the whole film. A similar dramatic irony is present in most character-led stories.

The next big dramatic irony, towards the end, is that we know Pat has found out that Tiffany has written Nikki's answer to his letter, but Tiffany doesn't know this until the climax, when this dramatic irony is resolved. Depending on whether we saw this coming or not, there might be a third dramatic irony for some of the audience, see below.

**Main Surprises:**

Danny wasn't allowed to leave the hospital. This is a minor surprise, but it's quite funny and it helps set up the characters.

Tiffany's presence at Ronnie and Veronica's dinner. With Pat, we were expecting Nikki to show up, so meeting Tiffany instead is a surprise.

Dr Patel's presence at the Eagles/Giants match. Although Dr Patel's appreciation of football had been planted earlier in the story, his appearance at the match is a minor surprise.

After Pat's speech to the "creep", we discover that Tiffany has heard the way Pat defended and protected her. It's a nice surprise which also sets up a small dramatic irony: Pat doesn't know she knows what he said about her.

Tiffany has written Nikki's answer to Pat's letter. This one could be a grey area because some might guess that Nikki never wrote the letter as it's not handwritten. For those who guess that Tiffany has written the letter, then a dramatic irony is set up when they understand. Pat is the victim, and the scene when he finds out is the resolution, which is surprising for Pat but not for the part of the audience that had guessed earlier. For those who don't see it coming, the resolution is a surprise both for them and the victim, Pat.

Nikki's presence at the competition. This a huge blow for Tiffany, as it wasn't planned. They lied to Pat to get him to do the dance, but they didn't know that Ronnie and Veronica would bring Nikki. This is not only a surprise for us and Tiffany, it's also a huge obstacle for her, as she was hoping that Nikki's no-show would help her to get Pat. It's also a nice reversal of the dinner scene, when we were expecting Nikki to come and Tiffany shows up instead. Here, we were not expecting Nikki and she suddenly appears.

As we said earlier, in most character-led stories the protagonist is victim of a very strong dramatic irony. We know something the protagonist doesn't, at least consciously. We're aware of the problem, of the need for the protagonist to change before they are. Later in the story, especially in romantic comedies, we often find a *reveal* scene, present in *Groundhog Day*, *As Good As It Gets* and *Silver Linings Playbook* as well. It's a surprising scene (for the audience) when we realise that the protagonist was more aware of the problem than we thought, has caught up with us without us knowing it. In other words, the resolution happened off screen, setting up a new dramatic irony with the audience as victim. This is the dramatic irony that is resolved in the *reveal* scene. Not a rule, just a way to surprise the audience and reverse the situation. In *Silver Linings Playbook*, the *reveal scene* happens during the climax, when Pat tells Tiffany that he fell in love with her the minute he saw her, but then he got stuck. This surprise doesn't mean that Pat lied to us over the whole film and knew this from the beginning, just that he realised a bit earlier, and kept it to himself. Unconsciously, he falls in love with Tiffany when he first meets her. This inciting event triggers his unconscious goal to change, but it takes him a while to bring this knowledge to a conscious level.

**Main Elements of Mystery:**

The main elements of mystery are related to the backstories of the two main characters. Everything we need to know about Pat's backstory is revealed by minute fifteen, which really helps our identification with him as we can then *become* the character. The mystery over Tiffany's backstory lasts longer, which isn't a problem as she isn't the protagonist but the catalyst. By the time she becomes more of a co-protagonist, we know enough about her past and her motivation to be able to identify with her too.

Otherwise, there is some mystery over Pat's intentions once he finds out that Tiffany has written Nikki's letter. This draws us slightly away from him for a short amount of time, but it's fine, because by then we can identify with Tiffany, who experiences more conflict than him over the last dramatic sequence of Act 2, until the mystery is resolved (we realise he had chosen Tiffany over Nikki and completed his evolution earlier).

**Main Elements of Suspense:**

There is a lot of suspense over the whole movie because we keep wondering if Pat will manage to control his condition or not, but the most suspenseful sequences are just before and during the dance competition (Will they do well enough to win the parlay bet, the danger being Tiffany's loss of hope?) and during the very last scene (Will they end up together, the danger being Pat's decision to be romantic and not to tell Tiffany what his intentions were, which means he might have lost her?). The dance rehearsals also bring in a nice time-lock, which adds tension to the story and increases suspense. They only have a limited amount of time to get ready before the competition starts. There is no literal ticking bomb in *Silver Linings Playbook*, but there are quite a few figurative ones.

## VISUAL STORYTELLING, PLANTING/PAY-OFF, EXPOSITION

### Planting/Pay-Off and Visual Storytelling:

Pat's picture, which Pat sees when he arrives at his parents' home, sits on the floor instead of hanging on the wall next to his brother's. It shows how his parents, and especially his father, see him as being not as good as his brother, as having fallen from grace. It also plants a nice visual pay-off at the very end, when we see Pat's father putting his picture back up on the wall, next to Jake's, to show the family's restored order and healed relationships.

When Pat's song is played for the first time and we understand what it's connected to (Pat's wedding and the incident with his wife and her lover), its significance is planted: it's a trigger. Then every time we hear it again (for example when he's out with Tiffany), we understand why he's having an episode. It's an example of planting to assign a specific meaning to an object, a character, a line of dialogue or in this case a song (as in *Casablanca*).

The letter device is used in many ways. First, it's a letter that Pat writes to Nikki. Then it's the supposed answer from Nikki, in fact written by Tiffany. The expression used by Tiffany ("If it's me reading the signs") is planted when Pat reads the letter, and pays off during Tiffany's face-off with Pat Sr. This is what allows Pat to understand that she loves him, using visual storytelling. Pat's last letter is a final pay-off because Tiffany is convinced it's another letter to Nikki, so she's surprised when she realised it's addressed to her.

Pat repairing the window is a nice visual metaphor showing that Pat has started mending himself, bringing order to the chaos of his life. It happens just after the fight at his parents'. When he takes his medication for the first time that morning, it also shows that he's realised he isn't doing as well as he thought. These two elements have been planted before and make it possible to use visual storytelling to convey a change in the protagonist.

In the last scene, both Pat and Tiffany have stopped wearing their wedding rings. It's a subtle but effective visual pay-off showing they have moved on from their respective ex-partners.

## Exposition:

*Silver Linings Playbook* deals perfectly with exposition, especially in its first act. In less than fifteen minutes we are given all the information we need to be able to fully identify with the protagonist. We learn everything that's relevant regarding Pat's backstory in the first few scenes, with his parents, with his therapist: what happened, his condition, what he knows about his condition, and we're even told what he has to do to get better, which is take his pills and find a way to control his trigger. Bringing the audience up to speed with the protagonist is a key point regarding identification. It's difficult to empathise with a protagonist who knows more than we do about something relevant to the story over a long period of time. It's not a problem to know *more* than the protagonist, as in *The Apartment*, but knowing *less* can be tricky and *Silver Linings Playbook* brilliantly avoids this.

There are a few other well-handled exposition scenes later. Tiffany's backstory, for example, is only gradually revealed, which creates enough mystery to tease and make us willing to find out more. It's not a problem that there is mystery about her for quite a while because she isn't the protagonist; she's the catalyst to start with. In fact, we start to care more about her and she becomes more of a co-protagonist as we find out about her past. Also, scenes delivering information about her use conflict to make the exposition more palatable. For example, the diner scene is first very funny, then we feel conflict both for Tiffany (who is hurt) and for Pat (who is unaware of his problem). Another poignant and beautifully written exposition scene comes during a rehearsal, when Tiffany tells Pat how Tommy died to show him what a feeling is.

Exposition can be the death of drama when it's mishandled, but *Silver Linings Playbook* provides an entertaining crash course for those interested in learning the craft. There is always conflict when exposition is handled. Either 1) because the information or the way it's given/received is conflictual or funny; 2) because characters don't want to hear what they are being told; or 3) because characters don't want to talk about what they are revealing. We never have a flat scene in which we're simply told about past events. Finally, we're not told things which are not important or relevant, and we're not told everything up front. There is just enough mystery at the beginning, first for Pat, then for Tiffany, for us to welcome the information when it's offered.

# The Intouchables

### Written and Directed by Eric Toledano and Olivier Nakache

Detailed Analysis

**Note: As usual it's best to watch the film just before reading the analysis.**

*The Intouchables* (*Intouchables* in France, *Untouchable* in the UK) is a 2011 French film directed by Olivier Nakache and Éric Toledano. Within a few weeks of its release, it became the second biggest box office hit in France, just behind the 2008 film *Welcome to the Sticks*. It was nominated for eight César Awards in France (Omar Sy winning Best Actor).

The film had a budget of €9.5M and generated a worldwide box office of €364M according to Wikipedia, most likely a profitability record. It was both a commercial and critical success and it is, to date, the most successful non-English language movie worldwide ever.

Adapted from a true story, the "real" Philippe (Philippe Pozzo di Borgo) first talked about his relationship with the "real" Driss (Abdel Yasmin Sellou, an Algerian not a Senegalese) in an autobiography, then in a TV documentary. He advised the filmmakers to make it a comedy, saying that in his condition, one looks for humour, not for people who pity you. He also said that the title for the movie was perfect, because it's a plural. It's the story of two untouchables, who, taken separately, are not people you'd want to spend any time with, but together become indestructible.

*The Intouchables* is another funny and moving character-led movie. It's primarily a buddy movie, a two-hander showing the evolution of the relationship between the two characters. In this way it's similar to romantic comedies such as *When Harry Met Sally* or *You've Got Mail* except it's about friendship, not love. Unlike *Groundhog Day* or *Silver Linings Playbook,* the story is told from the point of view of Driss (Sy), the catalyst character who pushes the protagonist to change, and not the protagonist himself, Philippe (François Cluzet).

Let's see how this plays out in a short synopsis of the story before digging further into the analysis.

00:01, at night in Paris, Driss is driving Philippe's Maserati at high speed. They are chased through the streets by the police, and eventually cornered. Driss claims the quadriplegic Philippe must be urgently driven to the emergency room; Philippe pretends to have a stroke and the fooled police officers escort them to the hospital.

00:10, the story of the friendship between the two men is told in flashback: Philippe, a rich quadriplegic who owns a luxurious mansion and his assistant Magalie (Audrey Fleurot) are interviewing candidates to be his live-in caregiver. Driss, a candidate, has no ambition to be hired. He's just there to get a signature showing he was interviewed and rejected to continue to receive his welfare benefits. He's told to come back the next morning to get his signed letter.

00:13, Driss in his mum's apartment in the suburbs, fighting with many children for the bathroom. We learn he's just reappeared after six months without giving any news. He says he was on holiday, but his mum isn't stupid. He gives her a Fabergé egg he's stolen from Philippe's house. His mum doesn't realise its value. She's given up on him, but she still has hope for her other children. She kicks him out and asks him not to come back.

00:19, the next day, Driss returns to pick up his signed paper, is given a tour of the house, finds out that the job comes with a separate studio apartment – and an en-suite bathroom. Philippe has signed his letter, but as Driss is about to leave, he offers him a month's trial for the job, betting that he won't last two weeks.

00:22, Driss accepts the trial and moves in. Despite his disinterest and lack of professional experience, Driss does well caring for Philippe, even if his methods are unconventional. Driss learns the extent of Philippe's disability and accompanies Philippe in every moment of his life, assisting him in all the ways needed (except one: emptying Philippe's bowels).

00:34, a friend of Philippe's reveals Driss's criminal record which includes six months in jail for robbery. Philippe states he doesn't care about Driss's past because he is the only one who doesn't treat him with pity. He says he won't fire him as long as he does his job properly.

00:37, Driss, helping Philippe file his mail, discovers that Philippe has a purely epistolary relationship with a woman called Eléonore, who lives in Dunkirk. He also jokingly suggests that they start a "prostitutes" file.

00:40, Driss turns out to be good at his job. He's able to calm Philippe down at night when he has "phantom pains". He shares a spliff with

Philippe to help with the pain, asks him if he's able to have a sex life (finds out his ears are the only erogenous zones Philippe has left). Philippe discloses that he became disabled following a paragliding accident and that his wife died without bearing children. He tells Driss that his real handicap isn't being in a wheelchair; it's living without his wife. He tells him that he's won the bet and is officially hired as his trial period is over. But he wants his Fabergé egg back.

00:51, Driss encourages Philippe to meet Eléonore, but Philippe fears her reaction when she finds out he's disabled. Driss forces Philippe to talk to Eléonore on the phone. Philippe, taken by surprise, is then delighted.

00:53, after exposure to modern art, Driss discovers opera – not his thing – and starts painting.

00:57, Driss convinces Philippe to send a photo of himself in a wheelchair to Eléonore, but Philippe then changes his mind and asks his aide Yvonne (Anne Le Ny) to send a picture of him as he was before his accident. Instead of getting rid of the wheelchair picture as instructed, Yvonne shoves it in the "prostitutes" file.

01:01, Philippe is led by Driss to be stricter with his adopted daughter, Elisa.

01:02, Driss oversees a "massage" session for Philippe, which features smoking pot and a lot of ear tickling...

01:04, for Philippe's birthday, a private concert of classical music is performed in his living room. Philippe tries to convince the friend who "warned him" about Driss to buy Driss's first painting, pretending it's by an exciting new artist. After the concert Driss plays Earth, Wind & Fire's "Boogie Wonderland" and Philippe has a more exciting birthday than usual.

01:15, a date between Eléonore and Philippe has been arranged. At the last minute Philippe is too scared to meet Eléonore and leaves with Yvonne before Eléonore arrives.

01:20, Philippe calls Driss and invites him to travel with him in his private jet for a paragliding weekend. On the way he gives him 11,000 euros in cash, what he managed to get for the sale of Driss's painting to his friend.

01:25, Adama, who we believe to be Driss's younger brother, and is in trouble with a gang, comes to fetch Driss at Philippe's mansion on the pretext of delivering mail. Overhearing, Philippe understands Driss's need to be supportive to his family and releases him from his job, suggesting he may not want to push a wheelchair all his life. We find out with Philippe that Adama isn't Driss's brother but his cousin, as his mum is in fact his aunt.

01:32, Driss leaves, just after having found out that Magalie's boyfriend, Fred, is in fact a girlfriend, Frédérique. Yvonne gives Driss a folder that they won't need anymore (the prostitutes' one). Inside, Driss finds the picture of Philippe they had agreed to send to Eléonore. He pockets it.

Driss returns to his neighbourhood, joining his friends. He reconnects with his aunt and manages to help his younger cousin. Thanks to his experience with Philippe, he gets a job at a courier company, having followed Philippe's advice to get his driver's license. In the meantime, Philippe has hired caregivers to replace Driss, but he isn't happy with any of them. His morale is very low and he stops taking care of himself, growing a beard, losing his appetite.

01:40, Yvonne becomes worried and contacts Driss, who arrives and decides to drive Philippe in the Maserati, which brings the story back to the first scene of the film, the police chase.

After they have eluded the police, Driss takes Philippe to the seaside. Upon shaving and dressing elegantly, Philippe and Driss arrive at a Cabourg restaurant with a great ocean view.

01:45, as they sit, Driss leaves the table, wishing Philippe good luck with his surprise lunch date and returning the Fabergé egg.

Moments later, Eléonore arrives. Touched, Philippe looks through the window and sees Driss outside, smiling at him. Driss bids Philippe farewell and walks away.

* * *

While the story is told mostly from Driss's point of view, Philippe experiences more conflict due to his condition and deep unhappiness. Although the story is quite balanced between the two characters, Philippe's problem – he needs to move on to be able to start a new relationship – is what really has to be solved in the film. Driss's problem with his family and his life in general is both a subplot and an obstacle, something that stands in the way of their relationship.

They both need to change, but Philippe's need is more acute.

Of course Philippe has an external problem – his handicap – but that's not the main problem in the story, which is good because there isn't much that can be done about it. What can be changed isn't Philippe's handicap, it's Philippe's attitude towards it. In fact, Philippe says it himself, when he admits that his real handicap isn't being in a wheelchair, it's living without his wife.

As soon as they first meet, we understand that the story is going to be about their relationship, and how they are going to change each other.

Thanks to Driss, Philippe becomes more confident, starts to enjoy life again, while Driss discovers art, music and painting and is led to sort himself out, accept his responsibilities and leave theft behind for a steady job.

So how can we define Philippe's evolution?

> **A** (start point in the story): Philippe is cynical, detached, blasé. He resents his condition. He doesn't believe he can be loved as he is. He functions, but he's lost his appetite for life.

> **B** (end point in the story): Philippe is hopeful, has accepted his condition and the idea that he might be happy and loved, like anyone else. He's alive again.

This is a pretty extreme change, so let's try to break it down to a few emotional or psychological steps, *map the change* so that Philippe's evolution is made more believable:

1. Driss doesn't pity Philippe. This is the reason why Philippe wants Driss and not someone better qualified to look after him. This is the first step towards change. If someone treats him like anyone else, maybe he can be like anyone else.

2. Driss makes Philippe laugh. This re-ignites Philippe's joie de vivre. He also re-discovers things he used to love: his sports car, paragliding, etc.

3. Philippe starts to consider the possibility of being happy again, of having a romantic relationship with someone else. He manages to talk to Eléonore, which raises our hopes as it's a big step, but he's not yet ready to show himself as he really is and can't find the courage to meet her.

4. Philippe realises that Driss has to help his family. He's aware that Driss isn't going to spend the rest of his life looking after him, so he selflessly lets him go. It's the low point in the movie, as Philippe gives up and starts to decline.

5. Finding out that Philippe isn't well, Driss engineers a lunch between Philippe and Eléonore. Philippe is touched, healed and

ready now to embrace life again and start a new relationship. He
has moved on.

Like all character-led movies, seen like this, it feels quite corny. So we
need a lot of humour, irony and energy to make it work. This is exactly
what the "real" Philippe suggested to the filmmakers: make it a comedy!

What makes the film work – beyond the excellent acting,
cinematography, use of music and directing – is the comedy generated
by the humour and gags in the movie, which it delivers in both quality
and quantity. Little by little, under Driss's influence, Philippe is forced to
change. And because of his exposure to Philippe and his world, Driss is
led to grow.

Like most buddy movies, a lot of the conflict – and humour – comes
from the contrast between characters who are complete opposites but
have to interact with each other. It's also a classic fish-out-of-water story.

There isn't much plot-led design for each sequence, but the film doesn't
feel episodic because 1) our interest is focused on the main evolution and
2) the many gags and strong humour in the film keep us entertained.
Therefore, it has less clearly defined sequences than the previous case
studies. This isn't a problem, especially in a character-led movie which
uses humour rather than the fractal aspect of story structure to generate
conflict. It would be a problem if the film weren't a comedy, because we
would likely feel that there isn't enough conflict, or that what's at stake
locally isn't clear or the story is episodic.

However, there are quite a few subplots in the story:

- Driss's problems with his family (poor communication with
his aunt due to the bad example he sets for her other children;
Adama's problems with the gang). This is related to Driss's inability to deal with his responsibilities. Looking after Philippe has
changed him. When he returns to the suburbs, he's able to sort
himself out, get a job, look after his aunt and get his cousin out of
gang trouble. It's a secondary evolution because Driss's problem
isn't as acute as Philippe's, but it's satisfying to see Driss change
and sort out his life too.

- Flirting with Magalie. This is mostly a running gag, which pays
off in the end one last time when we realise with Driss that she's a
lesbian (which is for him the only explanation as to how she could
have resisted him).

- Sorting out Elisa. This is connected to Philippe as he needs to
be stricter with his adopted daughter, but Driss also tries to help

3.5 CASE STUDIES 331

her in relation to her boyfriend and makes sure he treats her with respect.

• What happens with Eléonore isn't really a subplot. It's part of the main plot and helps to monitor Philippe's evolution, through successes and setbacks.

Also *The Intouchables* expertly uses classical tools to manage information and achieve a great deal of visual storytelling through planting and pay-offs, as we'll see in more detail in its STM Framework.

As in a romantic comedy, we want the two characters to become friends because we believe they should, even if they are not aware of this to start with. This is why the ending is so satisfying, because it delivers on all aspects (Philippe's and Driss's evolution as well as the evolution of their relationship). And like romantic comedies, the casting of the two main actors is crucial. Get the chemistry right and it works; get it wrong and nothing can save it.

Casting isn't less important in plot-led stories. It's just that in plot-led movies we have something at stake earlier, which is the conscious goal of the protagonist. In character-led stories, we have to like the character(s) enough to want them to change or become friends/lovers before they themselves want to, especially when there isn't a strong plot-led element in the movie (as in *Groundhog Day* or *Silver Linings Playbook*) to give us a frame of reference earlier.

If we look at Maslow's Hierarchy of Needs, what's at stake in *The Intouchables* mostly hangs in the middle of the pyramid, like most character-led movies. It's primarily about love/belonging (friendship, sexual intimacy), as well as esteem (self-esteem, confidence, achievement, respect of others, by others). But it frequently reaches down to the safety and physiological levels. Philippe's life is at stake when he feels suicidal. Many jokes are related to Philippe's inability to perform basic bodily functions: emptying his bowels, having sex, breathing, etc. This opens the movie to the base of the pyramid. But through its theme and some of its cultural and artistic elements, it also reaches up to the top (morality, creativity, spontaneity, problem solving, lack of prejudice, acceptance of facts). So overall *The Intouchables* has a high M-Factor. It spans all levels of the pyramid, which opens a wide potential audience. Its limited budget level also makes it a great candidate for crossover success.

The fact that it has a universal story, that it reaches out to all levels of Maslow's pyramid, that it uses classical tools to manage conflict and in-formation as well as a lot of planting and pay-off, making its storytelling

Emmanuel Oberg

as visual as possible, certainly helped it to reach such a large audience, not only at home but also abroad.

Like many successful European movies, there is no active protagonist with a strong conscious goal or a clear dramatic action defining what's at stake in the story and in clearly defined sequences in Act 2. Most of the classical tools are still used, but in a slightly different way, because it's a character-led movie. The dramatic action might not be clear, but the main evolutions (Philippe's, Driss's and the evolution of their relationship) offer a strong backbone to the story.

In fact, the best way to destroy a character-led movie is to try to force it into a plot-led box. A story like *Two Days, One Night*, which is a character-led story disguised as plot-led, tends to be the exception rather than the rule, at least on the European scene.

This is why it's essential for many independent producers, especially European ones, to put aside a strictly plot-led, Aristotelian approach to story structure when working on the development of their projects.

Let's take a look now at the STM (*Story-Type Method*) framework of *The Intouchables*. You'll find more information on this key development tool as well as a link to download a template in the *Story Design Tools* section of *Bringing It All Together*. As usual, there will be some repetitions between the analysis and the STM Framework. This is so that each part of the case study can be read independently.

# STM Framework for *The Intouchables*

## STORY-TYPE, M-FACTOR AND THEME

**Main Problem in the Story**: Philippe's inability to move on, to be happy again following the death of his wife, is the problem that needs to be solved by the end of the story.

**Story-Type**: Because the main problem lies within the protagonist, we're dealing with a character-led story. This is a close call, though, because we see the story from the point of view of Driss, the catalyst. Feel free to consider it a plot-led story or a hybrid if it makes more sense to you. Remember, story structure is subjective.

**M-Factor**: If we look at Maslow's Hierarchy of Needs, what's at stake in *The Intouchables* mostly hangs in the middle of the pyramid, like most character-led movies. It's primarily about love/belonging (friendship, sexual intimacy), as well as esteem (self-esteem, confidence, achievement, respect of others, by others). But it frequently reaches down to the safety and physiological levels. Philippe's life is at stake when he feels suicidal. Many jokes are related to Philippe's inability to perform basic bodily functions: emptying his bowels, having sex, breathing, etc. This opens the movie to the base of the pyramid. But through its theme and some of its cultural and artistic elements, it also reaches up to the top (morality, creativity, spontaneity, problem solving, lack of prejudice, acceptance of facts). So overall *The Intouchables* has a high M-Factor. It spans all the levels of the pyramid which opens a wide potential audience. Its limited budget level also makes it a great candidate for crossover success.

**Theme**: *The Intouchables* explores quite a few themes. The main one is about friendship: Can two characters who are different in almost every way become friends? Being different (one because of the colour of his skin, the other because of his disability) is another strong theme which explains why they become friends. Both are excluded, which unites them. Then we have themes related to social justice, racism and acceptance of facts.

## MANAGING CONFLICT

**Protagonist**: Philippe.

**Conscious Goal**: To find the strength to live.

**Unconscious Need**: Philippe needs to move on, to get better. He can't be happy after the death of his beloved wife following his accident, and he has to accept both his condition and the fact that his wife is gone.

**Motivation**: Philippe has lost his wife and with her the will to live. He's still trying though.

**Main Characteristic**: Philippe is disabled. It shouldn't be a main characteristic, but that's what defines him in our eyes, and in his.

**Secondary Characteristics**: Philippe has a sense of humour, loves classical music, painting and the arts in general. He's very rich. His ears are his only erogenous zone.

**Evolution (growth, change or steadfast)**: **Philippe** *changes*. He gets better and he moves on by the end of the story, as he's able to start a new relationship with Eléonore. **Driss** *grows* more than he changes. He has to sort out his life from a moral point of view, but psychologically he has less of an internal problem than Philippe. *The Intouchables* is like any buddy movie. We're interested in the evolution of the relationship between the two characters as much as in Philippe's evolution, driven by his need to change, and Driss's evolution, driven by his need to stop messing around and to accept his responsibilities.

**Main Characters**: Philippe and Driss. It's the story of their relationship.

**Main Plot**: The main plot is Driss trying to help Philippe find the strength to live.

**What's at Stake**: Philippe's happiness – and life, as suicide is always a possibility and becomes a reality towards the end.

**External Obstacles / Antagonist**: Philippe is his own antagonist, although his disability is an important external obstacle. Unfortunately, there is nothing that can be done about it. The only thing that Philippe can change is himself, his attitude to life and his handicap.

**Internal Obstacles**: Philippe lacks the confidence, the self-esteem to approach Eléonore. His depression in relation to the death of his wife is another obstacle.

**Catalyst:** Driss. He is the character who forces Philippe to change. What's original in *The Intouchables* is that the story is told from the point of view of the catalyst, not the protagonist, at least initially.

**Subplots**: There are quite a few subplots in the story:

- Driss's problems with his family (poor communication with his aunt due to the bad example he sets for her other children; Adama's problems with the gang). This is related to Driss's inability to deal with his responsibilities. Looking after Philippe has changed him. When he returns to the suburbs, he's able to sort himself out, get a job, look after his aunt and get his cousin out of gang trouble. It's a secondary evolution because Driss's problem isn't as acute as Philippe's, but it's satisfying to see Driss grow and sort out his life too.

- Flirting with Magalie. This is mostly a running gag, which pays off in the end one last time when we realise with Driss that she's a lesbian.

- Sorting out Elisa. This is connected to Philippe as he needs to be stricter with his adopted daughter, but Driss also tries to help her in relation to her boyfriend and makes sure he treats her with respect.

- What happens with Eléonore isn't really a subplot. It's part of the main plot and helps monitor Philippe's evolution, through successes and setbacks.

**Comedy:** There is of course a lot of comedy in *The Intouchables*. Most of the humour comes from the stark contrast between Driss and Philippe. The dialogue, based on the excellent characterisation, is another strong source of humour in the film. As in *Silver Linings Playbook*, comedy also helps to explore serious subjects, issues and themes, while delivering an uplifting, entertaining and moving story.

## FRACTAL ASPECT OF STORY STRUCTURE

**First Act:** The set-up is excellent. We enter not one but two worlds: Driss, in the suburbs; Philippe, his fancy environment. These two worlds collide and although the original story was told from Philippe's point of view, it's probably a good idea to take Driss's point of view initially. Yes, there are clichés in both worlds, but it's better to start with clichés than to end with them, as Hitchcock used to say. The main advantage is to create a clear fish-out-of-water situation for Driss, which causes a lot of conflict and humour.

**Inciting Event / Inciting Action:** The real inciting event is Philippe's accident and his wife's death. This is what caused the situation in which Philippe finds himself at the beginning of the story and will trigger his need to get better, to move on. However, there is a strong inciting event in the story: the meeting between Driss and Philippe. This triggers the beginning of their relationship, which will form the backbone of the story as we want to see how it will evolve.

**Beginning of Dramatic Act 2**: We understand that Philippe needs to get better quite soon in the story, but we have to wait until 00:40 to find out what happened to him (his accident and the loss of his wife). This is when we fully enter Act 2. We know enough about the protagonist to fully understand his conflict and be with him, rather than simply feeling sorry for him. This comes a bit late, but it's not a problem because the story has been very entertaining up to this point. Also, we start the story from Driss's point of view and it looks for a while as if what's at stake is for him to get a job, to get out of trouble, so we haven't been bored. Finally, the meeting between the two of them raises an important question, which is how their relationship is going to evolve. So even if we're not fully aware of the main problem, we have plenty to be entertained with.

**Sequences in Act 2**: The fractal aspect of the three-act structure isn't used much in *The Intouchables* to define clear sequences with clear subgoals. It's not a problem as conflict is generated differently, using humour, local scenes, managing information and subplots.

**Mid-Act Climax**: There is no mid-act climax in *The Intouchables*, as Philippe's need to move on, to get better, remains the same over the whole film. There is no clear midpoint either.

**Climax of Dramatic Act 2**: The climax is the last scene, when Driss leaves Philippe for his surprise meeting with Eléonore. Will Philippe chicken out again or rise to the challenge?

**Answer to the Dramatic Question**: *Yes*, thanks to Driss, Philippe is able to get better. When we see him talking to Eléonore, we understand that he's finally ready to move on, to start a new relationship, to embrace life again.

**Beginning of Dramatic Act 3**: We enter a very short Act 3 once we see Philippe smiling and talking to Eléonore in the restaurant. Driss and Philippe wave goodbye to each other, and as we watch Driss walk away, we get a few titles telling us what happened to them afterwards.

*Encore Twist*: There is no *Encore Twist* in *The Intouchables*, although the moment when Driss has to leave Philippe does feel like a low point, especially as we see Philippe losing his appetite afterwards and not looking after himself. But we never really believe it's over – we've seen the opening sequence; we know there is more coming – so there is no surprise launching the same action or evolution again.

**Does the Answer to the Dramatic Question Convey the Point of View of the Filmmaker(s):** *The Intouchables* is about friendship, tolerance and hope. The whole story comes through as a positive message, so the answer to the dramatic question is coherent with this humanist point of view.

**Does the Answer to the Dramatic Question Fit the Genre of the Story:** *The Intouchables* is a comedy. It would feel weird if it ended with the depression or suicide of Philippe. So yes, the answer to the dramatic question fits the genre.

**Is the Ending Satisfying**? Both characters deserve a happy ending. Neither of them has made decisions or done something bad enough to justify a punishment in the end. So the ending is both moving and satisfying. This friendship has allowed these two men to help each other. It's the perfect ending for the story.

**Duration of Dramatic Acts**: The three-act structure of *The Intouchables* is a bit loose because there is a lot going on, but Act 1 is about forty minutes long, Act 2 is sixty minutes long and Act 3 is one minute long.

## MANAGING INFORMATION
### Main Dramatic Ironies:
Thanks to the opening sequence, we know that these two characters are going to become friends. They don't know that for a while.

We know that Philippe is not really having a fit in the opening sequence, but the police don't. We know they make a bet about getting a police escort, but the police don't.

Most of us will know that the Fabergé egg is very valuable, but Driss's mother doesn't.

The friend who tried to warn Philippe about Driss doesn't know that the painting he's considering buying for 11,000 euros is by Driss, and that Driss isn't showing his work in London or Berlin.

Most of these dramatic ironies generate humour.
### Main Surprises:
Philippe is a quadriplegic. It's not obvious in the opening sequence, until Driss tells the police and we see the wheelchair.

Philippe knows that Driss has stolen the Fabergé egg but hasn't said anything.

Fred, Magalie's boyfriend, is in fact a girl, Frédérique.

Driss has secretly arranged a lunch with Eléonore in Cabourg.

**Main Elements of Mystery:**

At the end of the opening sequence, when Philippe asks: "So what do we do now?" and Driss says: "Leave it up to me", we don't know exactly what he means. We'll only find out after the long flashback, when we catch up with them.

Driss's backstory is only revealed gradually (the fact that he's done time for robbery, that his mother is in fact his aunt, etc). It's the same with Philippe's backstory, although it's not handled as a mystery. We simply find out about his past later in the story.

**Main Elements of Suspense:**

We worry about Philippe's well-being towards the end of the film, after Driss has to leave him. Apart from that, there is no strong suspense because it's mostly treated as a comedy.

## VISUAL STORYTELLING, PLANTING/PAY-OFF, EXPOSITION

### Planting/Pay-Off and Visual Storytelling:

- The fact that Philippe's ears are his only erogenous zones leads to a running gag that pays off many times during the movie: when they talk in the bar that same night and laugh about Philippe's ear hard-ons, then in the scene with the two masseuses, or at the end when Driss leaves Philippe before Eléonore's arrival and tickles his ears to tease him.

- Driss making fun of the modern art painting at the gallery when he finds out how much it costs plants the fact that he will start painting and that his own work will sell for a large sum too (pay-off).

- The theft of the Fabergé egg plants both Philippe's reveal that he knew about the theft (which shows that he appreciates Driss as he keeps him on nevertheless) and the moment in the end when Driss returns it, which shows that he's honest. It's also a symbolic gesture as we know that for Philippe each egg represents a year spent with his wife.

- The meaning of the white plastic gloves (used to empty Philippe's bowels) is planted in a very amusing way when Driss makes it clear that he'll never do that as a matter of principle. It pays off when he accepts the gloves later in the story, showing that he's now ready to do anything for Philippe. That's a great use of planting/pay-off to show a character change using visual storytelling.

- The picture of Philippe is planted when they agree to send it to Eléonore. What it means is that Philippe is ready to show who he really is to Eléonore. It pays off a first time when Philippe tells Yvonne to substitute it with another picture showing Philippe as he was before his accident, and when Yvonne hides it in the "prostitutes" files. It pays off again when she hands the file to Driss as he leaves the job. When Driss finds it, he understands that Philippe never sent it, and that sets up the final surprise, when Driss has arranged for Eléonore to come to meet Philippe in Cabourg.

- Driss teases Yvonne that she'll soon be having sex with the gardener. This joke pays off at the end when we see that Yvonne's date is indeed the gardener.

**Exposition:**

There is little exposition in *The Intouchables*. Most of it is related to the past of the two main characters. Driss's backstory is partially handled as a mystery and is revealed over the course of the film, while the main part of Philippe's backstory is conveyed relatively early, in the restaurant scene, when we find out about the death of his wife and how much he misses her. This is key to understanding Philippe and being able to empathise with him. It's well-handled, using humour, conflict and emotion to make the exposition more palatable. François Cluzet, like all great actors, does wonders to bring such a difficult scene to life. It's always hard to talk about the past without boring the audience, and he does it very well, with Omar Sy's help of course.

# 4. Developing a Theme-Led Story

## First Up

**We're going to use *Crash* (Paul Haggis) and *Cloud Atlas* as examples in this chapter, so it's highly recommended you watch these films before reading on.**

As discussed in the introduction, theme-led stories – often multi-stranded narratives or TV series – explore a unique theme or vision. They tend to illustrate a problem in society and/or make a moral, philosophical or spiritual point. They seem more difficult to develop because they don't appear to follow a classical structure, but that's only if you look at the surface of the story. Deep down, the same templates, the same tools are used. They are just handled in a less classical way.

While movies like *Short Cuts, Magnolia, Traffic, Parenthood, Amores Perros* or *Crash* might give the feeling that theme-led movies are a recent cinematographic phenomenon, it's not really the case. D. W. Griffith started the whole thing as early as 1915 with *Birth of a Nation*, which developed two main strands, and perfected it with *Intolerance* (1916) which had four distinct strands covering a few millennia. Without getting into the controversial content of his films, Griffith pioneered many aspects of the cinematic language, and his approach to storytelling was quite bold. The lack of a clear protagonist or main plot would leave some contemporary story analysts scratching their heads.

Also, TV series are often theme-led stories. Not always, for example *True Detective* is plot-led (what's primarily at stake is the resolution of the case) while *Breaking Bad* is character-led (what's primarily at stake is the evolution of the protagonist), but a series like *Game of Thrones* is definitely theme-led. While it looks like the first series places the Stark family at its centre to start with, it soon becomes apparent, as each strand is introduced (the Lannisters, the Night Watch, The Targaryen, etc), that there is no main plot but a series of subplots. This is confirmed with the shocking death of Ned Stark. Each subplot – each strand – is structured with a clear protagonist, a clear goal, clear obstacles, and all the subplots are connected by the same theme: the struggle for power and survival while all fight for the Iron Throne.

How do we deal with these different strands? Well, this is where the *Story-Type Method* really comes into its own and shows how the *dramatic* three-act structure can be used to design each strand, even if it's not used to shape the whole story. Let's see how this works.

If we go back to our initial definition of drama, here is how it's changed in a theme-led story as it becomes the *multi-stranded* form of drama:

# Structure (Theme-Led Story)

**Protagonists – Goals – Obstacles – Conflict – Emotion**

The *multi-stranded* form of drama:

- Various characters, the **protagonists of each strand**
- face different problems, plot-led or character-led, but all **linked to the same** *theme;*
- meet **obstacles** and
- experience **conflict** and **emotion**
- which **convey the filmmaker's** *vision* and force the audience to *think about the theme.*

We don't use the dramatic three-act structure to design the whole story, but we can still use it to structure each strand either as a plot-led or as a character-led subplot, thanks to the fractal aspect of story structure. Even if we don't use it for the whole story, we can still use it to structure each part: strands, sequences, scenes...

If we don't use the dramatic three-act structure to design a theme-led story overall, what do we do for the shape of the story as a whole? Well, we use a variation which defines three thematic acts instead of three dramatic acts, as we don't have a main dramatic *action* or *evolution* in a theme-led, multi-stranded narrative:

# Structure (Theme-Led Story)

## Why Three Acts?

In a theme-led story, we don't have three dramatic acts; we have three thematic acts:

1. The first act lasts until **the audience understands the theme of the story.**
2. The second act shows **various strands exploring the same theme.**
3. The third act reveals **the point of view of the filmmaker through the resolution of each strand.**

From a practical point of view, there are three main aspects to developing a theme-led story. We need to *nail the theme, sequence the strands* and *weave the draft.*

Although these steps don't necessarily happen in this order – most writers are probably not even aware that they apply these concepts – let's try to clarify the process. The order in which we focus on each design element and whether this work is conscious or not on the writer's part doesn't really matter as there is no single methodology that works for everyone. What matters is that these three main aspects are dealt with at some point as we develop a theme-led story.

When Paul Haggis explains the way he structured *Crash* with Bobby Moresco, he never mentions any of this. Consciously, they have used the *logistical* three-act structure and the 30–60–30 paradigm to shape the story.

In <u>Variety</u>, Haggis said this about the film's unconventional structure and its lack of a single protagonist:

*"When we finished it, I really didn't know if it was a script and in fact, when we shot it, I didn't know if it was a movie. Really, we stitched together this series of fables. I remember asking Bobby, 'How do we know when to stop?' And Bobby said, 'I think it's when the characters stop talking'."*

Still, I believe they have *nailed the theme, sequenced the strands, weaved the draft* and used the *dramatic* three-act structure as well as most of the tools we've discussed in this book (dramatic irony, planting and pay-off, visual storytelling etc) to structure each strand. The methodology used consciously, as well as the words used to describe it, don't matter. What's important is that at some point, the design is done and the story works.

This is often achieved subconsciously by talented writers such as Haggis and Moresco. Many writers, particularly descending writers – see *Are You or Are You Working with an Ascending or a Descending Writer?* – don't think consciously about story structure as they write. Thinking about the design of a story as you write can be the best way to come up with a cold, formulaic or didactic piece, especially if it's a theme-led story.

We'll dive into a detailed analysis of *Crash* at the end of this chapter, but for now, let's look at these three key aspects of developing a theme-led story.

# 4.1 Nail the Theme

I often read multi-stranded narratives in which the theme isn't clear.

This is usually a problem because a clear theme is what gives a backbone, a main direction to a theme-led story. If the theme isn't clear or if we have too many of them, then we only have a deconstructed, fragmented story. And quite often a fairly boring one, at least from an emotional point of view.

While a plot-led story is defined by a main dramatic *action* and a character-led story by a main *evolution*, a theme-led story is defined by a main theme or *vision*.

So *nailing the theme* is the first thing to do. Here are a few guidelines to help achieve this.

First, we want the theme to be clear, not only to the writer and everyone involved in the development process, but also to the audience. It's only when the theme appears clearly that we enter Act 2 in a theme-led story. When we understand – consciously or not – what the story is about. Every scene, every strand will explore the same theme. So we need to define exactly what the theme is.

We also want to make sure that the theme raises an interesting question. We could write a theme-led story about the importance of sleeping well in modern society. That's a precise theme, but one that's unlikely to interest many people. If, however, you slightly reword your theme and make it: "The way poor quality of sleep is killing modern society", it becomes more interesting. Simply rewording your theme can have a huge impact on the story you're developing, provided you follow up and implement this change of course.

The reworded theme becomes more interesting because it suggests conflict, which in turn will help you develop a more dramatic story. We could push this further and suggest that we make sure that the theme explores a conflictual issue. For example, racial tensions in Los Angeles as in *Crash*, or how drugs destroy lives in *Traffic*.

So to sum it up, when trying to *nail the theme*:

## Structure (Theme-Led Story)

### Nail the Theme

• Be precise. The theme will tie the story together, so look for clarity.

• Check that the theme raises an interesting question.

• Verify that the theme explores a conflictual issue.

# 4.2 Sequence the Strands

In a plot-led story, we *sequence the action* to break down dramatic Act 2 into more manageable units, finding ways for the protagonist to reach the conscious goal. We have a three-act structure because we have before, during and after a main dramatic *action*.

In a character-led story, we *sequence the evolution* to break down dramatic Act 2, finding ways for the protagonist to experience the conflict and emotions that are going to lead to an evolution towards an unconscious need. We have a three-act structure because we have before, during and after the main *evolution*.

In a theme-led story, there is no dramatic three-act structure because there is no main action or evolution. There is no main plot because we only have subplots, strands that explore the same theme or *vision*.

What we're going to do instead is *sequence the strands*.

First, we're going to define each strand in the story, around a character or a group of characters, making sure that each strand is connected to the same theme. If it's not, you need to cut it or find a way to connect it. Then, we're going to define a three-act structure for each strand (this is optional, like everything else in this book, yet still recommended at least for a majority of the strands):

# Structure (Theme-Led Story)

## Sequence the Strands

• **Define each strand** in the story (around a character or a group of characters).

• Check that each strand is **connected to the same theme.**

• **Design the three-act structure** for each strand.

To define the three-act structure for each strand, we're going to use the same tools we used at story level with plot-led and character-led stories thanks to the fractal aspect of story structure.

We're going to try to identify the main problem in each strand. If it lies outside the protagonist, in other characters or nature, it's a plot-led strand, structured around a main dramatic *action*. If it lies within the protagonist of the strand, the strand is character-led, structured around a main dramatic *evolution*.

If the main problem you explore in the theme hangs at the top of Maslow's pyramid, you might want to check that the problem in each strand reaches as low as possible, to widen your potential audience.

For example, the theme in *Crash* is linked to lack of prejudice, respect from others and for others, all elements that sit right at the top of the pyramid. Each strand, on the other hand, explores a problem connected to the theme but lying much lower in the pyramid: they are about love, protection of the family, business and property, or even survival. This helps to widen the potential audience of the movie as we explore problems which are meaningful to everyone.

Defining the three-act structure of each strand is a crucial part of *sequencing the strands*:

# Structure (Theme-Led Story)

## Define the Three-Act Structure for Each Strand

- Who is the **protagonist** of the strand?

- **What's at stake** in the strand?

- Is the strand **plot-led** or **character-led?**

- In each strand, **check that the problem isn't stuck at the top of Maslow's** pyramid of needs.

Once we've done this, we're going to develop each strand as a mini-story with a beginning, middle and end, with the added difficulty that each strand has to explore the same theme, and ideally each should be connected to at least one other, so that it becomes impossible to take one strand out without disturbing the entire story.

If we can cut a strand without disrupting the story, then it should be cut, or we have to find a way to make it part of the story in a genuine, non-artificial or superficial way.

Of course developing each strand can't be done separately from the overall story. Yes, each strand – or at least most strands – can have a three-act structure and be either plot-led or character-led around a main dramatic *action* or *evolution*, but they also have to, once combined, tell one story. You can plot them, design them and structure them individually, but only as part of a whole.

I call this *weaving the draft*.

# 4.3 Weave the Draft

Once we have *nailed the theme* and *sequenced the strands*, we can *weave the draft*.

This means, for example, finding the best way to introduce each strand. One of the great pleasures of theme-led stories is that we'll have a succession of inciting events, one for each strand, triggering the main dramatic action or evolution for each subplot. Make the most of this, because when done well, it feels like fireworks going off.

Similarly, towards the end of the story, as we close each strand, we'll find a succession of climaxes – one per strand – in a grand finale. Make sure you don't forget to close any one strand!

Another important skill to master when developing a multi-stranded narrative is finding the best way to cut from one strand to the next. Don't leave a strand for too long – unless it's intentional – and try to use a cliff-hanger (an unresolved conflict) before leaving a strand so the audience wants to go back to it. Set up a dramatic irony, or a mystery, or stage a surprise just before you leave a strand. This is what TV series do all the time, either when they move from one subplot to another, or at the end of an episode – or even a season!

You'll also want to make sure that each strand is connected to at least one other. This can be through a character involved in more than one strand or it could be more symbolically through a place or an object. Otherwise, it will feel like it's not part of the overall story.

A good way to achieve this is to make sure that there is causality between each strand: what happens in one strand has an effect on at least another one, showing that they are connected.

Using planting and pay-off really helps to bring in more causality, both within each strand and between strands.

A common aspect of multi-stranded narratives is that they tend to use coincidence more than other story-types. For this reason, you want to have as much planting and pay-off as you can, so that while your story might rely on coincidences, the audience will feel that the outcome is dictated by what happens in the story and not by fate. You try to counter-balance the coincidences – luck, bad luck, fate, accidents – with lots of causality – things happening because of what happened before in the story.

To sum up, here are the key points to keep in mind as we weave the draft of a theme-led story:

# Structure (Theme-Led Story)

## Weave the Draft

- Find the best way to **introduce** each strand.
- Check that you **don't leave a strand for too long.**
- Verify that **each strand is connected** to at least one other.
- Check that there is **causality between each strand.**
- Ensure that you **don't forget to close any strand.**
- **Use planting and pay-off to override coincidences.**

Let's now see how all this is applied in two case studies: *Crash* (detailed analysis) and *Cloud Atlas* (brief analysis).

# 4.4 Case Studies

## *Crash*

### Screenplay by Paul Haggis and Robert Moresco
### Directed by Paul Haggis

Detailed Analysis

**Note: As usual, it's best to watch the film just before reading the analysis.**

*Crash* is a 2004 ensemble drama written by Paul Haggis and Bobby Moresco, produced and directed by Haggis, about racial tension in Los Angeles. According to Haggis, it was inspired by a real-life incident involving his Porsche being carjacked outside a video store on Wilshire Boulevard in 1991.

The film received six Academy Award nominations, including Best Picture and Best Director for Paul Haggis, and won three for Best Picture, Best Original Screenplay and Best Film Editing at the 78th Academy Awards. It was also nominated for nine BAFTA awards, and won two, for Best Original Screenplay and Best Supporting Actress for Thandie Newton.

According to Wikipedia, it was made for only $6.5 million and grossed almost $100 million worldwide, so it was a very profitable movie.

Structurally, *Crash* is a perfect example of a theme-led story, in which there is no single protagonist or strong dramatic three-act structure over the whole film. Instead, we have many strands exploring the same theme, each structured in three dramatic acts, using the fractal aspect of the dramatic three-act structure.

Many TV series are designed in a similar way: there is no main plot overall, only subplots exploring the same theme. Each episode moves the subplots forward without a clear three-act structure as there is no main dramatic action. One of the best recent examples of such a story structure is *Game of Thrones*. Paul Haggis's and Bobby Moresco's experience in TV writing and producing probably led them to structure *Crash* the way they did and made the film a natural candidate for a TV series adaptation.

Let's see how the story unfolds in a detailed breakdown, then we'll take a look at each strand and how it's structured.

**STORY BREAKDOWN (Key Steps for All the Strands):**

0. Opening credits.

1. 00:03, opening sequence. We hear in voiceover, then we see African American **Graham Waters** (Don Cheadle) talking to an unseen woman: "It's the sense of touch. In any real city, you walk, you brush past people, people bump into you. In L.A. nobody touches you. We're always behind this metal and glass. I think we miss that touch so much that we crash into each other just so we can feel something". Reveal, they are in a vehicle; Waters is talking to **Ria** (Jennifer Esposito). We understand they've been in a car crash.

2. 00:04, Ria (Hispanic) argues with the other woman driver (Asian) about who is responsible for the crash. They both use offensive language and clichés about their respective origins. We realise that Ria and Waters are detectives, and they were arriving at a crime scene when the crash happened. The victim is a kid. Waters first looks at a piece of evidence – a trainer – and then freezes as he sees something off frame.

3. 00:06, flashback to the day before. **Farhad** (Shaun Toub), a Persian immigrant, and his daughter **Dorri** (Bahar Soomekh) argue with a Caucasian store owner as Farhad tries to buy a gun. The shop owner refers to him as "Osama", while Farhad insists that he is an American citizen. After the shop owner grows impatient and orders Farhad outside, Dorri finishes the gun purchase, which she had opposed. She chooses a random box of cartridges that fit the gun as the shop owner remains unhelpful.

4. 00:07, in another part of town, two African American young men, **Anthony** (Ludacris) and **Peter** (Larenz Tate) discuss racial prejudice.

5. 00:08, in the same neighbourhood, we meet **Rick Cabot** (Brendan Fraser) and his wife **Jean** (Sandra Bullock), both Caucasian. She's frustrated that he spends all his time on the phone. He gives her his phone battery to prove his goodwill.

6. 00:09, Anthony thinks Jean got scared when she saw them because they are the only African Americans in the neighbourhood. Surprise, Peter and Anthony have guns. They carjack Rick and Jean and steal their Lincoln Navigator. As they drive away, Peter sticks his St Christopher statuette on the dashboard.

7. 00:10, as the stolen SUV disappears, Waters and Ria arrive at the scene of a shooting between two drivers. The surviving shooter is a Caucasian male, identified as Wilshire narcotics police officer Conklin. The dead shooter, an African American male, is revealed to be an undercover police officer, William Lewis, from the Hollywood division. He was driving a Mercedes that didn't belong to him. Waters is suspicious of Conklin.

8. 00:11, later, at the Cabot house, Hispanic locksmith **Daniel Ruiz** (Michael Pena) is changing their locks when he overhears Jean complaining about having been carjacked by two African American men and now having to endure a Hispanic man changing their locks, fearing he'll give copies of the keys to "his other gang members". We understand that Anthony had read her correctly: she's furious she didn't do anything about her instinctive reaction to the two African American men. We realise Rick is L.A.'s D.A. He's concerned that the incident is going to make the news, and he's going to lose the "black" vote or the "law and order" vote.

9. 00:15, Caucasian LAPD officer **John Ryan** (Matt Dillon) argues on the phone with an African American lady (Loretta Devine) in charge of his father's medical insurance. Ryan's father is in pain due to a urinary tract infection and can't sleep, but this isn't an emergency and won't be covered. She offers to meet him to discuss this. When he finds out the lady's called **Shaniqua Johnson**, he makes a racist remark. She hangs up.

10. 00:16, Ryan joins his Caucasian partner **Tom Hansen** (Ryan Phillippe) in their patrol car. After witnessing a passenger performing fellatio on the driver of a moving Navigator similar to the one carjacked earlier, they pull the vehicle over, despite the

fact that the plate numbers and driver's description don't match. Hansen, who isn't racist like his partner, is unhappy about this. Ryan orders the driver, African American television director **Cameron Thayer** (Terrence Howard) to get out of the car.

11. 00:17, Cameron is cooperative, but his wife **Christine** (Thandie Newton) – who has had a few drinks – is argumentative, exits the car against Ryan's instructions and insults him as he holds her. This annoys Ryan, who manually molests Christine under the pretence of administering a pat-down while threatening to arrest them. Deciding it's better not to react so that the situation doesn't escalate further, Cameron apologises and politely asks Ryan to let them go. The shaken couple are released without a citation. Hansen is disgusted by Ryan's behaviour.

12. 00:22, at Farhad's shop, Dorri finishes loading the newly purchased gun and hands it to her dad disapprovingly. He justifies this with the fact that the guy who robbed them could have killed her mother. Farhad's wife tells him that the back door doesn't lock.

13. 00:23, at home, Christine wants to report the cops. When Cameron raises doubts that anyone would believe her, she expresses her anger at Cameron who did nothing while she was being molested. Cameron insists that he did the right thing, that they could have been arrested or killed. Christine thinks he was more concerned about his job. Cameron storms out, furious.

14. 00:25, Daniel arrives home from work long after dark. We see that he isn't a gang member as Jean suspected but a family man. He finds his young daughter, **Lara**, hiding under her bed after she heard a noise outside (Car? Gunshot?). We understand they've moved from a bad neighbourhood to this better one because of street violence. To comfort her, Daniel gives her an "invisible impenetrable cloak", to make her feel safe.

15. 00:30, in the carjacked SUV, Anthony and Peter, arguing and distracted, knock down an Asian man as they pass a parked white van. They argue about what to do with him as he's stuck under the SUV, then decide to get him out; otherwise, he'll die.

16. 00:33, the next day, at the police station, Hansen talks to his superior, **Lt. Dixon** (Keith David), about switching partners. Dixon,

an African American man, claims that Hansen's charge of Ryan as a racist could cost both Hansen and Dixon their jobs. Dixon suggests a transfer to a one-man car and mockingly tells Hansen that he should justify it by claiming to have uncontrollable flatulence.

17. 00:35, Peter and Anthony drop the wounded Asian man in front of the hospital.

18. 00:35, Daniel replaces Farhad's lock, but he tells him he has to fix the door. Farhad thinks Daniel is trying to take advantage of him, refuses to pay him, insults Daniel and asks him to fix the lock. Daniel tries to get him to realise that he needs to find someone to fix the door, then gives up, throws his bill into the bin and leaves without being paid. Farhad, furious, keeps asking him to fix the lock as he leaves, clearly misunderstanding the situation.

19. 00:36, Peter and Anthony bring the Navigator to the guy who commissioned the theft, but he rejects it due to the Asian man's DNA all over it. The SUV should be burnt to get rid of the evidence.

20. 00:38, Waters and Ria having sex. Waters takes a phone call from his mum, who is worried about Waters' brother. He refuses to go look for him, suggests she just waits for him to get back home. He calls Ria white, then Mexican, and they have an argument as Ria's parents are from El Salvador and Puerto Rico.

21. 00:40, Ryan looks after his father who's in pain, needs a pee and can't sleep. He helps his dad to the toilet. Once there, his father, embarrassed, asks him to leave him alone.

22. 00:41, in the morning, Farhad discovers that his shop has been broken into through the faulty door. It's a huge mess.

23. 00:42, Cabot finds out about Conklin's shooting, wonders if it's racially motivated and learns that Waters is on the case. He calls for a press conference at 4pm and asks for Waters to report only to him. He also asks for Flanagan to be found.

24. 00:43, Peter and Anthony, back in their neighbourhood, get into Anthony's car, which refuses to start.

25. 00:43, Jean, frustrated, tells off her cleaner Maria for not putting the dishes away. It seems unfair as Maria clearly does a good job

of taking care of their son James and had problems starting her car that morning.

26. 00:44, Anthony refuses to take the bus across town, as he believes the large windows on it are only there to humiliate the African American people forced to use it.

27. 00:45, Cameron is led to reshoot a scene because one of the actors feels an African American character isn't speaking "black" enough. Cameron gives in to the actor's veiled threat and reshoots the scene.

28. 00:46, Ryan, in plain clothing, visits Shaniqua Johnson, the insurance representative with whom he argued earlier on the phone. He explains that his father was previously diagnosed with a urinary tract infection, but he fears it may be prostate cancer. Ryan wants him to see a different doctor, but Shaniqua refuses. Ryan then proceeds to insult Shaniqua by calling her an affirmative action hire. He tries to explain that his father was a good man, who helped African Americans all his life and lost everything because he was white. He knows he's a prick, but he asks her to help his father, not him. Shaniqua has him escorted out of her office.

29. 00:49, Dorri arrives at the shop and discovers the mess while her father is calling the locksmith company, trying to get Daniel's name, obviously thinking he's responsible for the break-in. Dorri suddenly worries that the gun might have been stolen, but it's still there. Her mother is trying to clean graffiti from the wall. How can they call them Arabs when they are Persians?

30. 00:50, Waters goes to see his mum, who is mentally unwell due to hard drug abuse. She asks him – twice – if he's found his brother, and he says no. Twice. She asks him to tell his brother that she wants him to come home, that she isn't mad, even though she clearly is. Waters notices there is no food in the fridge. He joins Ria in their car, finds out that internal affairs have discovered something.

31. 00:53, Christine comes to the studio to apologise to Cameron but talks about the incident; how she was humiliated for him when that cop took away his dignity. Cameron walks away, cold, telling her to go home.

32. 00:55, Farhad and Dorri find out that the insurance company is refusing to cover the damage to the shop because the locksmith told Farhad to fix the door and he didn't. For the company, it's negligence. Dejected, Farhad grabs a bin, starts cleaning the shop, telling his daughter to go home and sleep.

33. 00:57, Ryan, aware that Hansen has asked for his transfer, shakes hands with him but warns him that he needs to spend more time on the job before making judgments on people. He doesn't even know himself yet. Ryan is teaming up with a new Hispanic partner. Hansen, on his own in a solo patrol car, is already the butt of flatulence jokes from his colleagues.

34. 00:58, Waters and Ria discover a huge amount of cash hidden in the spare tire of the Mercedes driven by Lewis, the black cop shot by Conklin.

35. 00:58, Cameron at work, thinking.

36. 00:59, Farhad empties the bin outside, comes back shortly afterwards, looking for something. He picks up the invoice Daniel threw away after their argument and finds his name: Daniel Ruiz.

37. 00:60, Ryan gets to the scene of a car crash. One victim is stuck in an overturned vehicle. It's Christine. When she recognises him, she becomes hysterical, doesn't want to let him touch her, but petrol is leaking from the tank and running downhill towards another car which has already caught fire. Ryan manages to calm her down and get her out, fighting his colleagues who are trying to pull him out. He rescues her just as her car bursts into flames.

38. 01:06, Waters meets **Jake Flanagan** (William Fitchner) who works with Rick Cabot to discuss the Lewis case, ten minutes before the press conference. Lewis was the third African American man "accidentally" shot by Conklin, which seems to make him a clear culprit. Waters lets him know about the $300 000 they found in the back of the Mercedes. The owner of the car, Cindy Bradley, has left town. Flanagan first tries to buy Waters with a promotion, then when Waters refuses to frame a potentially innocent man – he believes Lewis was full of coke at the time so might have shot first – Flanagan threatens him. Waters' brother is a car thief and Flanagan has a file on him.

39. 01:11, Waters meets Rick just before the press conference starts and tells him that given Conklin's history it's pretty clear what happened last night, sealing Conklin's fate in order to protect his brother.

40. 01:12, Farhad locates Daniel's home address and travels there with his gun. He sees Lara welcomed by her mother and waits for Daniel to show up.

41. 01:14, Anthony and Peter attempt to carjack Cameron, who has reached his limit of being pushed around and resists. Anthony tells Peter to shoot Cameron, but Peter doesn't. As police officers arrive, Cameron and Anthony both race for the car and jump in. Cameron drives away, with Anthony continuing to hold a gun on him.

42. 01:15, a car chase ensues. One of the police responders to the chase is Tom Hansen, who recognises the Lincoln Navigator. Cameron drives to a dead end, grabs Anthony's gun and gets out of the car, all the while yelling insults at the officers. Just before he pulls out the gun, Hansen convinces him to stop aggravating the situation and just go home. Hansen vouches for Cameron, promising the other officers that he will give him a "harsh" warning.

43. 01:19, Cameron, dropping Anthony at a bus stop, tells him that as an African American man, he embarrasses him and embarrasses himself.

44. 01:20, Daniel drives back from work. As Daniel's wife Elizabeth watches in horror, Farhad shoots Daniel just as Daniel's daughter Lara jumps into his arms to protect her father with the "invisible impenetrable cloak". It takes the grief-stricken parents a moment to realise that Lara is miraculously unharmed.

45. 01:23, Waters brings food to his mum's flat and fills up the fridge.

46. 01:24, Jean is complaining over the phone to Gloria, a friend of hers, that she's angry every day and doesn't know why. Just after, she slips and falls down a flight of stairs.

47. 01:26, at night, Peter, stranded, on his way home.

48. 01:26, Ryan, driving in his car, thinking.

49. 01:26, a car stops to pick up Peter who is hitch-hiking. It's Hansen. Peter sees Hansen's small statuette of St Christopher, just like his own. He begins to laugh as he realises that there is no difference between the two of them, but Hansen thinks that he's being racist. Peter then pulls his statuette out of his pocket to show him, but Hansen mistakes it for a gun and shoots and kills Peter. Hansen, shocked by his own action, dumps the body.

50. 01:30, as we get back to the first scene with Waters before the flashback, we understand that Peter is Waters' missing brother, now lying dead at the crime scene.

51. 01:31, Anthony, riding a bus, spots the white van owned by the Asian man that they had run over earlier. He gets off the bus. The keys are still hanging from the door and he drives the van away.

52. 01:32, the Asian man's wife, Kim Lee, arrives at a hospital looking for her husband, Choi Jin Gui, the man who was run over. We recognise her as the woman from the car crash in the opening sequence. Conscious and coherent, her husband tells her to go and immediately cash a check that he has in his wallet.

53. 01:33, Anthony has driven the white van to the same guy who refused the Lincoln, and as they inspect the van, a number of Asian immigrants are discovered locked in the back of the van, revealing that Choi was involved in human trafficking. Anthony is offered $500 for each person in the van.

54. 01:34, at the morgue, Waters supports his wailing mother as she identifies Peter's body.

55. 01:35, Dorri takes a phone call.

56. 01:35, still at the morgue, Waters promises his mum he'll find who is responsible. His mother tells him she blames him for his brother's death. He refused to look for him because he was too busy with his work. She's convinced that the last thing Peter did was to come home and bring her food while she was asleep. We know she's wrong, but Waters doesn't correct her.

57. 01:37, Dorri finds Farhad sitting in the shop, still shaken. He tells her that he shot a little girl, but that she's fine. He believes she was his angel, protecting him and his family. He asks his daughter to

take the gun away. Dorri checks the box of ammunition she had selected, and we realise they were blanks.

58. 01:39, Jean talks with Rick. She's okay thanks to Maria, the maid she had previously mistreated. She's the one who helped her when her friends let her down. Her anger seems gone. She tells Rick she loves him. He loves her too. She hugs Maria as she props her up in bed and tells her she's the best friend she's got.

59. 01:41, Hansen burns his car to get rid of DNA evidence linking him to Peter's death.

60. 01:42, Ryan, looking after his dad, still in pain in the bathroom, although this time his father allows him to hug him.

61. 01:42, Rick, at home, looking out of his window.

62. 01:42, Daniel, his little girl safe and asleep in her room, looking out too.

63. 01:43, Cameron, driving his car home. It's snowing. He stops and sees kids playing with Hansen's car, still burning. As he joins them, his phone rings. It's Christine. He takes the call and tells her he loves her.

64. 01:44, Waters, back at the spot where Peter's body has been found. He picks up something in the sand. It's the St Christopher statuette.

65. 01:45, Anthony parks the white van in Chinatown and sets the Asian captives free. As Anthony drives away, he passes a minor crash, which turns out to involve Shaniqua. Shaniqua and the other driver hurl racial insults at one another...

66. 01:47 – 01:52, end credits.

## MAIN STRANDS

Like most theme-led movies, there is no clear protagonist or main character in *Crash*. This is because what ties the story together isn't a main dramatic *action* as in a plot-led movie, or the main character's *evolution* as in a character-led movie, but a unique theme connected to the film-maker's *vision*.

In *Crash*, the main theme is how racial tension in L.A. connects and affects all the inhabitants of the city. This theme is introduced right away, in the opening scene. The story is theme-led because the main problem is located in society, rather than within the protagonist (character-led story) or outside the protagonist in other characters or nature (plot-led story).

Because there is no main dramatic action or evolution, there is no dramatic three-act structure over the whole movie. We only have subplots (strands) structured as a character-led or plot-led subplot (sometimes both). However, we have a *thematic* structure. Once we understand what the movie is about, the same theme is explored over the whole film. Also, thanks to the fractal aspect of story structure, each strand has its own dramatic three-act structure. *Crash* interweaves eight strands, some major and some minor:

**Strand 1 (major)**: Detectives **Graham Waters** (Don Cheadle) and **Ria** (Jennifer Esposito). This strand is connected to car thief Peter's story (strand 3), D.A. Cabot's story (strand 4), cop Hansen's story (strand 6) and Kim Lee's story (strand 8). It's structured around Waters as a protagonist, who has the conscious goal of solving the Lewis case. The inciting event takes place scene 7 at 00:10 when they get to the shootout scene. The mid-act climax takes place scene 39 (01:11 – 01:12) when Waters is forced to give up to protect his brother. What started as the subplot of the strand (Waters trying to care for his mum, and ignoring her requests to find his brother) becomes the main plot when we return to the first scene of the movie, as the body at the crime scene is revealed to be Peter, who has just been killed by Hansen. The emotional climax of this sub-plot-turned-main-plot takes place scene 56 (01:35 – 01:36) when Waters' mum tells him she thinks he's responsible for his brother's death. He's left with guilt and compromised ethics. He's probably the character who has lost the most and ends at the lowest point, along with Hansen. The first part of the strand is plot-led, the second character-led: the character-led subplot becomes the main plot and develops Waters' need to reconnect with his mum. This need isn't fulfilled by the end of the movie, so Waters fails on both, which feels quite bleak but nevertheless satisfying as we understand why and can learn from his failure.

**Strand 2**: **Farhad**, the Persian shop owner (Shaun Toub) and his daughter **Dorri** (Bahar Soomekh). This strand is only connected to locksmith *Daniel Ruiz's* story (strand 5). It's structured around Farhad as a protagonist who wants to protect both his business and family. His paranoia, fuelled by his less than perfect understanding of the English language, is the internal obstacle which triggers most of the external ones. When his wife tells him that the back door doesn't lock (inciting incident), he asks Daniel to come and fix it, which starts the whole revenge story. While this strand has a strong plot-led element, Farhad's need to be less paranoid is introduced right away, so this strand is primarily character-led. By the end of the movie, it looks like he has reached a kind of catharsis, so we hope he might have changed.

**Strand 3 (major)**: African American carjackers **Anthony** (Ludacris) and **Peter** (Larenz Tate). This strand is connected to Waters' story (strand 1), to Rick and Jean's story (strand 4), to Hansen's story (strand 6), to Cameron's story (strand 7) and to the human trafficking story (strand 8). This strand is one of the most directly thematic strands of the movie, as Peter and Anthony keep talking about racial prejudice. There is no clear inciting incident or dramatic action in the strand. They simply have the goal of dealing with the consequences of their carjacking, making the right or wrong choice each step of the way. It has a strong impact on the four connected strands: inciting incident of strand 4, climax of strand 6 and 7 and main obstacle of strand 8. Anthony has a clear need to develop a conscience, and it looks like he might have achieved that at the end when he does the right thing and releases the Asian captives. There is much less closure for Peter who dies stupidly, killed following a racially-induced misunderstanding by one of the most anti-racist characters in the movie. He's both a catalyst who challenges Anthony's beliefs, forcing him to change, and a bomb that explodes in Waters' and Hansen's face.

**Strand 4**: **Rick Cabot** the district attorney (Brendan Fraser) and his wife **Jean** (Sandra Bullock). This strand is connected to Waters' story (strand 1), Peter and Anthony's story (strand 3) and Daniel's story (strand 5). Contrary to Cameron and Christine's thread, these two are facing a different problem triggered by the same inciting event (scene 6 at 00:09). Rick's action is plot-led; he's in damage limitation mode following the carjacking, to keep his job whatever the cost. For Jean, the incident is more something that reveals her racism and the anger that she needs to deal with, so her side of the strand is character-led. By the end of the movie, it looks like Rick has managed to keep his job and Jean has overcome her anger. The conflict she goes through during the film changes her. The least satisfying event in the movie comes from her accidental fall, which seems to cause her to re-evaluate her friendships. It's purely coincidental, so it makes her evolution a bit forced. In fact, it's a small limitation of the multi-stranded aspect of the movie: such a big change might have been made possible if there were more room to develop it, but in a minor strand it feels a little contrived.

**Strand 5**: **Daniel Ruiz** (Michael Peña) the locksmith and his daughter **Lara**. This strand is connected to Rick and Jean's story (strand 4) and Farhad's story (strand 2). It's structured around Daniel's efforts to provide for his family and protect his daughter Lara. There is no inciting incident during the movie (he already has this goal when the film starts), but we realise it (entering dramatic Act 2 of the strand) as soon as we see him with Lara for the first time (scene 8 at 00:11). Although it's a plot-led strand (there is nothing wrong with either of them), we care about the characters because of what the theme subjects them to. The climax of the strand, when Farhad shoots Lara who is trying to protect her father, is one of the strongest and most moving scenes of the film. It combines dramatic irony, suspense, surprise, pay-offs and visual storytelling in a very powerful way. When we believe – with Daniel – that his daughter has been killed because of what he did scene 8 to try to comfort her, we feel his pain, his guilt, his shock, his anger. We feel the injustice. It's a great moment of cinema, a moment of pure drama. And when we realise – with him – that she isn't hurt, we feel his relief and utter puzzlement at what can't be explained yet.

**Strand 6 (major)**: LAPD Officer **John Ryan** (Matt Dillon) and partner **Tom Hansen** (Ryan Phillippe). This strand is connected to Waters' story (strand 1), Peter and Anthony's story (strand 3) and to Cameron and Christine's story (strand 7). It has a plot-led element structured around Ryan who is trying to do his job as a cop and care for his father. The inciting event isn't shown (he already has both goals at the beginning of the film), but we enter dramatic Act 2 right away (scene 9 at 00:15) as he's on a phone call with Shaniqua the first time we see him. There is no climax to this action, just a scene at the end when he seems a bit closer to his father. He needs to be less of a prick and achieves this by the end of the movie as saving Christine might at least partially redeem what he did to her at the beginning. We've seen the worst and best of him in twenty-four hours. The second part is character-led and structured around Hansen who is trying to deal with racism in the force (the inciting incident is the scene with Cameron and Christine) and needs to lose some of his naivety. Hansen doesn't entirely deserve what happens to him, but it feels very realistic and quite ironic. He certainly loses some naivety when he accidentally kills Peter at the end of the film (scene 49 at 01:26). This is when he realises that Ryan was right: he didn't really know himself.

**Strand 7 (major)**: TV director **Cameron Thayer** (Terrence Howard) and his wife **Christine** (Thandie Newton). This strand is connected to Ryan and Hansen's story (strand 6) and Anthony and Peter's story (strand 3). It's structured as a character-led strand, in which both characters need to change for their relationship to survive. The inciting incident (scene 11 at 00:17) reveals weaknesses in both of them. She needs to control her anger to be able to forgive him; he needs to stand his ground and stop being a pushover. She is able to forgive Cameron when the man who has molested her saves her life the next day (her climax). This is when her anger dies away. Cameron is able to go back to her when he confronts Peter and Anthony and then the cops (his climax). This is when he reclaims his dignity. While this strand isn't the longest, it's one of the most powerful.

**Strand 8 (minor)**: Human trafficker **Choi Jin Gui** (Greg Joung Paik) and his wife **Kim Lee** (Alexis Rhee). This strand is connected to Waters and Ria's story (strand 1) and Anthony and Peter's story (strand 3). Kim Lee has the car accident with Waters and Ria at the beginning because she's worrying about her husband on her way to the hospital. The strand doesn't have a strong structure apart from Choi Jin Gui trying to deliver his cargo, failing due to the accident and still getting his wife to cash the check. The strand is mostly there to put Anthony in front of two difficult choices. First, does he bring Choi Jin Gui to the hospital or let him die? Second, does he sell the immigrants for $500 a head or let them go? In both instances, Anthony does the right thing, which mostly proves that you can be a violent car thief and still grow a conscience.

## DETAILED ANALYSIS

What's at stake in the movie (the ability for people from different origins and cultural backgrounds to live together in the same city) is more intellectual than in most movies. Because the problem is in society, it isn't solved by the end of the movie (as suggested by the crash involving Shaniqua and the way the drivers involved react, mirroring the crash at the beginning with Waters and Ria). Nothing has changed in society. The main problem, the issue at the core of the theme is still there, as in most theme-led stories. It would be very unrealistic otherwise.

However, some of the individuals involved in each strand have resolved their racist attitude at least partially (Jean, possibly Anthony and Farhad) or our perception of them as being racists has evolved (Ryan). Some characters manage to resolve the way racial tension has impacted on their life, both private and professional (Cameron, Christine) or has threatened their job (Rick Cabot).

Some characters end up in a worse place (Waters, Hansen and definitely Peter). Of course, there is no solution given for the main problem, but on a personal level, some characters do evolve or seem to find a better way of coping. Giving a happy ending to all the characters wouldn't feel realistic, so the writers try to find a meaningful, satisfying ending.

One way to look at this is to ask the question: Does each character get what they deserve, according to their actions during the movie?

- **Peter** doesn't deserve to die, but what he did – carjacking – involves some risks and he pays the price. He also behaves in a way that makes it possible for Hansen to become afraid and then react in the way he does. He's not an entirely innocent victim. His actions – both during the film and in the last scene – contribute to his fate.

- **Hansen** doesn't deserve to become a murderer either, even an accidental one, but his holier-than-thou attitude needs to be addressed, and he too learns the hard way that he has racial prejudices (or Peter would still be alive).

- **Waters** doesn't deserve to be seen as being responsible for his brother's death. We know he does care for his mum and takes the time to look after her, but in a way he does privilege his work over looking for his brother. He also probably behaves for a while like she and his brother are not good enough for him anymore. So he might have a share of responsibility in the disintegration of the family unit, being an absent role model for his brother. It's not fair, but that's the price he pays for his social ascension.

- On the other hand, if **Lara**, Daniel's daughter, or **Daniel** himself, had been killed by **Farhad**, it would have been unacceptable because neither of them deserve such a fate. Farhad might have deserved it, but it wouldn't have allowed him to change in a positive way.

What's important in a negative – unhappy – ending is whether the characters (and through the characters, the audience) can learn from their mistakes. In *Crash*, this is the case, which is what makes the ending of each strand and therefore the ending of the movie satisfying. We can learn from Peter's, Hansen's or Waters' mistakes.

*Crash* is a challenging film which makes your brain work as you watch it, but not in a way that prevents entertainment and emotional involvement. We learn a lot about the theme as it's being explored, but *Crash* also delivers emotionally thanks to its wonderful writing and use of classical tools like planting/pay-offs, surprise, suspense and dramatic irony. It's a movie in which conflict and information are managed very efficiently.

For example, the scene when Anthony and Peter take their guns out and carjack Rick and Jean's SUV comes as a true surprise after their speech about racial prejudice in a posh neighbourhood.

The scene when Farhad is about to shoot Daniel is top-notch, classic writing. First because it's a pay-off for everything that happened before in both strands. The main elements – the gun and the impenetrable cloak – have been planted before and are paid off in this scene. But it also manages information brilliantly. It starts with dramatic irony and suspense (we know that Farhad is waiting for Daniel with a gun, but Daniel and his family don't). When this dramatic irony is resolved for Daniel, it triggers his goal over the scene, which is the same as his goal over the movie: to protect his family, and especially his daughter Lara. As he tries to do so while dealing with Farhad, we have suspense (Is Lara going to be killed trying to protect her dad with his gift?). Then surprise: she's been shot! This is such an injustice that like the other characters present, we can't believe what's just happened. When we think she might have died as a consequence of his fatherly love and her brave behaviour, the amount of pain for Daniel – and for us through identification – is unbearable. There is a great deal of conflict in the scene, and much of it comes from managing information, which adds depth to the conflict – it's not just two people fighting or arguing – and so delivers a huge amount of emotion. Then we have another surprise: Lara's still alive! Finally, we end with mystery: How is it possible that she isn't even hurt? The scene is also very visual, which gives it even more raw emotional power. There is little dialogue. Planting and pay-off is what gives meaning to actions and delivers emotions through visual storytelling, not spoken words.

The same goes for the scene of the crash involving Christine, one of the most powerful in the film. It's another example of fractal structure applied at a scene level. The protagonist of the scene is Ryan, who is simply trying to do his job as a cop and rescue the victim of a car crash. He first has to fight external obstacles: the driver is stuck; the fire is threatening to spread... Then the tone shifts and the stakes are raised when we discover that the crash victim is Christine. When she realises who is trying to rescue her, she becomes hysterical which makes it even more difficult for him to do his job. Christine is an external obstacle, but with an internal origin. It's only because of what he did to her earlier in the movie that she reacts that way. She wasn't panicking before. She has to accept being saved by Ryan, her former tormentor. It's a great pay-off for what happened before in the movie, and shows that there is rarely pure evil or pure good in a human being (or a well-rounded character). Ryan has to find a way to calm her down to stand a chance of saving her. There is a strong element of suspense in the scene (presence of a danger, the petrol and fire in the other car threatening to reach the car they are stuck in) with a clear time-lock (he has a very short amount of time to extract her before the car catches fire and explodes). The fact that he behaves in a truly heroic way, risking his life and coming back for her when his colleagues had dragged him to safety, awards him a partial redemption we never thought he would deserve. In fact, Ryan doesn't evolve much during the film. It's our perception of him that changes, which is a form of evolution. The look they exchange at the end of the scene, as she's walked away by other officers, is truly moving. She can't believe that the same man who abused her yesterday has today risked his life to save hers. This scene is the climax of her strand. It's the scene that allows her to move on, let go of her anger and forgive Cameron.

Another strong surprise is when we realise that Peter is Waters' brother. It shapes the whole movie with a kind of teaser flashback (see *Flashback: To FB or Not to FB* in *Craft the Draft*). Because we don't see what Waters sees before we go back in time, it sets up a mystery rather than a conflict the audience can understand or a dramatic irony. So it's more of an intellectual teaser flashback than an emotional one, as in *Goodfellas*, *Run All Night* or *John Wick*.

One thing about causality: while there are many coincidences in *Crash* – as in most theme-led movies – the story doesn't feel contrived because of the impressive amount of planting and pay-off present. Yes, Ryan stumbling upon Christine's car, Hansen driving past Cameron and Anthony's car or picking up Peter as well as many other plot points are coincidences. But these moments also pay-off past events and plant future pay-offs. While there are coincidences, they are part of the enjoyment of a theme-led story. We want to see how apparently disconnected strands are going to connect, ideally generating meaning in the process.

Theme-led movies can deal with more coincidences as long as there is enough planting and pay-off to make it feel like there is causality in the story. A string of coincidences wouldn't generate any meaning or emotion. This is where many fail when trying to develop a theme-led movie. The fact that there are coincidences in life doesn't make them acceptable in a movie. It might be life-like, but it feels contrived unless planting and pay-off are used to override the coincidence and make it moving and meaningful.

So while *Crash* is clearly not structured classically, it uses classical tools 1) to design each strand around a plot-led or character-led action, with a clear dramatic three-act structure and 2) to generate conflict and emotion in the story, as well as causality and meaning.

Crucially, while the film deals with social issues that sit quite high on Maslow's pyramid of needs (racial tension, morality, prejudice) each strand explores more visceral notions (safety, protection of family, survival, healing of relationships). We see this through each character: solving a crime and being a good son and brother for Waters; protecting his material belongings and providing for his family for Farhad; dealing with the consequences of carjacking for Peter and Anthony; keeping his job as a D.A. for Rick and dealing with her anger for Jean; protecting his daughter and family for Daniel; caring for his father for Ryan; dealing with rampant racism in the force for Hansen; healing their relationship for Cameron and Christine; profiting from their trafficking for Choi Jin Gui and Kim Lee. Each strand goes at least one level lower than the theme in Maslow's pyramid, even reaching the lowest level when the characters' lives are at stake.

This, combined with the low budget of the film, gives *Crash* a medium-high M-Factor and helped the film reach the commercial success it did. It's not a theoretical, political or moral pamphlet on racial prejudice in society. It's a moving story grounded in the gripping preoccupations of all the characters involved. What's at stake in the story is survival in a life-threatening environment. This is key in giving a theme-led story a chance of reaching a wider audience. Because the theme (the main problem) sits high in Maslow's pyramid, each strand has to reach down to lower levels to increase its potential audience (more on this in *Is Maslow Running the Show?*).

Here is what Paul Haggis said about *Crash* in an interview for Hitfix:

> *"What I decided to do early on was present stereotypes for the first thirty minutes. And then reinforce those stereotypes. And make you feel uncomfortable, then representing it to make you feel very comfortable because I say: 'Shh, we're in the dark. It's fine, you can think these things. You can laugh at these people. We all know Hispanics park their cars on a lawn, and we all know that Asians can't drive in the dark. I know you're a big liberal, but it's okay, nobody's going to see you laugh.'*
>
> *As soon as I made you feel comfortable, I could very slowly start turning you around in the seat so I left you spinning as you walked out of the movie theatre. That was the intent. Now if you saw "EZ Streets", you know that I don't usually write stereotypes. But that was what I decided to do.*
>
> *So when the criticism came later – 'Oh my God, it's full of*

> *stereotypes' – I went: 'Oh my God, you're a genius. Really? Wow! That's remarkable, really! I should have corrected that.' No. So when you're doing something that's different, I think people are always going to say things, but it amused me more than anything."*

Like most theme-led movies, *Crash* is highly reliant on the ability of the director to attract the right cast. A solid script with great parts never hurts, but because the story isn't classically structured, financiers often need the reassurance of A-list actors. This is what made movies like *Magnolia*, *Crash*, *Traffic* and *Cloud Atlas* possible.

A detailed strand by strand analysis (or strands map, see *Story Design Tools* in *Bringing It All Together*) of *Crash* is available as a free download at www.screenwritingunchained.com. It shows the timing of each strand, when each strand connects with others, as well as the inciting event and the climax of each strand.

# *Cloud Atlas*

## Written and Directed by The Wachowskis and Tom Tykwer

## From a novel by David Mitchell

### Brief Analysis

**For a short synopsis, please check the** Wikipedia **article, but as usual it's best to watch the film just before reading the analysis.**

**Logline**: Everything is connected.

The official synopsis describes *Cloud Atlas* as "An exploration of how the actions of individual lives impact one another in the past, present and future, as one soul is shaped from a killer into a hero, and an act of kindness ripples across centuries to inspire a revolution".

This is the spiritual theme that connects everything in *Cloud Atlas* and makes it a theme-led, multi-stranded narrative.

As in *Crash*, each strand is connected to at least one other and what happens in one strand has direct consequences in the others.

On top of that, because *Cloud Atlas* is not only multi-stranded but non-linear, there are other symbolic/spiritual connections, with the use of the same actors to illustrate the journey of each soul through different human beings across centuries.

It takes a while to get into it, but once/if you're hooked into the concept, it becomes a fascinating journey.

It's mostly an intellectual puzzle, but it does manage to deliver strong emotional moments, especially towards the end, when everything starts to pay off and each strand reaches a climactic conclusion and the film's message (everything is connected) is revealed and demonstrated.

Tom Hanks's character's evolution is probably the most satisfying, as he manages to redeem his betrayal and become a true hero not only in his main strand as Zachry but also through the whole movie, as his soul evolves through each strand from murderer to accidental hero to saviour.

The whole movie, however, isn't character-led, because we don't give his character in each strand the unconscious goal to evolve. What's at stake in the movie isn't his evolution; this is only something we can understand, decode and appreciate towards the end.

Let's try to define for each strand whether it's plot-led or character-led, who the protagonist is, and to which other strands it's primarily connected:

**Pacific Islands, 1849**: Protagonist Adam Ewing (Jim Sturgess), character-led strand. His conscious want / goal is to conclude a business arrangement for his father-in-law. His unconscious need is to realise that he's on the wrong side of slavery. He gives up his goal in the end (burns the contract) and joins the anti-slavery movement. This is what we were hoping for him. Linked to the next strand as Frobisher reads Ewing's journal, to the Luisa Rey strand as Goose becomes Isaach Sachs, and to the Big Isle strand as Sachs becomes Zachry.

**Cambridge/Edinburgh, 1936**: Protagonist Robert Frobisher (Ben Whishaw), plot-led strand. His conscious goal is to find the time and inspiration to complete his musical work, "The Cloud Atlas Sextet". He achieves his goal but commits suicide. Linked to the previous strand as Frobisher reads Ewing's journal and to the next one as Frobisher's work is a key part of Luisa Rey's investigation.

**San Francisco, 1973**: Protagonist Luisa Rey (Halle Berry), plot-led strand. Her goal is to reveal a conspiracy regarding a nuclear reactor. She's the protagonist (with Joe Napier as a co-protagonist for some of the strand). She succeeds. Links to the previous strand through the "Cloud Atlas" sextet record. Linked to the Pacific Island strand and the Big Isle strand as Isaac Sachs is the link between murderer Goose and hero Zachry.

**London, 2012**: Protagonist Cavendish (Jim Broadbent), plot-led strand. Cavendish, once tricked by his vengeful brother into a nursing home, has a clear goal: trying to escape (with his inmates as co-protagonists). He reaches this goal and becomes a successful writer. Linked to the next strand as his adventures become the movie watched by Sonmi.

**Neo-Seoul, 2144**: Protagonist Sonmi (Doona Bae), character-led strand. She needs to discover freedom and how she's being lied to. It's mostly character-led, although there is a strong plot-led aspect as she also tries to escape and survive with Hae-Joo Chang once she's outside. She does evolve and becomes free but pays the price and dies. However, she manages to broadcast a message which starts a new era, so her death isn't pointless. This strand is linked to the previous one through the movie of Cavendish's exploits and to the next as she's believed to be a deity by Big

Isle's inhabitants.

**Big Isle, 106 winters after The Fall**: Protagonist Zachry (Tom Hanks), character-led strand. Zachry needs to redeem himself for having left his brother-in-law and nephew to be killed by the Kona. He needs to overcome his fear. So it's mostly a character-led strand, although the second half has a strong plot-led aspect around helping Meronym, to pay her back for saving his niece. Both the character-led and the plot-led climaxes are linked as he manages to kill the Kona chief (Hugh Grant) and overcome his fear. Directly linked to the previous strand, and symbolically to all the others through the evolution of Zachry through the centuries, especially from Goose the thief / murderer to Sachs the accidental hero / whistle-blower to Zachry the full-blown – though conflicted – hero.

* * *

Overall, *Cloud Atlas* is a hugely ambitious, incredibly risky, fascinating construction that gives your brain an intensive workout and still manages to touch your heart (if the theme resonates with you). Without Tom Hanks's indefectible support, it might never have got made.

Like *Crash*, it shows that even when the dramatic three-act structure isn't used to design the whole story, you can still use it to shape each strand as plot-led or character-led, and of course all the other tools to generate conflict, manage information and achieve visual storytelling.

# 4.5 Hands-On: Getting Stranded

Hands-on

Take any theme-led movie – one you are developing, or a produced one – and work out the different storylines. It can be a single paragraph per strand as we did with *Cloud Atlas* or a strands map as detailed as the one we made for *Crash*, with a beat by beat analysis of each plot point and which strand it's connected to. It's entirely up to you.

Once you've identified the various strands, separate the minor from the major ones, and decide whether each strand is plot-led or character-led (sometimes they are both), who the protagonist is for each strand and what's at stake in it (main action or main evolution).

Try to be as precise as possible. If the movie has a sound structure, you'll find that most strands are likely to be using a dramatic three-act structure, related to the main action or evolution of the protagonist of the strand, and are exploring a theme common to all the strands.

Then try to pinpoint the main structural events in each strand: inciting incident or inciting action? Climax? Answer to the dramatic question? Mid-act climax possibly (but not necessarily)?

*Encore Twist?* You could go as far as writing the STM Framework for each strand, but that's rarely necessary. It could be useful to do so for the most problematic strands, once you've identified them, to troubleshoot them further.

If the movie is well-developed, you'll probably see that the first logistical act of the movie or screenplay (the first thirty minutes or so) is full of inciting events, one for each strand, that the last logistical act (last thirty minutes) is full of climaxes, and that we cut between each strand at a faster pace as the movie reaches its conclusion.

If there are issues in a screenplay developed as a theme-led story, you'll struggle to find a common theme or enough connections between the strands; you'll lose a strand for too long or will stay in another for too long; there won't be cliffhangers before leaving each strand to hook the audience into each storyline; there will be a lack of causality between each strand (events in a strand won't be caused by events in another strand, and/or won't cause events in other strands). Sometimes there might be a clear main plot, a strand significantly stronger and more important than the others – usually because what's at stake is stronger, or because we care more about the characters involved in that strand – in which case the story might be better handled as a plot-led or a character-led story, with fewer subplots. Often the pace won't pick up as the story unfolds and you might reach the end having understood little about what it was about. This is exactly what we should try to avoid.

While there is no dramatic three-act structure as such over the whole film in a theme-led story (there is not one main dramatic *action* or *evolution* to define one), we have a *thematic* three-act structure: As soon as we – the audience – understand what the main theme is, we enter thematic Act 2 as we start to follow the *vision* of the filmmaker. Usually this happens fairly early in the story. First, because we see many strands starting and are unable to identify one as being more important than the others. Second, because we notice that they all explore the same theme, that each strand explores a different aspect of the same problem.

There is rarely a clear Act 3 in theme-led movies because the thematic problem is almost never conclusively solved. Still, after the climax of each strand, we have a third act showing the consequence of the action or evolution of the protagonist of the strand. Hopefully, we are also left with a better understanding of the problem (usually in society) and we get closure in some of the strands (some of the characters find a way to deal with the problem, while others don't).

Also, try to look at the way other structural tools are used, especially dramatic irony, mystery and surprise. Managing information often plays a strong part in theme-led stories. Look for planting and pay-offs and check that visual storytelling is used as much as possible. You'll see that you can come up with a framework for each strand, like a mini-movie. Often, music takes a very important part in theme-led movies because it helps to unify the story and bring out emotion.

Theme-led stories use classical tools and templates in an unclassical way. It's hard to achieve and requires a very specific talent, but it's not impossible. Your mission, should you accept it, is to look at the evidence and see how a story that seems to have no structure can in fact be very tightly structured.

# 5. Developing Something Else: Hybrids and Exceptions

# 5.1 Story-Types Are Structural Templates, Not Rigid Formulas

Having spent quite a bit of time trying to define three main story-types – plot-led, character-led and theme-led – I'd like to explain why these are flexible guidelines rather than rigid models. Not every movie has to fit a single story-type, or any combination of story-types.

Many problematic screenplays are exceptions that don't work, in which case the *Story-Type Method* might help get them into shape, but some great movies don't fall clearly into one of the story-types we've defined. They are hybrids or exceptions that work and should be identified, respected and even protected as such during the development process.

So I'm going to pick a few exceptions which tell a story that reached a wide audience, using all the tools and principles we've looked at, just in a less classical way. Each of these screenwriting gems creates a unique *fusion* of the main story-types, brilliantly combining dramatic *action*, *evolution* and *vision*. They go free-style, and there is nothing wrong with that.

Although I tried to pick examples from different genres and countries, the selection of films I've picked in this book, including in this chapter, inevitably reflect the kind of cinema I like, my personal taste, as well as my age, gender and origins. Still, I hope that these examples will help you to identify your own favourite hybrids and exceptions.

This chapter is possibly the most important because **the one crime we don't want to commit in development is failing to identify an exception that works**. It's a capital sin for anyone involved in the process.

A screenwriting theory is only valid if it helps us create and understand stories that work for their intended audience. The way they achieve this doesn't matter. No theory can encompass all exceptions. If it tries to, it gets so overcomplicated, cluttered with so many special cases that it becomes close to useless.

In other words, we're not trying to define a structural model to make sure that every story fits it rigidly. Three story-types might be better than just one, but it's still limiting. It might cover more of the existing repertoire, but it's still not exhaustive. **We need a theory that helps us understand the design of successful movies and develop original stories that work. Not a theory that limits the kind of stories that can be invented.**

Most of the examples that follow could have been ruined by the development process if anyone had tried to force them into any single structural model.

When we approach a story, as a writer or anyone involved in its development, it's much more interesting to ask ourselves: "Does it work?" and if it doesn't: "Why doesn't it, and how could it work better?" rather than: "Does it fit a model?" and if it doesn't: "How can we make it fit?". Following a model or a paradigm doesn't give any guarantee of success. The only thing it might guarantee, if done unimaginatively, is boredom.

This is why it's so important to understand the principles, the tools, and be open-minded regarding the way they can be used creatively. At the same time, be aware that you can use classical tools and templates to design a working exception, without having to reject them entirely.

*The Story-Type Method* can help screenplays that don't work yet to fire on all cylinders, but like any wrongly used theory it could also ruin stories that work in their own way if taken too literally. **Story-types are flexible structural templates designed to stimulate creativity and channel inspiration, not rigid formulas that have to be followed religiously.**

Remember, William Goldman (screenwriter of *Misery*, *Butch Cassidy and the Sundance Kid*, *The Marathon Man*, *The Princess Bride*) says **structure is everything**, but he also suggests that as far as which film is going to be a commercial success, **nobody knows anything**. I wholeheartedly agree!

There is no "right" or "wrong" way to tell a story. There is only one commandment in the unwritten screenwriting Bible: *Thou Shalt Not Be Boring*. The way to get there is up to each creative team. As we can't make it "right", let's make it exciting, moving, entertaining and if possible meaningful, whether we follow a story-type or not.

We've already discussed an exception with *Citizen Kane*, when looking at flashback structures, but to illustrate this point further, let's take a look at the following films:

# Developing Something Else

## Hybrids and Exceptions

- *Edge of Tomorrow* (D. Liman)
- *The Lives of Others* (F. H. Von Donnersmark)
- *Birdman* (A.G. Inarritu)
- *The Secret in Their Eyes* (J.J. Campanella)
- *L.A. Confidential* (C. Hanson)

Despite being less detailed than usual, the following case studies contain many spoilers. If you haven't watched some of them, please watch those you think might be relevant to your project before reading on.

# 5.2 Case Studies

## *Edge of Tomorrow*

*Edge of Tomorrow* (also known by its tagline *Live. Die. Repeat.*) is a 2014 American science fiction film based on a screenplay adapted – by an army of successive writers including Christopher McQuarrie and Jez & John Henry Butterworth – from the 2004 Japanese light novel, *All You Need Is Kill,* by Hiroshi Sakurazaka and directed by Doug Liman. Made with a budget of US$175 million, *Edge of Tomorrow* grossed US$100.2 million in North America and US$269 million in other territories for a worldwide total of US$369.2 million according to Wikipedia.

Structurally, it's a cleverly designed hybrid that starts out as a character-led movie and becomes plot-led once the character has changed enough. Like Robocop was half-man, half-robot, 100% cop, *Edge of Tomorrow* is half character-led, half plot-led, 100% kick-ass sci-fi action movie. Let's see how Doug Liman and his writers managed to pull that one off.

At the beginning of the movie, Earth is under attack by an alien race. Major William Cage (Cruise) is a U.S. Army public relations officer who excels at recruiting new soldiers but has no inclination to go to the front line himself. Which, if we're honest, makes him very much like most of us. He isn't a hero. He is an ordinary man.

When the call-to-action comes in the form of a U.K. superior (Brendan Gleeson) telling him he's sending him to the battleground with a crew to film and sell the war to the population, Cage's first reaction is to refuse. Not in an artificial way, because that's what the hero's journey is supposed to be. No, in a genuine way. He's clearly scared shitless at the idea of seeing an actual weapon in action. When he threatens his superior with blackmail, he gets arrested as a deserter, stripped of his rank and sent to the front anyway. Hats off to Tom Cruise for making his character both entirely believable and likeable despite his extreme cowardice at the beginning of the movie.

Just as in character-led romantic comedies such as *Groundhog Day, As Good As It Gets* or *Silver Linings Playbook*, we have to like the character despite his or her initial flaw, which means that the actor needs a lot of charisma. Tom Cruise, like Jack Nicholson, Bill Murray or Bradley Cooper, has it in spades.

Anyway, back to *Edge of Tomorrow*. Not only does Cage refuse the initial call-to-action, when he ends up on the front line, he's still trying to cop out. He's not a hero like Luke Skywalker in *Star Wars* who longs to fight but can't because he has to help his aunt and uncle, whose timely deaths free him to go and have fun piloting X-wings. No, Cage is a genuine coward who is unprepared, unskilled, ungifted and is promised a certain death as soon as he reaches the battlefront. He knows it. We know it. And it's only thanks to the repeat of the same day ending with the same fate (Cage's death) that he's going to be able to change and turn into not only a fighter but a heroic one. As in *Groundhog Day* – a clear source of inspiration for the movie, which could have been pitched as *Groundhog Day* meets *Starship Trooper* – it's the endless repetition of the same day which can convincingly turn a coward into a hero, as he learns various skills and strengthens his character.

This is what makes *Edge of Tomorrow* such an original action movie. The action is great, the special effects are top-notch, the acting is first-class, but what grips us from the beginning is a character-led question: Will Cage manage to change and overcome his cowardice? More generally, will he manage to become less self-centred and more altruistic, because his cowardice comes primarily from the fact that he's only interested in himself, and not at all in others.

His ability to save the world is only interesting in as far as it illustrates his change. We are not that concerned with knowing whether the world will be saved (at least during the first half of the movie). We're much more interested in knowing whether he'll manage to change or not and whether he'll end up with Rita.

*Edge of Tomorrow* is a character-led movie to start with because what's primarily at stake in the movie at the beginning *is* the internal problem of the protagonist. Cage *wants* to find a way out, but we know that he *needs* to change and face his fears. He has to grow out of his cowardice, and give up his conscious goal so that he can embrace his mission. Which is why we – the audience – give him the unconscious goal to change, especially before we find out that he's the one who can save the world, which coincides with the moment when he has changed enough, thanks to Rita, for the story to become plot-led.

Initially, Cage doesn't want to save the world because he wants a way out. He's only interested in saving himself. It's in the second half of the movie, once he's changed – by love of course – that he can embrace a more altruistic quest and try to save both the world and Rita Vrataski (Emily Blunt), which of course creates a dilemma because he can't have both.

We'll dig further into *Edge of Tomorrow* and its fascinating structure another time, but for now let's look briefly at a few other hybrids or exceptions in different genres.

## *The Lives of Others*

*The Lives of Others* (original title: *Das Leben der Anderen*) is a German debut feature film written and directed by Florian Henckel von Donnersmarck. It won the 2006 Academy Award for Best Foreign Language Film after having won seven Deutscher Filmpreis awards, including Best Film, Best Director, Best Screenplay, Best Actor and Best Supporting Actor, setting a new record with eleven nominations. It was also nominated for Best Foreign Language Film at the 64th Golden Globe Awards. *The Lives of Others* cost US$2 million and grossed more than US$77 million worldwide according to Wikipedia, which made it, beyond a critically appraised movie, a highly profitable one.

Let's start with a short log-line: In 1983 East Berlin, dedicated Stasi officer Gerd Wiesler (Ulrich Mühe), doubting that famous playwright Georg Dreyman (Sebastian Koch) is loyal to the Communist Party, receives approval to spy on the man and his actress-lover Christa-Maria Sieland (Martina Gedeck). Wiesler becomes unexpectedly sympathetic to the couple, then faces conflicting loyalties when his superior takes a liking to Christa-Maria and orders Wiesler to get the playwright out of the way.

*The Lives of Others* is a true exception because it starts from the point of view of the antagonist, Gerd Wiesler, who personifies the threat from the regime to the famous playwright and his actress-lover Christa-Maria. Most of the conflict in the story comes from a strong dramatic irony: we know the couple are being spied on, but they don't. This is what leads us initially to identify with them rather than with Gerd. They are the characters who experience the most conflict through this dramatic irony, even if they themselves don't actually experience it until later.

Over the story, Wiesler discovers, through spying on them, a world that he didn't know and realises that the world he used to believe in is corrupted. He starts to care about them and evolves from antagonist to co-protagonist, trying to save them. Although the antagonist does change, it's not truly a character-led story because we never dare to hope that he will change initially. His change almost takes us by surprise, although it's completely believable.

We're fascinated by his evolution as it happens and we start to care for him as much if not more than for our initial co-protagonists, because we know the risk he's taking to protect them and understand the conflict he experiences. Gradually, he starts to experience more and more conflict, which increases our identification with him. Wiesler fails to save Christa-Maria but does save Georg Dreyer, the writer, who doesn't know who helped him. This strong dramatic irony has to be resolved, which is what happens when the writer looks in the archives years later, realises the sacrifice Wiesler made for them and ends up writing a book about him: the story of a good man.

It's very difficult to say if the story is plot-led or character-led, as it depends on who we see as the protagonist. To start with, we identify with the couple, who, victims of a strong dramatic irony, are the characters experiencing the most conflict, even though they don't have a strong conscious goal. We're simply lending them the goal to find out they are being spied on. Gerd Wiesler is clearly introduced as an antagonist, even if we share his point of view as the story unfolds. But then, as his world and values collapse and as he starts to help the co-protagonists, he becomes a co-protagonist himself. While the characterisation is excellent, and despite the strong evolution of one of the main characters, in the end we're not dealing with a character-led story because the main problem remains external to the protagonist(s): it's the oppressive regime and its corrupt leaders.

*The Lives of Others* is an extremely moving story, relying on managing information and especially dramatic irony as its main structural tool to generate most of the conflict. The character who changes most, as in *Billy Elliot*, is the antagonist turned co-protagonist, not the initial co-protagonists. In this movie, the victims of the dramatic irony are the initial protagonists, like in *The Hand That Rocks the Cradle*, not the antagonist like in *Misery*, but it works equally well to generate tension and emotion.

Overall, *The Lives of Others* perfectly illustrates how dramatic irony can be used as a structural tool and how a main ironic question (How and when will the victim of the dramatic irony find out?) can replace or work alongside a main dramatic question (Will the protagonist reach the goal?), at least for a while. It also proves that some supposed rules such as "the protagonist is the character who changes most in a story" aren't based on anything.

Story structure is often much more complex than that.

## *Birdman*

*Birdman* is a 2014 American satirical dark comedy / drama directed by Alejandro González Iñárritu and written by Iñárritu, Nicolás Giacobone, Alexander Dinelaris, Jr. and Armando Bo. The story follows Riggan Thomson (Keaton), a has-been Hollywood actor best known for playing the superhero "Birdman", as he struggles to mount a Broadway adaptation of a short story by Raymond Carver.

The film was shot in New York City with a budget of US$16.5 million and grossed more than US$103 million worldwide according to Wikipedia. It won the Academy Award for Best Picture as well as Best Director, Best Original Screenplay and Best Cinematography from a total of nine nominations, which made it the most nominated film of the Academy's 87th annual awards ceremony along with *The Grand Budapest Hotel*. It also won Outstanding Cast in a Motion Picture at the 21st Screen Actors Guild Awards, as well as Best Actor in a Musical or Comedy for Keaton and Best Screenplay at the 72nd Golden Globe Awards.

Structurally, *Birdman* is at the same time plot-led, character-led and theme-led. Although we do explore a few subplots – like the relationship between Riggan's daughter, Sam (Emma Stone), and actor Mike Shiner (Edward Norton), it's not a multi-stranded narrative because there is a clear main plot, around Riggan's struggle with the production of his play. What makes *Birdman* such a fascinating exception is that it's impossible to know whether the main problem is external (other characters causing problems for Riggan, be it his lead actor, his girlfriend, his daughter or an ill-intentioned critic), internal (his schizophrenia and paranoia) or in society (There is nothing wrong with him; he's only trying various ways to deal with a world he doesn't belong in).

Towards the end, suicide looks like the only possible way out. It feels more and more unavoidable and yet we still hope and fear because we empathise with the protagonist. After the first attempt on stage, which could be a legitimate ending for the film, we are surprised to find out he isn't dead. It feels too happy. It's not possible. It doesn't feel real. Could the filmmakers have gone for an artificial, unsatisfying happy ending? Then, we realise that while he failed to kill himself (which would have been a success in a way), his problems are still there. His daughter is still obsessed with social media (although we feel he has found closure with her, so there is a positive evolution). His best friend doesn't really care about the fact that he's just tried to commit suicide; he's only concerned with the success of the play. So even if Riggan has managed to silence his inner voice (Birdman), it still feels like death is the only way out.

If a failed suicide can't solve his external problems, Riggan probably has to die because society remains the same, his daughter and his best friend remain the same. He doesn't fit this world. Death feels like a relief more than a depressing outcome.

Although we are offered a semi-open ending with the last shot showing his daughter looking ecstatic, my interpretation of the ending – there are many others – is that this shot is still from his point of view. He would have wanted to see his daughter react in amazement when she realises he isn't dead but is flying, free at last. I guess this shows I'm an optimist!

An interesting point to note is that if we look at Maslow's Hierarchy of Needs, what's at stake in the main plot seems to sit quite high in the pyramid, as it's about creativity, self-esteem, achievement, respect by others. His relationship with Sam and his ex-wife means that it's also about family, but more importantly, it's made very clear that Riggan is taking more and more risks to make the play happen. He's co-producing it, then he decides to pay his actor's fee himself, which leads him to remortgage his house – the one that was supposed to become his daughter's – so he's risking everything on this project. If he fails, he's finished creatively and bankrupt financially.

Raising the stakes like this helps to shift the story to a level far more people can relate to: it becomes about survival, security of employment, resources, family, health, property. And of course the danger of suicide, the threat of Riggan's death, brings it down to the lowest level, security of the body / homeostasis. This greatly contributes to widening the potential audience of the film. Storytelling choices like this can make the difference between an arthouse movie and a crossover or commercial success. It doesn't give any guarantee – nobody knows anything – but it simply increases the commercial potential of the movie.

In relation to this, there is a huge difference between a passive, depressive character who simply wants to commit suicide – this can feel alienating as there isn't much the character or the audience can do about it – and a character like Riggan. Here, the protagonist struggles with an internal foe – his schizophrenia – as well as external pressure from critics and other antagonistic characters – the world he lives in. Riggan is constantly active. He has a very strong conscious goal – reviving his career through this play – and is fighting his alter-ego. He is a protagonist, struggling in the front row of a war raging both within himself and outside of him.

This is why it's possible to empathise with Riggan. We understand his conflict and can follow his dramatic action. There is a dramatic question that remains open until the end. We never feel that we can guess the outcome, so we remain emotionally and intellectually engaged. It's all about understanding not only the conflict, the problem, but also what can be done about it. It's not enough for the audience to identify the problem. To create a dramatic action, we also need to understand who is trying to do something about it, consciously or not. And to create dramatic tension, we need to perceive what stands in the way of a resolution.

Beyond the technical achievement – *Birdman* appears to be almost a single shot and feels much less claustrophobic than Hitchcock's *Rope*, the last notorious attempt to date – what makes *Birdman* such an exciting exception from a storytelling point of view is how it manages to be so meaningful, at so many different levels, yet moving and entertaining at the same time. It's impossible to decide whether it's plot-led, character-led or theme-led, and it doesn't matter.

Like *Tootsie* – another masterpiece – it blurs the line between story-types and achieves something unique yet universal. Films like *Birdman* remind us why we have to keep an open mind when looking at story structure. Many stories follow more familiar patterns and story-types, while others are working exceptions. These still use the same tools – for example, *Birdman* manages conflict and information brilliantly, uses planting and pay-off, has a strong time-lock, etc – but they remind us that like each human being, each screenplay is unique.

## *The Secret in Their Eyes*

*The Secret in Their Eyes* (*El Secreto de Sus Ojos*) is an Argentinian crime thriller directed by Juan Jose Campanella and written by Eduardo Sacheri and Campanella from Sacheri's novel, *La Pregunta de Sus Ojos* (*The Question in Their Eyes*). It won an Academy Award for the Best Foreign Language Film and the Spanish equivalent, a Goya Award, for Best Spanish Language Foreign Film in 2009. It was a very profitable movie with a budget of US$2 million for a box office of US$34 million according to Wikipedia. This is no doubt one of the reasons that led to a US remake in 2015, written and directed by Billy Ray, with Chiwetel Ejiofor, Nicole Kidman and Julia Roberts.

From a story design point of view, it's an exception with an intricate flashback structure.

The present-time story is centred around protagonist Benjamin Esposito (Ricardo Darin), writing his book about the Liliana Coloto case. It might seem plot-led, but it's in fact character-led as it's mostly about Benjamin getting what he needs: the woman he's loved all these years, Judge Irene Menendez Hastings (Soledad Villamil). Everything in the past, shown through flashbacks, moves the present-time story forward, both regarding Benjamin's relationship with Irene and our understanding of the case. In order to find a satisfying ending for his book, Benjamin needs to solve both the case and his love life.

The past-time story is more directly about the investigation, so is more plot-led, but the main subplot is character-led and about Benjamin's love for Irene.

Thematically, the movie is about missed opportunities and the power of love, both for Ricardo Morales, the young man who lost his wife, and for Benjamin, who lost Irene in the past (but might still get her in the present).

While it's not a classically structured movie, *The Secret in Their Eyes* nevertheless uses all the tools and principles we've discussed. Managing information is a large part of its structure, although unlike *The Lives of Others* it's based more on mystery and surprise than dramatic irony. The main dramatic irony, as in a romantic comedy, is that we know Benjamin and Irene are meant for each other. We feel their pain as they keep denying their feelings, hoping they will end up together.

Both storylines have a strong, clear structure. They are firmly linked to each other as the subplot in the past becomes the main plot in the present. As a result, we never feel like the dramatic action stops when we switch from one time-line to the other, which is a common problem in stories based on an ill-designed flashback structure. Here, the past and present storylines tell the same story and we're hooked from the beginning to the end.

*The Secret in Their Eyes* is a fascinating exception, entertaining, moving and meaningful. Like many other stories, it proves that with exceptional craft and talent, a flashback structure (see *Flashbacks: To FB or Not to FB* in *Craft the Draft*) can indeed produce a gripping, original, effective story.

# L.A. Confidential

*L.A. Confidential* is a 1997 American neo-noir crime film directed, produced and co-written by Curtis Hanson. The screenplay by Hanson and Brian Helgeland is loosely based on James Ellroy's 1990 novel of the same name, the third book in his L.A. Quartet series. Like the book, the film tells the story of a group of Los Angeles Police Department (L.A.P.D.) officers in 1953, and the intersection of police corruption and Hollywood celebrity. The title refers to the 1950s scandal magazine *Confidential*, portrayed in the film as *Hush-Hush*.

Critically acclaimed, *L.A. Confidential* was nominated for nine Academy Awards, winning two: Basinger for Best Supporting Actress and Hanson and Helgeland for Best Adapted Screenplay.

Made for a budget of US$35 million, *L.A. Confidential* grossed US$64.6 million in North America and US$61.6 million in the rest of the world, for a worldwide total of US$126.2 million according to Wikipedia.

Structurally, it's a hybrid between a theme-led, character-led and plot-led story, which explores three main strands, each one with a clear story-type:

The **Ed Exley** (Guy Pearce) storyline is plot-led. Exley wants both a career and justice. What's at stake in the strand is his ability to resolve the Nite Owl case. It has a strong character-led element though, which is that Exley needs to drop his by-the-book approach to policing. It pays off in the end, when he takes the advice of Captain Dudley Smith (James Cromwell) who states that a detective should be willing to shoot a guilty man in the back for the greater good, as Exley kills Smith himself to prevent his corrupt superior from getting away with his crimes.

The **Bud White** (Russell Crowe) storyline is also plot-led. White is initially obsessed with punishing woman-beaters, but his goal soon becomes to solve the same Nite Owl case after his partner, Dick Stensland, is fired due to Exley's testimony in the Bloody Christmas scandal and turns out to be one of the Nite Owl's victims. There is a character-led element in White's need to control his own violence, which pays off in the scene when, manipulated by Smith, he almost kills Exley but manages to control his anger just in time.

The **Jack Vincennes** (Kevin Spacey) storyline is character-led. Jack used to be a good detective but his advising role on TV series *Badge of Honor* and the tip-offs he provides to Sid Hudgens (Danny DeVito) – publisher of the *Hush-Hush* tabloid magazine – to perform celebrity arrests and make money on the side, have made him forget what the job is really about. He's become corrupt in a way he probably considers minor until the death of actor Matt Reynolds (Simon Baker), for which he feels responsible. He decides to find Reynolds' killer and get his pride back, which is what he needs. He reaches his goal and dies, but he does redeem himself and allows Exley to understand that Smith killed him and is the bad guy thanks to the Rollo Tomasi trick.

The three protagonists are trying to solve the same problem – corruption in the L.A. police department – in different ways, from different angles, and separately, at least to start with, as Exley and White strongly dislike each other for various reasons. They don't act as co-protagonists until the last part of the film. Neither Exley nor White are corrupt, which is why their strands are plot-led, but Jack is corrupt himself, even if in a small way, because he's not thinking about the consequences his actions have on the lives of those he entraps. He's part of the problem he's decided to solve and his death is a way to pay for what happened to Reynolds.

So *L.A. Confidential* is a kind of theme-led story with three main strands converging in the end. However, because the main problem is more contained (L.A.P.D versus society) and because we have a clearly identified antagonist we can dispatch by the end of the film (Dudley Smith), the problem is more solvable – at least on the surface and temporarily – than in a typical theme-led story, which contributes to making it a hybrid/exception.

In the end, Vincennes dies after redeeming himself, but Exley and White, who have opposed each other over most of the film, team up and defeat the bad guys. The three storylines are thematically linked (they explore different ways to approach the same problem), they focus on three very different characters, but they tell the same story. Although the three main characters are confronted with the same problem, they are not consciously co-protagonists because they – and we – only realise this as the story unfolds.

Overall, *L.A. Confidential* is a beautifully working exception and a modern classic. A story with three protagonists, a hybrid between a theme-led, character-led and plot-led story. It doesn't fit in any box, but it uses all the tools we've discussed, just in a slightly different way. It manages conflict and information brilliantly and delivers meaning, entertainment and emotion in an original yet effective way.

# 6. Bringing It All Together

## From the Original Idea to the Shooting Script

While I have tried to make the first part of the book as practical as possible, using examples and case studies, it's still mostly theory. We had a look at how we could use the *Story-Type Method* to develop plot-led, character-led or theme-led stories; we looked at a few case studies for each story-type; we even discussed how we could develop something else and deal with hybrids or exceptions. Now let's look at the development process and see how we can turn this theory into practice.

Of course the approach will be different depending on your role in the process. A writer, director, producer, development exec or story editor all have different talents and agendas. However, all have the same goal: to develop the best possible screenplay and ultimately get the movie made.

If we look at the film experience as a communication process from the filmmakers to the audience, the development process – from the original idea to the shooting script – can be seen as a way to improve this communication.

With some creative teams, it's probably better for everyone but the writer/director to take a back seat, because what the audience wants is their fresh, original view of the world, so why interfere? I certainly wouldn't try to put Terry Gilliam, Frederico Fellini, David Lynch or Lars von Triers through a classic development process. It kind of misses the point. I'd buy the time they need, send them away, protect them and hope it all comes out right.

However, if a writer or writer-director is looking for a first audience during the development process to test their ideas and check if their design works, then feedback from producers, story editors and development execs through meetings and notes can be invaluable.

# What We Want to Avoid: Script Doctors!

For a writer, getting a script doctor on board is like having to rush to hospital when you were set to have a natural birth at home. Even if it's sometimes unavoidable, it often feels like a failure.

This is especially the case when a script doctor, hired at the last minute – i.e. a few weeks, sometimes a few days before production, occasionally during production – takes over the whole project and completely changes it. Sometimes, that's needed and helpful. Often, it's pointless because it's simply too late to do any good.

So how do we work on a project in such a way that we don't have to get to that point?

This is where story editing skills come into play. We have to get the story design right before we can work on the surface of the screenplay.

# Story Editing Skills Should Prevent Last Minute Fixes

The ability to work on story design during development is the best way to keep script doctors at bay. This means that all parties involved need to be able to discuss story structure rather than getting bogged down in the screenplay itself.

The first, and possibly the most important trick, is to make the distinction between problems and symptoms. Very often, people focus on the symptoms rather than the problems, which makes it almost impossible to resolve them. We'll keep rewriting the ending which clearly doesn't work when that's only a symptom of an unclear structure or a weak evolution. We'll work on the characters when the issue is with the plot, and vice-versa. We'll try to change the way we manage conflict when the problem is with the management of information. The result? Instead of getting a better draft, we get a draft that's different. It becomes rather easy to think we're dealing with a fifth draft, when we only have a fifth version of a draft zero, a draft still weak structurally. A first draft is like the foundation of the building. It has to be sound enough for us to be able to build on it. Otherwise, as soon as we add some weight, it will collapse.

So how do we get a better draft, and not simply a different draft with the same problems and different symptoms, or sometimes even a new set of problems?

There are many tools at hand to develop the story over the whole development process. Some are well-known, others less so. Some writers are already using these tools or will embrace them; other writers find it difficult to work on anything other than the screenplay itself.

You'll have to find what works for you – if you're a writer – or for the writer you're working with, but what's key here is to make the distinction between story design tools and selling documents.

So let's dive in.

## Development Stages: Selling Documents and Story Design Tools

Here lies one of the main hurdles to a smooth development process: the confusion between selling documents and story design tools. Producers tend to need selling tools, so they ask for a pitch, synopsis or treatment. Writers tend to need design tools, so they'd rather work on index cards, beat sheets, step outlines or scene breakdowns.

This confusion often happens when development is financed by regional, national or even international organisations, as is frequently the case in Europe. In order to raise development funds, producers have to comply with the requirements of various financing sources. So this is what they ask their writers to provide. As a result, writers often struggle to design a story using selling documents.

This approach rarely works, or at least doesn't work optimally, especially when writers are good at writing design documents such as a step outline or scene breakdown but not that good at writing selling documents such as a synopsis or treatment. These often require a healthy dose of literary talent to be effective, which is a talent not all screenwriters – even good ones – have.

Let's try to separate selling documents and story design tools. Then we might be able to decide which document is appropriate at a given stage and who is the best candidate to write it, as it's not always the writer.

# 6.1 Selling Documents

Selling documents are meant for the outer development circle: financiers, distributors, TV commissioners, regional, national or European organisations...

Whether a script is already written, or whether you're looking for development funds to get to a first draft, these documents are meant to sell the project to whoever can help move it forward.

One might wonder why someone would want to read a synopsis when a script is already written, but the reason is simple: lack of time. Shorter documents help a potential partner to decide whether they should take the time to read the script or not.

These shorter documents should be written to make the most of what can be conveyed on paper. They are meant to be read, while screenplays are meant to be seen and heard on screen. It's a different kind of writing, which is why some screenwriters won't feel comfortable using them.

Still, let's see what each selling document is meant to achieve and how we can design them as efficiently as possible.

# The Story-Type Method®

## Selling Documents

- Pitch
- Synopsis
- Treatment
- Screenplay
- Package

# Pitch

A pitch can be a dozen different things, from the one sentence elevator pitch to a full-blown pitch including every single plot point. One could write a whole book on pitching, so I'll try to stick to the key points.

As a selling tool, a pitch is simply a way to convey – most often orally – the essence of a project in order to sell it, whether we're after development funds or production finance. A pitch doesn't necessarily tell the whole story. It can be as simple as a one-liner or even a couple of words describing a high concept, like "Jaws in space" for *Alien*.

A short pitch is often used as a hook to capture the imagination and convince the pitchee to invest more time in the project (set up a meeting, read the screenplay, etc).

Honing and delivering a good pitch is an art in itself and a crucial weapon to master for anyone involved in screenplay development. Whether you pitch to a buyer, colleague, boss, director, potential partner, it's a fantastic selling tool. Like writing, pitching requires both an understanding of the theory and a lot of practice before we get it right, so if you're not yet good at it, I'd encourage you to research and develop this essential skill.

This is beyond the scope of this book, but I'm going to try to provide a few pointers for a short pitch (1–5 lines) and suggest how the *Story-Type Method* can help us approach each project slightly differently.

Often, a good pitch will suggest the main source of conflict and describe a clear main dramatic action, as well as "what's at stake" in the story, but that's not always possible depending on the story-type of the project, so let's take a look at some of the possibilities.

**Plot-led stories** are clearly easier to pitch: define in one or two sentences who wants what and why, what stands in the way, what's at stake if the protagonist fails and you're mostly done. Plot-led stories are often genre movies – which definitely helps sell them, and not only at pitch stage – plus they usually have a high M-Factor, which suggests a large potential audience. If there is a dilemma and/or a strong character-led element as in *Midnight Run* or the *Bourne Trilogy*, try to include it in the pitch as it will add subtlety or depth to the story. If there is a strong, structural dramatic irony (as in *Back to the Future*, *The Departed* or *Avatar*), try to make it part of your pitch. It can even be more important than the dramatic action itself and become the core of the pitch. With a good pitch for a plot-led story, you can raise both development and production finance, even without a director or cast attached. In fact, it can be easier to raise funds with the pitch than with the script, because it might sell the concept better than an early draft of the screenplay. Sometimes less is more: sell the sizzle, not the sausage.

**Character-led stories** tend to be slightly more difficult to pitch, because what's at stake lies at the individual level and they often have a lower M-Factor because they are usually about love, belonging, relationships, self-actualisation, which immediately suggests a smaller audience – hence why it's a good idea to keep the budget reasonable. It's about who *needs* what and why, and how the protagonist struggles to change. A high concept (as in *Groundhog Day*) really helps to sell a character-led story in a pitch. Remember, you're usually not selling a dramatic action in a character-led story; you're selling an evolution. This is the core of the story, so it should also be the core of your pitch, unless you disguise your character-led story with a very strong plot, as in *Little Miss Sunshine or Two Days, One Night*, in which case you can sell the plot. You might also want to use the way catalyst characters influence the protagonist or the evolution of their relationship.

As with plot-led stories, if there is a strong dramatic irony shaping your story, as in *Tootsie,* make sure you use it. Otherwise, having a director on board and some kind of cast might be necessary to raise interest, especially if the budget is significant. Not trying to rain on anyone's parade, just helping to manage expectations. You need to be aware of the specificity of each project to come up with the right pitch for it, and knowing the limitations of a character-led story from a "pitch appeal" point of view will help you come up with the right elements for a successful pitch.

**Theme-led stories** are often the most difficult to pitch, especially in early development stages because what's at stake usually lies in society (as in *Crash, Traffic* or *Magnolia*), or is abstract, philosophical or spiritual (as in *Cloud Atlas*).

Therefore, instead of trying to sell what's at stake, it's the theme itself, or the most exciting journeys in the strands, which will feed the pitch. Remember, you're selling a filmmaker's *vision* in a theme-led story, not a single dramatic *action* or *evolution*.

So don't try to pitch the plot of a theme-led story. It's likely to be both confusing and boring for the pitchee. Instead, sell the theme, the complexity, the characters, the background, the concept, the irony or even the special effects and action sequences (as with *Cloud Atlas*).

Also, as the main problem in a theme-led story usually sits at the top of Maslow's pyramid, try to suggest how each strand is rooted at a more universal level to raise its M-Factor.

Unless we're talking about a very low budget – say Alejandro G. Iñárritu with his 2000 debut feature film *Amores Perros* – no one jumps until at least an established director able to attract the cast is attached (Steven Soderbergh, The Wachowskis, Paul Thomas Anderson, Alfonso Cuarón, Robert Altman and so on).

So until you have a great director and stellar cast attached, pitching a theme-led movie can be painful. It's probably best not to waste too much time looking for development funds for a theme-led movie. Get it written or at least co-written by the director as it's a vision-led project, get a fantastic cast, and then pitch it. You're unlikely to sell it to the audience without the cast, and decision-makers in the industry know that.

To illustrate this, here is how Bobby Moresco, co-writer of *Crash*, described the way Paul Haggis approached him:

> *"What happened was Paul Haggis called me up one morning and said, 'Listen to me. I have these pages, this idea for a story. Nobody is ever going to pay us to write it and nobody is ever going to make it.' I responded, 'That sounds good.' He sent it to me, and I called him up and said, 'You're right. Nobody is ever going to pay us to make it, but it is a story worth telling."*

It was a good pitch, and it worked. Moresco was on board (they knew each other well and had already worked together). We're sure glad these two believed enough in the story to write it on spec. Their self-awareness about the chances for the project to raise interest at an early stage saved them a lot of energy.

With **exceptions or hybrids**, I'm afraid you're mostly on your own, but the best hook to pitch these is often the originality of the project, its structure, its subject, whatever leads it to be a hybrid or an exception. Embrace its difference and wear it with pride!

Unless there is a high concept, or a writer/director who is a known quantity to carry it, selling an exception – especially at pitch stage – is often as difficult as developing it, because people don't know what they are dealing with and tend to be afraid of the unknown.

Be aware of that in the pitch and highlight the potential reward associated with the risk: it's different; it's fresh; it's never been done before! Try to find the universal, the human journey in your exception that means an audience will relate to it despite the fact that it's different. Make sure you use its originality as an asset; otherwise, its difference might become a liability.

Asking a question such as: What if...? or Did you know that...? to start your pitch can be useful, because it can help anchor the story in reality.

One last thing, a pitch is different from a tag line, which is the one liner on the poster. For *Alien*, the pitch was "*Jaws* in space"; the tag line was "In space, no one can hear you scream".

## Synopsis

A synopsis is a summary of the whole story over 1–5 pages.

It usually contains no dialogue and tells the beginning, middle and end of the story. But don't just tell the plot. That's likely to be boring. Use the appropriate style to make it pleasant to read, but keep to the point. If it's a comedy, try to make it funny or at least suggest how it will be. If it's a thriller, make it suspenseful. If it's a horror, make it scary.

Don't try to put every plot point in a synopsis. Sometimes, we can summarise a whole dramatic sequence that takes twenty minutes in the screenplay in just a few lines. Sometimes, we're going to have to expand a key moment because from a character or theme point of view, it requires clarity.

Some writers have a simple technique, which is to write one page per thirty minutes of the movie, which means that for a two-hour film, we get one page for the first logistical act, two pages for the second logistical act (one page for act 2.1; one page for act 2.2) and one page for the third logistical act.

Of course, this method is centred on a logistical approach to the three-act structure (the 30–60–30 paradigm), but for a synopsis, it forces you to be brief and allocate roughly the same space for each part of the story.

I prefer to concentrate on the dramatic structure of the screenplay, but as long as the design is sound, such a method allows the story to fall within an expected shape, which might be relevant if you're writing a genre movie. It's also a nice productivity tool if you have to write a synopsis before writing the script. It gives you more manageable units (around one page per thirty minutes for a two-hour film) and can help to get the job done.

In a synopsis, we usually have enough room to suggest one or two sub-plots if they are important in the story. Overall, a good synopsis should convey the following elements:

- **What's at stake in the story?** Why will we want to know what's going to happen next? What happens if the protagonist fails (to reach the goal, or to evolve)?

- **What's the theme?** This is relevant irrespective of the story-type. Make sure the story is about something. This is usually obvious with theme-led stories, fairly obvious with character-led stories, but sometimes it has to be pushed out of a plot-led story. A strong theme, especially at synopsis stage when you can't wow the reader/audience with funny dialogue or brilliant action scenes, can make the difference between a sale and no sale.

- **How is it designed structurally?** Is there a main protagonist? Is there an antagonist? If it's a plot-led story, focus on the main dramatic *action* and the protagonist's conscious goal. If it's a character-led story, focus on the *evolution* of the protagonist. If it's a theme-led story, make sure you suggest how the various strands are connected to the same theme, and how they express the filmmaker's unique *vision*.

- **Does the ending convey a clear point of view, in connection with the theme?** Are the subplots connected in some way to the main plot (or to the same theme in a theme-led story)? The climax, the ending, like in the film itself, is crucial in a synopsis, because this is what will convey most of the meaning of the story. So make sure it's clear. It doesn't have to be profound, or even original, but it should be clear. And because it's what you're going to leave the reader with, make sure it's good too. A final twist can help if it's not cheap or predictable.

Emmanuel Oberg

# Treatment

A treatment is more detailed than a synopsis. It also tells the whole story, but because there is more room, we have space for more subplots and characters, a few well-chosen bits of dialogue if it's a comedy, to try to convey the tone and style of the script.

We're talking here about treatments as a selling tool. Some call a treatment what we'll call a scene breakdown, which we'll discuss in the next section on story design tools. A treatment is a selling document intended to be read outside of the inner development circle (writer, director, producer, development exec, story editor or consultant). It's a document designed to go out in the industry to sell the project and raise funds for the next stage of development. If you already have a script, use it unless it's not working or you've completely changed the story for the next draft, or use a synopsis if a short document is required.

A treatment can be anything from five pages to around fifteen pages long. I wouldn't advise making it any longer than this because it becomes harder to read beyond that length, especially by a non-technical reader.

All the points listed for a synopsis apply, so I'll only add a few pointers:

- Because treatments are longer than a synopsis, **the literary style is even more important**. A good treatment conveys a story that is well-designed dramatically using a literary style to sell the design as well as possible. It's a hybrid, even more than the synopsis, between a literary and a dramatic document. Yes, it has to convey a story designed for the screen, but it also has to be written in such a way that it's exciting to read.

- **Because writing a good treatment requires a healthy dose of literary talent, many screenwriters hate writing them**, and it's easy to understand why. Writing a screenplay requires a different set of skills to writing a novel.

- Although it's possible to include a few lines of dialogue in a treatment – unlike in a synopsis – **only include dialogue if it's necessary and adds to the document**. A few lines of hilarious dialogue, a verbal running gag or a poignant line of dialogue that pays off a key moment in the story might help convey the style, tone and genre of the film. As in the screenplay itself, it's the quality of the dialogue that counts. So use dialogue sparingly in your treatment and when you do, make it count.

- Because you have more space, **try to make sure that you include as much planting and pay-off as you can**. This will add causality to the story, and show the reader that the story is designed with the screen in mind.

- Also **try to include as many visual storytelling moments as you can**, which will again suggest that the story is designed with the screen in mind.

- Finally, because you have more time than in a synopsis, also **try to convey how you're going to play with information in the screenplay**. Make sure a few surprises – and if possible one or more dramatic ironies – prevent the story from being linear or predictable.

- Overall, while you're using a literary style to sell the story, **check that the treatment implies a story using drama and visual storytelling**. Don't use the fact that you can write in a literary way to keep suggesting what the characters think or feel. You want a literary style that helps the reader to get excited about a dramatic story, which is designed for the screen but has to be on paper at this stage. You don't want the reader to feel that the treatment is pleasant to read, but suggests a novel.

## Screenplay

Of course, a screenplay can be a selling tool too, to raise further development or production finance. So what should it look like?

For some a screenplay should only describe what we're going to see and hear on screen. While this is usually true, it can result in a dry, hard-to-read document.

There is a compromise to be found between a theoretically well-written script, which only describes what we'll see and hear on screen, and a literary script, which misleads the reader by constantly providing information that won't reach the audience.

If something that's written can be conveyed by an actor's look or attitude or if we're describing a character for the first time and adding a few words might help us picture that character, that's fine as long as what's written is dramatised through action and dialogue over the next few pages.

We want to do everything we can to help the reader experience something that's going to be as close as possible to the finished movie. If that means using brief literary descriptions here and there, if it makes the script more pleasant to read because it's less dry and more lively, then great. Just make sure you don't cross the line between making the script more enjoyable to read and conveying essential information that won't be dramatised, or that won't be conveyed until much later in the story. Oh, and try to avoid adverbs too!

Regarding length, a screenplay shouldn't be longer than one hundred and thirty minutes, unless you're Peter Jackson or Oliver Stone. One hundred to one hundred and ten minutes seems to be a good length for most stories, as it gives enough space to develop characters, plot and theme. It's often shorter for children's movies, say around eighty to ninety minutes, because they tend to have a shorter attention span.

# Package

A package is anything that can help sell your project beyond or in combination with the previous documents.

In an ideal world, a great script is all you need. In reality, putting together a strong package might help to 1) get people to read the script, which should never be taken for granted 2) make up for the script's weaknesses while it's still in development or when the type of project means it needs a little help to sell and 3) convince the financiers that the gain opportunity of the project is stronger than the risk of financial loss.

So along with the screenplay – if you already have one – you can add an exciting synopsis to give a sense of the story and entice the reader to read the script. Include a short pitch to show it's possible to sell the project in a few words; mood boards or storyboards to suggest the visual approach; notes from the writer or director to support their vision – very popular in Europe, often requested by various funding bodies – or director name and a cast list of course if any significant names are attached. Even music, if that's relevant and important for the project.

Use any of these, but don't go overboard. If you have a strong script and an efficient pitch, that's probably enough (apart from the cast and director's name if already attached of course).

If your project is hard to pitch (say it's a theme-led story or it relies on improvisation) or if the script needs a lot of work, sometimes not sending the existing script but including a good treatment and rewrite notes can be a more effective strategy.

# 6.2 Story Design Tools

Story design tools and documents are meant for the inner development circle: writer, director, producer, head of development, story editor or consultant, and whomever you trust to be willing and able to read these technical documents.

In general, they are not meant to be sent outside this inner circle to raise development or production finance. They are meant to help the writer design the story and help whoever is involved in the development process to clarify their thoughts on the screenplay.

Some writers, especially ascending writers – see *Are You (or Are You Working with) an Ascending or a Descending Writer)* – will feel familiar with many of these documents, might already be using some of them and would gladly embrace the new ones. Other writers will shiver at the idea of working on anything other than a screenplay. That's fine. Good writers use the tools that suit them to get the work done. Select the tools that work for you, make them yours, invent new ones, until you've found the right methodology. There is no single blueprint that works for every writer.

Those working in development – producers, directors, development execs, story editors – should make themselves familiar with all these tools without necessarily forcing them on a writer. In fact, you should probably avoid having a technical discussion unless you know the writer expects that and is comfortable with it. Story design tools are meant to help you clarify your thoughts, define what you think isn't working yet in the screenplay and inform a discussion using non-technical words to convey these issues.

Here is the list of the tools we're going to look at:

# The Story-Type Method®

## Story Design Tools

- Pitch
- Story Structure Framework / STM Framework
- Character Outline / Character Pages
- Evolution Map / Character Breakdown
- Relationships Map
- Strands Map
- Step Outline / Index Cards / Beat Sheet
- Scene Breakdown
- Screenplay

# Pitch

The pitch isn't only a selling tool. It can also be a useful design tool as it helps the writer to define in one sentence – through a dramatic *action*, *evolution* or *vision* – what the film is about and what's at stake. In this way, a pitch can help a writer to encapsulate the essence of the story, the backbone of its dramatic structure. This can be a precious guide through the whole development process.

We've already discussed tips on writing a pitch according to the story-type of a project in the selling documents section above, so let's move on.

# Story Structure Framework

A story structure framework provides a summary, over a few pages, of the main structural elements in the story. It identifies the structural engine of the story. It gives an indication of the theme, plot and characters, the main structural choices, the general design and how conflict and information are managed in the story.

It's not a tool for everyone and it's perfectly normal for some to freak out when first exposed to it. It's not meant to be used on every project, but if it's relevant, it can be very powerful.

As a design tool, it's most useful for plot-led or character-led stories and less directly relevant for theme-led stories, hybrids or exceptions. For theme-led stories, we might use a simpler framework for each strand, or we could use a strands map (more on this other design tool later), as we did in our analysis of *Crash*.

I created an advanced story structure framework which I call the STM (short for *Story-Type Method*) Framework. Overall, an **STM Framework** answers the following questions:

1. What is the main problem in the story, which leads us to the **story-type, M-Factor and theme** of the story? These three elements are key to the development process.

2. How do we play with **managing conflict**: Who is the protagonist? What is the conscious goal? The unconscious need? What about motivation? Characteristics? Evolution (change, growth, steadfast)? What is the main plot? What's at stake? What are the external obstacles? Internal obstacles? Is there an antagonist? A catalyst? What are the subplots? Who is the main character? Any comedy – which can be a great way to generate conflict?

3. How is the **fractal aspect of story structure** used in the project? How good is the set-up, how well is the story-world introduced and defined in the first act? Is there an inciting event or inciting action? When do we enter dramatic Act 2? What are the subgoals? The main dramatic sequences? Is there a mid-act climax? What is the climax? When do we enter dramatic Act 3? What's the answer to the dramatic question? Is there an *Encore Twist*? Does the answer to the dramatic question convey the point of view of the filmmakers? Does it fit the genre of the story? Is the ending satisfying? What's the duration of the dramatic acts?

4.   How do we play with **managing information**: Main dramatic ironies? Main surprises? Elements of mystery? Suspense?

5.   Finally, how do we play with other tools such as **visual story-telling, planting/pay-off, exposition**? These are slightly less structural than the first ones, but they can still have a huge impact on the overall structure of the story.

Few writers will come up with a story structure framework at the beginning of the writing process, and that's not a problem. Most of the time, this work is done subconsciously. Some ascending writers – those who start with the structure, then break it down into a beat sheet or index cards, then design a scene breakdown and finally write a draft – would probably find it very useful, even if they complete it as they go i.e. not necessarily as a rigid first stage. Or they could write one if they feel something is amiss in their screenplay but can't pinpoint exactly what. The STM Framework becomes a fantastic troubleshooting tool in the right hands.

However, it's best not to ask a descending writer (those who work on an intuitive draft and then pump some structure and design into it) even to look at a story structure framework, especially before they have a sound first draft. They'll look at you like you're some kind of lunatic.

This being said, while a story structure framework might be too abstract for some writers and not necessarily a good design tool for others, it can be a precious diagnostic tool for many writers, producers, development execs and story editors.

For example, writing down an STM Framework for a draft is a great way to prepare for a meeting. It can provide a snapshot of the status of the project, showing its strengths but also what needs work.

The STM Framework is a clinical tool though, so beware. In the wrong hands, or used badly – i.e. too literally or mechanically – it can do more harm than good. But used appropriately (as a flexible design or diagnostic tool, as a thinking tool, as a snapshot of the project status at a moment in time and not as a rigid checklist) it can really help troubleshoot the most important structural problems in a project. Think of it as a cheat sheet, a way to write down the essence of the structure of a project over a few pages. You'll find an STM Framework for most of the detailed case studies at the end of each chapter.

Let's take a closer look at a detailed STM Framework. Should you feel like writing one for your project, a template is available as a free download at www.screenwritingunchained.com.

# STM Framework Template

## STORY-TYPE, M-FACTOR AND THEME

**Main Problem in the Story**: What has to be dealt with in the story. Its location (within the protagonist; outside the protagonist in other characters and nature; in society) should help determine the story-type. This is not necessarily the same as the goal. For example, in *Alien*, the main problem is... the alien. The protagonist's goal changes because the problem evolves as the alien grows in strength and becomes more of a threat to the survival of the crew. In plot-led stories, when there is an antagonist, that's the main problem. In character-led stories, the main problem lies within the protagonist, so the protagonist *is* the antagonist. In theme-led stories, the main problem tends to lie in society. For more information on this, see *If We Know the Problem, We Know the Story-Type*.

**Story-Type**: Use the location of the main problem above to determine the story-type of your project. Story structure frameworks are best suited to plot-led and character-led stories. Theme-led stories, hybrids and exceptions can still use them, but in a modified form. For example, for a theme-led story, one could write a mini-framework for each strand, but it's usually more efficient to come up with a strands map like we did for *Crash* (more on that later). Remember, many stories are hybrids or exceptions, so keep an open mind! You don't want to force each story into a rigid box; you want to use these tools as flexible structural templates to make sure the story engine fires on all cylinders. If you need help identifying the story-type of your project, please visit www.thestructurator.com. There you'll find *The Structurator*, a free interactive video guide that should allow you, through a series of questions, to find out if you're dealing with a straight story-type or a hybrid / exception.

**M-Factor**: First, identify where the main problem lies in Maslow's Hierarchy of Needs, from the most universal layer, physiological, all the way up to self-actualisation. Remember, this is about what's at stake in relation to the main problem, not the goal or subgoals. For example, in *Bicycle Thieves*, what's at stake is safety (of employment, resources, health, morality, family). Not just getting a bicycle back. Then, can you find parts of the story that complement or strengthen the above in relation to Maslow? For example, elements that raise the stakes in the subplots, as in *Billy Elliot*, or in each strand as in *Crash*. Or are there some psychological or thematic elements which open up a story otherwise anchored at the bottom of Maslow's pyramid, like the dead daughter's backstory in *Gravity* or the creativity theme in *Misery*? All this contributes to the overall M-Factor. With a medium to high M-Factor, you're probably doing okay, but with a low to medium one, you might want to take another look at the design of the story. For more information on the M-Factor, see *Is Maslow Running the Show?* in the first chapter.

**Theme**: Even plot-led and character-led stories have a theme, which is what the story is about and is directly linked to the filmmaker's *vision*. Plot-led simply means that the main problem in the story lies outside the protagonist. It doesn't mean we shouldn't work on the characters or theme. Likewise, character-led means that the main problem lies within the protagonist. Plot and theme still need attention. A theme can be as simple as "Good triumphs over Evil" (most horror/thrillers and action/adventures), or "Everyone deserves love" (as in most romantic comedies) or "If you try hard enough, you can succeed" as in any triumph over adversity movie such as *Billy Elliot* or *The Pursuit of Happyness*. But it can also be more complex, as in *Edge of Tomorrow* which is about cowardice on the battlefield or "Does the end justify the means?" as in *Prisoners*. Defining the theme of a plot-led movie helps you make it more interesting, relevant, unique. We have seen many plot-led movies with a simplistic or nonexistent theme, so finding an original theme and making the most of it will help a plot-led movie to stand out. Most of the meaning in a plot-led movie is conveyed through one or more subplots, as well as in the ending (Is the problem solved or not, and how?). In character-led movies, the theme is often linked to the evolution of the protagonist. See *Theme* in *Craft the Draft* and *Developing a Theme-Led Story* for more information on the theme.

## MANAGING CONFLICT

**Protagonist**: The character – or group of characters sharing the same goal – experiencing the most conflict in the story.

**Conscious Goal**: What the protagonist wants. This dramatic action is what generates the most conflict in plot-led stories. The goal can change as the problem evolves, for example the goal of the protagonist in *Alien* changes as the threat evolves. This is not a problem as long as it's always connected to the same problem. Sometimes, we have a first goal for the first half of dramatic Act 2, then after a mid-act climax a second goal, logically connected to the first one. Often, the goal is the same over the whole movie. Make the distinction between a new goal (what the character wants) and subgoals (ways the character tries to reach the goal). We're talking about goal(s) here, not subgoals. In plot-led stories the protagonist usually has a unique goal over the whole story as the goal defines the main dramatic *action*, which is the structural backbone of the story. In character-led stories, the protagonist can have different conscious goals as the dramatic backbone is defined by the unconscious need of the protagonist and the main dramatic *evolution*. In theme-led stories, we have many protagonists and many goals, many actions or evolutions connected to the same theme and *vision*. More in this in *Managing Conflict* in *Behind the Scenes*.

**Unconscious Need**: The protagonist of a plot-led story doesn't always have a strong need. It can add depth to the story though, so there is frequently an unconscious need which defines a problem less important than the main one and will lead the protagonist to grow (stronger in the same direction) rather than change (wrong direction that needs correction). In character-led stories, the unconscious need defines the main problem – and the main evolution – in the story. The story is shaped by this unique unconscious need; however, the protagonist can explore different conscious goals, which are mostly ways to generate the conflict that is going to lead the protagonist to change, move on, heal. In theme-led stories, each strand can be structured as a plot-led or character-led subplot, leading the conscious want or the unconscious need of each main character to define the dramatic backbone of the strand. More on unconscious need in *Developing a Character-Led Story*.

**Motivation**: Why does the protagonist want to reach the goal? Why does the protagonist have this unconscious need? Sometimes it's quite obvious. Sometimes, it's not. Motivation should always be clear to the audience, even if it's not spelt out, because it often defines what's at stake.

**Main Characteristic**: What is the single character trait that dominates the others, that defines the archetype of this character? For example, for Salieri in *Amadeus*, it's jealousy. This is not a necessity, but it can really help to get a handle on the character.

**Secondary Characteristics**: What are the few secondary characteristics that turn the archetype defined by the main characteristic into a human being, that makes him or her unique? To keep the Salieri example in *Amadeus*, it's his love of food (to compensate for his sexual abstinence), his relative mediocrity (compared to Mozart's talent) and his singular relationship to God. This makes him very different to Othello, another jealous character. More on this in *Characterisation* in *Craft the Draft*.

**Evolution (growth, change or steadfast)**: Does the protagonist grow, as in most plot-led stories, or change, as in most character-led stories? Or does the character remain steadfast, as in many franchises like *Indiana Jones*, *James Bond*, *Mission Impossible* or *The Avengers*?

In a plot-led story, the growth of the protagonist is a subplot (an internal problem less important than the external problem defining the main plot but connected to it). If it becomes more than that, we're probably dealing with a character-led story, although sometimes it can be the evolution of a relationship, as in a buddy movie (*Midnight Run*) or a romantic comedy (*When Harry Met Sally*).

The evolution is a key part of character-led stories, as it's what defines the structural backbone of the story.

In theme-led stories, each strand will have its own story-type, therefore its own dramatic action or evolution.

More on this in *Don't Forget the Subplots* in *Sequence the Action* (for plot-led stories), *Sequence the Evolution* (for character-led stories) and *Sequence the Strands* (for theme-led stories).

**[Optional but Can Be Useful]**: Try to answer the questions above (goal, motivations, main and secondary characteristics, evolution) for the most important characters in the story, including the antagonist. The protagonist and antagonist – if present – usually have a unique (conscious or unconscious) goal over the whole story, but the goal of other characters can change as it's not their dramatic action (or evolution) that shapes the story.

**Main Character**: The most interesting, fascinating character in the story. The character the story is about. Often, it's the protagonist. Occasionally, it's another character. For example, in *There's Something about Mary*, the protagonist is Ted (Ben Stiller) but the main character is Mary (Cameron Diaz). Sometimes, as in many horror/monster movies (*Jaws, Alien, Misery*), the main character is the antagonist (the monster). We identify emotionally with the protagonist (Chief Brody, Ripley and the Nostromo crew, Paul Sheldon), but the most fascinating character is the antagonist (the shark, the alien, Annie Wilkes). More on this in *Protagonist vs Main Character* in *Craft the Draft*.

**Main Plot**: What is the main dramatic action, the action that shapes the story and gives it a three-act structure? Usually, it's simply a case of deciding who *wants* what (and why). This main dramatic *action* is only expected in a plot-led story. In a character-led story, it's the main *evolution* that shapes the story (who *needs* what and why) and in a theme-led story, it's the main theme or *vision*. More on this in *Sequence the Action* and *Sequence the Evolution*.

**What's at Stake**: One of the most important questions in any story. What happens if the protagonist fails to reach the conscious goal or the unconscious need? Can you define something so negative that failure isn't an option for the protagonist? Can you also make sure that success seems possible but hard to obtain, until the end of the story? This is what increases the tension for the audience. We can – and often should – raise the stakes as the story unfolds, to give it a bit of a boost. What's at stake overall is usually clearer in plot-led and character-led stories than in theme-led stories, where we need to define what's at stake in each strand instead. More on this in *Hands-On: What's at Stake* in *Developing a Plot-Led Story*.

**External Obstacles / Antagonist**: If we have a single or main source of external conflict for the protagonist, a character or a group of characters whose goal is in direct opposition to the goal of the protagonist, then we have an antagonist. It can also be antagonistic forces, for example nature in a disaster movie. Otherwise, we only have different sources of conflict and obstacles for the protagonist. This isn't a problem as long as obstacles are not random or weak.

If there is an antagonist in the story, check if the goal of the antagonist is in direct opposition to the goal of the protagonist. If protagonist and antagonist have the same goal (such as to win a race or seduce the same love interest), make sure that only one of them can succeed, and if possible give them different motivations for reaching it. Protagonists and antagonists often illustrate two opposing views of the world, so try to embed that in their design, even if they are in fact much closer than it seems (as in *Heat*). In character-led stories, the protagonist *is* the antagonist as most of the conflict comes from within the protagonist. More on obstacles in *Managing Conflict* in *Behind the Scenes*, also see *Protagonist vs Antagonist in Craft the Draft*.

**Internal Obstacles**: Which character trait or element of backstory is making it more difficult for your protagonist to reach this specific goal in this specific story? Try to make it specific and relevant, not random. For example, Indiana Jones' fear of snakes is pretty random. His reluctance to destroy an archaeological artefact of significant value is more related to character, therefore more interesting. In a character-led story, the main internal obstacle is related to the evolution of the protagonist. More on this in *Behind the Scenes*, as well as in *Developing a Character-Led Story*.

**Catalyst:** In many character-led movies, there is a character who forces the protagonist to change. These catalyst characters can cause a lot of conflict for the protagonist, but they aren't antagonists; often they are a co-protagonist regarding the unconscious goal/need of the protagonist, even when they seem to stand in the way of the conscious goal. For example, in *Silver Linings Playbook*, Tiffany is the catalyst. She pretends to be helping Pat to get his wife back when in reality she's trying to get him to realise he has to move on because she's the one for him. In *The Intouchables*, it's Driss, who forces Philippe to change and move on. It's Carol in *As Good As It Gets* and Rita in *Groundhog Day*, because when the protagonist meets them, it triggers their unconscious need to get better in order to deserve them. You can also find catalysts in plot-led movies or hybrids. For example, Mrs Wilkinson is Billy's catalyst in *Billy Elliot*. She's not only Billy's ally and co-protagonist, like all mentors and good teachers she also pushes him to grow, to develop his potential. Jonathan Mardukas is the catalyst for Jack Walsh in *Midnight Run*. While he's more of an antagonistic force on Jack's conscious want, he's primarily a catalyst on Jack's unconscious need, as well as a co-protagonist forcing him to grow and even to change, which is what makes *Midnight Run* such a complex near-hybrid. More on this in *Grow the Draft*.

**Subplots**: What are the subplots, the smaller problems or actions developed and resolved in the story, connected to the main plot in some way? If a subplot isn't connected to the main plot, find a way to connect it or consider getting rid of it. If you only have subplots and no main plot, you might be developing a theme-led story, a multi-stranded narrative. Subplots often help to convey meaning or subtlety as there is more room than in the main plot to do so. You don't need subplots in a plot-led or character-led movie – especially real-time or near real-time ones like *High Noon* or *Gravity* – but they can provide more depth or a different point of view, so it's a good idea to consider them, as long as you don't get lost in them. In theme-led stories, we have only subplots (defining strands) and no main plot. More on this in *Sequence the Action* and also in *Developing a Theme-Led Story*.

**Comedy:** While it's not necessarily a structural element, it can help to see if there is some comedy in the story, and how it's generated. There are few stories which wouldn't benefit from a little humour, even if only for comic relief.

## FRACTAL ASPECT OF STORY STRUCTURE

**First Act / Set-Up:** How efficient is everything that happens in the story before we understand what's at stake and what the main *action* (plot-led), *evolution* (character-led) or *vision* (theme-led) is going to be? How strong are the opening pages? How good is the set-up? How well is the story-world defined and introduced? See *Hands-On: What's at Stake* in *Developing a Plot-Led Story* as well as *A Good Set-Up* and *Story World* in *Craft the Draft*.

**Inciting Event / Inciting Action:** Is there an inciting event in the story, a clear plot point in Act 1 which triggers the conscious goal of the protagonist as in *Gravity* (the cloud of satellite debris hitting the space shuttle)? Or do we have an inciting action as in *Misery*, a succession of plot points in dramatic Act 1 which lead the protagonist to take action? Does the inciting event take place during the story (usually in dramatic Act 1), or does it take place before the story starts, as in *Once Upon a Time in the West* or *Memento*? If there is no clear inciting event, would showing one in Act 1 help kick-start the story, or help the audience to understand the goal or the motivations of the protagonist? In a character-led movie, is the need to change already there, or does a *character* inciting event – such as meeting a catalyst character or experiencing a psychological trauma – trigger it? See *Inciting Incident vs Inciting Action* in *Craft the Draft*.

**Beginning of Dramatic Act 2**: When do we understand who wants (or needs) what and why? It's not always when the protagonist decides to pursue a goal. Sometimes, the protagonist already has a goal at the beginning of the movie, but it's not necessarily the goal of the movie, just the initial goal. For example, many instalments of *Indiana Jones*, *James Bond* or *Mission: Impossible* start with the end of the last mission, which is not always connected to the present story. Sometimes, the protagonist already has the goal of the story from the start, but we'll only enter dramatic Act 2 when the audience understands that goal and motivation. Check that it doesn't take forever, like in *Once Upon a Time in the West*. This is because until we understand what the main problem is, we can't understand what's at stake in the story and therefore get emotionally involved in it. Sometimes, we have a better understanding of the problem than the protagonist, as in *Misery*, and we're waiting for the protagonist to catch up with us, which is fine (unlike the opposite, when we know less than the protagonist, which could go against a strong identification, as in *Cake*). In character-led stories, we enter dramatic Act 2 when we understand what the character needs, or when we realise that what the character needs is more important than what the character wants. In theme-led stories, we enter a thematic Act 2 when we understand what the story is about, what the vision of the filmmaker is. More on this in *Behind the Scenes, Cold Start, Developing a Character-Led Story* and *Developing a Theme-Led Story*.

**Sequences in Act 2**: In a plot-led story, how do we cut the main goal into subgoals, tasks, things that the protagonist can actually do to reach the goal? Each of these subgoals usually defines a dramatic sequence, which allows us to cut a long dramatic Act 2 – often taking most of the film – into more manageable units, almost like mini-movies. There can be one or two sequences in dramatic Act 1 especially when it's longer than usual, but usually it's Act 2 which is cut into four to six dramatic sequences. Dramatic Act 3 only includes one or more dramatic sequences if there is an *Encore Twist*. In character-led stories, conscious subgoals and sequences are not necessarily ways to reach a main conscious goal; they are often ways to generate the conflict that is going to force the character to change. Because the main evolution defines the structural backbone of a character-led story, the protagonist can have different conscious goals. More on this in *Sequence the Action* (plot-led story), *Sequence the Evolution* (character-led story) and *Sequence the Strands* (theme-led story).

**Mid-Act Climax**: Is there a mid-act climax in the story? A midpoint doesn't mean much structurally, except to mark the middle of the script. A mid-act climax around the middle of dramatic Act 2 brings a first dramatic answer in a first climax to the first goal of the protagonist. The protagonist then tries to reach another goal, which is a logical consequence to the first one, in the second half of dramatic Act 2. In some stories, this can happen at the end of Act 1, when a first goal reaches a climax which triggers the actual goal of the story. For example, in *Alien,* the first goal of the crew of the Nostromo is to investigate the possibility of non-human life, before they have to deal with the consequences of having found it. Although we can't call this a mid-act climax, structurally it's very similar. See *Midpoint vs Mid-Act Climax* in *Craft the Draft.*

**Climax of Dramatic Act 2**: This is the scene or sequence during which the protagonist faces the biggest obstacle, bringing an answer to the dramatic question. If the protagonist doesn't face the biggest obstacle (or doesn't experience the most intense confrontation with the antagonist) during the climax, we risk an anti-climax. In a character-led movie, it's usually the moment when we wonder for the last time if the protagonist will manage – or has managed – to change or not, and will overcome his or her internal flaw. More on this in *Climax vs Ending* in *Craft the Draft.*

**Answer to the Dramatic Question**: Does the protagonist reach the goal or not? Does the protagonist get what they want or need? Is the main problem in the story solved? In relation to this, a couple of important questions...

**Beginning of Dramatic Act 3**: Can we pinpoint the moment in the story when the goal (conscious or not) is reached for good, when the main problem in the story is solved and we start seeing the consequences of the action or the evolution of the protagonist? Or the moment when the protagonist has to give up and has definitely failed? Open endings are not always an issue, but they are often a cop-out. Either because the problem has no solution – in which case designing the story as theme-led might be a better option – or because the filmmaker has no clear point of view, lacks the courage to take a stand. More on this in *Behind the Scenes* (plot-led story), *Developing a Character-Led Story* and *Developing a Theme-Led Story*.

*Encore Twist*: Is there a first climax, towards the end, which gives a first answer to the dramatic question – the protagonist succeeds or fails, and stops trying to reach the goal – followed by a surprise which starts the same dramatic action, until a second climax provides a second answer to the same dramatic question? This is very common in genre movies, especially action/adventure, thrillers or romantic comedies, but it can also be found in arthouse, character-led movies like *Two Days, One Night*. Sometimes, the dramatic answer is simply reversed and there is no *Encore Twist*. For example, at the end of *There's Something about Mary*, it looks like Ted (Ben Stiller) has lost Mary (Cameron Diaz), has failed to get her back, but she tells him he's the one she wants. This isn't an *Encore Twist*, only a final twist, a simple reversal of the dramatic answer. See *Encore Twist* in *Craft the Draft*.

**Does the Answer to the Dramatic Question Convey the Point of View of the Filmmaker(s):** This is a big one. Meaning is expressed less by the story as a whole than by the ending, and a huge part of this is related to the answer to the dramatic question. This is why forcing a happy ending on a story that needs to end in tears to be meaningful, or forcing an unhappy ending on a story that should end well, is rarely satisfying. This is also why, when a problem cannot find a believable solution because it's too broad, a theme-led story can be an interesting option. Showing different characters confronted with the same problem, and how some might find a way to resolve it while others don't, might allow you to explore the problem without having either a depressing ending or a superficial, unbelievable ending. More on this in *Happy Ending vs Satisfying Ending* in *Craft the Draft*.

**Does the Answer to the Dramatic Question Fit the Genre of the Story:** This one is crucial too. For example, thrillers and horror movies are all about overcoming life-threatening forces. At least one character is expected to survive, mostly unscathed (or with injuries that don't mean a permanent disability). This is why the amputation in the novel of *Misery* was rightly turned into a softer hobbling in the movie. If we kill all our co-protagonists in a horror, thriller or disaster movie – or if the two main characters don't end up together in a romantic comedy – it might be surprising, but it's rarely satisfying. That's because while there is value in a story that shows how a character or group of characters survive against all odds, there is little value in showing that they all die. Similarly, showing that two characters don't find true love, while being plausibly realistic, doesn't really help us to cope with a solitary life. It's fine if it's well-handled, for example if you warn the audience right at the beginning, as in *500 Days of Summer*, otherwise you might end up in trouble. Again, anything is possible, but make sure you manage the expectations of the audience, so that the story can be surprising or unconventional without being disappointing.

**Is the Ending Satisfying?** This is another big one, of course, because the ending is one of the most important factors for word of mouth. It's what you leave the audience with. A good movie can be ruined by a poor ending. Few stories can be great without a satisfying ending. What's most important here is to make the distinction between a *happy* ending and a *satisfying* one. A satisfying ending can be sad or unhappy if the failure (or even the death) of the protagonist is necessary to give meaning to the story or achieve greater good. For example, farmer Dan's death in the remake of *3:10 to Yuma*. The protagonist dies but reaches his goal to provide for his family and gets his son's respect back. This shows that a protagonist can die and succeed (it's in fact the definition of a tragic hero, a character who dies for the greater good). Getting the ending right is crucial. More on this in *Climax vs Ending* and *Happy Ending vs Satisfying Ending* in *Craft the Draft*.

**Duration of Dramatic Acts**: How long are dramatic Act 1, Act 2 and Act 3? The answer is almost never 30–60–30 minutes, so you might want to forget about this logistical way to look at story structure and concentrate on what happens before, during and after the main dramatic *action* in a plot-led story. How long before we understand who *wants* what and why in the movie (Act 1)? How long before we get, in the climax, an answer to the dramatic question: "Does the protagonist reach the goal or not?". Is the external problem solved or not (Act 2)? And what are the consequences of the protagonist's *action* in the world of the story (Act 3)? In a character-led story, replace this with what happens before, during and after a main *evolution*; how long before we understand who *needs* what and why; does the protagonist manage to change or not (Is the internal problem solved?) and what are the consequences of the protagonist's *evolution*. More on this in *Behind the Scenes* and *Developing a Character-Led Story*.

## MANAGING INFORMATION

### Main Dramatic Ironies:

Is there a dramatic irony that shapes the story and is part of its structure? Global dramatic ironies over most of the story as in *Infernal Affairs* and its remake *The Departed*, *The Lives of Others*, *Tootsie*, *Back to the Future*, *City Lights* or *Avatar*? Or dramatic ironies that are resolved halfway into the film, as in *The Apartment* or *Bolt*? Important things that the audience knows and some characters don't, which allow the writer to generate humour, suspense, drama, gags and thrills?

For each major dramatic irony, it's a good idea to check when it's set up and resolved, and who the victim is. If it's not resolved, make sure that's not a problem.

Also check that a strong dramatic irony isn't causing structural issues in the story, especially regarding identification, whether the protagonist is the victim or not. More on this in *Behind the Scenes*.

### Main Surprises:

What are the unexpected plot points in your story? Which piece of information, which character action or decision creates a shock for the audience and provides a turning point in the story? Is there a final surprise? Is there an *Encore Twist*? Or a surprising reversal of the answer to the dramatic question? We want to know where the story is heading, but we like to be surprised along the way. Check that you have at least a couple of major surprises in the story, especially in genre movies. More on this in *Behind the Scenes*.

### Main Elements of Mystery:

Which information is partially revealed but not enough to be fully understood by the audience? Is it used as a hook, an appetiser at the beginning as in many thrillers, or is it the main course, as in a whodunit? If you do use mystery over the whole story, check that you're also using other tools to manage information, such as surprise and dramatic irony, so that we don't feel that we are kept in the dark just for the sake of a final surprise. Also try to ensure that we know as much or more than the protagonist, not less. It's very difficult to identify with a character who keeps important things from us over a long period of time. More on this in *Behind the Scenes* and in *Cold Start*.

**Main Elements of Suspense:**

Do you tell the audience about a danger (physical, psychological or emotional) so that we can see where it's coming from and fear for the protagonist? While dramatic irony is often used to generate suspense (the audience knows where the danger is coming from but not some of the characters), we can have suspense without dramatic irony (everyone knows where the danger is coming from). But if the audience doesn't know where the danger is coming from, there is no suspense, only a potential surprise.

Overall, the key thing in this section is to make sure that there is some variety in the way information is managed. All these tools are useful and work well together, but if you use only one, make sure it's dramatic irony or suspense and not mystery, unless you want to privilege the intellectual involvement over the emotional involvement of the audience.

Managing information is part of story structure, especially if there is an important dramatic irony that shapes the story. It's what gives a third dimension to an otherwise two-dimensional narrative. When the story is predictable or linear, it's often because we need to work on the way information is managed in the story, so don't neglect it! More on this in *Behind the Scenes*.

## VISUAL STORYTELLING, PLANTING/PAY-OFF, EXPOSITION

### Planting/Pay-Off and Visual Storytelling:

How is information handled in the story? Mostly through dialogue, or using as much visual storytelling as possible? Is planting/pay-off used to achieve this, as well as to bring in more causality? Can we switch scenes or sequences around easily? If that's the case, there is not enough causality in the story (cause and effect, what happens in the story happens because of what happened earlier) so we probably need more planting/pay-off. More on this in *Behind the Scenes*.

### Exposition:

Is there a lot of information regarding past events (things that happened before the start of the movie)? Is it handled visually? Is it dramatised? Do we use flashbacks to *show* us what happened, or does someone *tell* us what happened? More on this in the *Silver Linings Playbook* case study.

# Character Outline

A character outline provides a kind of snapshot of each character: conscious goal, unconscious need, motivations, growth or change, main and secondary characteristics, brief backstory, etc.

Some of this information can be put into a story-type framework, especially for the protagonist, but it can be useful to write it down separately as an outline for all the important characters.

In a TV series, it's part of the "Bible" – the document that describes all the key elements of the series so that each writer can refer to it.

# Character Pages

Character pages are an interesting variation on character outlines. While a character outline provides an analytical view of the character from the outside, character pages give you an opportunity to get a more intuitive perspective of the character, from the inside.

You write character pages either by telling the story as if you were one of the characters, from that specific point of view, or by writing their backstory (where they come from; what they have done; what their aspirations are, etc), also from their perspective.

While it's a bit more literary than any of the other tools, it gives us a chance to get into each character's head, understand their motivations better, sometimes find what's missing in their design. Often, it's a great way to "find the voice of the character".

One set of character pages per character. There can be as little or as much of it as you want/need. You could write half a page and be done with it, or you could write five pages every morning from the point of view of your protagonist. Just don't forget to write the screenplay!

# Evolution Map / Character Breakdown

A character evolution map (or character breakdown) allows us to map the evolution of a character in detail (start point, end point and four to six psychological/emotional steps). It's clearly useful in character-led stories, to map the evolution of the protagonist (a change related to an unconscious need), but it can also help to map the growth of the protagonist in a plot-led movie (or the evolution of any other character).

The key here is to make the distinction between what the character unconsciously *needs* and what the character consciously *wants* in the story.

We also have to differentiate between the life-goal (ambition of the character) and the goal in the story. What we're talking about here is the evolution of the character in the story.

See the *Map the Change* and *Sequence the Evolution* in *Developing a Character-Led Story* chapter for more detail on this process.

# Relationships Map

A relationships map takes this one step further, and helps to chart the evolution of more than one character. So instead of defining a start point, an end point and four to six psychological/emotional steps just for one character, we're going to do this for a relationship between two characters: How can we define the relationship between two characters at the beginning of the story, at the end and the steps leading to this evolution?

Often, the relationship will change because of what happens in each character's evolution. The idea is to try to see some cause and effect between what happens in the story and not only how each character changes, but also how the relationship evolves.

You can expand this to more than one relationship. For example, you could have an evolution map for the protagonist, one for the antagonist, and one for the love interest. Then map the evolution of the relationships between the protagonist and love interest, the protagonist and antagonist or the antagonist and love interest.

A good way to illustrate this is to use rows and columns. In columns, you put single characters or pairs. In rows, you list events chronologically. You can also do the opposite, but as the number of characters/relationships tends to be more limited than the number of events, I find it easier to do it this way.

You should be able to read each column (say one character, or one relationship) from the top (beginning of the story) to the bottom (end of the story) and go through all the steps that make this specific evolution possible. Each column read this way should make sense; otherwise, you're probably missing a step or have a flawed step somewhere.

Finally, you should be able to see connections between the columns. For example, one event in one column happens because of something that happened earlier in another column, and leads to another event in another column. The more connections, the more causality in the story.

Ascending writers should find this tool really useful, especially to add depth to the characters in a plot-led or character-led story. Descending writers might find it too abstract or analytical, which is fine. It can still

be used by other people involved in the development process to spot potential issues in the evolution of characters and/or their relationship, and
then put it to the writer in non-technical terms, without ever mentioning
– or worse, showing them – the relationships map itself.

Most of these documents are great for identifying problems but are
not necessarily appropriate as design tools, depending on the way each
writer works and whether they are ready to embrace them or not. See *Are
You (or Are You Working with) an Ascending or a Descending Writer?*

## Strands Map

A strands map is a combination of beat sheets, character breakdowns and
relationships map that can be used to structure (or troubleshoot) theme-
led stories / multi-stranded narratives. It allows you to split the strands
so that each one can be followed separately, and at the same time check
that what happens in each strand is connected with at least another one
and that everything happens with the right timing. For example, it helps
ensure that you don't lose a strand for too long, and that the pace at which
you cut between strands increases as you get closer to the end.

It's a complex document so it might help to look at the one mentioned
in the detailed analysis of *Crash*. Again, I doubt that Paul Haggis and
Bobby Moresco felt the need to come up with one of these as they wrote
the screenplay, but as a tool to troubleshoot a theme-led story and identify
potential structural or timing issues, or even to simply understand how
theme-led stories (including many TV series such as *Game of Thrones*) are
structured, it's extremely useful.

This detailed strand by strand analysis of *Crash* is available as a free
download at www.screenwritingunchained.com. It shows the timing
of each strand, where each strand connects with others, as well as the
inciting event and climax of each strand.

As with a relationships map, I'd be careful before discussing a strands
map with film writers inclined to write theme-led stories (TV writers
should be fine; they do this all the time). They tend to be descending
rather than ascending writers, so they usually prefer to work in a more
intuitive way, at least with early drafts.

This doesn't make the tool less useful to someone working on such a
project and wanting to prepare for a development meeting. It will inform
a non-technical discussion and help raise the right questions to the writer.

# Step Outline / Index Cards / Beat Sheet

These are the more commonly known story design tools.

A step outline is usually about five to ten pages long. A beat sheet (on index cards, in a short document or even on a flip chart) tends to have anything from fifteen (coarse) to one hundred or more (detailed) beats/cards/steps.

You can pick any of these depending on which one fits your writing style and methodology best; they all achieve the same thing.

Those who prefer to keep working on the computer will write a step outline or a beat sheet in a normal document. Those who enjoy leaving the computer aside will use physical index cards on a cork board or large table. You can even visualise a cork board on a computer screen with the right software, if that's your thing. It doesn't really matter.

What's common to these tools, irrespective of the way they show each step (as a beat, a card or a few lines) is that they provide an opportunity to get an overall view of the story, without unnecessary details, over a few pages / flip chart or one cork board. Of course TV series storylines can populate many cork boards / flip charts, but let's keep it simple for now.

The great thing about these tools is that as you're working on the story, you can get a whole dramatic sequence on a single card/step/beat. For example, "They escape from jail" is one sequence, and can be one beat/one index card/one sentence in the step outline, even if in the screenplay it will become a fifteen-page exciting action sequence made of seven dramatic scenes and one of the set pieces of the movie.

In *The Apartment*, the entire broken mirror sequence – see the full analysis in the planting and pay-off section in *Behind the Scenes* – would be a single line in a step outline, a single index card or beat: "Bud finds out that Fran Kubelik is Sheldrake's mistress". That's it. One line. One story beat. Well, to be precise, we would have to add another story beat before that one: "Fran finds out from Sheldrake's secretary that he's only having a fling with her". Still, it's a very short description for fifteen pages of script. It's the essence of the sequence. The reason for each story beat.

There is no dialogue; the style is direct – these documents aren't meant to be seen/read by anyone outside the inner development circle. The idea is to try to describe each step of the story in a few words, so that we know what happens and/or what we learn, without focusing on how it happens or how we learn it (I call this adaptation, more on this in the next section).

This is the best way to test things like story logic and causality. If you take one step out, or if you swap two steps, does the story still make sense? It shouldn't!

These tools also detach the writer from the details, and force the writer to concentrate on the function of each story element (characters, scenes) rather than on the form. In short, to concentrate on what is *needed* in order to tell the story, instead of what is *liked* (especially if it's about rewriting an existing script, or if the writer tends to write great dialogue which, like paint or wallpaper, can cover many cracks).

Also, step outlines / beat sheets / index cards can be used to start checking for visual storytelling (especially through planting and pay-off).

## Scene Breakdown

In a step outline (or if we use a beat sheet / index cards) we only have one step/card per story beat. A full dramatic sequence can be a single line, because we try to focus on what happens and what we learn in the story.

In a scene breakdown, we're going to split dramatic sequences into scenes – we want to list all the steps in the jail escape sequence for example – and we're going to focus on how things happen, and how we learn them.

However, we still won't use dialogue, which will force us to be as visual as possible. We'll use a lot of planting and pay-off to both bring in causality and increase visual storytelling. Instead of getting a character to say something, can we plant a specific meaning for an element (object, character, situation) so that seeing the element later means something for the character and the audience?

This is what I call adaptation. In a step outline, we define what happens and what we learn. In a scene breakdown, we go one step further and try to find the best possible way – the most dramatic, visual way – to make a step happen or convey information.

Note: We change scene numbers in a scene breakdown when what's at stake dramatically in the scene changes, not necessarily when the location changes. For example, a couple might start arguing about their upcoming wedding in the kitchen, fight in the bathroom and make up in the bedroom. This is just one dramatic scene even if, from a logistical point of view, we'll change location three times in the screenplay (int. kitchen, int. bathroom, int. bedroom).

In other words, a scene breakdown tends to be the whole script, without the dialogue. It's about fifteen to fifty pages long (for a two-hour feature film). Any shorter, it should be a step outline, any longer and you should probably be writing the script instead.

Contrary to a treatment, the style isn't important in a scene breakdown because it's an internal document, only meant to be read by the writer and inner development circle. It's not a selling tool; it's a story design tool.

Many writers who hate writing treatments will love writing scene breakdowns instead because they can use them to work on the story design, as screenwriters.

So if you're working with a writer who refuses to write a treatment, make sure it's not because they hate the selling tool but would actually love the story design equivalent.

# Screenplay

Each draft of a screenplay is always a failed attempt at telling the story until the final one... if we're lucky!

My advice is to read as many screenplays as you can, old and recent, from movies you love and also from successful movies you haven't necessarily enjoyed. Not only to see what the story looks like on the page, to learn from the writer's style and so on, but also to get a sense of what's in the screenplay compared to what's on the screen. Sometimes, it's very close. Sometimes, there are very significant differences. Try also to read screenplays from newcomers who got their film produced, as this gives a sense of what has to be achieved on paper to get a movie made without a significant track record.

Thankfully, it's now very easy to find ways to read produced screenplays. Many of them have been published and are in print, and the producers of most movies nominated for an Academy Award make the screenplay available for download in the run-up to the ceremony.

You'll see that the styles are diverse and that the old school advice: "Only write what you'll see and hear on screen" doesn't strictly apply. Still, good screenplays are not novels, and few ever describe what takes place in a character's head (a.k.a. cheating). Good screenwriters find ways to dramatise the characters' thoughts and feelings through action and dialogue.

Irrespective of your style and the kind of movies you're developing, I'd highly recommend reading any screenplay by William Goldman (especially *Butch Cassidy and the Sundance Kid* and *Misery*), James Cameron (*Aliens* and *Terminator II*), Tony Gilroy (*The Bourne Trilogy*) and Diablo Cody (*Juno, Young Adult*) to get a sense of what can be achieved with great dialogue and characterisation, strong visual storytelling and excellent action sequence writing (where applicable). These screenwriters find ways to make the screenplay exciting, visual, clever, with a very distinctive style, without resorting to any literary artifice.

# 6.3 The Rewrite Stuff: 12 Ways to a Stronger Screenplay

I'd like to end this journey with a few practical steps so you can take action on your project, because that's where the real fun begins.

As we know, writing *is* rewriting, so let's take a look at the rewrite stuff and map *12 Ways to a Stronger Screenplay*.

At this stage, you might have identified some areas that need work, especially if you have written down an STM Framework for your project.

If that's the case and you're all inspired and fired up, feel free to skip the rest of the book and get busy!

Otherwise, if the amount of work ahead feels a bit overwhelming or if you're not sure where to start, my advice is to relax and tackle each potential issue in the screenplay, one by one.

Based on the thousands of scripts I've read and analysed, I've made a list of twelve key areas to look at when rewriting any story, irrespective of its story-type, genre or budget level. Each elements is connected to at least one aspect of the *Story-Type Method*. Here they are:

Not all these elements are important or relevant in every story, so the following list shouldn't be taken as a step by step recipe. It's a pick and choose process, not a do them all.

# The Rewrite Stuff
## 12 Ways to a Stronger Screenplay

1. Identify the **story-type** (plot-led, character-led, theme-led, hybrid or exception) of your project.
2. Define **what's at stake** and work out your **M-Factor**.
3. Clarify the **theme**; check it raises an interesting and conflictual question.
4. Re-work the **set-up** and define the **story-world**.
5. Use **the fractal aspect of story structure** to break down acts or strands into **sequences and scenes**, and don't forget the **subplots**.
6. Look at **managing conflict**: want vs. need; protagonist vs. obstacles.
7. Play with **managing information** and audience POV: dramatic irony, surprise, mystery, suspense.
8. **Change, growth or steadfast?** Design the main characters, their relationships and their evolution.
9. **Antagonist or catalyst**: Who is testing your protagonist?
10. Think of a **time-lock** to increase dramatic tension.
11. Maximise **planting, pay-off** and **visual storytelling**.
12. Craft a **satisfying ending**: moving, entertaining and meaningful.

Let's take them one by one:

1. Identify the **story-type** of your project. This will help you develop the project accordingly, using the same set of tools, just in a different way. Remember that some stories are hybrids or exceptions, so keep an open mind. I would also suggest, if applicable, to clarify the **genre**. **If you're stuck,** read *If We Know the Problem, We Know the Story-Type* and check out *The Structurator®* at www.thestructurator.com. You might also want to read *Genre* in *Craft the Draft*.

2. Clarify **what's at stake** and work out your **M-Factor**, identifying where the main problem and other elements in the story, like strands or subplots, stand in Maslow's Hierarchy of Needs. This might allow you to raise the stakes and widen your potential audience. **If you're stuck,** read *Is Maslow Running the Show?* and *Hands-On: What's at Stake* at the end of *Craft the Draft*.

3. Clarify the **theme**. It doesn't have to be highly philosophical, but it helps to know what the story is about, especially for character-led stories and, even more, theme-led ones. Does the filmmaker have a strong vision? Does the theme raise an interesting and conflictual question? With plot-led stories, an interesting, original, relevant

theme is often what's going to lift a project above B-movie territory. Think about movies like *Gravity* or *The Matrix*. It's their theme that makes them stand out. **If you're stuck**, read *Theme* in *Craft the Draft* (*Developing a Plot-Led Story*) and *Nail the Theme* (*Developing a Theme-Led Story*).

4.   Re-work the **set-up**, define the **story-world**. Do we understand what's at stake in the story within the first fifteen minutes? Are you using dramatic irony, mystery or suspense to make sure we want to know what's going to happen next, if the main problem hasn't been defined yet? If the story-world is unique and different, take the time to show that your characters might look different, but are just like any of us: human beings (or aliens, robots and animals behaving like human beings). We also need to feel that we know them, as individuals, to be able to care about them when disaster strikes. **If you're stuck**, read *A Good Set-Up* and *Story World* in *Craft the Draft*.

5.   Use the **fractal aspect of story structure** to break down acts or strands into sequences and scenes, and don't forget the subplots. Even if the story isn't structured in three dramatic acts overall, using the three-act structure to design strands, sequences and scenes can significantly improve the story. Don't forget the **subplots**, either to add some depth to a plot-led story with a character-led subplot, or to design a multi-stranded narrative. **If you're stuck**, read *Key Point 2* and *Key Point 4* in the first chapter and, depending on your story-type, *Sequence the Action* in *Developing a Plot-Led Story*, *Sequence the Evolution* in *Developing a Character-Led Story* or *Sequence the Strands* in *Developing a Theme-Led Story*. You can also take a look at any of the STM Frameworks for the main case studies, especially *Misery*, *Silver Linings Playbook* and the strands map of *Crash*, which is available as a free download at www.screenwritingunchained.com.

6.   Look at **managing conflict**: *want* versus *need*; protagonist versus obstacles. Use drama, conflict and emotion to give the story a strong dramatic backbone. We'll care for the protagonist if they're the character in the story who experiences the most conflict, if we understand what the protagonist wants/needs, why and what stands in the way. Frustration and anxiety, two of the most basic human emotions, are embedded in the protagonist–goal–obstacle

device. Using it will show your character to be like any other human being; it will bring empathy and universality to the story. If you develop a theme-led story, check that this backbone is present in most strands. **If you're stuck**, read *Managing Conflict* in *Behind the Scenes*.

7. Look at **managing information** and audience POV: dramatic irony, surprise, mystery and suspense. All these tools are part of story structure. Some stories use dramatic irony as their primary structural tool, like *Infernal Affairs* and its remake *The Departed*, *Tootsie*, *Avatar* or *The Lives of Others*. Some are based on mystery and surprise like *Sleuth*, *The Usual Suspects* or *Psycho*. Just check that 1) you rely on more than one tool to manage information and 2) the way you do it doesn't prevent an emotional identification with the protagonist, such as when we know less than the protagonist over a long period of time. **If you're stuck**, read *Managing Information* in *Behind the Scenes*.

8. **Change, growth or steadfast?** Design the main evolutions in the story. In a plot-led movie, it will be how the protagonist grows. In a character-led story, how the protagonist changes. In a theme-led story, a combination of growth and change in the various strands. A change or growth can also be related to the evolution of a relationship, as in a buddy movie or romantic comedy, or the way we perceive the antagonist, as in many monster/horror movies. **If you're stuck**, read *Map the Change* and *Hands-On: Growth, Change or Steadfast?* in *Developing a Character-Led Story*.

9. **Antagonist or catalyst:** Who is testing your protagonist? In plot-led movies, we often have an antagonist, a main if not unique source of obstacles and conflict for the protagonist. In character-led movies, while most of the conflict comes from within the protagonist who is resisting change, a catalyst often pushes the protagonist, forcing the protagonist to change. Identifying that character and acknowledging their importance is key, especially in near-hybrids like *Midnight Run* or *The Intouchables*. **If you're stuck**, read *Protagonist vs Antagonist* and *Villain vs Antagonist* in *Craft the Draft* (*Developing a Plot-Led Story*) as well as *Grow the Draft* (*Developing a Character-Led Story*).

10. Think of **a time-lock** to increase dramatic tension. This isn't only useful in action or disaster movies such as *Apocalypto* (limited

amount of time for the protagonist to rescue his pregnant wife and child) or *Gravity* (limited amount of time before running out of oxygen). *12 Angry Men*, *High Noon* or *Two Days, One Night* use a strong time-lock to add suspense and emotional intensity in the story. Just like the three-act structure, you don't need to have a time-lock over the whole story, but thanks to the fractal aspect of story structure you could use a time-lock in scenes, sequences, strands and subplots to increase suspense and dramatic tension. **If you're stuck,** read *Time-Locks* in *Craft the Draft*.

11. Maximise **planting, pay-off** and **visual storytelling**. Planting and pay-off will increase causality in the story (cause and effect) and potentially help to generate emotion, especially at the end. It will also help with visual storytelling, an essential asset for a story which aims to cross borders (*The Artist; Apocalypto*). If you're stuck, read *Planting and Pay-Off* and *Visual Storytelling* in *Behind the Scenes*.

12. Craft a **satisfying ending**: moving, entertaining and meaningful. The ending is what you leave the audience with. It's one of the most important factors of word of mouth. An unsatisfying ending can kill a great story. Just as we want to hook the audience early, we want to leave them on a high note (even if it's a sad or even tragic ending). **If you're stuck,** read *Climax vs Ending* and *Happy Ending vs Satisfying Ending* in *Craft the Draft*.

So what's the next step? The first thing to do is assess which of these areas need your attention in the next draft. On rare projects, it will be just one or two, on many others, especially those at an early stage or from new writers, most areas will benefit from some rethinking.

Again, the STM Framework was designed to assess the strengths and weaknesses of a project, so if you feel like writing one, it should help you to pinpoint the areas on which you need to focus.

Ultimately, the way you achieve this doesn't matter. What's important is to go beyond the symptoms and identify the structural problems so you can come up with the right solutions and end up with a better screenplay, not just a different one.

So from that point, it's up to you really.

If there is a lot of work to do, you might decide to focus on just a few areas for the next draft and leave others for later. Sometimes doing the work in stages feels less overwhelming.

You could decide to tackle them all and spend one week on each relevant area, one pass per week, focusing exclusively on the element of the week, and get up to twelve minor rewrites done in up to twelve weeks.

You could start with the hardest one, the area that needs most work and will generate most changes, and reassess the other areas once you're done with that one.

You could begin with the easiest, the one that inspires you most, the simplest one to implement in your story, and work your way up.

You could roll a pair of dice and surprise yourself with a different area each week. This might make it more fun (as well as unpredictable).

You might just be able to hold everything in your head and try a single rewrite addressing all the areas needing work.

You might prefer to work on the screenplay, or you might find it more appropriate to use one or more of the story design tools we've just discussed to tackle the issues and come back to the screenplay afterwards.

Every writer and every project is different. I know from personal experience that rewriting is hard work, but it can also be fun, especially if we feel like we have the machete, map and compass we need to get through that damn jungle.

*With 12 Ways to a Stronger Screenplay*, I've tried to provide such a survival kit. Now it's up to you to figure out the best way to reach your destination...

# Conclusion

## Tools, Not Rules: Keep an Open Mind

What we've discussed in this book are tools, not rules. Principles that help us to understand how existing stories are written but shouldn't dictate how future stories have to be designed.

The *Story-Type Method* doesn't define a single, monolithic structural model. It only provides a selection of tools for working creatively on a screenplay during the development process. Even story-types are only used to explain general principles, not to define rigid templates for any specific story. You can pick and choose what you like, embrace what makes sense to you and discard what doesn't. Again, tools, not rules.

As we know, there's no formula for artistic or commercial success. Take any paradigm, it can apply equally to the latest success and the most embarrassing bomb at the box office.

The only thing we know for sure is that we don't know.

Structure might be everything, but *Nobody Knows Anything*.

So keep an open mind. When writing or assessing a screenplay, be careful not to force it into any model.

There is only one thing that truly matters in a story: Do we want to know what's going to happen next?

If the screenplay works, if we want to turn the pages, if it delivers meaning, entertainment and emotion, that's what counts. Whether it fits a story-type, whether it's structured classically or not, is irrelevant.

So let's put technique where it belongs. Sure, it can help to design and troubleshoot a story, but it always comes second to talent, both in the invention of ideas and the creativity involved in playing with the tools and principles.

## Trust Your Instinct; Follow Your Passion

Our instinct offers a gate to the sum of our knowledge.

It's usually more trustworthy than any conscious analysis.

So once you've mastered the principles described in this book, put them aside – consciously – and trust your instinct. Don't think about what you're doing as you're doing it.

The aim is to go from conscious competence to unconscious competence.

This is true for writers – the more we think about what we're writing, the worse it tends to get – and for those working in development. It's very easy to let technique get in the way.

Passion is the fuel that keeps us going. That's why we want to write, direct or produce a project. It's what allows us to make the right choices and convince others to get on board.

So trust your instinct, and follow your passion.

## To an Easier Development Process!

Well, that's about it for now.

I hope that *Screenwriting Unchained* has brought you a comprehensive set of story design tools, a clear explanation of the principles and the beginning of a method leading to an easier screenplay development process for all involved. Less conflict and drama in the meeting room, more conflict and emotion on the page and on screen. That's the general idea.

Finally, I hope that *Screenwriting Unchained* has inspired you in some way and that you enjoyed reading it as much as I enjoyed writing it.

May the Force be with you!

# Hands-On Solutions

## What's Your Type?

### *Jaws* (PL)

The protagonist is a group of three characters, police chief Brody (Roy Scheider), marine scientist Hooper (Richard Dreyfuss) and shark hunter Quint (Robert Shaw) sharing the same goal: to kill the man-eating shark which is feeding off Amity's beaches. Our main emotional point of view in the story is Brody, as we start with and feel closer to him, just like we feel closer to Ripley in *Alien*. He represents the common man, while his co-protagonists represent science (Hooper) and brute force (Quint) and illustrate different ways to solve the same problem.

The antagonist and main problem in the movie is the "monster", the giant shark. As in most horror or monster movies, this makes *Jaws* a straight plot-led movie as the main problem lies outside the protagonist. In many ways, the shark is also the main character of the movie, as it's the most fascinating one.

The main problem defines a survival issue, so it lies right at the bottom of Maslow's pyramid, giving *Jaws* a high M-Factor. While it was one of the first blockbusters, it had a limited budget, which made it a highly profitable movie.

### *Silver Linings Playbook* (CL)

When he's released from psychiatric hospital, protagonist Pat (Bradley Cooper) has a very strong conscious goal, which is to get back together with his estranged wife Nikki (Brea Bee). While this conscious goal shapes most of the story, what's at stake is never really "Will Pat get his wife back?" but instead "Will he move on?" and "Will he get better?". We know that wanting to get his wife back isn't a solution but is part of a problem. This is a strong dramatic irony, and we want to see when he'll realise that he's going in the wrong direction.

So while his conscious *want* is to get his wife back, his unconscious *need* is to move on, and that's much stronger. Also, most of the conflict comes from himself and his own actions or decisions, rather than from antagonistic characters. He has to tame his demons to get better. This makes it a character-led movie disguised as plot-led, like *Two Days, One Night*.

The main problem lies at the top of Maslow's pyramid (self-actualisation, esteem), but the romantic comedy element reaches down to love and belonging. Pat's bipolar disorder affects physiological areas like his sleep and sex life, which lie right at the bottom of Maslow's Hierarchy of Needs. This gives *Silver Linings Playbook* a medium-high M-Factor. You'll find a detailed case study of *Silver Linings Playbook* in *Developing a Character-Led Story*.

### *Parenthood* (TL)

While there is a clear main character in *Parenthood*, as father Gil Buckman (Steve Martin) is at the centre of the story and in many ways experiences the most conflict, he's not a very active protagonist as he doesn't have a strong conscious goal, apart from dealing with whatever life throws at him (which is too vague a goal to shape a movie). There isn't anything wrong with him, so it's not a character-led story either. We don't hope that he'll change, in fact he's quite endearing the way he is.

*Parenthood* is a theme-led story which explores the theme defined in the title though many different strands, all connected to the same problem: How difficult it is to be a parent or a child. All the characters are part of the same family, and three generations are involved: the parents, the grandparents and the children. Each strand explores a different side of the problem, so we see how the grandfather spoils one of his grandsons, how the sister-in-law and her husband raise their genius daughter, etc.

As often in theme-led stories, we find a stellar cast and an A-list director, and the fact that it's really funny doesn't hurt. It's not for everyone though, as like most theme-led stories, if you don't connect with the theme, its lack of dramatic three-act structure might give it a slightly episodic feel. Also, the main problem sits in the middle of Maslow's pyramid (love, belonging), with little transversal exploration up or down, which gives *Parenthood* a medium M-Factor.

### *Game of Thrones* (TL)

The whole series doesn't have one main protagonist. It's structured with many strands, most of them plot-led, all of them connected by the same theme: power. The main problem lies in society. It's related to the inability of all the clans and tribes in *Westeros* to live in peace together, which leads them to fight for the *Iron Throne*.

This makes it a theme-led story, the main overall question being who will end up ruling this world?

While this problem sits at the top of Maslow's pyramid, each strand explores lower layers in the Hierarchy of Needs, being about survival, sex and power as well as love and belonging, esteem and lack of prejudice. This gives *Game of Thrones* a high M-Factor.

### *Billy Elliot* (PL)

This classic triumph over adversity story is plot-led. Once he has overcome his own resistance, the main obstacles preventing Billy (Jamie Bell) from becoming a ballet dancer stem from prejudice in other characters (his father; his brother). Billy's father (Gary Lewis), the antagonist, is the character who changes most in the story, as he becomes a co-protagonist in the last part of the film, once Billy finds the strength to stand up to him (which defines Billy's own growth in the movie).

While the main problem sits right at the top of the pyramid (creativity, self-actualisation), the subplots in the story contribute to grounding it, making it relevant to a much wider audience. The miners' strike subplot is about security and survival; the emotional subplot is about love and belonging. So overall a medium-high M-Factor.

### *Saving Mr Banks* (CL)

This might look like a plot-led movie with Walt Disney (Tom Hanks) as a protagonist trying to get P.T Travers (Emma Thomson) to let him do a movie adaptation of *Mary Poppins* without her getting in the way. In fact, it's a character-led story with P.T. Travers as the protagonist whose need is to overcome her traumatic childhood and her inability to save *Mr Banks*, her father.

She's Walt Disney's antagonist (main source of conflict for him and his team) on the main plot, but she is the true protagonist of the movie because she's the one who experiences most of the conflict in the story, especially through the flashbacks showing the evolution of her relationship with her father. On that main storyline, P.T. Travers is her own antagonist. The flashbacks explain who she is and what she needs in the present time.

Walt Disney isn't an antagonist; he is the catalyst who is forced to understand her problem in order to solve his, and will lead her along the road to recovery as a co-protagonist.

The main problem lies at the top of the pyramid. It's about

self-actualisation and esteem, but the flashbacks explore themes related to love and belonging, as well as survival (her father's life is on the line). Overall, *Saving Mr Banks* has a medium-high M-Factor.

### *Traffic* (TL)

There is no clear protagonist in *Traffic*, which is a multi-stranded narrative. Its many strands are all related to the theme of drug trafficking and its consequences, which is a problem in society. This makes it a theme-led movie.

Each strand has a clear protagonist and is either plot-led or character-led, but there is no protagonist over the whole story, except maybe Robert Wakefield (Michael Douglas) as his strand is about the main investigation and is connected to a few others.

As often with theme-led stories, the problem lies at the top of Maslow's pyramid (problem-solving), but because drugs destroy lives it also reaches down to lower levels. Each strand has a clearly defined problem showing different ways for this to happen. Protecting your family and your loved ones is a universal drive. We're not all directly concerned by drug abuse, but we can all relate to parents trying to protect their children. So overall a high M-Factor for *Traffic*.

### *Interstellar* (PL)

Astronaut protagonist Cooper (Matthew McConaughey) tries to save the world. The main problem lies in the lack of resources which are causing our planet to die. This makes the story plot-led, as the main problem lies outside the protagonist.

It has a very strong character-led subplot though: the relationship between Cooper and his daughter Murph (Jessica Chastain). She feels like he has abandoned her, and this feeling gets worse when she finds out, or believes, his sacrifice was all for nothing. Ultimately he's vindicated and they find closure, although by then she's on her death bed as she grew old when he didn't. She dies in peace with all her children and grandchildren. He can deal with that because he's saved them all and didn't sacrifice his life with his daughter for nothing.

The main problem is not only about the protagonists' lives but the future of humanity itself, so it's anchored right at the bottom of the pyramid (survival). Like all stories in space (*Gravity*, *Apollo 13*, etc), it goes down to the primal level (physiology) as breathing is not possible in space. Through the relationship with the daughter, the story explores themes of love / belonging which gives it a heart, and its time travel high concept also reaches the top of the pyramid (problem solving) to give it more depth. So *Interstellar* has a very high M-Factor overall.

### *Little Miss Sunshine* (CL)

*Little Miss Sunshine* seems to be plot-led on the surface because the story is all about getting Olive (Abigail Breslin) to California to support her bid to become Little Miss Sunshine, a mini-miss beauty pageant. In reality the film is about the need for a dysfunctional family to come together. Because the main problem lies within the protagonist (the family and their relationships), it makes *Little Miss Sunshine* another character-led story disguised as plot-led, like *Silver Linings Playbook*, *Savings Mr Banks* or *Two Days, One Night*.

It's an interesting case of a character-led story in which the protagonist is a group of characters sharing both the same conscious goal (supporting Olive in her bid to win the contest) and the same unconscious need: to get better as a family, to resolve their issues. So the winning-obsessed father (Greg Kinnear), his wife (Tony Colette), the depressive uncle (Steve Carell), the vow-of-silence-pilot-wannabe brother (Paul Dano) and the grandfather (Alan Arkin) are all involved in this evolution, which will lead the father to support his daughter unconditionally, the uncle to get out of his depression and the brother to start talking again. There was nothing wrong with the mother, the grandfather or Olive, so these don't need to change.

The main problem is about love, belonging, esteem and even survival as Steve Carell's character is suicidal. So overall *Little Miss Sunshine* has a medium-high M-Factor.

### *Finding Nemo* (PL)

Pixar's screenplays are amongst the best, and *Finding Nemo* is one of their strongest stories, topping their box-office results if we use figures adjusted for ticket price inflation.

While it's a clear plot-led story (the main problem being that Nemo has been taken away and has to be rescued), there is a very strong character element in it: Nemo's father Marlin is overprotective and is partly responsible for Nemo's ordeal (and his).

What's primarily at stake in the story is finding Nemo and bringing him back to safety, but Marlin also needs to grow and allow his son to separate from him. What happens to Nemo, and the conflict that Marlin experiences through the movie, allow Marlin to change by the end and become a better father.

Marlin is the protagonist of the film, with Dory as co-protagonist, and Nemo himself is the protagonist of the only subplot of the film, trying to escape from the dentist's aquarium with his new finny friends. *Finding Nemo* is a great example of a plot-led story with a strong character-led element. The main problem in Maslow's Hierarchy of Needs lies in survival, love and belonging, which gives *Finding Nemo* a high M-Factor.

# What's at Stake?

## *Jaws*

In *Jaws*, what's at stake is initially the safety of Amity's population as well as its economic survival (the island heavily relies on its tourism industry), then it becomes the survival of co-protagonists Brody (Roy Scheider), Hooper (Richard Dreyfuss) and Quint (Robert Shaw) in their struggle against the great white shark.

The negative consequences of the protagonists' failure to capture or kill the shark would be more locals and tourists dying, the economic death of the town and the physical death of the protagonists themselves. That's what's at stake in the story.

## *Silver Linings Playbook*

What's at stake in *Silver Linings Playbook* is Pat's (Bradley Cooper) ability to get better. There can't be any happiness for him if he doesn't find a way to cope with his bipolar disorder – and everything that makes it worse. Will he give up trying to get back with his estranged wife Nikki (Brea Bee) so he can move on? Will he heal his relationship with his father Pat Sr. (Robert De Niro)?

As soon as we introduce the romantic comedy element with Tiffany (Jennifer Lawrence), what's at stake also becomes their happiness as a couple: Will Pat and Tiffany end up together? All this is explored through Pat's evolution in the story. If Pat fails to change, he won't be happy, and neither will the people close to him (his brother; his father; his mother; Tiffany). At best, Pat will end up with a woman who doesn't love him (his wife Nikki), at worst he'll be sent back to jail or psychiatric hospital.

## *Parenthood*

This is a theme-led story and as such what's at stake isn't as clear as in a plot-led or character-led story. Also, it's a comedy, so as long as there are enough gags and we find them funny, we don't care that much about what's at stake. As in *The Court Jester*, *Airplane*, *This Is the End* or *The Naked Gun*, what we really care about is how funny the story is rather than what's at stake plot-wise. Still, we recognise the theme and in *Parenthood*, its universality reaches out to many.

However, if we had to pinpoint it, it's the happiness of the family as a whole which is at stake, especially for Gil Buckman (Steve Martin) and his wife Karen (Elisabeth Mastrantonio) who are about to have another child at what seems to be the worst possible time. What's at stake for them is their ability to overcome this and remain happy as a couple, which is what they achieve in the end.

### Game of Thrones

The stakes are high in the series as a whole. The story world itself is threatened by what lurks north of the Wall. Most strands are about survival, of the protagonists, their family, their clan or tribe over the others.

### Billy Elliot

What's at stake in the film is Billy's ability to be himself. We don't want him to conform to society's expectations. We want him to realise his potential. This is a very universal theme, an aspiration that everyone can relate to, because it's not only connected to creativity but to self-actualisation.

What's also at stake is his relationship with his father: Will it get better? Will they both manage to overcome the death of Billy's mother? This is the emotional core of the story which connects the main plot with the subplots and impacts on Billy's relationship with his father.

### Saving Mr Banks

What's at stake primarily in the film is apparently Walt Disney's (Tom Hanks) ability to get *Mary Poppins* made. In reality, the story is about P.T. Travers' ability to move on, to overcome the traumatic death of her father. It's a good example of a character-led story disguised as plot-led. If P.T. Travers (Emma Thomson) can't change, she'll never be happy (and *Mary Poppins* might never get made).

### Traffic

What's at stake in the story as a whole is whether society can solve the problem that drug trafficking represents. Each thread has something more personal at stake, but it's connected to that same theme. Survival is often at stake in each strand, either because fighting the traffickers is a high risk activity, or because taking drugs threatens the lives of the characters.

### Interstellar

What's at stake in *Interstellar* is primarily the survival of the human race, including the lives of all the main characters, and at a more personal level Cooper's (Matthew McConaughey) ability to mend his relationship with his daughter Murph (Jessica Chastain), who never forgave him for having left her. If Cooper fails, the human race dies, and his daughter will never understand why the personal sacrifice he made for the greater good was necessary.

### Little Miss Sunshine

Here it looks like what's at stake is to get Olive (Abigail Breslin) to the beauty pageant on time, but what's really at stake is the ability of this dysfunctional family – especially the father (Greg Kinnear), the uncle (Steve Carell) and the brother (Paul Dano) – to get better, which is what the external journey will allow them to achieve. This is another example of a character-led story disguised as plot-led.

While it's the characters' evolution which is primarily at stake, the external goal gives the story a clear direction and strong time-lock to maximise the conflict and cause the characters to change.

The fact that Olive doesn't win the pageant, but that her father and the rest of the family end up supporting her, shows that the pageant itself is only an excuse, a reason to force the characters to spend some time together and experience the conflict which is ultimately going to lead the family to become less dysfunctional.

### Finding Nemo

What's at stake is both Nemo's survival (we know he'll die if he's given to the dentist's horrible daughter) and his father's happiness (if he manages to survive the various threats on his way). Marlin is partially responsible for Nemo's ordeal and will never forgive himself if he doesn't find his son and rescue him. Of course during the journey, Marlin and Dory's lives are also frequently under threat. At a more personal level, Marlin's ability to tame his overprotecting habit is also at stake and constitutes the main evolution – growth – in the story. If Marlin doesn't become less overprotective, we know that father and son won't be happy even if Nemo is rescued. The death of Nemo's mother at the very beginning seeds Marlin's overprotective behaviour and Nemo's desire for more independence.

# Growth, Change or Steadfast?

*Jaws*

Chief Brody (Roy Scheider), the main protagonist, doesn't change. There is nothing wrong with him as a character. However, he does *grow*. He overcomes his fear of water in order to kill the shark. He ends up stronger but not changed. It's a plot-led movie.

Co-protagonist Hooper (Richard Dreyfuss) doesn't change – there is nothing wrong with him, which is why he ultimately survives – and neither does Quint (Robert Shaw): his inability to change and accept defeat and his stubbornness will lead to his death. Both co-protagonists are *steadfast* characters.

*Silver Linings Playbook*

Pat (Bradley Cooper), the protagonist *changes*. Pat's need to change is measured through the evolution of his relationship with Tiffany (Jennifer Lawrence), who we immediately identify as the right girl for him. We want them to end up together – that's the romantic comedy element – so we want him to realise that Tiffany is the one. She's a catalyst (a character forcing him to change) and a co-protagonist helping him to move on.

Tiffany *changes* too, as she needs to stop her promiscuous, self-damaging behaviour with men following the death of her husband Tommy, for which she feels guilty. Pat helps her to get her self-worth back. So the two main characters change, which allows them to end up together.

This is why when Pat fails to reach his conscious goal at the end of the movie and doesn't get back together with his wife, it doesn't feel like a failure but a success: he's moved on; he's let go of his wife; he's reached his unconscious goal, and as a reward he's got Tiffany. It's a happy and satisfying ending for an equally funny and moving story.

*Parenthood*

Each strand shows its own evolution (or lack of it). Some of the characters change; some grow; some remain steadfast. Gil (Steve Martin), the main character, *grows* as he realises that having another child is more important than his job. He doesn't really change because he's not introduced as a character who has a strong internal flaw. He simply has common fears and insecurities.

### Game of Thrones

Most characters *change* or *grow* in each strand. That's one of the great things about a TV series: you have the time and space to handle the evolution of multiple characters. They are going through a lot of conflict, which has to cause some sort of evolution. The most drastic evolutions are related to the youngest characters, who are forced to find a way to cope with extremely hard situations: death of a father, captivity, etc. They don't necessarily have a problem to start with, but the problem in the story forces them to adapt, to grow in order to survive. Daenerys Targaryen (Emilia Clarke) undergoes one of the most extreme transformations, from victim (forced wife) to Khaleesi and Mother of Dragons.

### Billy Elliot

Billy (Jamie Bell) *grows* as a character. He finds the strength to stand up to his father Jackie (Gary Lewis) but doesn't change because there is nothing wrong in him, apart from his own prejudice against male ballet dancers. He overcomes this fairly quickly in the story, so it's never handled as a main problem. Even his ability to deal with the death of his mother isn't a real problem for him. He's coping very well overall. He's finding ways to keep a connection with her – through music and dancing – but it's healthy, not morbid.

On the other hand, Jackie, his father *changes* quite drastically in two ways. First, thanks to Billy's action he overcomes his prejudice and decides to support Billy in his quest, and second, he finds a way to deal better with the loss of his wife. Instead of rejecting everything that reminds him of her – like Billy playing the piano or wanting to dance – he accepts it, which allows them to heal their relationship and gives Billy a chance to succeed.

### Saving Mr Banks

P.T. Travers (Emma Thomson) *changes* as she learns to move on from her traumatic childhood. Walt Disney (Tom Hanks) is a steadfast character in the film; he doesn't really change. His understanding of P.T. Travers changes. He finds more compassion for her as he gets to understand her, so he *grows* in a way.

*Traffic*

Each protagonist in each strand either grows or changes:

In the **Mexico storyline**, police officer Javier Rodriguez (Benicio Del Toro) *grows* as he decides to stop working for Salazar when he realises he's in cahoots with the cartel. There was nothing wrong with Javier, but he's wiser at the end of the story.

In the **Wakefield storyline**, judge Robert Wakefield (Michael Douglas) *changes* when he realises that his dedication to his work is part of the drug problem his daughter Caroline is a victim of. He starts to look for her, rescues her and in the end resigns when he recognises that the War on Drugs implies a war even on some people's own family members.

In the **Ayala/DEA storyline**, Carl Ayala's pregnant wife Helena (Catherine Zeta-Jones) *changes* when she's forced to take control of her destiny to survive. She gradually leaves behind her old self as she learns the truth about her husband's illegal activities and engineers both her husband's release and her lawyer's punishment.

*Interstellar*

Cooper (Matthew McConaughey) doesn't change. He suffers from his daughter's rejection, but he understands it, and we understand why he's doing what he's doing. It's a sacrifice, not a mistake. We never wonder what's wrong with him, or want him to realise that spending your life with your daughter is more important than saving the human race, because like him, we believe he's doing the right thing, even if it's difficult.

Cooper is a fairly *steadfast* character, except he's vindicated in the end, which gives him closure on the emotional subplot. His daughter (Jessica Chastain) *changes* when she realises that her father was right, that his sacrifice of her childhood was worth it.

*Little Miss Sunshine*

The characters who have an internal problem all *change* in the film: the father (Greg Kinnear) learns to love his daughter unconditionally; the brother (Paul Dano) starts speaking again; the uncle (Steve Carell) overcomes his depression. The mother (Toni Colette) and the grandfather (Alan Arkin) have no need to change and are *steadfast* (although one of them dies, which is kind of a major change). Olive (Abigail Breslin) *grows* because despite the fact there is nothing wrong with her, it means a lot for her to perform the way she does during the contest and see her whole family supporting her.

### Finding Nemo

*Finding Nemo* is a plot-led movie (the main problem is clearly outside the protagonist), yet Marlin *changes* as a result of his action. He stops being over-protective (which is what causes the external problem). Nemo *grows*. Because his father isn't constantly limiting his freedom, he doesn't have to fight for it anymore. He's also proved his worth, being instrumental in freeing his co-inmates from the aquarium and releasing Dory and the other fish from the net. Dory *grows* too. She finds a friend in Marlin and seems to remember things a bit better by the end of the movie.

# Recommended Reading

*Writing Drama* by Yves Lavandier, Le Clown et L'enfant (Paris), 2005 [English translation of *La Dramaturgie*, first published in 1994]

Back in 1987, I joined an informal screenwriting workshop started by Lavandier – then a fresh graduate from Columbia University in New York where he was taught by Frank Daniel, Milos Forman and Stefan Sharff between 1983 and 1985 – shortly before I designed and ran my own very first screenwriting workshop in 1989. In *Writing Drama*, Lavandier further develops the content shared in his early workshop and offers a very thorough analysis of dramatic irony, especially how this essential tool can impact on story structure. He also brilliantly explores, amongst many other topics, key notions like diffuse dramatic irony and suspense, dramatic acts and logistical acts, the link between Mandelbrot's theory of fractals and storytelling, external obstacles with an internal origin, preparation, and what he calls the modified structure, which laid the foundation for my *Encore Twist*. Lavandier doesn't focus solely on screenwriting, he studies all forms of drama – cinema, theatre, TV, even comic strips and opera – from Europe and the rest of the world. *Writing Drama* was a significant reference for the *Developing a Plot-Led Story* chapter of *Screenwriting Unchained* and I'm grateful to Lavandier for this substantial work, seen by many as a remarkable contribution.

*Dramatic Construction* by Edward Mabley, Chilton (New York), 1972

Unfortunately out of print, Mabley's seminal book can be found with a bit of patience from online booksellers and in a few libraries. It was Frank Daniel's main theoretical reference and as soon as I managed to find a second-hand copy, it became one of mine. Mabley succinctly introduces in *Dramatic Construction* all the classical tools, including the protagonist–goal–obstacles–conflict device, the dramatic three-act structure, its fractal aspect in scenes and sequences (the foundation for Daniel's famous *Sequence Approach*), dramatic irony, surprise, mystery, theme, characterisation and unity as well as preparation and less structural tools like activity, dialogue, exposition or effects. He also offers a detailed analysis of more than twenty theatre plays and one film, *Citizen Kane*. Mabley greatly influenced the study of dramatic writing and his ideas, rooted all the way back to Aristotle's *Poetics*, were relayed and built upon by many teachers and theoreticians. *Dramatic Construction* was another significant reference for the *Developing a Plot-Led Story* chapter of *Screenwriting Unchained*, along with various unpublished documents related to Daniel's teaching, which I collected over the years.

*The Tools of Screenwriting*, by David Howard and Edward Mabley, St. Martin's Griffin (New York), 1993

Howard, another of Frank Daniel's former students, wrote this excellent adaptation of *Dramatic Construction* without ever meeting Mabley, who passed away in 1984. A fascinating foreword by Gregory McKnight explains the genesis of Mabley's book up to its publication in 1972; how it then went out of print and lay dormant until Daniel discovered it and adopted it for his own use as a teacher, recommending it to his students for many years as an excellent and concise introduction to dramatic theory; finally, how a former student of Howard introduced Mabley's book to McKnight who, after acquiring the rights, asked Howard if he'd like to rewrite the text in order to reflect the way its principles apply to screenwriting. It also features an insightful introduction by Frank Daniel, who never wrote about his own influential approach to screenwriting. If you can't get hold of a second-hand copy of the original Mabley, *The Tools of Screenwriting* is the closest you'll get to it. As Howard's focus is on cinema – primarily American – rather than theatre, this makes it more directly relevant for many contemporary readers, especially those interested in the study of Hollywood movies. *The Tools of Screenwriting* is an essential book from the man who wrote (with Robert Gordon) the hilariously entertaining *Galaxy Quest*. I'm grateful to David Howard for both of these achievements.

*Making a Good Script Great* (**2nd edition**) by Linda Seger, Samuel French Trade (Hollywood),1994 (1st edition 1987)

In this accessible and practical book, Seger, one of the most well-known script consultants, gives first-class advice on screenwriting, especially regarding character development and the rewriting process. When I first read her book two decades ago, Seger's description of the link between character evolution and story structure planted one of the early seeds for the *Developing a Character-Led Story* chapter in *Screenwriting Unchained*.

*Adventures in the Screen Trade* by William Goldman, Abacus (London), 1989

Few know more about writing in Hollywood than William Goldman, one of the most gifted writers of his generation, who gave us, amongst others, the screenplays of *Butch Cassidy and the Sundance Kid*, *Marathon Man*, *Misery*, *The Princess Bride*... You'll find in this book invaluable advice and entertaining anecdotes from a true master of the craft, delivered with wit and class. It was after reading *Adventures in the Screen Trade* that I stopped believing there was such a thing as objectivity when assessing a screenplay, which completely changed my approach to script development and greatly impacted on the *Bringing It All Together* chapter of *Screenwriting Unchained*.

*The Writer's Journey* by Christopher Vogler, Michael Wiese Productions (San Francisco), 1999

Inspired by the work of Joseph Campbell, his teacher and mentor, Vogler wrote one of the most influential books on screenwriting for stories with a mythical element, a classic example being *Star Wars*.

*The Hero with a Thousand Faces* by Joseph Campbell, Princeton University Press, 1949

Brilliant exploration of mythical storytelling and the main source of inspiration for *The Writer's Journey*. Not focused on screenwriting like Vogler's book, but nevertheless ground-breaking.

*Conversations with Wilder* by Cameron Crowe, Alfred A. Knopf (New York), 1999

Fascinating exploration of Wilder's work through a series of interviews with the filmmaker.

*How to Write Groundhog Day*, by Danny Rubin, Kindle and Apple eBook, 2012

Rewarding journey into the development process of this much loved movie, full of insight, humour and advice, penned by the writer of the original screenplay himself.

*Hitchcock*, by François Truffaut, Simon and Schuster (New York), 1967

Iconic series of interviews with the filmmaker by the film critic. In relation to story structure, it reveals – amongst many other topics – how the Master of Suspense and his screenwriters used dramatic irony to generate conflict and tension, especially in thrillers.

# If You Want to Find Out More...

At **www.screenwritingunchained.com**, you'll find additional documents available as free downloads, such as a ready-to-use template for a *Story-Type Method* Framework, a strands map for *Crash*, as well as a sampler of the first fifty pages of the book with the most important illustrations in colour. This should be useful to those who purchased the black and white paperback and not the colour hardcover or those with a black and white e-book reader.

At **www.screenwriterstroubleshooter.com**, you'll be able to download a free sampler (first fifty pages) of the second volume in the series. This sampler includes the table of contents, the introduction and the first ten problems (out of forty in the book).

If you haven't done so already, you might want to give *The Structurator*® a try at **www.thestructurator.com**. I designed this free interactive video guide as an introduction to the *Story-Type Method* and a way to help you identify the story-type of your screenplay.

Finally, you'll find some information on my 3-day Advanced Development Workshop as well as upcoming online courses and publications at **www.screenplayunlimited.com**.

CPSIA information can be obtained
at www.ICGtesting.com
Printed in the USA
BVHW022021041121
620782BV00004B/222

9 780995 498129